PROFESSIONAL ORIENTATION TO COUNSELING

PROFESSIONAL ORIENTATION TO COUNSELING

Third Edition

Nicholas A. Vacc
Larry C. Loesch

BRUNNER-ROUTLEDGE
ALERE FLAMMAM
Taylor & Francis Group

USA	Publishing Office:	BRUNNER-ROUTLEDGE *A member of the Taylor & Francis Group* 325 Chestnut Street Philadelphia, PA 19106 Tel: (215) 625-8900 Fax: (215) 625-2940
	Distribution Center:	BRUNNER-ROUTLEDGE *A member of the Taylor & Francis Group* 7625 Empire Drive Florence, KY 41042 Tel: 1 (800) 634-7064 Fax: 1 (800) 248-4724
UK		BRUNNER-ROUTLEDGE *A member of the Taylor & Francis Group* 27 Church Road Hove E. Sussex, BN3 2FA Tel.: +44 (0) 1273 207411 Fax: +44 (0) 1273 205612

PROFESSIONAL ORIENTATION TO COUNSELING, Third Edition

3 4 5 6 7 8 9 0

Printed by Edwards Brothers, Lillington, NC, 2000.
Cover design by Nancy Hagan Abbott

A CIP catalog record for this book is available from the British Library.
∞ The paper in this publication meets the requirements of the ANSI Standard Z39.48-1984 (Permanence of Paper).

Library of Congress Cataloging-in-Publication Data
Vacc, Nicholas A.
    Professional orientation to counseling / Nicholas A. Vacc, Larry C. Loesch.—3rd ed.
        p. cm.
    Includes bibliographical references.
    ISBN 1-56032-851-7 (alk. paper)
    1. Counseling. 2. Counseling—Practice. 3. Counselors—Training of. 4. Counselors—Professional ethics. I. Loesch, Larry C. II. Title.

BF637.C6 V33 2000
158.3'023—dc21

00-034294

CONTENTS

ACKNOWLEDGMENTS

We would like to thank Brian M. Gmutza, Simone F. Lambert, Ruth E. Lubik, A. Keith Mobley, Keith A. Nilsen, and I. Marc Strickland for helpful comments and suggestions concerning the preparation of this edition of *Professional Orientation to Counseling.*

PREFACE
TO THE THIRD EDITION

Just because everything is different doesn't mean anything has changed.
—Irene Peter

We began the previous edition of this book with these words from Irene
Peter (widow of humorist Dr. Laurence Peter) because they were an apt
description of the evolution of the counseling profession since the first
edition of this book was published. We retain them here because they still
apply. The counseling profession continues its positive evolution. In fact,
the nature and status of the counseling profession are very much different from what they were when the earlier editions of this book were
presented. The counseling profession now has a much stronger and more
positive identity among the various helping professions and enjoys a widespread and growing recognition by the general public. As we suggested in
the preface to the second edition, this situation appears to be the result of
advancements in counselor credentialing, improved counselor preparation standards and increased adherence to those standards, greater
governmental and other third-party payer recognition of counselors' competence, and better, more ethical, and more accountable professional practices by counselors, among other factors. In many ways, the counseling
profession is at last in good shape as the new millennium proceeds. For
perhaps the first time in the history of the counseling profession, the vast
majority of persons who identify themselves as counselors feel good about
who they are and what they do as professionals. It is a hard-earned, well-
deserved feeling for counselors, and one to be savored. There is reason for
counselors to celebrate (but not to become complacent).

Why and how these advances for the counseling profession have been
achieved are of course matters for speculation. However, primary among
the reasons is that counselor licensure laws now exist in the vast majority
of states. This status has enabled counselors to be on a par with other
publicly and legally recognized professions, and it has concomitantly
empowered them in ways that were not previously possible. In particu-

lar, counselors have become much better and stronger advocates for themselves and for the various clienteles they serve. There have been positive changes within the profession as well. For example, many more counselors are now competent to provide marriage and family, addictions, substance abuse, brief or short-term, physical and/or sexual abuse, or multicultural counseling services. The popular media, including the Internet, also have helped to improve the counseling profession by greatly extending recognition of counselors as distinguishable from other helping professionals. These are good trends and serve the counseling profession well.

Despite recent gains, however, much remains to be done and accomplished for and within the counseling profession. Passage of counselor licensure laws in the few remaining states not having them would universalize the legal status of the counseling profession, as would greater uniformity in reciprocity agreements among states having such laws. Stabilization and extension of counselor preparation standards would instill even greater public confidence in counselor competence. Clarification and specification of how new educational trends, such as distance education, are to be implemented into counselor preparation practices would facilitate professional and public understanding of who and what a counselor actually is. Improved and increased individual and program evaluation practices by counselors would move them to the forefront of the helping professions in regard to accountability. And finally, continued, improved, and increased self-monitoring of professional practices would allow counselors greater freedom in control of their own profession. So while much has improved in and for the counseling profession, there remain to be addressed many of the same needs that historically have been important.

In preparing this third edition of this book, we sought to update the information in it to the greatest extent possible. We also sought to make other changes that would make it a better professional resource for counselors. For example, we have reorganized the book to align it more closely with the Council for the Accreditation of Counseling and Related Educational Programs (CACREP) core curriculum area standards because they remain the primary framework for counselor preparation in the United States. We also have extended the coverage of topics in each of the sections and included additional topics not covered in the previous editions. However, there is one important aspect of this book we have not changed. We want this book to be most useful for persons who identify themselves as professional counselors.

June, 2000

Nicholas A. Vacc, Ed.D., N.C.C., CCMHC
Greensboro, North Carolina

Larry C. Loesch, Ph.D., N.C.C.
Gainesville, Florida

THE COUNSELING PROFESSION

Section 1: Professional Counseling

Professional Counseling: A Point of View

What is counseling? Professional responses to this question have been many, diverse, and varied. For example, Nugent (1994) wrote:

> Professional counseling is a process in which a trained counselor helps an individual, groups of individuals, or family members gain self-understanding and understanding of others in order to solve problems more effectively and resolve conflicts in everyday living. This voluntary and confidential process involves a professional relationship in which counselors and clients jointly participate in problem resolution. (p. 5)

Similarly, Miars, Burden, and Pedersen (1997) wrote:

> In the helping [counseling] relationship, individuals work together to resolve a concern and/or foster the personal growth and development of one of the two people. (p. 65)

Others have emphasized that counseling is a process. For example, Hansen, Rossberg, and Cramer (1994) wrote:

> The counseling process consists of establishing a cooperative interaction and using that relationship to help clients explore themselves and their situations, gain a clearer understanding of both, and then try out appropriate actions. The therapeutic process extends over a considerable period with numerous interviews that gradually produce changes in how clients view themselves and lead to overt or covert behavior changes. (p. 189)

A similar emphasis on counseling as a relationship was supported by Capuzzi and Gross (2000).

Peterson and Nisenholz (1999) focused on the importance of counseling as a relationship between individuals and wrote:

> The counselor is the most important element in the helping [counseling] relationship; the next most important element is the **therapeutic alliance**, or working relationship, between the counselor and client. (p. 71)

Nystul (1999) characterized counseling as both an art and a science and wrote that:

> The art and science of counseling represent an extension of the scientist-practitioner model. From this perspective, the science of counseling generates a knowledge base that has been shown to promote competency and efficacy in counseling. The art of counseling involves using this knowledge base to develop skills that can be applied sensitively to clients in a multicultural society. (p. 2)
>
> ***
>
> To call counseling an art suggests that it is a *flexible, creative process* whereby the counselor adjusts the approach to the unique and emerging needs of the client. (p. 3)
>
> ***
>
> The science of counseling provides a balance to the art of counseling by creating an objective dimension to the counseling process. (p. 4)

Still others have chosen not to define counseling directly, but rather to focus on the knowledge, skills, characteristics, and abilities effective counselors must possess, specifically including mutlicultural competence (e.g., Axelson, 1998; Corey, 1996; Egan, 1997; Gladding, 2000; Ivey, Ivey, & Simek-Morgan, 1996; Kottler & Brown, 1999).

So what *is* counseling? Obviously no simple answer to this question exists. Therefore, it may be more helpful to look at the question from a slightly different perspective and ask, what is the general professional agreement about relative to counseling? There does appear to be professional agreement about at least ten aspects of what counseling is. First, counseling is a **process**; it is not a singular, one-time event or action. Second, the essence of the counseling process is the **relationship** (or therapeutic alliance) between the person(s) giving assistance and the person(s) receiving that assistance. Third, the persons providing the assistance are known as **counselors** (or sometimes simply as helping professionals). In most counseling relationships, one counselor provides the assistance. However, there are some situations (e.g., in co-led group counseling) in which more than one counselor may be fully involved in the counseling process. Fourth, the counselor is a **professional**. In this context, professional means that the counselor has appropriate (usually postbaccalaureate) academic and experiential preparation, holds credentials widely recognized and honored by members of the counseling profession, and adheres to standards of behavior in counseling that are established and endorsed by members of the counseling profession. Fifth, the persons receiving the assistance are known as **clients** (or sometimes as helpees or counselees). Clients may receive counseling individually, as members of a group, or as members of a family unit. Sixth, counseling proceeds through an orderly, evolving, and identifiable set of **stages**. Seventh, counseling is a **multidimensional** process that necessitates consideration of a wide variety of characteristics of the client(s) and of the counselor. Eighth, counseling potentially can be provided through a **variety of modalities**, although the efficacy of counseling provided through emerging, nontraditional modalities has not yet been evaluated fully. Ninth, counseling may be provided from within either **remedial** or **preventive** perspectives, or both. And finally, counseling is based on an identifiable knowledge base, is practiced in a manner in which the relationship between the knowledge base and counseling behaviors can be identified, and is **amenable to evaluation** through application of professionally accepted methodologies.

This multifaceted characterization acknowledges the comprehensiveness of the activity known as counseling. To help clients enhance their lives, professional counselors apply knowledge, skills, and techniques derived from the areas of human growth and development, the social and behavioral sciences, and from counselor education. Their work may involve individual interpersonal relationships, social or small-group interactions, or community-wide involvements. They also may be involved with personal, social, familial, or vocational concerns. Finally, they may be involved with either direct or indirect service delivery.

The comprehensive nature of the activity known as counseling leads to the conclusion that no one person can, or does, practice all aspects of it effectively. Thus, counseling activities are more commonly clustered in **counseling specialties**. Typically, counseling activities (and counselors) are subdivided under the general rubrics of mental health counseling, school counseling, and family counseling. However, these broad areas are usually subdivided into even more distinctive counseling specialties. Sometimes a counseling specialty designation reflects the nature of the counseling service modality, such as individual, group, or marriage counseling. In other cases, a counseling specialty designation reflects the nature of the type of problem being addressed, such as addictions, gerontological abuse, physical abuse, sexual abuse, or career counseling. And in still other cases, a counseling specialty designation reflects the setting in which counseling is provided, such as community agency counseling or counseling in business and industry. A brief overview of some of the counseling specialties follows.

☐ Specialities in Counseling

Mental Health Counseling

Mental health counseling emphasizes the provision of services in the community, business or industry, or in private practice. Within these settings, professional counselors are involved in the provision of many types of mental health counseling services. For example, they may provide family, adult, adolescent, or child counseling services; administer preventive mental health programs; provide consultation services; or help people find and achieve appropriate vocational goals and placements.

Marriage and Family Counseling

The specialty of marriage and family counseling views the family unit as having unique characteristics that require special knowledge and skill in order for counseling to be effective. Professional counselors working in this specialty are interested in specific problems that impede effective family functioning. Counseling practice with a focus on the family includes working with couples concerning training in parenting skills, relationship enhancement, or premarital counseling. These areas of focus, as well as implementation of systemic intervention, are directed toward assisting a significant portion of the family (i.e., those who are defined as a part of the family, whether remarried, part of a stepfamily, a single parent, divorced, or a significant other) achieve an effective, functional, and mutually beneficial identity as a family unit.

Counseling in Student Affairs Practice

Student affairs practice in higher education refers to the other-than-academic services provided for students on college or university campuses. Student affairs practice is based on the recognition that undergraduate and graduate students' problems have to be considered in the context of the total college or university environment. Professional counselors in higher education settings have special concern for the university community and problems unique to it. They may be occupied with recruitment (admissions), managing a counseling program, overseeing student residence life, career planning and placement, addressing student mental health, advising on student activities (e.g., fraternities and sororities), advocating for special student groups (e.g., students with disabilities, foreign students, and students requiring educational opportunity programs), administering student discipline, retention, advising, or student development in general.

School Counseling

Professional counselors in this specialty area view the school as a unique community that must be understood distinctly if the people in that environment are to be assisted with their educational, personal, and social developments. All people working in the school (e.g., administrators, supervisors, teachers, cafeteria workers, secretaries, custodians, volunteers, and teacher aides) are viewed as important contributors to the achievement of educational goals and to the quality of life in a school. However, the professional counselor in the school setting specializes in facilitating the development of children and adolescents, with emphases on interactions among children, school personnel, and parents.

Counseling in student affairs practice in higher education and school counseling share a concern for understanding the settings in which behavior occurs. Professional counselors in these settings bring their knowledge, skills, and techniques to the situations, and apply them to the problems presented within these special environments (i.e., unique places in which people live, work, and study).

Rehabilitation Counseling

This counseling specialty involves provision of counseling services to persons having relatively substantial physical ability challenges, such as visual, auditory, skeletal, muscular, or neurological impairments. These counseling services are often provided in conjunction with medical services to assist persons to cope with the psychosocial and personal difficulties associated with their physical ability challenges. There is also considerable emphasis in the rehabilitation counseling profession on helping individuals with physical ability challenges find effective, meaningful, and satisfying vocational adjustments. Rehabilitation counseling services are often provided through community agencies, although there is an evident increase in private practice rehabilitation counseling.

These counseling specialty designations are helpful for discussion purposes. However, they should not overshadow the reality that there is much in common among the specialties and the professionals who provide the respective specialized counseling services. In particular, counselors distinguish themselves by the applied nature of their work. In addition, there is much commonality in the counseling activities used for the various counseling recipient groups, problem types, and settings. Regardless of specialty, a common bond exists among professional counselors: the goal of helping people to cope and to find effective solutions for problems that can arise at any point in the lives of otherwise primarily normal people.

Collectively, the above information provides a sense of what professional counselors are and do. Yet, it is an incomplete description because it does not fully address the question, what do counselors actually do in their daily activities? This question has been asked often by both professionals and laypersons and, although responded to by a wide variety of professionals, is usually answered only incompletely. In an attempt to provide a more complete response to this question, Loesch and Vacc (NBCC, 1993) conducted a job analysis of professional counselors. In essence, they undertook a systematic examination of the nature and features of professional counselors' work behaviors. The results of their analyses provided information on work behavior similarities among professional counselors of all specialties and in so doing were useful in clarifying the congruence of activities that take place among professional counselors.

The primary purpose of the investigation was to gain an understanding of the nature of work behaviors among professional counselors. Data were gathered in regard to how often respondents engaged in each of the work behaviors presented and how important efficacy in each of the behaviors was to each respondent's professional functioning. The primary result from factor analyses of their responses was a scientifically meaningful description of what professional counselors do across specialties in the form of a simple representation of counselor job behaviors.

Presented in Table 1.1 are the five orthogonal factor solutions that describe counselors' work behavior frequencies. The five clusters, encompassing 136 specific work behaviors, are ordered from highest to lowest by weighed combination of the frequency of a behavior with its importance (e.g., being able to access the potential for a client to harm self or others would be highly important). The 722 responding counselors reported that they engaged in five major categories of work behaviors: fundamental counseling practices, counseling groups, counseling families, counseling for career development, and professional practice. Loesch and Vacc's work thus provided the profession with an empirical description of actual counseling practice.

A primary use of the results of the work behavior study was as a component of the conceptual framework for the National Board for Certified Counselors National Counselor Examination. Because it is good psychometric practice to investigate the conceptual bases for an examination on a periodic basis, the work behavior study was repeated, under the direction of the senior author here, in 1998. As a prelude to this second study, the original list of work behaviors was reviewed and slightly revised by a carefully selected group of counseling professionals. Subsequently, the

(text continues on page 12)

TABLE 1.1. Results of the 1993 NBCC Work Behavior Study

Fundamental Counseling Practices

1. Counsel clients concerning personal change
2. Establish counseling goals
3. Assess potential for client to harm self/others
4. Evaluate client's movement toward counseling goals
5. Evaluate extent of client's psychological dysfunction
6. Counsel adults
7. Clarify counselor/client roles
8. Develop comprehensive treatment plans
9. Assist with client's evaluation of counseling
10. Reframe client's problem
11. Identify source-of-problem alternatives
12. Obtain client's informed consent prior to counseling
13. Counsel clients concerning lifestyle change
14. Inform client about ethical standards and practice
15. Clarify client's support systems
16. Assess psychosocial needs
17. Systematically observe client behaviors
18. Evaluate need for client referral
19. Evaluate existing (precounseling) client data
20. Conduct precounseling diagnostic interview
21. Use "active listening" skills
22. Maintain case notes, records, and/or files
23. Use cognitive-oriented counseling techniques
24. Self-evaluate counseling effectiveness
25. Inform client about legal aspects of counseling
26. Use behavioral-oriented counseling techniques
27. Determine DSMIII-R classification
28. Analyze cost-benefit of treatment alternatives

Counseling For Career Development

29. Assist client in understanding test results
30. Facilitate client's development of decision-making skills
31. Use test results for client decision-making
32. Use interest inventories
33. Evaluate client's educational preparations
34. Use self-report personality inventories
35. Use test/inventory results for intervention selections
36. Evaluate client's occupational skills
37. Use occupational information in counseling
38. Provide career/vocational education
39. Facilitate client's development of job-search skills
40. Use achievement tests
41. Provide career counseling for adolescents
42. Use print and other media in career counseling
43. Select appraisal instruments/techniques for counseling
44. Provide career counseling for adults
45. Use nontest appraisal techniques

(continued)

TABLE 1.1. (*Continued*)

46. Use aptitude tests
47. Use career resources library
48. Use intelligence tests
49. Use computerized career counseling resources
50. Provide career counseling for persons with disabilities
51. Provide group vocational counseling
52. Provide career counseling for older adults
53. Provide out-placement counseling
54. Use computerized "counseling" software

Counseling Groups

55. Assist with group members' feedback to each other
56. Identify harmful group-member behaviors
57. Evaluate progress toward group goals
58. Resolve conflict among group members
59. Self-evaluate group counseling effectiveness
60. Determine group counseling termination criteria
61. Inform clients of group counseling guidelines and goals
62. Systematically observe group members' behaviors
63. Use "structured" activities during group counseling
64. Use group-centered group counseling leadership techniques
65. Use leader-centered group counseling leadership techniques

Counseling Families

66. Counsel persons in crisis
67. Counsel clients concerning substance use/abuse
68. Counsel clients concerning sexual abuse
69. Counsel adolescents
70. Counsel concerning family member interaction
71. Counsel clients concerning personality change
72. Counsel clients concerning physical abuse
73. Develop family conflict resolution strategies
74. Counsel concerning family change
75. Clarify family counseling goals
76. Clarify familial behavior norms
77. Inform family members of family dynamics/roles
78. Inform family members of family counseling guidelines and goals
79. Clarify client's moral/spiritual issues
80. Counsel concerning divorce
81. Counsel children
82. Counsel concerning human sexuality
83. Counsel concerning divorce-conflict reduction
84. Interview client's significant others
85. Use behavioral family counseling techniques
86. Counsel concerning marriage enrichment
87. Use structural family counseling techniques
88. Use strategic family counseling techniques
89. Use multigenerational family counseling techniques
90. Counsel concerning premarriage

(*continued*)

TABLE 1.1. (Continued)

Professional Practices

91. Serve as a liaison with other agencies
92. Provide consultation services for ethical or legal dilemmas
93. Participate in case conferences
94. Administer counseling program
95. Conduct prevention-oriented developmental activities
96. Participate in staffing decision-making processes
97. Engage in professional/community public relations
98. Participate in continuing education/skill enhancement
99. Conduct community outreach
100. Correspond orally with others to maintain professional communications
101. Evaluate counselors' performance
102. Establish programmatic service goals
103. Read current professional literature
104. Write to other professionals to maintain professional communications
105. Participate in professional organization activities
106. Assess programmatic needs
107. Review legal statutes and regulations
108. Supervise staff
109. Provide counselor skill-development training
110. Review ethical standards
111. Provide consultation services for interpersonal skills training
112. Provide consultation services for human relationships development
113. Provide consultation services for human resource needs evaluation
114. Engage in formative evaluation of counseling program
115. Engage in summative evaluation of counseling program
116. Supervise counselor trainees
117. Provide consultation services for professional skill development
118. Prepare developmental/preventive media
119. Develop program-related reports
120. Allocate financial resources for counseling program
121. Conduct self-development training for nonclients
122. Provide consultation services for organizational development
123. Provide multicultural training/education
124. Use computers for program data management
125. Engage in data analyses
126. Write communication for noncounseling, professional activities
127. Collaborate in research with other professionals
128. Engage in counseling outcome research
129. Engage in counseling process research
130. Write for publication
131. Provide career counseling for children
132. Develop appraisal instrument/technique
133. Engage in field/observational research
134. Evaluate computer software
135. Conduct fund-raising activities for program development/maintenance
136. Engage in experimental/laboratory research

work behavior study was repeated using the same methodology and data analyses. Preliminary results indicate that the results of this study will be very similar to, although not exactly the same as, the results of the first work behavior study. Unfortunately, the final results of the second work behavior study were not available as this book went to press. Final results of the study should be available from the NBCC in the year 2000.

Although the results of the work behavior studies are helpful in providing information about what counselors actually do in the professional activity known as counseling, what they do not provide is information about the relationship of counseling to other mental health specialties such as psychology or social work. To make comparisons among groups of mental health professionals, we must continue to rely on general descriptions of respective roles, functions, and responsibilities.

☐ Differences Between Professional Counselors and Other Mental Health Specialists

Mental health professionals, other than counselors, include applied and academic counseling and clinical psychologists, social workers, marriage and family therapists, and psychiatrists.

Applied psychologists focus primarily on psychological pathology, or what is commonly viewed as abnormality, illness, or disease. They are typically involved in the diagnosis of personality problems with an emphasis on personality reorganization (i.e., rebuilding the structural and functional effects of a person's personality), and are concerned with maladaptive behavior (i.e., psychopathology). Applied psychology is usually subdivided into school, counseling, clinical, industrial, and community psychology. In contrast, academic psychologists are primarily concerned with areas in basic psychology (e.g., perception, history, physiology, and experimental psychology). Typically, **academic psychologists** conduct research in laboratory settings on the many factors that influence animal and human behavior, with careful control of variables or factors extraneous to those being investigated. Psychologists who work in academic settings are typically concerned with obtaining data that help the understanding of human and animal behavior and that lead to generalizations.

Social workers have a special concern for community problems that may lead to psychopathology (e.g., intrafamily problems, unemployment, urban decay, or poverty). The complex social system and delivery of social services are emphasized, usually in the context of the medical model (i.e., remediation of existing problems). Major focal points in social work are: (1) social advocacy, which includes social program delivery and planning, (2) clinical practice, which typically emanates from comprehensive community mental health hospitals and centers, and (3) mental health consultation to community organizations, families, and individuals. In the latter context, social workers often gather and interpret pertinent information about patients' personal history and social situations, thereby providing data that may assist physicians with diagnoses and treatments.

Marriage and family therapists have much in common with social workers because of their interest in the family as a unit of the community. However, they tend to be primarily occupied with family psychotherapy (i.e., the client is all members of the family as opposed to individual family members). Many times, marriage and family therapists are members of another professional group such as social workers, psychologists, or relatively recently, counselors. A distinction, although slight, is sometimes made between marriage and family therapists and marriage and family counselors. The former group aligns itself primarily with the American Association of Marriage and Family Therapists while the latter aligns itself primarily with the American Counseling Association. Other than these professional alignments, however, it is usually difficult to discern differences in their respective practices.

Psychiatry is frequently confused with applied psychology because professionals in these two areas direct their interest toward the diagnosis and treatment of psychopathology. Psychiatrists, however, are medical specialists who hold a degree in medicine (M.D.), study the characteristics of people, and explore topics such as abnormal behavior, motivation, drives, and anxiety, and the medical and psychological conditions that affect these dynamics. Typically, psychiatrists conduct their work in hospital settings. In sharp contrast to psychologists, psychiatrists often use psychopharmacological drugs (medications) in the treatment of psychopathological disorders. However, in a few hospitals, some clinical psychologists who have received special training have the privilege to prescribe psychopharmacological medications.

Psychotherapist is a generic term that generally is unregulated. That is, in many states, anyone may call himself or herself a psychotherapist because use of this title is not regulated by state (counseling) licensure or other law. It is true that many mental health professionals holding legitimate professional credentials refer to themselves as psychotherapists because it connotes the nature of the services they provide. However, use of this term is not recommended because of the significant possibility that persons not having substantive professional preparation for counseling can use it and thereby misrepresent the counseling profession in any of a variety of ways that would be detrimental to professional counselors.

To distinguish completely among various mental health professionals is impossible. However, differentiation on the basis of commonly held perceptions is possible. For example, mental health problems may be conceptualized along a continuum from rather minor adjustment problems for otherwise normal people to abnormal behavior (i.e., severe psychopathology). Similarly, the work orientations of mental health professionals may be conceptualized as being on a continuum from scientist, with an emphasis on theory development and research, to practitioner, with an emphasis on affective interactions. A combination of these continua forms a quadrant system based on descriptions of the extremes. Mental health professionals may be placed in the quadrants as illustrated in Figure 1.1. Presently insufficient research data are available for determining which quadrant placement is best for a given profession, but Figure 1.1 may be used to convey general, relative positions of several of the professions discussed.

Illustrative Case—Keith

The approach to a given problem varies by specialty and perhaps can be best explained through an example. Consider Keith, a 27-year-old male

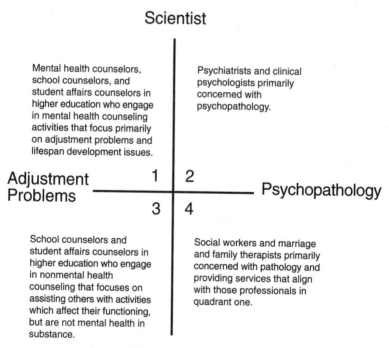

FIGURE 1.1. Mental health service delivery continuum.

struggling unsuccessfully to advance himself within a large retail firm. According to his wife, he is very nervous and becomes tense when he leaves for work. He does not concern himself with responsibilities in the home, and he annoys his wife with unprovoked verbal assaults on their 6-year-old son. Keith appears unhappy at work, and his wife is unhappy about her inability to comfort him. Despite the necessary oversimplification of this example, certain distinctions among the various mental health specialties can be illustrated.

A social worker would most likely view Keith's presenting problem in the context of the occurrence of various factors in a population. Consideration would be given to the kind of neighborhood in which Keith resides, his income, his educational background, and whether his wife works (i.e., socioeconomic factors). Also of interest to the social worker would be elements of the couple's lifestyle such as possessions, what is being purchased on installment plans, club memberships, religious affiliations, childhood history, and past individual medical or psychological problems. The social worker might believe that a referral is necessary, or might view the particular problem as solvable through meetings with the couple to discuss family dynamics.

Based on this information, the social worker might refer Keith to a psychiatrist and would provide the latter with a picture of generalities based on his or her knowledge of family dynamics and adult behaviors. An important role for the social worker is to contribute to the understanding of a problem by providing information about the psychosocial variables in Keith's life.

Marriage and family therapists also would consider demographic and contextual variables. However, the primary focus of their concern would be intrafamily dynamics. The therapist would arrange an interview with the couple, perhaps including the child, and would focus attention on whether their problems are with interpersonal relationships within the family or with social situations with other groups of people. The marriage and family therapist would focus primarily on the problems of adjustment as they relate to the intra- and interpersonal relationships of the family members. During therapy, the marriage and family therapist would have cogent and useful advice to offer Keith and his wife on how to improve their interpersonal relationships, based on the premise that Keith's improved interactions would be a benefit in helping his entire life.

The psychologist would probably interview Keith and perhaps administer a battery of psychological tests. The psychologist might view Keith's problem as hostility toward authority figures, or that he has not matured sufficiently to maintain adequate control of his impulses. Keith could also be viewed as anxious because he is not achieving to the level of expectations held for him by himself or others, or both. From the psychologist's perspective, these factors may be contributing to a low level of self-esteem or valuation which creates feelings of unworthiness. This interpretation of Keith's situation is based on psychoanalytic-personality theory, but psychologists are not confined to this approach in viewing people's problems. For example, other psychologists might base the problem on the work of the behavioral psychologist B.F. Skinner, using knowledge from learning theory, and they may employ behavior modification techniques.

The psychiatrist, like the psychologist, is concerned initially with diagnosis. An interview with Keith would be arranged and information from significant others in Keith's life more than likely would be requested. For example, demographic information and family history, including family interactions and past occurrences of problems, could be gained from a social worker or clinical psychological tests or from both. The psychiatrist would be interested mainly in determining causes or reasons or, at the very least, gaining a good understanding of the symptoms in order that appropriate treatment could be prescribed. The treatment might be medication to reduce the anxiety and general impulsive behavior, or therapy with the psychiatrist or, more typically, with a social worker.

The professional mental health counselor (sometimes known as a community counselor) working with Keith would consider the same data as the other mental health service providers but would apply the data to life span development (i.e., vocation, career, family, childrearing, interpersonal and intragroup relationships, and the person's context of a quality life). These professional counselors would recognize the type of environment in which Keith is employed and the values associated with it. Like social workers and marriage family therapists, professional mental health counselors would try to understand family dynamics. However, they might depart from the other professionals by deciding jointly with Keith to administer a battery of psychological, interest, and educational tests if sufficient information existed following interviews with Keith. The professional mental health counselor might conclude that Keith and his wife could benefit from joint counseling, or that there is a need for a referral because of the severe degree of pathology present with Keith. Whether or not a referral is made, the professional mental health counselor would conduct counseling sessions with Keith to help him formulate an appropriate plan of action (i.e., proper referral or continued counseling).

In sharp contrast to the other specialists, the professional school counselor's involvement with Keith and his family would begin with the son. The assumption is made that the family dynamics have affected a change in the child's behavior (e.g., the child is exhibiting learning difficulty or acting-out behavior in the school) and his teacher has sought help from the school counselor. Because the focus of concern is the child's behavioral changes, the school counselor must work closely with the teacher in order to help the child. The school counselor utilizes the same data as that considered by the mental health counselor, but they are applied to the school situation. A school counselor tries to understand a student based on (1) the child's perspective, (2) prior knowledge of the school and the teachers, (3) observations of the child in the classroom, (4) interviews with the child, and (5) data contained in the child's cumulative school file. The latter contains information concerning achievement and intelligence test data, family background, academic record information, and previous teachers' comments. However, if insufficient information is available, the school counselor subsequently may decide that an interview with the parents could be beneficial. In this situation, interviewing Keith and his wife might aid the school counselor in determining whether (1) the core problem of the child's school learning or overt-behavior problems is due to interpersonal problems at home, and (2) the parents could benefit from counseling. The school counselor would focus primarily on improving the child's behavior and performance in school, but would also help the child to cope with problems at home.

Of course, many overlapping areas are addressed by mental health service providers, and the illustrations and distinctions cited above are not as clear-cut as described. For example, social workers and marriage and family therapists may be knowledgeable of and have skills in career development and testing, and some professional counselors may function as psychologists. However, what professional counselors have in common are (1) knowledge and skills in human growth and development, social and behavioral sciences (especially psychology), helping relations, group interactions, assessment and appraisal, and research methodology; and (2) a profound respect for the scientific approach.

☐ Assumptions for Professional Counselors

The counseling profession is based on certain assumptions, some of which are definitive and fully agreed upon by professional counselors. Others, however, are implicit; not specifically stated or readily acknowledged and, in many instances, not clearly perceived. Two factors that most professional counselors view as important to successful practice are the professional counselor's (1) knowledge and skills, and (2) personality. Without useful knowledge, a professional counselor is unable to practice effectively. Likewise, in order to practice effectively, the professional counselor needs to be able to respond to clients in ways and with skills that promote willingness to profit from the counselor's efforts. Relatedly, a professional counselor must exhibit personality characteristics that allow clients to be receptive to the counselor's efforts.

Knowledge and Skills

A professional counselor needs to be knowledgeable of those aspects of mental health that relate to the development, relief, and solution of an individual's emotional and other concerns which are associated with quality of life. In addition, the professional counselor must be aware of the effect that biological and societal influences may have upon an individual's behavior. Therefore, it is widely recognized in the counseling profession that counselor knowledge and skill development should include preparation in eight areas:

1. human growth and development;
2. social and cultural foundations;
3. the helping relationship;
4. group dynamics, processes, and counseling;
5. life style and career development;
6. appraisal of the individual;
7. research and evaluation; and
8. professional orientation.

These are the core preparation areas recognized and endorsed by the Council for Accreditation of Counseling and Related Educational Programs, the American Counseling Association, and the National Board for Certified Counselors. In addition, they have been found by faculty in counselor preparation programs to be highly relevant to preparing counselors (Vacc, 1992).

Human Growth and Development.   This area involves an understanding of the nature and needs of individuals at all age levels. Included are studies in human behavior, personality theory, and learning theory. The study of human growth and development allows the professional counselor an opportunity to gain an understanding of how psychological, sociological, and physiological factors influence behavior at all developmental levels.

Social and Cultural Foundations.   Included in this area are studies of change, ethnic groups, subcultures, sexism, changing roles of women, urban and rural societies, population patterns, cultural mores, use of leisure time, and differing life patterns. Knowledge of traditional disciplines such as the behavioral sciences, economics, and political science is emphasized. Studies in this area help the counselor to understand contexts in which people live and function, and how factors in those contexts influence human behavior.

The Helping Relationship. Knowledge of the helping relationship includes counseling and consultation theory, development of self-awareness, and an understanding of how and why clients do what they do. Development of helping relationship skills for the successful practice of counseling is emphasized. Studies in this area help the counselor develop actual counseling behaviors.

Group Dynamics, Processes, and Counseling. Theories of group behavior, group practices, methods for working with groups, group dynamics, and observational and facilitative skills are covered in this area. Studies in this area help the counselor to develop skills to work with several clients simultaneously, as well as to be able to facilitate other types of group interactions.

Life Style and Career Development. Vocational-choice theories, the relationship between career choice and life style, sources of occupational and educational information, approaches to career decision-making processes, and approaches to career exploration constitute this area of knowledge development. The intent is to enable the professional counselor to be of assistance to clients in their personal, social, emotional, and vocational choices and with the activities in their daily living.

Appraisal. The particular knowledge, skills, and experiences necessary to enable a professional counselor to gather information to use in making judgements about clients and environmental settings make up this area. Included are methods for gathering and interpreting data (i.e., use of tests), individual and group testing, observation techniques, alternative types of assessments, standards for the practice of testing, and general skills necessary for the assessment and appraisal of individuals' behaviors.

Research and Program Evaluation. Effective functioning as a professional counselor necessitates a knowledge base in the areas of statistics, research design, and development of research and demonstration proposals. Professional counseling practitioners, regardless of specialty, must be able to contribute through research to the body of literature in the profession. Studies in this area enable counselors to be familiar with and competent in a variety of evaluation procedures such as those used for evaluation of counseling processes and counseling program evaluation.

Professional Orientation. This area includes knowledge of the basic components of the counseling profession (i.e., professional organizations, codes of ethics, legal considerations, standards of preparation, certification, and licensing). In addition, the role identity of the professional counselor and other human service specialists is explored. Studies in this area help the counselor to be a fully involved member of the professional counseling community.

Personality

Even the most knowledgeable and well-trained professional counselor will be unable to help others if she or he does not possess appropriate personality characteristics; failure to evidence these characteristics will cause clients to be unreceptive to the professional counselor's behaviors. Although the qualities of personality that promote effective counseling are elusive, researchers have identified several personality characteristics that are important in promoting a productive counselor-client relationship.

Security.   Prerequisites to security are self-confidence, self-respect, and freedom from fear and anxiety. Secure counselors feel comfortable about themselves and therefore provide healthy models for their clients. The professional counselor who doubts self, lacks respect for personal competence, and is suspicious and questions everyone's motives is unlikely to be of help to others. Fear and anxiety are associated with the diminished ability to attend to the client during an interview.

As a personal quality, security in a counselor is more likely to allow clients to be themselves. Counselors who are comfortable with themselves do not seek to satisfy their own needs by shaping the client in their own image or in their image of what the client should be. They have the capability to allow clients to develop at their own rates and in their own directions.

Trust.   Trust, in its most elementary form, is to be able to give, receive, and depend on others, a quality that is highly important in determining the professional counselor's attitude toward people. Trust, which develops during the early stages of life, is difficult to learn if not acquired when young. In counseling, the absence of trust may cause a counselor to act in ways that do not benefit clients. The most unfortunate part of lack of trust is that counselors who cannot trust others also cannot trust themselves, and thus are generally ineffective in all aspects of counseling.

Courage.   All human beings appear to have an innate desire to be loved, recognized, and respected. Professional counselors, however, must be able to put aside their own needs within the context of counseling in order to find gratification. For example, the professional counselor must be willing to absorb a client's anger, and to accept a sense of "aloneness" as the client progresses and becomes autonomous from the counselor. Analogous to professional counselors working with clients are parents allowing their growing children to mature and develop. During a counseling relationship, the client initially relies upon the counselor, shares personal thoughts, aspirations, and behaviors which are rarely made public, and seeks direction and order in his or her life. Subsequently, counselors must be emotionally capable of relinquishing their clients' dependency and allowing them to gain control of their own lives.

In summary, professional counselors need to have enough self-security, self-trust, and courage to relinquish a part of themselves when helping others. In addition, Bardon and Bennett (1974) found that other particular personality qualities of helping professionals affect their behavior when making judgments about clients. They suggested that professionals working with clients need to possess personality qualities that include genuineness, positive skepticism, and empathy. These qualities also are important and relevant to professional counselors.

Genuineness.   Genuineness involves a concern for what happens to people. To understand the importance of this quality, reflect upon the role professional counselors play in the lives of their clients. Counselors are empowered (by their clients because counseling is most often entered into voluntarily) to tell others what to do and they have great authority in this capacity because they are viewed as experts. Such power in relationships with their clients can only be regulated or controlled by a sincere and overriding concern for the welfare of others, a value that is integral to preventing potential misuse of authority.

Positive Skepticism.   Another important personality quality is an attitude of positive skepticism. Skepticism, as viewed by Bardon and Bennett (1974), reflects an understanding of the imperfections of the current state of knowledge, instrumentation, and methods. Unfortunately, professional counselors often have to act without the security offered by the exactness available in other disciplines (e.g., the hard sciences). However, because of the nature of their involvement with real-life situations that require assistance and because better alternatives typically are unavailable, professional counselors must act. A cautious, skeptical, and yet critical approach that makes use of past successes and failures must be an abiding value of professional counselors when assisting clients. The adjective "positive" has been included to suggest that skepticism should be linked with a willingness to persist and try new approaches. This is most important because professional counselors will have disappointments, immediate results may be lacking, and occasionally, clients may be uncooperative. Therefore, an optimistic outlook, despite discouragement, is required.

Empathy.   Empathy is the ability to identify and connect with others emotionally. Professional counselors on many occasions work with people whose values and life experiences are very different from their own. Also, clients often enter a counseling relationship being extremely antagonistic toward the counselor; the counselor is perceived as threatening and reflective of the troublesome social system that most likely prompted their seeking assistance. To function well when people are hostile, angry, and negative can be difficult. Professional counselors, however, must develop an understanding of how their clients feel and must be able to respect those feelings even when they appear to be making the counselor's job difficult.

Although the personality qualities presented above are not explicit, they are highly important in determining how the professional counselor functions. Perhaps the personality qualities are more reflective of the attitude professional counselors take toward the nature of their work than is knowledge. However, knowledge is ultimately more useful for professional counselors, enabling them to approach the problems that confront them regarding human behavior when they possess these various personality characteristics.

The Counselor as Scientist

A final assumption about professional counselors, the sine qua non, is that the professional counselor is a scientist; a view that is consistent with the earlier assumption of positive skepticism as a desirable characteristic of the professional counselor. If an individual's behavior can be altered and the individual is capable of making that change as a result of the counseling relationship and process, then the professional counselor must observe the effects of his or her procedures as they affect individuals by carefully measuring and evaluating change. Professional counselors are continuously confronted with measuring and evaluating the effects of their counseling in order to derive specific conclusions about efficacy. Therefore, there is a scientific aspect of the practice of counseling.

The counseling practitioner as scientist has been described by Barlow, Hayes, and Nelson (1984) as involving three interrelated activities or roles. First, the counseling practitioner is a consumer of research findings reported in professional journals and at professional meetings. The information gained involves either initial or reexamined assessments of approaches for the practitioner to put into practice. In the second role, the practitioner is an evaluator and appraiser of approaches that use empirical methods which would increase effectiveness and accountability. Finally, the practitioner is a researcher who produces and analyzes data and who reports these data to the scientific community at professional meetings and in professional journals.

Conceptually, the research basis for practice or professional activities and judgments of counselors is illustrated in Figure 1.2. A majority of what is known about human behavior derives from research in the social and behavioral sciences, much of which is conducted under circumstances that are less than ideal. With numerous replications, however, the scientific credibility of research findings is enhanced and enables the scientist to draw conclusions. When professional counselors try to determine something about a client's behavior, they must take into account many factors or variables, some of which cannot be ignored, such as developmental stage, age, gender, situational events, attitudes, personality, personal habits, and cultural considerations. Literally, the professional counselor is confronted with an almost limitless number of confounding variables when counseling.

FIGURE 1.2. The influence of research and practice as they affect the outcomes of a professional counselor working with clients.

Illustrative Case—John

Consider John, an adolescent whose offensive behavior alienates others. To understand John's behavior and to help him alleviate his inappropriate behavior, the professional counselor must understand (1) what is known about adolescent behavior, (2) how behavior is changed, (3) how John perceives what is happening to him with regard to others and different aspects of his life, and (4) other special problems John brings with him to interpersonal relationships. The professional counselor, working with John, must help him by using two resources at once. One resource is the existing data that have been derived by other practitioner-scientists as established, accumulated laws or rules for people in general. The other resource is existing data specific to John, his behaviors, and his life situation. The former is termed *nomothetic*, which pertains to general laws and principles, while the latter is termed *idiographic*, which pertains to laws and rules of behavior specific to an individual, in order to explain individual cases.

☐ The Professional Counselor as a Practitioner-Scientist

Professional counselors, to be most effective in helping individuals, must integrate information, reconcile differences, and view themselves as scientists. All evidence needs to be considered and evaluated and a decision must be derived through distillation of all available knowledge, information, and experiences. As a practitioner-scientist, the professional counselor is engaged in a scientific experiment in which questions are raised and examined, and results and conclusions are changed as new evidence becomes available. Counseling involves a series of formative evaluations and action plans. When professional counselors take a course of action or discuss what is happening during counseling, they must judge the probability of the validity of change made in a client's behavior against the data.

Competent professional counselor practice, recognizing that the practice is scientific, takes place when knowledge, both nomothetic and idiographic, is filtered by the professional counselor. Competent professional practice is also the interaction between the professional counselor and knowledge in a setting, an interaction designed to foster helpful behavior. Ultimately, professional counselors are only as useful or as valuable as the amount of knowledge they have gained. This book is dedicated to the assumption that the content of counseling is never removed from scientific methods.

In addition to knowledge and techniques, effective counselors must have skills in scientific inquiry, not only to enable them to be fully functioning professionals, but to establish themselves as self-regulating professionals. This viewpoint is neither original nor new; the scientist-practitioner model has long been used by counselor preparation programs approved by the American Psychological Association (APA) (Hock, Ross, & Winder, 1966).

Adoption of the APA training procedures is not being suggested for professional counselors, but the practitioner-scientist viewpoint, as opposed to the scientist-practitioner approach, makes considerable sense for the future of professional counseling. Moreover, this viewpoint is consistent with the existing Code of Ethics and Standards of Practice of the American Counseling Association (1999). These Standards state that counselors must gather data on their effectiveness and use the findings to guide them in the counseling process. The spirit of scientific inquiry, therefore, must pervade the perspectives of professional counselors, with the manifestation of the spirit being the common rule rather than the exception.

Inherent in the practitioner-scientist approach is viewing scientific inquiry in counseling from a much broader perspective than has been characteristic in the past. As mentioned earlier, the core of this view is the professional counselor's development of a habitually inquiring, critical attitude about practice. Thus, scientific methods are equated with inquiry as well as traditional methods of normative data gathering. This means that professional counselors must continually engage in careful, scientific review of all their activities. Common to both scientific inquiry and practice is the necessity for a questioning attitude, a method of problem solving, a high regard for evidence, and methods for self-monitoring and improvement. The practitioner-scientist approach, then, is more than just data gathering and analysis; it is a way of approaching all professional activities.

The distinctive feature of the practitioner-scientist approach is the need for professional counselors to have competent training in the knowledge and techniques associated with counseling and research methods. Being a professional counselor, therefore, means being competent in facilitating science as well as human development. Although a major part of a professional counselor's time is spent in practice or direct service, a part of the direct service must be devoted to the improvement of and subsequent changes in services as determined through scientific inquiry. An important element of the practitioner-scientist approach is that it encourages professional counselors to examine and compare client behaviors for decisions about counseling goals, intervention strategies, and effectiveness of the counseling process. This approach guides the professional counselor to promote sensitive counseling that is uniquely suited to each client. Many people view the practitioner-scientifist approach as a one-time activity. However, counseling and data gathering are continuous processes throughout a relationship with a client; they are activities that establish direction for the counseling process. The practitioner-scientist approach is a means for obtaining and using information to generate and establish counseling goals and intervention strategies, and to determine the effectiveness of counseling.

The focus of this ongoing process is not to find the "truth" for working with people, but, rather, to use information in a way that helps clients develop. In this respect, the professional counselor can be viewed as an experimenter who is continually assessing and conceptualizing the relationships among the information obtained, counseling goals, and counseling approach. The effectiveness of the professional counselor, therefore, is maintained by the counselor's ability to gather data in a scientific manner and to use it for making ongoing modifications to the counseling process. Without the scientific component, the counseling process becomes merely an act of faith.

☐ Summary

Professional counselors apply knowledge, skills, and techniques derived from the areas of human growth and development, the social and behavioral sciences, and counselor education. In addition to professional counselors, there are many types of mental health professionals (e.g., applied psychologists and social workers) who use counseling techniques and who work in many settings such as private practice, community agencies, and higher education. However, as members of a group of mental health professionals, counselors distinguish themselves by the applied nature of their work. Further differentiation among the many mental health professionals can be made on the basis of commonly held perceptions with regard to mental health problems. These can be conceptualized along a continuum from adjustment to abnormal behavior. In addition, differentiation can be made between mental health professionals regarding work orientations that range from scientist to practitioner.

The counseling profession is based on a number of assumptions. To be successful, counselors must possess certain essential personal characteristics such as security, trust, and courage. Relatedly, counselors also are assumed to have mastered a body of knowledge and skills. Finally, the professional counselor is a scientist. This latter role is important because counselors are increasingly required to evaluate the effects of their counseling and to read as well as produce research findings for professional publications and other (e.g., electronic) resources. Counseling, then, encompasses a diverse number of settings and involves basic assumptions about what is required to be successful.

So again, what is counseling? It is an activity about which we know and believe a great deal, but which we cannot define succinctly. We know at a minimum that it is helping from a caring perspective. Yet this statement is entirely too simplistic because it belies the many complexities of counseling and fails to differentiate what professional counselors do from the many other lay uses of the term (e.g., financial counseling, real estate counseling, or fitness counseling). Thus, counseling as an activity engaged in by specialized mental health professionals is something that needs to be explained at length; there is no easy way to explain counseling.

II

CORE KNOWLEDGE AREAS FOR PROFESSIONAL COUNSELING PRACTICE

Life Span Development

The purpose of this chapter is to assist the reader in obtaining an understanding of the material that is generally associated with textbooks focusing on developmental psychology. Summarized concisely is an overview which conveys the main points of issues viewed as life span development within the contextual framework of the counseling profession. We have tried in this chapter to maximize information and directness rather than produce elegant prose. A brief glance at the topics will indicate that the focus is that of a social developmentalist; primary theoretical underpinnings of human development are featured as well as the outcomes of social and personality development and its implications for later development. A limited emphasis is provided on the physical development of individuals.

☐ Nature Versus Nurture

One of the broadest and most basic issues in human development is the *nature versus nurture* controversy. The longstanding argument refers to the relative contributions of heredity and environment in the development of personality and behavior in individuals.

One undeniable factor influencing human development is genetics. Scientists have produced much research regarding the influence of heredity on an individual. Researchers have suggested that genetic factors account for approximately 40–50% of differences in cognitive skills, 30–

40% of differences in temperament, and 20–30% of emotional character-istics. However, environmental factors also have been shown to heavily influence human behavior development. For this reason, it has rarely been assumed that approximately 50% of any human trait is linked to genetic factors. Likewise, counseling and related research has shown that significant change is possible across the life span. As could be expected, genetics alone cannot sufficiently account for all factors in the develop-ment of an individual, although genetics does serve as the basis for the shared experience of human existence.

Internal Models of Experience

Often emphasized in the field of counseling is the concept of internal paradigms of experience. These internal paradigms are sets of assump-tions or conclusions about the world, about the self, and about relation-ships with others which are derived from the interpretation of life events. The long-range effect of a given experience, interaction, or environmen-tal circumstance lies not within the objective properties of the event it-self, but within the individual's interpretation of the event and the mean-ing that is associated with it. This meaning is generalized beyond the event and then continues to affect the manner in which one interprets future events. This paradigm of learning helps account for continuity of behav-ior over time as well as the nonuniformity of effects manifested by indi-viduals who have similar experiences.

Ecological Perspectives

A broader perspective of the influence of environment on human devel-opment is that of human ecology. To understand the overall influence of the environment on the individual, it is important to understand the con-text in which an individual exists. Complex patterns of interaction and development can be observed beyond the individual and his or her fam-ily. A neighborhood, a school system, and a community can all have sig-nificant effects in either enhancing or inhibiting the personality and so-cial development of individuals. This ecological perspective places the individual and his or her family at the core of the developmental process, but also considers the influences outside of this core and, in turn, the influences upon these influences, which cause a ripple effect within the ecological system. This broad perspective takes into consideration social problems, parenting styles, economic and employment factors, and soci-etal status.

☐ The Psychoanalytic Perspective of Development

Two individuals most frequently associated with the psychoanalytic per-spective of human development are Sigmund Freud and Erik Erikson. A more recent contributor is Arthur Chickering. Succinct summaries of the contributions of each are presented below.

Sigmund Freud

Many of the ideas about human, social, and personality developments stem from Sigmund Freud's psychoanalytic theory. His approach charac-terizes human beings as being blueprinted from inborn biological needs (i.e., innate or inborn determinants of personality and social behavior).

Much of the theory of Sigmund Freud, a physician whose practicing specialty was neurology, evolved from observations of his neurotic pa-tients. These observations led him to believe that human beings are born with two types of urges or instincts: Eros, the life instincts, and Thanatos, the death or destructive instincts. Freud concluded that these instincts were the source of all psychic or mental energy used by individuals to think, learn, and perform other mental functions that satisfy the individual's inborn goals or motives.

Freud's point of view was that a newborn infant has an undifferenti-ated personality consisting of instincts (Eros and Thanatos) and some ba-sic reflexes. These instincts are divided among three components of one's personality: id, ego, and superego. The id component of personality rep-resents all of one's basic needs, wishes, and motives. The ego is formed as psychic energy that involves cognitive processes such as perception, learn-ing, and logical reasoning, which are designed to assist in finding realistic methods of gratifying the instincts. The superego is the ethical compo-nent of personality which develops from the ego. Its function is to deter-mine whether the ego's method of satisfying the instincts is moral.

According to Freud, the social and personality development of an indi-vidual progresses through a series of five psychosexual stages: oral, anal, phallic, latency, and genital. These psychosexual stages parallel the matu-ration of sex instincts. Freud assumed that the activities and conflicts that emerge at each psychosexual stage would have significant influences on personality development over time.

Eric Erikson

A student of Freud, Eric Erikson extended Freud's theory by concentrat-ing less on the sexual instincts and more on sociocultural determinants of human development. Erikson (1968) argued that individuals progress through a series of eight psychosocial stages with each stage characterized by a particular social conflict or crisis that the individual must successfully resolve in order to develop as a healthy individual. The first five stages correspond with Freud's five psychosexual stages. The last three stages, which occur during young adulthood, middle age, and old age, are significant extensions of Freud's developmental approach. A comparison of Erikson's developmental stages and Freud's psychosexual stages is presented in Table 2.1. As indicated, Erikson's developmental stages, which are continuous, do not end at young adulthood as do Freud's stages.

Arthur Chickering

Arthur Chickering (1987) proposed a developmental model that builds upon Erikson's stages and outlines sources of impact in the college environment. Chickering sees the traditional-age college student as a person in a distinct psychosocial phase defined by the emergence of certain inner capabilities and needs which interact with the demands of the environment. Chickering expanded Erikson's identity stage to include seven vectors or dimensions of development that occur in young adulthood. These include developing competence, managing emotions, developing autonomy, establishing identity, freeing interpersonal relationships, developing purpose, and developing integrity. Chickering postulated that existing within each of these dimensions or vectors are a series of developmental tasks, a source of concern, and a set of outcomes. The vectors characterize the primary concerns the student will have, the tasks that will confront them, and what will be the sources of preoccupation or worry. Chickering further postulated that development along each dimension or vector involves cycles of differentiation and integration; at each of the seven vectors the student continually apprehends more complexity and shifting. More differentiated perceptions and behaviors serve to create a coherent picture of the student. Accordingly, growth along the vector is not simply the result of maturational unfolding but rather results from stimulation. Students do not develop in unison; they are developmentally diverse.

Abraham Maslow

Abraham Maslow (1968) proposed a humanistic approach to human development. Maslow's model concerns the development of motives and needs without the emphasis on pathology that pervaded psychoanalytic

TABLE 2.1. Erikson's and Freud's Stages of Development

Approximate age	Erikson's stage or psychosocial crisis	Corresponding Freudian stage	Erikson's viewpoint: Significant events and social influences
Birth to 1 year	Basic trust versus mistrust	Oral	Infants need to learn to trust others to care for their basic needs, with the key social agent being the parent(s) or primary caregiver. If rejected or if care is inconsistent, infants may view the world as an unsafe place with untrustworthy or irresponsible people.
1 to 3 years	Autonomy versus shame and doubt	Anal	Children need to learn to be autonomous in caring for themselves with the key social agent continuing to be the parent(s). Children who are unable to achieve this autonomy may doubt their own abilities and feel shameful.
3 to 6 years	Initiative versus guilt	Phallic	Children will try to act grown up and accept responsibilities beyond their capability. This may produce conflict with parents and other family members who are key social agents, making the children feel guilty. Children need to maintain a sense of initiative while not impinging on the rights, privileges, or goals of others.
6 to 12 years	Industry versus inferiority	Latency	Children need to master important social and academic skills with key social agents being their teachers and peers. Success results in becoming self-assured. Failure can result in feelings of inferiority.
12 to 20 years	Identity versus confusion	Early genital	As part of the transition between childhood role and adolescence maturity, with key social agent being peers, adolescents struggle with establishing basic social and occupational identities or remaining confused about their role as an adult.

(continued)

TABLE 2.1. (*Continued*)

Approximate age	Erikson's stage or psychosocial crisis	Corresponding Freudian stage	Erikson's viewpoint: Significant events and social influences
20 to 40 years	Intimacy versus isolation	Genital	At this stage, strong friendships are formed including a shared identity with another person. Failure in this area may result in feelings of loneliness or isolation. Lovers, spouses, and close friends are key social agents.
40 to 65 years (middle adulthood)	Generativity versus stagnation	Genital	Adults become productive in their work, raise their families, and look after the needs of young people. Those not assuming these responsibilities become stagnant and/or self-centered. Spouse, children, and culture norms are key social agents.
Old age	Ego integrity versus despair	Genital	As one reflects, life will be viewed as either meaningful, productive, and happy or a major disappointment, based on one's life experiences.

approaches. Maslow described these drives as **deficiency motives** and **being motives**. Deficiency motives include drives for physical and emotional homeostasis such as food, water, shelter, sex, and respect and love from others. Being motives are defined as those that drive individuals to understand themselves and humanity, have spiritual experiences, display altruism, and experience emotional growth. Maslow described these needs for being as basic drives to reach one's full potential or to become self-actualized. Maslow posited that these needs are constructed in a hierarchical sequence with the deficiency motives of **physiological** and **safety needs** at the base of the sequence, followed by needs for **love, belonging,** and **basic self-esteem,** and finally **self-actualization** at the apex. According to the hierarchy, needs at the beginning of the sequence must be effectively met in order for an individual to begin attaining higher order needs. For this reason, Maslow suggested that this hierarchy was a potential sequence which may not be accomplished by all individuals.

☐ Social Learning Theory

John Watson has generally been accepted as the most significant early proponent of behaviorism. Strongly influenced by Pavlov's work concerning the conditioning of animals, Watson applied Pavlov's findings to children's development by demonstrating the classical conditioning of an 11-month old child who was afraid of a rabbit. Classical conditioning has been illustrated with older children as well as with infants, and its power to instill complex meaning and social attitudes has been demonstrated by researchers. Watson also was a proponent of the concept that newborn infants are "tabulae rasae," conditioned by their environments to become socialized (e.g., feel, think, and act in certain ways). Watson believed that children's learned associations between stimuli and responses or habits are the building blocks of human development. Consistent with this approach, social and personality development was viewed as a continuous process marked by the gradual acquisition of new and more refined behaviors. These behaviors were viewed by Watson as habits that may be acquired by repeated exposure to a stimulus through classical or operant conditioning, or observational learning.

Since Watson's work in the early 1900s, various theorists have built upon his explanations of social and personality development. These movements have been characterized by various names, including the Neohullian theorists who assumed that one's personality consisted of a set of habits, each of which was formulated through learned associations. Neohullians also advocated that human behavior is motivated by primary and secondary drives and behaviors which reduce drives become learned and are established as habits; the goal is to help children acquire habits that are socially acceptable.

Another important movement is Skinnerian. A name given to operant learning theorists who advocated that drives played little or no role in human social learning. Instead, our actions become either more or less probable as a function of their consequences. Accordingly, human behavior is controlled by external stimuli through reinforcement or punitive events rather than anything internal.

More recently, Bandura has been the principle proponent of cognitive social learning theory which attributes habits and personality to responses acquired by observing the behavior of social models. Bandura views learning as a cognitive activity that occurs as an individual attends to activities even before the behavior is reinforced. According to Bandura, reinforcers and punitive events are performance variables that motivate learners to engage in activities that they have already learned. Proponents of Bandura's point of view believe that children play an active role in their own socialization. They regulate their own behavior by rewarding acts that are consistent with learned standards of conduct. This process is a continuous and reciprocal interaction between personal, behavioral, and environmental elements; the environment affects the child, and the child's behavior affects the environment. The importance of Bandura's contribution has been the idea that individuals influence their environment, which influences their development.

Appealing elements of the social learning approach to development are its objectivity, its practical applications, and the amount of information it has helped generate about developing children and adolescents. Perhaps the greatest criticism of the social learning approach is that it discounts or only minimally emphasizes the importance of biological and cognitive contributions to the personal and social development of individuals.

☐ Cognitive-Developmental Theory

The major contributor to cognitive-developmental theory is Jean Piaget. Piaget and his students view children as curious, active explorers who respond to the environment according to their understanding of its essential features. From this perspective, any group of children might react very differently to some aspect of the same environment because they may interpret it differently. Accordingly, to predict how a child will respond to a nurturing mother, a scornful police person, or an authoritarian teacher, one would need to have knowledge of how the child perceives or construes the event.

According to Piaget (1964), the term cognitive development refers to the changes that occur in the mental abilities over the course of an individual's life. Piaget advocated four major stages of cognitive growth between birth and early adulthood with each successive stage representing a new and more complex method of intellectual functioning. Piaget described children as active, inventive, curiosity seekers who are constantly construing a "schemata" to conceptualize what they know and modifying these cognitive structures as their knowledge is extended. The latter involves organization (i.e., rearranging existing knowledge into higher order schemata), adaptation (i.e., adjusting to the environment which occurs through either assimilation and accommodation), assimilation (i.e., the process by which a child tries to interpret new experiences within the framework of existing schemata), and accommodation (i.e., modifying one's existing schemata in order to interpret or cope with other new experiences). Intellectual growth results from the interplay of assimilation and accommodation, which in turn creates a need for further assimilation and accommodation.

The stages in which growth takes place according to Piaget (1964) are defined as sensory motor (birth to 2 years old), preoperational (between ages 2 to 7), concrete operations (ages 7 to 11), and formal operations (ages 11 to 12 years and older).

During the **sensory motor stage**, the infant gains knowledge and understanding of objects and events by acting on them. Children in this stage engage in the behavior of adapting to their surroundings which eventually is internalized to form mental symbols, enabling them to understand the permanence of objects, including people, to imitate the behavior of others, and to solve simple problems. The sensory motor period is followed by the **preoperational stage** whereby symbolic reasoning becomes increasingly apparent. During this time children begin to use words and images in their activities in inventive ways. Children become more and more knowledgeable about the world in which they live, but their thinking is quite limited in comparison to that of adults. During this period children are described as very egocentric because they view events from their own perspective and have difficulty understanding another person's point of view. Also, their approach is characterized by "centration," which is described as the ability to focus on one aspect of a situation only rather than being able to evaluate or merge several pieces of information simultaneously.

During the **concrete operation stage**, children begin to think logically and systematically about concrete objects, events, and experiences. This period is characterized by performing arithmetic operations mentally and being able to order in sequence physical actions and behaviors. The final stage, **formal operations**, is characterized by rational, abstract, and deductive reasoning such as might be characteristic of a scientist. During this period individuals are able to think about thinking and to engage in ideas as well as physical objects. Piaget has made a tremendous contribution to science, not only in terms of his theoretical point of view, but by legitimatizing qualitative study. However, his perspective is not without its critics, mainly because of the lack of specificity relative to movement through stages and the reasoning for why or how a child progresses from stage to stage.

As identified by King (1978), Piaget's contributions to cognitive development can be summarized as follows. First, the development of individuals proceeds at irregular rates, and movement from one stage to the next higher stage involves two phases—a readiness phase during which a person gathers the prerequisites, and the attainment stage during which a person becomes able to employ the behavioral characteristics for the next stage functioning. Second, there exists a process of within-stage development whereby an individual's use of the highest elements within that stage of operations is gradually expanded to a wider range of content areas. Third, Piaget identified a "state of mind" that appears to accompany phases of the developmental process such as egocentrism, which involves an element of self-consciousness that seems to develop when a person takes on new tasks or new operations of a new stage. Finally, as a person moves forward in development and is able to deal with higher order stages, the developmental process is accompanied by "decentering," a shift of focus from self to the larger world.

Lawrence Kohlberg

Influenced by Piaget, Lawrence Kohlberg is recognized because of his accomplishments in understanding development. Kohlberg viewed social and personality development through a sequence of qualitatively distinct stages that are influenced by the individual's level of cognitive development and the kinds of social experiences encountered. Kohlberg (1966) used Piaget's theory as a conceptual framework for theorizing about social phenomena such as emotional attachments, social ability, gender identities, sexual typing, and moral reasoning, and he stressed that cognitive and intellectual development are interrelated. He is perhaps best known for his prescriptions relative to **moral reasoning**. Kohlberg proposed three major sequential levels of moral development. During the first stage of Kohlberg's model (Level I: Preconventional Morality), moral judgements are based on externally imposed consequences from authority figures, personal gains, or both. During the next stage of moral reasoning (Level II: Conventional Morality), individuals begin to incorporate or internalize the norms and rules of the group to which they belong, whether the group is family, peers, or a community. The third stage of moral reasoning (Level III: Principled or Postconventional Morality), involves a shift from the source of authority to self-chosen principles which have been critically analyzed and questioned by the individual. Kohlberg did not posit that each level is associated with a specific age range nor that all individuals progress through all of the levels and stages of moral reasoning. He contended, however, that this sequence of moral development is both universal and hierarchical.

Carol Gilligan

Carol Gilligan offers a somewhat different perspective on moral development. Gilligan contended that gender differences in overall social development account for variations in the development of moral reasoning. She therefore suggested that Kohlberg's theory was more applicable to males. According to Gilligan, social development in males tends to focus more on separation and individuation while female development is based more on connections and relationships with others. These differences in gender development foster a moral system based more on justice and fairness for males and on caring and compassion for females.

William Perry

Perry (1970) initiated a model which outlined both ethical and intellectual development of college students that originated from the work of Piaget. He postulated a 9-position scheme which characterizes the development in students' thinking concerning the nature of knowledge, truth, and values, and the meaning of life and responsibilities. Similar to Piaget, Perry described steps in which a student moves from a simplistic categorical view of the world of right and wrong to the realization of the congruent nature of knowledge, and to relative values in the formation and affirmation of their own commitment. Perry addressed the issue of the interrelationship between one's developing intellect or understanding of the world and the nature of knowledge and an individual finding identity relative to the meaning of his or her role in the world (i.e., How do I know who I am and can be?).

Perry's theory represents a continuum of development divided into nine positions or sequences that are characterized into four general categories, the first of which is **dualism** (positions 1 and 2). During the dualistic period, students view the world in discreet, concrete, and absolute categories to understand people, knowledge, and values; elements exist absolutely. Therefore elements such as alternative perspectives are not yet acknowledged and views and evaluations are stated as if they are self-evident.

The second category is known as **multiplicity** (positions 3 and 4), which is characterized by the students' view of the world involving multiple perspectives with individuals accepting others who hold different beliefs; individuals with different beliefs are no longer seen as being simply wrong. In contrast to dualism, which is viewed as single answers or dichotomist, the area of multiplicity is characterized by multiple answers. During this level students have difficulty evaluating points of view and tend to view opinions as all equally valid and therefore not subject to evaluation.

Category three is **relativism** (position 5 and 6). At this level, students recognize that knowledge is contextual and relative in contrast to the level of multiplicity where the existence of different perspectives was simply acknowledged. In relativism, different perspectives are seen as pieces which fit together into a larger gestalt. Accordingly, the context in which the point of view exists is established. This level is sometimes characterized by students seeing the big picture. During this period students are able to think analytically, evaluate their own ideas as well as others' ideas, and accept authority and value judgments of others. However, during this level students typically resist decision making.

With category four, **commitment in relativism** (position 7, 8, and 9), the upper level positions on Perry's scheme are characterized by students taking responsibility in a pluralistic world and establishing their own identity in the process. Such personal commitments as marriage, religion, and career are renewed and committed upon; students begin to establish their own identity and lifestyle in a way that is consistent with their own personal views, values, and themes.

☐ Early Growth and Development

Studies of premature infants have shown a relationship between low birth rate and low IQ, as well as physical and neurological defects. These findings have caused the health profession and social policy makers to focus increasing attention on the conditions that affect the mother prior to the infant's birth. Some general principals that have been accepted concerning the physical development of infants include the following: (a) growth and functional development occur from the head to the tail region (cephalocaudally) and from the center axis toward the extremities (proximodistally), (b) body size shows especially rapid growth during infancy and early childhood and again during adolescence, (c) an individual's growth follows a biologically determined curve which permits some prediction of its course and extent, (d) motor and perceptual development is characterized by an initial increase in simple motor actions or differentiation in later hierarchal integration of simple actions into more complex units, and (e) maturation does not ensure skilled development. Most studies have confirmed that skills are usually optimally learned at times of maximum biological readiness. Fairly apparent is that the basic structure of growth is predetermined through genetic determinants and may be capitalized on through the social environment. The capitalization on events in the environment is referred to as learning.

The word "learning" has multiple meanings. As it relates to human development, however, learning is generally viewed as a process through which an activity originates or is changed based on situations encountered in the environment. Embedded in this definition is the exclusion of reflexes, maturation, or temporary states occurring to the organism. Critical to development are associative, instrumental, and observational learning. The concept of classical conditioning introduced by Pavlov (1927) is a type of associative learning. For example, using a dog and meat powder which is an unconditional stimulus (UCS), with a metronome which is the conditional stimulus (CS), the dog eventually salivates, known as the conditional response (CR), upon presentation of the metronome alone. Pavlov also reported that such acquisition of a conditional response could be extinguished by prolonged presentation of the condition stimulus without the unconditional stimulus. As cited earlier, Watson (1930) demonstrated that classical conditioning could be employed with infants as well as older adults. Thorndike (1932) focused much of his work on instrumental learning and formulated the Law of Effect, which states that recurrence of an act depends upon the positive or negative consequences it has received in the past. Building on Thorndike's earlier work, Skinner (1938), who designated instrumentally conditioned acts as operants, is widely recognized for many of the principles of instrumental learning.

As a result of Thorndike's and Skinner's earlier work, the belief that behavior is positively reinforced if the satisfaction of a basic need is accomplished or a secondary reward achieved has been generally accepted. Behavior is negatively reinforced if an adverse stimulus is removed, reduced, or avoided. In either situation, the probability of extinction of the behavior increases accordingly when reinforcement is no longer present. Reinforcement may occur on a continuous or partial schedule depending upon whether the reinforcer follows every stimulus response or just some of them. Partial schedules of reinforcement, which may be either fixed or variable, have been demonstrated to be more effective in maintaining behavior than have continuous schedules.

☐ The Preschool Years

A significant task of social development in infancy is attachment. This concept involves the crucial development of early reciprocal bonds between infant and caregiver. This two-way attachment is necessary for infants to experience adequate security in order to engage in further exploration of their environment. This concept is based on the position that infants have innate tendencies for survival, bonding with others, and exploring their environment. While striving to survive through exploring their environment, infants' behaviors such as crying and rooting reflexes, emotional responses, and verbalizations are reinforced by caregivers. This contingent responsiveness of the caregiver appears to be the common denominator in the formation of secure attachment. Many theorists suggest that secure attachment in infancy is necessary in forming subsequent affectional bonds with others throughout the life span. The consequences of insecure attachment have been reported to include problems in later life such as marriage difficulties, personality disorders, or poor self-concept. Overall, the concept of attachment relates to Maslow's hierarchy of needs, Erikson's first stage of psychosocial development, object relations theory, and social learning theory.

During the preschool years, a child's personality becomes richer, more complex, and more highly differentiated. During this period of time, both new personality characteristics and motives emerge at the same time that already established ones may become modified. The forms and amounts of various behavior characteristics depend on the child's social experiences. For example, factors affecting the establishment of aggressive behavior include the type of reinforcement received for such behavior, observation and imitation of models, and the degree of anxiety or guilt associated with aggressive behavior. Frustration is frequently associated with increased aggression, but children differ widely at this age in the ability to tolerate frustration and in the intensity of their reactions to it. Researchers have demonstrated that children who tend to be highly aggressive during the preschool years are also likely to be highly aggressive in later adulthood.

While dependency tends to be a relatively constant characteristic during the preschool years, situational factors such as social context influence the expression of dependency. That is, children who are highly dependent on their mothers also are more apt to generalize their dependency responses on others. While many attributions have been given to dependent children, one that appears in the literature with some frequency is the syndrome of "withdrawal of love" (i.e., giving love and affection when children behave as significant others want them to and withholding these rewards when they behave in a disapproved way). The withdrawal of love syndrome tends to produce children who frequently manifest dependent behavior at home.

Dependency, autonomy, and independence tend to be characteristics that are formulated in the preschool years but remain evident through later childhood, adolescence, and adulthood. Research has demonstrated that mature, confident, and independent preschool children have family settings that are highly consistent, warm, loving, and in general, secure. These situations give the child a degree of independence but maintain firm lines relative to expectations.

☐ Development in Middle Childhood

During the middle childhood years, a child is exposed to an ever increasing number of influences outside the family. A child's family remains important, but children are also greatly influenced by peers and others in their social environment. Also, during this period, the child's personality tends to mature and become more stable.

Middle childhood years are reflective of a critical period in the developmental continuum of children. According to Piaget, prior to age 7 or 8, a child's concept of justice is based on rigid and inflexible notions, however, between the ages of 8 and 11, a progressive equalitarianism develops. Beginning about age 11 or 12, the element of equity comes into play. Ethnic, racial, and religious identifications become fairly well established during the middle childhood years, and prejudice can have serious consequence for the child's personality development and self concept. Generally accepted is that attitudes of children during the middle childhood years are primarily learned from parents, peers, and society.

Depending on how children embrace the environment about themselves, the social environment can expand markedly during the middle childhood years. An important force in this expanded social environment is a child's peers. The peer group provides an opportunity to learn to interact, to deal with hostility and dominance, to relate to a leader, to lead others, to work with social problems, and to further develop one's self-concept.

During the early years of middle childhood, informal groups sometimes classified as gangs form. These groups, as do most other activities, involve same-gender peers. There is a general tendency for children to conform to the values and attitudes of other members of their peer group, but there are wide variations in the strength of these tendencies. While we often unquestioningly view conformity as an indication of maladjustment, it is a normal adaptive process during middle childhood years.

☐ Adolescence

Traditionally, adolescence has been viewed as a critical period in the developmental process. Many behavioral scientists have tended to agree that adolescence represents a period of particular stress in our society. Influencing this stress are such factors as the adjustment required by the physiological changes associated with puberty including an increase in sex hormones and changes in body structure and function, cultural demands of our society concerning interdependence, heterosexual and peer adjustment, and vocational, career, and educational choices. Important to recognize is that in other cultures adolescence is not viewed as a particularly stressful period of adjustment.

The important part of becoming a mature adult is developing a sense of one's identity. During adolescence, establishing one's identity becomes particularly problematic as a result of the rapid physical and physiological changes of puberty in addition to the increase in and changing social demands. The task of identity is further complicated depending upon the values, expectations, and opportunities of the social structure in which the adolescent is functioning.

Among the most dramatic of developmental events to which all youth must adjust is the interrelated physiological and sociological changes occurring during the early adolescent period, usually from about ages 11 to 15. Strictly speaking, puberty begins with the gradual enlargement of the ovaries and related organs in females, and the prostate glands and seminal vessels in males. A brief overview of some issues in this physiological process are highlighted below.

Endocrinological Factors in Development

Many of the physiological and body changes that occur during this time are due in part to an increased output of activating hormones by the anterior pituitary gland, which is located immediately below the brain. The pituitary hormone stimulates the activity of the gonad or sex glands, and therefore increases the production of sex hormones and the growth of mature sperm and ova in males and females, respectively; these hormones, including testosterone in males and estrogen in females, combine with other hormones of the bodies and stimulate the growth of bone and muscles.

Growth Spurt

Frequently, the accelerated rate in height and weight that occurs with the onset of adolescence is referred to as a growth spurt. The growth spurt varies widely from one child to another, in intensity and duration, and in age of onset. However, the variations in development frequently cause concern to adolescents and their parents.

Sexual Maturation

As is the situation with the height and weight growth spurt, there are considerable individual differences in the age and onset of puberty among adolescents. The beginning age of sexual maturation for girls ranges from approximately 8 to 13, and among boys from 9 and 14.

Sexual Identity Development

Sex role identity is a facet of identity formation that requires consideration in a comprehensive view of life span development. Genetic endowment is the most significant influence upon sexual identification. Heredity and hormones largely determine sexuality and orientation. However, as discussed earlier, no behavior is entirely controlled by either nature or nurture. Environmental influences on sexual and gender identification begin at a very early age. As preschoolers, children begin to develop their sexual identity as a consequence of their own cognitive development. Gender identity comes about first in the formation of gender schema and subsequently with identification of the self accurately into either category. The stability and constancy of gender occurs through the Piagetian concept of conservation. After these cognitive changes take place in children, behavioral differences in sex roles such as same-sex imitation, preferences for same-sexed playmates, and preference for sex-stereotyped toys begins to occur. Another Piagetian concept, assimilation, helps to explain early formation of sexual identity. Children assimilate behavior preferences of others through observation and begin to incorporate gender-typed behaviors. Although Freud proposed that sex-typed behavior is a function of identification which he thought occurred around 4 years of age, sex-role behaviors clearly begin prior to this age. Social learning theorists emphasize the roles of parenting and peers in the formation of sexual identity and sex-role behavior. These theorists state that sex-typed behaviors are reinforced through environmental interactions and both instrumental and associative learning. During adolescence, the fixed rules associated with gender specific behaviors become more flexible, and a wider range of behaviors become incorporated.

The Road to Maturity

Because adolescence and development are so complex and interrelated, to describe the process in an easily understandable manner is difficult. However, one way to conceptualize development is to describe the tasks and adjustments associated with progression through life. Havinghurst (1972) has summarized the kind of demands and adjustments that people at different points in their lives meet if they are to be satisfied and successful. As mentioned earlier, one of the transitions of adolescence is puberty, a time which brings noticeable physical changes. Physical maturation also has social consequences because children who develop early tend to experience immediate social advantages. During this period of time, cognitive changes are occurring and, according to Piaget, formal operations emerge. Erikson described this period as a critical struggle for adolescents to discover who they are and what they are to become. Erikson viewed this period as involved in endless discussion, fantasy playing of various roles, and hero-like worship of others. As researchers have indicated, peer group participation becomes very important, and, concomitantly, identification with the family and acceptance of its norms and values seem to decrease. Peers play a significant role in other adolescents' lives as each emerges. They provide a same-age standard and an opportunity for wider experience to support some forms of institutionalized behavior. Unfortunately, the influences of peers on occasion lead to behaviors defined as juvenile delinquency, behavior that violates social cultural codes. During the adolescent years the use of drugs seems to increase to include alcohol and psychoactive drugs.

☐ Adulthood and Older Adults

As an individual's chronological years increase, physiological and psychological changes continue to take place. Commencing in adulthood, some physical decline becomes evident in a variety of systems. However, as during the early years of life, changes differ among individuals and systems. As they mature, individuals tend to evaluate their physiological state relative to their age. Acute illness can appear at any age and throughout the life span although it is accepted that chronic illnesses increase with age. Contrary to stereotypes, mature and older adults retain interest and engage in sexual behavior despite the fact that reproductive systems decline. For example, most menopausal women report no change in sexual behavior, and as has been reported by some researchers, sexual activity in later years seems to correlate with that of the earlier years.

Although there are many physiological changes during adulthood and older adulthood, intelligence seems to remain constant. Some researches have demonstrated a slight decline in IQ scores which occurs perhaps at age 65, a change that has been attributed primarily to a decline in the ability to perform perceptual-spatial tasks. Otherwise, little change or decline is evident with intelligence.

There are changes in older adults' lifestyles because their living circumstances, including vocational position, economics, and residence usually change as their needs change; children are out of the house, more disposable income is available, and less energy is directed towards tasks of achieving or acquiring wealth and a desire to experience life. A critical aspect of the aging process is retirement and, as has been reported, retirement seems to be more difficult for professionals (white collar workers) as opposed to nonprofessionals (those classified as blue collar workers).

Work and changes in work patterns are an important facet of life span development that occurs concomitantly with other developmental sequences. Many career theorists have proposed models of development regarding early childhood interests and abilities, but perhaps the most prominent career theorist was Donald Super. Super (1990) proposed a sequential stage model of vocational development (Figure 2.1). Central to Super's framework is the role of self-concept in the career development process. Super believed that, although sequential in nature, the stages which he proposed are flexible and should not be rigidly associated with age. Each stage could be interrupted, resumed, and recycled throughout the life span. Super also created an archway model which delineates how biographical, psychological, and socioeconomic factors influence career development.

Work for adults plays a very significant role in their lives and has a great deal to do, in addition to money, with how they think of themselves (self-esteem). However, economic well being is consequential in addition to affecting self-esteem because it affects health care opportunities and the ability to engage in activities as well as in some social situations. The importance of social interaction in adulthood varies, but it appears that the more friends individuals have often affects their outlook on life.

A significant aspect of aging is the adaption to death. The frequency of death thoughts tend to increase with age and when physical illness is present. Obviously death means different things to different people; (i.e., a new life, a sensation of life, being reunited with those already dead,

BIRTH	Curiosity
GROWTH	Fantasies Interests Capacities
EXPLORATORY	Tentative Transition Trial
ESTABLISHMENT	Trial and Stabilization Consolidation, Frustration and Advancement
MAINTENANCE	
DECLINE	Deceleration Disengagement Retirement

FIGURE 2.1. Super's Life Stages and Substages.

being isolated from others, or being rewarded). Some individuals even welcome death, and the ability to cope with the prospect of death is influenced many times by religious beliefs and close relationships with family. Individuals face death by a variety of methods including such things as denial, including rationalization and suppression or withdrawal, and by attempting to master death through cognitive acceptance.

☐ Summary

In this chapter we have examined some of the issues concerning human growth and development. Provided was a cursory overview of theories, trends, and effects of society and the environment that concerns life span development. Also discussed were some fundamental concepts concerning learning. A most important generalization emerging from the information is that differences exist among individuals within the broad framework of human development. Also, the environmental influence of one's family of origin upon personal development is indisputable. Important to this premise is the fact that every family, regardless of its configuration, is a dynamic and fluid system. It is therefore requisite to examine the family life cycle as an important dimension of development across the life span. Both continuity and change can characterize any family system. Changes can be sudden and disruptive to a family system (e.g., unexpected financial problems, death of a family member, divorce, teenage pregnancy, or the birth of a disabled child). Changes also can be more developmental and inevitable in nature such as the birth of children and grandchildren or increased autonomy through entering school or college, adolescence, marriage, or retirement. In each of these examples, any change can produce long-lasting or permanent modification to the roles and transactions within the family system which, in turn, can affect development.

Multicultural and Diverse Populations: Social and Cultural Issues Concerning Counselors

☐ Cultural Diversity and the Counselor

It is generally agreed upon in the press and elsewhere that American society today is more multiethnic and diverse than at any other time in the recent past (Holcomb-McCoy & Myers, 1999). This change was described by *USA Today* (1992) with the following headline: "'Diverse' Fits Nation Better Than 'Normal'." The social structure of the United States is changing because of this increase in diversity, which is likely to entail significant social, cultural, and economic transitions. As a result, professional counselors are continually being called upon to provide services to an increasingly diverse clientele. Effectively meeting this need requires a high level of awareness, flexibility, and sensitivity, and a willingness to extend one's knowledge and understanding about traditions, beliefs, and values that may be unfamiliar.

Working well with culturally diverse clients involves more than simply learning about other cultures. As Sue (1998) indicated, counselors need to develop "multicultural counseling competence," which includes an awareness and appreciation of the values and characteristics of one's own culture as well as those of others.

Culturally skilled counselors are actively in the process of becoming aware of their own assumptions about human behavior, values, biases, precon-

51

ceived notions, personal limitations, and so forth. They understand their own world views, how they are products of cultural conditioning, and how this may be reflected in their therapeutic work with culturally different groups (p. 38).

The increasing importance of multicultural issues in counseling was highlighted by Pedersen (1999), who indicated that multiculturalism is the emerging "Fourth Force" or dimension in the behavioral sciences. Counselors will need to develop competencies in working within the context of this Fourth Force. Therefore, this chapter provides an overview of some of the basic demographic, social, and cultural considerations within our growing multicultural society, of which counselors need to be aware.

☐ Demographic Changes

Several changes are or will be occurring within our society as we enter the new millennium. Included are modifications in the number of individuals by age groups, level of education, family structure, and ethnic groups. These demographic changes, in turn, will have an impact on the role of the professional counselor.

Age Groups

Because our citizens are living longer, America is becoming a nation of older persons. The life expectancy for Americans has grown from 68.2 years in 1950 to 75.7 years in 1994 (Wattenberg, 1991; Tidwell, 1997). Further, the Census Bureau projects that by the year 2030, the average age of American citizens will have risen from its current level of 32 years to 41 years (Fosler, Alonso, Myer, & Kern, 1990). Individuals 75 and older are the fastest growing segment of the population, while the group of 18- to 64-year-old individuals is expected to grow only slightly over the next 20 years after which time their number will begin to decline (Butler & Lewis, 1982; Fosler et al., 1990). These changing demographics will have a significant impact on social policymakers and on the economics of the nation's tax base, and consequently entitlement programs such as health care, social security, and education.

Level of Education

More persons are receiving high school and college educations than ever before. In 1950, the high-school dropout rate among individuals who were between 25 and 29 years old was 50%, and only 8% of the group had completed four or more years of college. In 1988, the high-school dropout rate among this same age group was 14.1%, and 22.7% had completed four or more years of college (Wattenberg, 1991).

Family Structure

The family unit has also undergone change in recent years. Bumpass (1990) estimated that the level of marital disruption among recent first marriages was approximately 60%. As a result, approximately half of the children in American society will live part of their childhood years in a single-parent family. A majority of these single-parent families will be due to a divorce with the children remaining in a mother-only family for the balance of their childhood (Bumpass & Sweet, 1989; Castro Martin, & Bumpass, 1989).

Bumpass (1990) also cited a change in the formation of relationships as having profound implications on family life. The percentage of first marriages preceded by cohabitation increased from 8% in the late 1960s to 49% in 1985–86. Further, it is likely that 50% of persons in their 30s have been in a cohabitating relationship.

Additional changes in childbearing and parenting have also affected the structure of the family. The proportion of children born to unmarried mothers doubled from 1970 to 1987, with 31% of our children being born to unmarried mothers in 1993 (Tidwell, 1997). The unusually high birth rate among unmarried, teenage mothers, which increased from 5.9% in 1950 to 30.2% in 1987, is an important element of unplanned fertility (Bumpass, 1990; Trussell, 1988; Wattenberg, 1991).

Cultural Diversity

The United States has moved into an era of cultural pluralism (Lee, 1997). In 1990, the composition of the United States population was: European American, 76%; African American, 12%; Hispanic, 9%; and Asian and other, 3% (Usdansky, 1992). Wattenberg (1991) estimated ethnic changes in the population by the year 2080 as follows: European American, 55%; African American, 16%; Hispanic, 19%.

Impact on Professional Counselors

Fosler, Alonso, Myer, and Kern (1990) listed three current points of stress created by these demographic changes: rising health care costs for the over-85 population, a diminishing and poorly prepared pool of young employees, and a chronically unemployed or underemployed lower class. Future stress points include the increasing number of poorly educated children who could expand the size of the under-class and debilitate the workforce, and the projected increase in both the number and proportion of elderly people after the year 2010. These stress points, in total, will result in professional counselors likely encountering changes in the racial and demographic characteristics of their clientele, and the nature of presenting problems.

☐ Understanding Diversity

It is important for counselors to have a working knowledge of terms used in reference to various groups and populations. For example, some counseling professionals have used the terms race, culture, and ethnicity interchangeably. However, counselors need to understand and be able to differentiate among such terms. The following terms and concepts are central to a basic understanding of diversity.

Culture.   Pedersen (1988) defined culture as a "shared pattern of learned behavior that is transmitted to others in the group" (p. 54). Different ethnic groups within a single racial group may have different cultures. Likewise, there may be different cultures within a single ethnic group (Pedersen, 1988).

Race.   Race refers to biological differences of physical traits or genetic origin that might distinguish one group from another. Differences in race include biological requirements of differentiation and genetic relationships. Race does not include or explain differences in social behavior.

Ethnicity.   Persons preserve ethnic group values, beliefs, and behaviors when ethnic identification is strong (Hernandez, 1989). The term ethnicity is used to identify the customs, language, religion, and habits one generation passes to the next in an effort to provide a social and cultural heritage (Pedersen, 1988).

Minority.   Atkinson, Morten, and Sue (1989) defined the term minority as a physically or behaviorally identifiable group that makes up less than 50% of the United States population. Thus, in addition to racial and ethnic minorities, this definition encompasses the aged, poor, gay and lesbian persons, people with disabilities, substance abusers, and prison populations (Atkinson et al., 1989).

Prejudice. Prejudice has been defined by Axelson (1998) as a preconceived opinion or judgment without just grounds or sufficient knowledge. Further, it is an irrational behavior or attitude directed against a group, an individual, or their supposed characteristics.

Contextualism. Contextualism refers to the idea that any behavior must be appraised in the context of the culture in which it occurs.

Discrimination. Discrimination is the creation of unjust or unfair competition in which categories of people are treated differentially on arbitrary grounds and without reference to their actual behavior (Axelson, 1998). Axelson further indicated that discrimination serves to perpetuate or maintain social distance through the possible inclusion of segregation, isolation, or personal acts growing out of prejudice.

Racism. Racism, which is grounded in the belief that some races are inherently superior to others, exists in three categorical forms: individual, cultural, and institutional (Axelson, 1998).

☐ Characteristics Across Cultures

The challenge in writing about the characteristics of a given culture is the risk of perpetuating stereotypes about that culture. Yet, discussing such characteristics provides general guidelines that can be used when working with persons of a different culture. It is important for counselors to realize the limitations of such guidelines and to exercise care in treating clients of any cultural background as individuals with a unique set of beliefs and feelings.

African Americans

African Americans are presently the largest ethnic minority group in the United States. The African American population totaled 33.1 million in 1995 compared with 26.8 million in the 1980 census. The African American population has grown faster than the growth of the total population during the past two decades, increasing from 11.8% of that total in 1980 to 12.6% in 1995. This growth in the African American population in all likelihood will continue to be greater than the growth of the European American population because of the relative youthfulness of the African American population (Baruth & Manning 1991; Tidwell, 1997).

Given the highly prevalent population of African Americans, counselors practicing in the United States should have the knowledge and skills to work with this ethnic group. Much literature exists that describes some of the characteristics that are unique to the African American culture. First, there is a strong collectivist spirit among African Americans that is, in large part, a product of a shared history of oppression and discrimination. This is manifested in an emphasis on group cooperation, interdependence, and shared responsibility among group members (Priest, 1991). Second, the African American culture emphasizes the importance of family, with the family structure most likely including extended family members and close friends (Paniagua, 1998). Counselors may wish to take advantage of these strong family ties by including family or extended family members as a part of an African American client's treatment. Third, although religious involvement varies among African Americans as a whole, the African American culture generally tends to emphasize spiritual issues more than U. S. culture overall (Lee, 1997). Counselors should be willing to incorporate these issues into the therapeutic experience.

African Americans share a history of hardships that has become a part of their rich cultural heritage. Counselors working with African American clients should not be surprised to address issues related to racial discrimination or difficulties in cultural adjustment. These issues can also manifest themselves in the therapeutic relationship, particularly when the counselor is of another race. However, it is important to avoid stereotypes about how African American clients "typically" respond, recognizing that each client is an individual with unique ideas and feelings.

Hispanic Americans

Hispanic Americans include Mexicans, Mexican Americans, Chicanos, Spanish Americans, Latin Americans, Puerto Ricans, Cubans, Guatemalans, and Salvadorans. While all of these groups are recognized as being of Hispanic background and share many values and goals, certain aspects of their culture suggest a highly heterogeneous population (Baruth & Manning, 1991; Gonzalez, 1989; Green, 1995). The number of Hispanic Americans grew from 6.9 million in 1960 to 27 million in 1995 (National Association of Hispanic Publications, 1995; Wattenberg, 1991). During the decade from 1980 to 1990, the Hispanic population increased by 34% or approximately 5 million people (National Association of Hispanic Publications, 1995). Based on the high rates of immigration and fertility among the Hispanic population, demographers estimate that the Hispanic population in the United States will exceed the African American population during the first decade of the this century (Herr, 1989). Further, it is projected that 22% of the U.S. population will be Hispanic by the year 2050 (National Association of Hispanic Publications, 1995).

A review of the literature by Atkinson et al. (1989) suggested that the Hispanic population is seriously underrepresented among mental health clientele despite a need for more of such services. This finding appears due to a number of high stress factors that are present among many Hispanics and that apply to many low-income individuals, thus aggravating the need for more mental health care. These factors include poor English skills, limited education, low income, depressed social status, deteriorated housing, minimal political influence, the continuation of traits from a rural agricultural culture that are relatively ineffective in an urban technological society, the necessity for some to migrate seasonally, and adapting to a prejudiced and unfriendly society. Because of these stress factors, it can be expected that counselors will likely see increasing numbers of Hispanic American clients as their population in the United States grows in the years to come.

Hispanic American individuals, as with other minority groups, emphasize collectivism and the family. They tend to value interdependence and often rely on extended family members, including friends or clergy, for support and assistance (Lee, 1997). Counselors can build upon these strengths by incorporating family work into therapeutic sessions. Often highly affective and demonstrative, Hispanic American clients may benefit from a more responsive and affective counseling style. In addition to these issues, counselors should be sensitive to cultural gender-role norms which Hispanic American clients may hold. Hispanic American women may feel pressured to present themselves as pure, submissive, sentimental, and self-sacrificing, while Hispanic American men may feel the need to maintain an air of *machismo*: strong, proud, capable, and less sentimental (Green, 1995). Counselors may need to help clients process issues related to these role expectations, particularly when they may conflict with expectations of the majority culture.

Asian Americans

Asian Americans include persons from Asian cultures such as Chinese, Japanese, Korean, and Asian Indian. The Asian American population increased 70% from 1980 to 1988 (i.e., 3.8 million to 6.5 million), and made up almost 3% of the U.S. population by 1990 (Wattenberg, 1991). The inflow of Southeast Asians to the United States over the past 20 years has further underscored the diversity of the Asian culture. For example, cultural features of the Southeast Asians who originate from countries such as Vietnam, Cambodia, Laos, and Thailand, differ from those of the more populous groups of Japanese and Chinese. Also, great differences exist among individuals from the various Southeast Asian countries. As with Hispanic Americans, Asian Americans constitute a richly diverse and heterogeneous group (Uba, 1994). Thus, counselors must avoid any temptation to make generalizations about clients of Asian descent. Therefore, they need to take time to understand the culture as each individual presents it.

The prevailing stereotype of Asian Americans is that they are model minorities and problem free (Sue & Sue, 1995). This stereotype has resulted in limited financial and moral support from the government. According to Sue and Sue (1985), Asian Americans display a bimodal distribution formed by a highly educated and successful group, and a group typified by little formal education and limited success. Asian Americans as a group are confronted with the same problems as many other minority groups: overcrowded living conditions in urban areas, unemployment, economic exploitation, limited access to health care, concerns over immigration status, educational stress caused by strange surroundings and a lack of competence with the English language, and conflict created by continual exposure to the majority values and norms. Also, Asian American students have reported more feelings of isolation, loneliness, and distress than European American students (Sue, Ino, & Sue, 1983).

Common cultural norms among Asian American groups include an emphasis on respect for authority figures, a hierarchical family structure, a belief in the importance of harmony in interpersonal relationships, and a preference for less direct communication styles (Sue, 1998; Sue, Ivey, & Pedersen, 1996; Uba, 1994). Asian American clients may react with discomfort to forms of counseling that include a lot of direct confrontation, or to approaches that emphasize an egalitarian relationship between counselor and client. Sue et al. (1996) offer a succinct description of some less traditional ways that counselors might work more effectively with Asian American clients.

> For many Asian-Americans, the helpful counselor may be one who gives advice, avoids confrontation and direct interpretation of motives and actions, indirectly discusses personal issues, does more initial talking than the client, and evidences a formal interactive approach. (p. 39)

Native Americans

Unlike other ethnic groups in the United States, the number of Native Americans is showing a downward trend. Their population has decreased from its highest point of about three million to just above one million (Atkinson et al., 1989). Roughly 65% of Native Americans live on or close to a Native American reservation, with the remaining number living in urban or predominately European American areas (Anderson & Ellis, 1995; Axelson, 1998).

Native Americans face a great deal of adversity in the modern world. In addition to addressing the effects of centuries of injustice and discrimination, Native Americans are confronted with additional hardships including an alarming incidence of suicide, low educational attainment, poverty, and a high incidence of alcoholism (Anderson & Ellis, 1995; Green, 1995; Lee, 1997). Native Americans also continue to have difficulties overcoming myths that their culture is evil, savage, and inferior (Baruth & Manning, 1991). On the contrary, most Native American cultures embrace ideals related to harmony with nature and others, cooperation, respect for elders, and reverence for a rich cultural heritage (Green, 1995; Lee, 1997). Counselors need to be respectful of these ideals, and to look for ways to incorporate them into the counseling process. However, as with most minority populations, Native Americans vary greatly by groups and tribes, so it is essential that counselors avoid stereotyping and allow clients to share information about their own unique culture.

☐ Biases Among Counseling Theories

In recent years there has been increasing discussion related to the cultural biases inherent in many theories of human behavior and counseling. Advocates for change have correctly pointed out that traditional theories, including psycho-dynamic, humanistic-existential, and cognitive-behavioral theories, do not necessarily apply well to all cultural groups (Ivey, Ivey, & Simek-Morgan, 1997; Lago & Thompson, 1996). This fact should not be surprising given that these theories were developed by and for members of a predominantly Caucasian Western culture and thus permeated by a Western world-view and value structure (Aponte, Rivers, & Wohl, 1995). However, in response to these observations and a growing awareness of multicultural issues, counselors and other professionals from the behavioral sciences have taken the initiative in developing greater advocacy efforts to address multicultural issues in working with clients. In addition to providing increased training in multicultural issues, professionals are developing more comprehensive counseling theories that can encompass the diversity of cultures and values of a global society (Ivey, Ivey, & Simek-Morgan, 1997; Sue, Ivey, & Pedersen, 1996). They emphasize the contextual influence of culture on individuals' world views and values and integrate, as appropriate, constructive elements from traditional theories.

☐ Barriers to Effective Multicultural Counseling

Essential to effective counseling with clients of diverse cultures is recognizing and accepting diversity. Yet, counselors often lack knowledge in critical areas concerning multicultural counseling. Thus, it can be a challenge for many counselors to identify and overcome some of the misconceptions and biases that are the product of years of cultural indoctrination. Moreover, clients may enter the counseling process with their own set of biases and misunderstandings.

Bacon (1990) suggested a number of barriers that counselors and clients of different cultures might face. The effectiveness of counselors can be limited if they (a) attempt to deny racism or racial elements as realities in society, (b) base interactions with minorities on myths or negative stereotypes, (c) lack an understanding or respect for cultural diversity, (d) lack or have had limited exposure to persons of different cultures, and (e) lack knowledge about the needs of minority communities. Clients of different cultures face barriers to effective counseling if they are (a) unwilling to seek help from someone outside their cultural group, (b) lack knowledge about available services, and (c) feel unwelcome to participate in the counseling services.

Lack of understanding can create further barriers to the counseling process. Failing to recognize and address cultural differences in communication style, for example, can create significant misunderstandings (Lago & Thompson, 1996; Vacc et al., 1995). Counselors without an adequate understanding or appreciation of diversity also risk imposing their own values on clients, which is both unethical and detrimental (Sue, 1998). These risks necessitate that professional counselors engage in a continual process of learning about their own values and biases, and develop a broad base of knowledge about diverse populations.

☐ Appreciating Differences and Similarities

A pitfall of counseling individuals from minority cultures is the assumption that all people from a specific group are the same (Lee, 1997). As mentioned earlier, differences within groups can be greater than differences among groups, a fact that is all too easy to overlook. The challenge for the counseling professional is to learn to integrate cultural awareness with a respect for the uniqueness of each individual. Despite differences within and among groups, some common characteristics exist across cultures that are important to the counseling process. Features that are present in every culture include a family unit, marriage, parental roles, education, medicine, forms of work, and forms of self-expression (Axelson,

1998). Furthermore, people from all cultures share many of the same basic desires, needs, and feelings such as love, friendship, joy, and sorrow. The skilled multicultural counselor is able to draw upon all of these commonalities while attending to specific cultural considerations.

Preparation for Counselors

As described by Vacc, Wittmer, and DeVaney (1995), there are a number of assumptions basic to effective multicultural counseling.

1. An individual focus rather than the use of mass methods is needed when working with clients of different cultural backgrounds.
2. The individual is primarily a person and secondarily a member of a group.
3. Social aspects of an individual's life (e.g., environment at home, school, and work) are important.
4. Accurate information is a necessary foundation for providing services.
5. Counselor preparation in the areas of social and cultural issues is essential.

Thus, the basic foundation of effective multicultural counseling is a combination of accurate knowledge about diversity and good counseling skills, both of which are facilitated through counselor education experiences. Specific knowledge about working with diverse populations is available through counselor education course work and a wide variety of scholarly resources. Counselors also can gain valuable insights by being more inquisitive with friends and acquaintances of other cultures and taking the initiative to spend time with people of diverse cultural backgrounds. In sum, effective counseling skills can be mastered through counselor education, training, study, and supervised practice.

Loesch (1988) presented four additional skills especially important in counseling diverse populations: active listening, individual and group appraisal, vocabulary adjustment, and confrontation. Counselors who practice effective active listening are able to encourage self-disclosure, build trust, and create a comfortable atmosphere by mirroring clients' verbal and nonverbal behavior. Sound appraisal skills allow counselors to assess and meet clients' needs better. Such skills include the ability to discern whether standardized testing or other assessment techniques are appropriate for a given population. Vocabulary adjustment involves attending to and responding correctly to the verbal and nonverbal nuances of individuals with a different cultural background. Finally, counselors skilled in multicultural counseling are able to use confrontation with culturally appropriate discretion and care.

☐ Ethical Issues

Ethical issues exist concerning a counselor's ability to work with diverse populations. Counselors are ethically bound to provide services to individuals and groups only when they can do so competently. Lack of knowledge about counseling issues specific to another culture can be detrimental to the counseling process, even when accompanied by the best of intentions. Counselors who have not been adequately prepared to work with individuals from other cultures should not do so. Also, as part of informed consent procedures, it is a good idea for counselors to discuss with clients at the outset of counseling, their training and limitations in working with individuals with their cultural background.

☐ Summary

Counseling with multicultural populations can be an exciting and rewarding experience, but effective multicultural counseling requires adequate training, culture-specific knowledge, and an open approach that addresses clients both as individuals and as members of a culture. Increasing attention on multicultural counseling has provided more training opportunities and resources than ever before. New multicultural counseling theories also provide means for counselors to address the needs of clients within the context of their beliefs, values, and traditions. However, the challenge remains for counselors to continue to develop, through research and practice, more effective and equitable ways to meet the needs of clients from diverse cultural backgrounds.

CHAPTER

Helping Skills

The construct of helping skills runs the gamut of applications to include those used by car salespersons, neighbors, social science researchers, or licenced professional counselors. Helping skills vary in form, depth, purpose, and content, and they cover a wide range of issues.

For the purposes of this book, we focus on helping skills as methods that are useful in the social sciences in general, and counseling in particular. Because we recognize that much of what will be discussed can be generalized to less therapeutic usage, the discussion that follows focuses on methods that seem to have universal value and are intentional.

Intentional and Unintentional Helping Skills

The distinction between intentional and unintentional helping skills is the interviewer's mindfulness in applying methods that have been documented in the literature. With intentional helping skills, behaviors and structures are deliberate and are guided through the use of a model or theory of intervention. Models and theories provide a structure that allows the information gathered to be comparable from client to client, which is an essential principle of professional practice. Because the professional counselor's purpose is to differentiate among clients with respect to the intervention(s) or issues under consideration, the use of unintentional methods introduces error into the process.

Proponents of intentional helping skills seem to agree that using similar methods with clients assists in making comparisons possible among clients. However, the use of helping skills may become particularly complex when considering the different interpretations of language that can occur. While the same words may have different interpretations among different groups and wording may therefore vary, the meaning or the intent of helping behavior does not vary. Being sensitive to client differences therefore, may require variations in language as needed with different clients. It is best for a counselor to use words that have equivalent meanings for different clients, even if those words are not objectively similar. However, standardization of the behavior and language used by counselors serves very well in most situations since there is great commonality of meaning for most words among people speaking the same language.

Thus far, the value of intentional helping skills is that they

- incorporate a basic principle of theory and models of helping therefore making information comparable client to client,
- are more reliable,
- minimize errors of intervention,
- permit a degree of standardization of meaning, and
- offer flexibility.

The use of intentional helping skills also is a multidimensional activity that serves to establish rapport with the client and to form a base of information for the counselor. Further, helping skills need to be viewed as a means for obtaining and using information to generate interventions or strategies when counseling clients. Also of importance is viewing helping skills as a continuous process rather than a one-time activity. The focus of this ongoing process is not to find a "truth," but to use information in a way that is helpful to the client. Without intentional helping skills, counseling in some situations becomes an act of faith.

Professional counselors may not know all there is to know about helping skills, but they do know enough not to divorce themselves from the knowledge available. Helping skills are not the beginning and end of counseling. Rather, they are a useful element when employed by skilled and knowledgeable counselors.

Helping skills produce outcomes. The use of helping skills during counseling influences what the counselor and client do in sessions and the outcome and success of counseling. To master these elements, the beginning counselor must develop a repertoire of helping skills as well as a theory of counseling that directs their application. This is no easy task. Research on counseling and psychotherapy outcomes indicates that no single superiority exists for any particular approach (Smith & Glass, 1977). Also, there is no consensus among professional counselors about the best approach to counseling. Many professional counselors, therefore, describe themselves as doing what works best for their clients.

Offered in this chapter is a paradigm of therapeutic constructs and help-ing skills methods derived from research, the literature, and licenced pro-fessional counselors' practice. Counselors can use these to begin strength-ening their helping skills with a client. The therapeutic constructs and helping skills methods discussed are fundamental and basic to the coun-seling process.

☐ Therapeutic Constructs

A professional counselor's attitudes are fundamental to the counselor-client relationship, and they establish the foundation for effective com-munication skills. The more positively a client perceives a counselor, the greater the likelihood that the client will be willing to offer trust and to take risks in changing his or her own attitudes, thoughts, and behaviors. Carl Rogers (1951) popularized three core features of professional helpers that are hypothesized to be essential for building a therapeutic relation-ship, or rapport, and producing basic facilitative conditions. These core features are empathy, genuineness, and unconditional positive regard.

Empathy

Empathy can be described as the desire and ability to understand a client's presenting issues accurately. Empathy implies that, in addition to having knowledge and an evaluative understanding of a client's concerns, the professional counselor can share the client's experience through deep and subjective understanding.

Overall, empathy can assist in forming and maintaining the therapeu-tic relationship and can assist clients in experiencing counseling at their preferred pace. For a client, the first cue that a counselor desires to under-stand without judgment may be the use of attending skills such as atten-tiveness and listening. Attending skills can be demonstrated through body positions, facial expressions, and verbal reactions (e.g., "okay," "uh-huh") which convey to the client that the counselor is receiving the information and is interested in hearing more. The counselor's receptiveness, interest, and full attention also are conveyed facing the client squarely, having an open-body posture without the arms or legs crossed, maintaining eye contact with the client, leaning slightly forward, and smiling or nodding when appropriate. These attending skills are a precursor to listening ability. Professional counselors generally view themselves as skilled listeners, but effective listening does not develop without extensive practice. Effec-tive active listening involves being sensitive to and aware of the client's feelings. Listening is a selective process during which professional counselors choose from the things around them those that most fit their needs, purposes, and desires (Wittmer, 2000). Active listening is the intentional use of attending abilities which include awareness of a client's verbal and nonverbal messages and emotional experiences. Actively listening to a client can result in the accurate reflection of implicit messages in the client's statements.

Genuineness

The genuineness of a professional counselor is defined by appropriate role behaviors and authenticity. An effective counselor in a therapeutic relationship, therefore, is open, spontaneous, and expressive.

The congruence of a professional counselor's inward experiences and outward and observable behaviors is what defines a counselor as trustworthy and honest in the client's eyes. Such counselors are able to provide authentic emotional responses accurately and to convey sincere concerns for the client's situation while maintaining the client's respect and dignity.

Unconditional Positive Regard

Respect for the client is referred to as positive regard. While attempting to understand and respond to a client's experiences accurately, effective counselors should ensure that they are accepting of the client without conditions or judgment. Counselors are not expected to be free of values in a relationship with a client because such behavior would lack authenticity. Through positive regard, client behaviors and emotional responses are neither condemned nor condoned. Rather, they are accepted without condition.

Warmth and immediacy in interactions also communicate acceptance and positive regard as well as commitment to the client. These elements of positive regard are provided, in part, through nonverbal behaviors such as body posture, eye contact, and facial expression as previously discussed.

☐ Helping Skills Methods

Establishing basic therapeutic conditions and effectively gathering initial information from a client is the beginning of facilitating effective change. This is all done in conjunction with the use of helping skills.

Helping skills are useful in moving beyond the client's frame of reference to include gathering information and perceptions about the client.

Wittmer (2000) described six helping skills methods: (a) advising or evaluating, (b) analyzing and interpreting, (c) reassuring and supporting, (d) questioning, (e) clarifying and summarizing, and (f) reflecting and understanding of feeling. One other frequently used helping skill is confrontation. As discussed below, these seven helping skills methods vary in the degree to which they facilitate client response.

Advising and Evaluating

The counseling interview includes legitimate times when the counselor must give information and data to the client such as the provision of specific information about employment, legal issues, or lifestyle adaptations. As another example, Transactional Analysis and cognitive-behavioral therapies require the counselor to educate the clients about the theories and techniques of the process. However, important differences exist between giving information and advising and evaluating. With advising and evaluating, the professional counselor recommends or prescribes the course of action a client should consider taking based on the information gathered.

Of concern is the advising and evaluating provided by an unskilled interviewer. Because advising is based on the counselor's values and not the client's cognitive process, it generally is not effective in the long-term behavior change of the client. Advising also can foster undue dependence of the client on the counselor or can cause the client to project blame on the counselor for faulty or misinterpreted advice. As with advising, evaluating a client's behavior is based on the value system of the client and can be detrimental to the core therapeutic conditions discussed previously. Moreover, evaluating a client's behavior can block effective listening skills and therefore inhibit further disclosure from the client.

Analyzing and Interpreting

Analysis and interpretation are often associated with psychodynamic theories. However, many other theoretical perspectives (e.g., Transactional Analysis, Adlerian Psychology, and some cognitive-behavioral theories) also use analyzing and interpreting as a means for promoting insight or presenting hypotheses of clients' behavioral patterns.

Generally, analysis and interpretation differ from other types of helping skills in that they deal with the implicit parts of client messages or behaviors rather than direct or explicit implications. Analysis and interpretation can be used to assist a client in making connections among thought, feelings, and behaviors and can produce insight which may be a precursor to change. To interpret information effectively for a client or to present a hypothesis, many factors must be considered such as timing, wording, abstraction, and appropriate motivation of the professional counselor.

Analyzing and interpreting are not considered to be the most effective helping skills. Although clients may at times have difficulty recognizing their own patterns or motivations, the responsibility of an interpretation remains with the professional counselor. Also, interpreting or analyzing could be inaccurate or beyond the cognitive or emotional readiness of a client. As a result, defensiveness or decreased disclosure can occur rather than increased self-awareness and insight.

Reassuring and Supporting

Statements that offer reassurance and support often are intended to do one or more of the following: (a) instill a belief in the client, (b) recognize potential for problem-solving, or (c) foster empowerment. Research data indicate that reassuring or supporting statements are one of the most popular responses used by counselors (Wittmer, 2000). However, data also indicate that statements of this type have little effectiveness in producing positive change (Wittmer, 2000).

Reassuring and supporting statements can often produce negative effects, despite how well intended they may be. Reassuring statements have a tendency to diminish or dismiss client feelings as "normal" or "common," with the implication being that the client should not feel this way but if he or she does, it should not be for very long. Instead of communicating acceptance or understanding, these statements deny clients the right to experience their own emotional responses.

These statements also may send an unintended message to the client that the counselor does not want to explore or discuss negative emotions or client experiences further. Reassurance also tends to come from a somewhat superior position (Wittmer, 2000) which, in turn, can sometimes create separation in the client-counselor relationship.

Questioning

Questioning is irreplaceable in the interview process. Questions or inquiries are excellent methods for beginning interviews, obtaining critical information, encouraging participation and elaboration from the client, and having clients engage in self-exploration. There are two main types of questions: closed and open.

Closed questions require only a yes, no, or short answer from the client, and they typically begin with *Are, Do, Can, Is,* or *Did.* These questions are useful in obtaining specific information and focusing on a particular problem or issue. Questions of this nature, however, should be limited because excessive use can discourage discussions as well as provide the client with opportunities to avoid sensitive subjects.

Open-ended questions are preferred in therapeutic interviews. They usually begin with the words *Could, What, Why,* or *How,* and they allow the client to discuss more fully selected concerns or issues. Open-ended questions are invitations to share, and they can provide the professional counselor with subjective viewpoints, feelings, and thoughts of the client while minimizing the provision of direction or structure for the client response.

Questioning should be used judicially for several reasons. First, questioning needs to maintain its significance in the interviewing process. Second, appropriate questioning can ensure that a client doesn't become alienated or feel interrogated. Finally, questioning should not become the center of the communication pattern between client and therapist.

Clarifying and Summarizing

Clarifications are effective statements or questions for facilitating accurate communication. The use of clarification enables professional counselors to check out the accuracy of their perception or processing of a client's ambiguous or vague statements.

Summarizations are statements to the client that convey what has been communicated over a period of time (Ivey, 1994). They may occur at the beginning or end of an interview, when making transitions from one topic to another, or after a lengthy or complex client statement. While summarizations generally are used to assist clients in organizing their thinking, Cormier and Cormier (1991) stated four purposes for summarizations: connecting multiple elements of client disclosure, identifying a theme, regulating the pace of a session and giving focus, and reviewing progress.

Clarifying and summarizing are effective helping skills which also convey to the client the professional counselor's use of listening skills. In addition, clarifying and summarizing responses can be used deliberately to assist clients in hearing what they have stated. The effects of clients hearing what they have said can be numerous. Clients are able to gain a sense of whether the professional counselor has effectively listened to and understood what they have stated. Clarification statements often promote personal inquiry and insight, and they present a client with hypotheses about behavioral patterns or themes about which they may not be fully aware. This nonjudgmental manner of providing hypotheses about the presenting issues by rephrasing the client's comments or asking for elaboration allows the client freedom to reject the professional counselor's interpretations while maintaining the dignity and basic elements of the therapeutic relationship.

Reflecting and Understanding Feeling

While clarifications and summarizations tend to focus on the cognitive aspects of client input, the helping skill of reflecting and understanding feeling emphasizes the affective component. The first step in reflecting and understanding feeling is to identify emotional words in client statements or to observe nonverbal cues of emotional responses such as facial expression, voice quality, and body posture. Next the client's sentiment and the tone of the statement is adapted into different words that convey similar intensity and the content of the client's original statement. An added skill is to reflect emotions conveyed in client statements using words that match the client's sensory preferences through phrases that begin with it "looks like," "sounds like," or "feels like." Finally, restatements of what a client has delivered should be assessed for accuracy or effectiveness in order to ensure that the client's disclosures have been understood. In summary, focusing on feelings should not be confused with reflection of content statements which focus on ideas or information.

Reflecting and understanding feelings is considered a powerful helping skill for several reasons. First, if used accurately, reflecting and understanding feeling allows clients to know that they have been heard and understood, which is critical to the therapeutic conditions discussed previously. Second, clients attempt to communicate further when they feel others are attempting to understand them. This, along with other basic attending skills, encourages greater levels of client disclosure, particularly of emotional experiences. Third, reflecting and understanding feeling is useful in assisting clients to learn effective ways of communicating and coping with their emotions.

Confrontation

The important counselor skill of confrontation, which involves many of the above stated counselor responses, is an effective tool to offer growth-directed and constructive feedback that is neither critical nor disapproving. As such, it can have a negative or aggressive connotation.

The main purposes of confrontation are to assist clients in taking a different perception of themselves in a situation or to increase a client's awareness of inconsistent messages or behaviors. With confrontation, the professional counselor provides verbal responses that describe discrepancies, conflicts, and mixed messages that are apparent in the client's expressed feelings, thoughts, or actions (Cormier & Cormier, 1991). These discrepancies or mixed messages occur between or among any combination of verbal statements, nonverbal messages, or behaviors.

Care must be taken to ensure that a confrontation is directed toward growth and increased awareness of the client rather than establishing the professional counselor's expertise or venting frustration. Relatedly, a confrontation should include specific examples of behaviors or statements rather than vague or imprecise comments. It also should focus on the incongruity as the problem rather than focusing on the client as the problem or on the values, opinions, or judgements of the counselor.

Counseling Theory and Practice

In addition to helping skills as discussed in the previous chapter, two other elements help differentiate professional counseling from other forms of communication and conversation: (a) professional training, which includes subsequent endorsement from the profession through certification, licensure, or both, and subscription and adherence to professional standards; and (b) reliance on the use of a theoretical model or rationale. Thus, professional counseling is a process of communication which, in some ways, is similar to that used by many in society. However, it also is different because it is guided by an explicit theoretical rationale, is developed in the context of specialized training, and is conducted within the context of professional standards.

☐ Individual and Group Counseling

The use of helping skills usually is discussed within the context of training for or the practice of individual or group counseling. However, a very practical problem for professional counselors, particularly those working in institutional settings, is having adequate time to provide counseling services to all the people who desire them. When, for example, school counselors decide to see students for individual counseling, they make a substantial commitment of time (typically weekly or biweekly), and thereby decrease the time they have available for counseling services for others. The professional counselor has to decide whether such a large portion of time is appropriately spent working with individual students. An alternative is group counseling, which evolved from individual counseling as counselors realized they were limited in the amount of time available to reach individually all persons who desired help (Kemp, 1970).

Group counseling typically involves use of some of the helping skills employed in individual counseling. However, counseling more than one individual simultaneously makes some elements of the group counseling process much different from those of individual counseling. Professional counselors doing group counseling must consider special and often additional issues that are of little or less concern when counseling a single client; these include selection of group members, size and composition of the group, initiation of the group, and duration of the counseling process.

Group counseling is often considered to be counseling *by* the group (i.e., rather than counseling *in* the group), and this forms a major difference between individual and group counseling. With group counseling, group members learn to accept responsibility for helping others within the group as well as themselves (Sonstegard, 1998). In this perspective, productive change can take place within individuals as a result of the behaviors of the individual, the group counselor, and the other group members. Trotzer (1989) referred to this composite phenomenon as constructive influence through harnessing the power of the peer group.

As with most small-group situations, powerful norms usually develop in the group. Group counselors strive to facilitate (as opposed to impose) development of helpful norms within a group. One typically sought norm is open communication while another is collaboration among group members for the purpose of resolving problems. Thus, in group counseling opportunities are available for members of the group to be helped and for members to be helpers for others, a condition rarely present in individual counseling. As members witness others giving and receiving help, they become more willing to do both themselves. This spectator-type counseling process increasingly enhances each group member's opportunities for feedback and assistance. Group members develop the ability to think and perform for the good of others and to ask for feedback for themselves, with the group leader reinforcing the right of and necessity for members to make their own decisions (Kemp, 1970; Trotzer, 1989).

Group and individual counseling are applied in many settings. However, practical considerations, such as time, resources, and costs, make group counseling particularly suitable for schools, businesses, and some community agency settings. Group counseling can be designed in a variety of ways to serve the needs of either homogeneous or heterogeneous groups. In the former, the group is made up of similar individuals (e.g., adolescents, young adults, or single parents) who have a common concern (e.g., interpersonal relationship difficulties, self-development, or self-awareness). In the latter, different individuals (e.g., elderly people, adolescents, married couples, and the bereaved) with individual manifestations of their respective concerns are brought together for discussions. The counselor facilitates the development of common goals among members of a counseling group. Thus, a feeling of safety in numbers often develops in group members, along with the feeling that they and their concerns will be accepted by the group (Trotzer, 1989).

Because counseling groups consist of individuals with diverse backgrounds, interests, and life situations, each group becomes a social laboratory in which many beliefs, coping strategies, and practices are shared, compared, and examined. Through observation and experimentation under the leadership and facilitation of the group counselor, members of a group have the opportunity to learn and improve interpersonal, behavioral, and social skills that closely approximate those in society (e.g., caring, challenging, intimating, and refuting) (Corey, 1996).

Group counseling is usually considered to permit the counselor to make more effective use of time by working with several people simultaneously. The rationale is that counselors are able to expand their sphere of influence beyond that which is possible in individual counseling by drawing upon the resources of group members and channeling them appropriately. Recognition must be made, however, that some situations or problems do not readily lend themselves to rectification through a group counseling process. In fact, individual counseling is by far the most predominant form of counseling used by professional counselors. It is often characterized by terms such as personal, face-to-face, and a relationship between two people. The major difference between group and individual counseling seems to be the persons (clients) being helped in a given block of time. In addition, all elements of what is thought of as counseling in groups take place within individual counseling except for interactions among members (clients). Individual counseling does have the advantage over group counseling of providing a setting which is perceived by many as safer. Therefore, counseling may progress more quickly because the client has maximum personal contact with the professional counselor. In summary, both individual and group counseling are very important activities for professional counselors.

☐ Theoretical Models

By virtue of professional preparation, a counselor beginning a counseling process has a theoretical model in mind no matter how vague, ill-formed, or undefined it may be. As a client's problems become clearer, so too does the theoretical model to be used by the counselor. The theoretical model provides direction for the counseling process. Although this direction initially may be quite hazy, it exists in every counseling situation and ranges from a clearly articulated single model to one whereby the counselor has merged two or more models. The importance of theory in the counseling process is illustrated in Figure 5.1.

Several theoretical models describe the development of and are suitable for both individual and group counseling. Such models typically necessitate that professional counselors have comprehensive knowledge of personality and human development in order to use them. Equally effective counseling outcomes can result from many different theoretical models. However, no professional counselor is equally effective with each theoretical model.

Moreover, little is known about how professional counselors can be most effectively matched with particular theoretical models in order to gain the greatest benefits; the selection of a theoretical model is at the discretion of the counselor. But, regardless of the model(s) selected, theories serve as maps for helping clients by providing direction and goals, clarifying the counselor's role, explaining what takes place during the counseling process, and evaluating the effectiveness of counseling.

Hopson (1982) discussed five schools of thought for classifying most of the theoretical models used by professional counselors: psychoanalytic, client-centered, behavioral, cognitive, and affective. Within each school the theories that are used most frequently by professional counselors are briefly summarized.

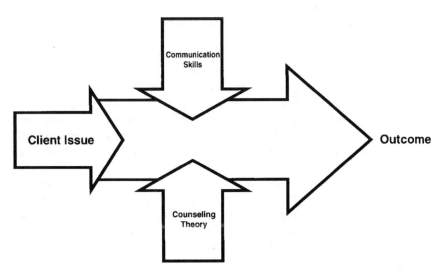

FIGURE 5.1. Professional Counselor.

Psychoanalytic Models

This model, in its general form, was historically the first, and approaches based on it concentrate on the past history of the client, understanding the dynamics of the person's personality, and the relationship between the client and the counselor.

Freudian Psychoanalytic Theory. This theory is based on the fundamental principle that an individual's behavior is controlled by desires to seek pleasure and to avoid pain, with the mind functioning as an expression of these conflicting forces. Freud (1911), the founder of the theory, referred to this concept as the "pleasure principle." It is viewed as operative throughout life, but experienced mainly during an individual's early years.

In Freudian psychoanalytic theory, an individual's present mental functioning is causally connected to past experiences, and current behaviors are determined by antecedent conscious and unconscious forces and events. Of importance are the effects which unconscious forces have upon an individual's mental processes and activities; mental elements are evaluated by their degree of consciousness or repression. The latter is important if an individual is repressing selected mental elements with the purpose of avoiding pain and displeasure. Consideration also is given to the manner in which libidinal (i.e., thought to be primarily sexual) drives interact with aggressive drives and the effect that this interaction has upon an individual's behaviors. Finally, the psychoanalytic approach indicates that an individual's behaviors can be traced to important experiences and events in childhood and subsequently generated fantasies, wishes, and dreams.

Proponents of Freudian psychoanalytic theory view a person's ultimate personality structure as influenced and determined by a culmination of biological factors and experiences. This includes the development of libidinal drives through the oral, anal, and phallic phases or stages of development, and the latency and adolescence periods of life. The oral phase, from birth to approximately 18 months of age, involves libidinal gratification through the mouth, lips, and tongue. Libidinal gratification during the anal phase (approximately 18 months to three years of age) involves activities related to the retention and passing of feces. During the phallic phase (approximately three to six years of age), the genitals become the central focus of libidinal gratification. Beginning with the latency period, which exists from the phallic phase to puberty and adolescence, the final development of an adult identity is initiated through socialization and education with significant others in the environment. Dominant within this developmental period are the **id** (i.e., the effect of libidinal and aggressive desires upon the mind), **ego** (i.e., the individual's self-identity), and **superego** (i.e., conscience).

Counseling based on the Freudian psychoanalytic theory emphasizes the client making rational responses and choices in response to unconscious conflicts, as opposed to the client responding automatically to them. Clients learn to control their lives through self-knowledge of their neurotic symptoms and behaviors which represent manifestations of their unconscious conflicts.

Counseling using this theory includes four main phases, all of which are related to transference: opening, developing, working through, and resolving. Transference involves feelings and expectations of the client that a counselor elicits by engaging the person in a therapeutic process. The client casts the counselor in a role (e.g., parent, spouse, or sibling) that meets the client's needs. A closely related phenomena is countertransference, which occurs when the counselor's own needs become entangled in the client's needs. Countertransference may be reflected in the counselor's attraction for or dislike toward certain clients.

Adlerian Theory. Adlerian theory, which is also referred to as individual psychology, focuses upon the belief that behavior exists only as the process of individuals interacting with each other. Of importance in this theory are the concepts that behavior takes place in a social context and that individuals cannot be studied or understood in isolation (i.e., without understanding the social context of the individual). An individual's behavior may change throughout life depending upon the constancy of his or her life style and the alternatives with which the individual is confronted. Through self-determinism, individuals have choices about goals to be pursued. Heredity and environment, which are viewed in the context of how an individual uses them in reaching goals, do not cause a person's *being* or determine a person's behavior. Instead, individuals focus on *becoming* through striving for mastery and superiority in self-selected goals (Adler, 1972), completion (Adler, 1958), and perfection (Adler, 1964). Individuals face challenges through solving the "life tasks" of society, work, and sex with the key element being interdependency; for "the benefit of the society," individuals must learn to work together with members of the other sex. In Adlerian theory, all individuals are *mitmenschen*, or equal, fellow human beings.

The Adlerian theory approach to counseling is based on the premise that individuals give their own meaning to life and behave according to their self-selected goals. As a result, they have control in shaping their respective internal and external environments and assume appropriate attitudes toward the outcomes of their selections. Individuals are also viewed as creative, self-consistent, and capable of change.

In Adlerian theory, the primary social environment for children is the family constellation. By observing, exploring, and seeking feedback from their environment (i.e., home and family), individuals learn what is right and wrong, and what fosters their personal success. To be successful in attaining goals, an individual has to solve the aspects of life tasks, or compensate in some way for unresolved tasks. A counselor following the Adlerian approach examines with the client his or her life style and aims to change behaviors within the client's existing life style rather than changing the life style.

Analytical Psychotherapy. Developed by Carl Jung, analytical psychotherapy (counseling) focuses upon the relationship between the conscious and the unconscious. These two subsystems form the psyche, a self-regulating system that controls an individual's behaviors. Analytical psychology emphasizes the need to become more aware of the conscious and of one's being by developing a greater understanding of the unconscious. The unconscious subsystem is viewed as contributing greatly to providing direction and meaning and enabling one to be creative, but it also creates problems for the individual if neglected.

Jung advocated that an individual's behavior is both consciously and unconsciously motivated, with the two systems being compensatory to each other. If an individual consciously develops a strong attitude in a given direction, the counterpoint attitude becomes strongly developed in the subconscious. These differences become evident through observation of relationships with others, communication skills, work habits, and analysis and interpretation of messages from the unconscious provided through dreams.

Proponents of analytical psychotherapy believe that each individual experiences the instincts of hunger, thirst, sex, aggression, and individuation, which is striving to achieve a true self or the attainment of wholeness based on conscious and unconscious factors. A person's behaviors are influenced in part by current experiences and in part by what may happen in the future as a result of the present behaviors. While conscious forces are evident and available to an individual, unconscious forces are available only through symbols which are interpreted as guiding messages. During counseling based on this model, individuals experiencing difficulties or conflicts are helped by appropriate translations of the symbolic messages provided through their dreams.

Counseling from the analytical psychology perspective is concerned with the purposeful and prospective functioning of the psyche, which is composed of the ego, personal unconscious, and nonpersonal unconscious. While past experiences are important in the development of personality and individuation because of the effect they may have upon present functioning, future outcomes also must be considered. Conscious elements are referred to as the ego. Previously conscious elements that can be readily retracted to consciousness are considered the personal unconscious. The final component of the psyche, the nonpersonal unconscious, is composed of factors (i.e., archetypes) that are unavailable to consciousness, but which affect behaviors. Examples of nonpersonal unconscious elements include (a) the hero archetype, (b) the Wise Old Man, (c) rebirth, (d) that which we do not want to be, (e) feminine and masculine principles, and (f) the need to experience meaning in life, centeredness, and wholeness.

Counseling within the context of analytical psychology is viewed as a process of helping clients find self-knowledge, achieve self-education, reconstruct their personality, or all three. Individuals with conflicts experience unconscious messages that need to be addressed. After a complete analysis of an individual's consciousness, the unconscious is explored, mainly through dream interpretation, with a focus not only on antecedent causes, but on future behaviors as well. Enlarging upon given data through interpretation enables a client to perceive previously unconscious connections, motivations, and feelings. The goal is to make the client aware of the unconscious as much as is possible.

Client/Person-Centered Model

Person-centered counseling, which was originally termed client-centered counseling, focuses on developing self-actualization (i.e., an individual's inherent tendency to develop all capacities in order to maintain or enhance oneself). Developed by Carl Rogers during the 1940s, this model and its adaptations are based on an "if-then" principle and place substantial faith in the client's problem-solving abilities. If the counselor conveys genuineness, accurate empathic understanding, and unconditional positive regard, and the client perceives these attitudes, then the client will achieve beneficial change by moving toward self-actualization and overcoming self-internalized restrictions.

Counselors who use the person-centered theoretical approach to counseling assume the role of being themselves with their clients; their inner experiencing is permitted to be present during the counseling relationship with the client. Through inner experiencing of the counselor's own feelings (i.e., genuineness), an understanding of the client's feelings (i.e., empathic understanding) is achieved. This is accompanied by an acceptance or respect for the client's individuality (unconditional positive regard) which is derived from a trust in the self-directed capacity of the client. As the client's awareness of inner experiencing develops, positive changes come from within the client.

Within person-centered counseling, present experiencing is important and provides the resources for the client's personal growth and change.

The counselor assumes the role of facilitator and helps clients establish and attach meaning to their inner experiencing. Any expression that could be interpreted as evaluative in nature is avoided by the counselor, as are probing questions and descriptions of the client.

Person-centered counseling fosters a relationship with the client that includes warmth and responsiveness from the counselor, freely expressed feelings influenced by a permissive climate, and the absence of coercion or pressure. In the relationship, the counselor is often referred to as the "helper" and the client is the "other."

An important assumption in person-centered counseling, as stated earlier, is that people are born with a tendency toward self-actualization, a basic motivation to enhance the organism. With growth, the client develops an ability to discriminate between positive and negative inner experiencing, and to acquire a sense of self. Thus, the client's self-concept and sense of self-regard develop. Self-regard is affected by the reactions of others and the introjections of conditions of worth. Conflict can arise when a client's self-regard is incongruent with his or her organismic needs and desires as they relate to the interactions with significant others in the environment. If negative organismic needs persistently prevail over self-regard needs, intervention may be needed. The intent of person-centered counseling, therefore, is to enable individuals who are experiencing conflict to incorporate previously denied organismic urges within their self-concept.

Behavioral Models

Within behavioral models for counseling, principles of learning and behavior modification are applied to the resolution of clients' problems. Two widely used approaches based on this model are behavior therapy and multimodal therapy.

Behavior Therapy. Changes in the principles of behavior therapy have been continually occurring since its beginnings in the 1950s, primarily because of updated research findings. As a result, four conceptually different approaches are used in behavior therapy: applied behavior analysis, neobehavioristic stimulus-response, social learning theory, and cognitive behavior modification. However, the primary hypothesis for behavior therapy remains unchanged: behavior modification techniques are used for treating all abnormal or maladaptive behavior. In contrast with previously discussed models, behavior therapy clients' previous thoughts are considered of little or no value in counseling, as are unconscious conflicts. Rather, current causes of behavior are the focal point, with treatment techniques varying according to clients' needs.

All behavior therapy is based on an educational model of human development as well as a commitment to scientific methodology. With the **applied behavior analysis** approach, behavior is viewed as a function of its consequences. Actual behavior rather than cognitive processes are of concern, with the behavior modification techniques of stimulus control, reinforcement, punishment, and extinction being emphasized. The **neobehavioristic stimulus-response** model of counseling focuses on anxiety. Intervention techniques involve systematic desensitization and covert conditioning for the purpose of extinguishing the underlying cause(s) of the anxiety. Overt behaviors and covert processes are assumed to follow the same laws of learning. Cognitive mediational processes, external stimuli, and external reinforcement are three focal points in counseling based on **social learning theory**. Current behaviors, cognitive processes, and environmental factors are viewed as interacting influences upon behavior. Cognitive processes, which are affected by environmental events, determine the treatment for environmental influences as they affect the individual. The client, however, determines what behaviors will or will not be changed, with behavioral change being directly related to the client's self-directed capabilities.

With the fourth approach, **cognitive behavior modification**, cognitive restructuring is emphasized. This involves using techniques for the purpose of gaining an understanding of individuals' interpretations of their experiences as they affect their respective behaviors. Alteration of irrational ideas, perceptions, and interpretations of significant individual experiences is emphasized.

Success within behavior therapy is dependent upon the client's willingness to make changes, and the interactions between counselor and client. The client is an active participant in the process and is encouraged by the counselor to be completely involved in determining and setting goals. The counselor's initial responsibility is to identify the existing concern. Toward this end, assessment techniques may be used, including psychological tests, behavioral observations, self-reports and self-monitoring, roleplaying, and imagery. Techniques used for treatment may include training in social skills or assertiveness, self-control procedures such as progressive relaxation and biofeedback, cognitive restructuring such as rational-emotive therapy, and real-life, performance-based techniques such as behavior modification programs used in classrooms.

Multimodal Therapy. Arnold Lazarus developed multimodal therapy during the 1960s and 1970s. With this model, behavioral psychology is extended to include assessment procedures and the interactions between sensory, imaging, cognitive, and interpersonal factors. Central to multimodal therapy is individual behavior which is determined through the "BASIC ID," an acronym for Behaviors, Affective processes, Sensations, Images, Cognitions, Interpersonal relationships, and Drug/biological functions. The component of "behaviors" involves an individual's activity level. Emotions and feelings, and reactions to these two elements are included under affective processes. Personal awareness of reactions to bodily sensation (e.g., pain or pleasure) is considered under sensations. Imagination is addressed through the images component, and an individual's analytical, planning, and reasoning skills are comprised in the cognition component. Relationships with others and the amount of emphasis placed on these by an individual are addressed by the interpersonal relationships component. Finally, the general health and physical well-being of an individual are addressed under drug/biological functioning, which also includes biochemical and neurophysiological elements such as personal hygiene, exercise, diet, and medications used.

Multimodal counselors believe that a client's abnormal behavior is due to a multitude of problems (e.g., conflicts, unhappy experiences, and social deficits) that need to be treated using a multitude of intervention techniques (e.g., biofeedback, imagery, bibliotherapy, audiotherapy, assertiveness training, or roleplaying). Likewise, because each individual is unique, therapy is approached through an individualized intervention plan based on the central hypothesis of who or what is best for the respective individual. Of concern are the interactions among the modalities within the client's BASIC ID, as well as external influences upon behaviors. During the initial interview, a **Modality Profile** (i.e., a list of problems and prospective interventions) is charted based on excessive and deficient modalities across the client's BASIC ID. Once the counselor determines problem areas, bridging and tracking procedures are employed. The counselor first addresses the client's preferred modality and then gradually bridges (i.e., leads or guides) the client into other modality areas that need attention. The direction of these bridges and the appropriate intervention technique to select for each problem are determined by tracking the preference order of modalities exhibited by a client. The preference order, referred to as **firing order**, varies across individuals and across situations. The counselor's role is to help clients understand influential antecedent factors affecting their respective behaviors and to use appropriate interventive techniques. The counselor also conducts an ongoing assessment of the client's progress and adjusts the Modality Profile accordingly.

Cognitive Models

Approaches based on a cognitive model focus on how clients conceptualize and cognitively organize their worlds. The common focus is to help clients change conceptualizations, and subsequently their associated feelings and behaviors. Three widely used approaches based on this model are rational-emotive behavior therapy, reality therapy, and transactional analysis.

Rational-Emotive Behavior Therapy. Albert Ellis, who developed the theory of rational-emotive therapy during the 1950s, advocated that emotional consequences are mainly created by an individual's belief system and not by significant activating events. Within his theory, the focal point of an individual's intrapersonal and interpersonal life is his or her growth and happiness. An individual is born with an innate ability to create or destroy, to relate or remain isolated, to select or not select, and to enjoy or dislike, abilities that are affected by the individual's culture/environment, family, and social reference group. Primary goals in rational-emotive behavior therapy are to help behavior individuals (in rational and emotive ways) to desire rather than to demand, to work at altering elements of their being that they would like to change, and, with understanding, to willingly accept aspects of their lives that are beyond their control.

Ellis and Dryden (1997) indicated that several main propositions of rational-emotive behavior therapy exist. He proposed that individuals have innate abilities to be both self-preserving and self-destructive and to be rational as well as irrational. In addition, being influenced by others is most pronounced during the early years and therefore, individuals are greatly influenced by their early-life family environments. Because an individual is able to perceive, think, emote, and behave at the same time, cognitive, connotive, and motoric behaviors are also coexistent. Both normal and abnormal behavior are viewed as functions of perceptions, thoughts, emotions, and actions, and therefore, these elements are essential in any rational-emotive behavior therapeutic relationship between the counselor and client. Also important is the need for the counselor to be accepting of a client and yet at the same time be critical of the client's behaviors, pointing out deficiencies where necessary and strongly stressing self-discipline and autonomous functioning if the client remains dependent. Finally, the strong cognitive emphasis in rational-emotive behavior therapy makes it unnecessary to establish a warm relationship between client and counselor. With its purpose of helping individuals achieve deep-seated cognitive changes that could involve alterations in basic values, rational-emotive behavior therapy uses a variety of methods, including didactic discussion, behavior modification, bibliotherapy, audiovisual aids, activity-oriented homework assignments, role playing, assertion training, desensitization, humor, operant conditioning, suggestion, and emotional support. Rational-emotive behavior therapy includes a general form, which involves learning rationally appropriate behaviors, and a preferential form, which involves learning how to internalize rules of logic and scientific method while also learning how to dispute irrational ideas and inappropriate behaviors. Typically, general rational-emotive behavior therapy is included as a part of preferential rational-emotive behavior therapy. Eliminating emotional problems involves disputing disturbance-creating ideas through logical and empirical thinking. The real causes of an individual`s problems are viewed as dogmatic, irrational, and unexamined beliefs that need to be exposed through objective, empirical, and logical evaluation. Individuals who are experiencing difficulty need to be made aware that the problem (a) is of their own making because of their beliefs rather than antecedent causes or conditions, (b) will continue unless addressed, and (c) can be extinguished or minimized through rational-emotive thinking and actions.

Rational-emotive behavior therapy is a highly active-directive approach that views the client holistically, and stresses the biological components of personality development. When necessary, counselors strongly challenge a client's irrational beliefs. The major goal is to help individuals minimize their self-defeating outlooks by developing more realistic and acceptable philosophies of life. Identifying a client's basic irrational beliefs is of immediate importance to the counselor, who then proceeds to expose them and work with the client to develop more rational points of view.

Reality Therapy.   Developed by William Glasser, reality therapy embraces the theory that the brain functions as a system that controls behaviors by fulfilling needs built into the environment. Individuals experiencing difficulties are doing so because they are unable to control or act upon elements in their environment in a satisfactory manner. The goal of reality therapy, therefore, is to help individuals focus upon choosing actions that are appropriate for satisfying the basic needs of staying alive, reproducing, having power, being free, and having fun.

Reality therapy views behavior as an integration of an individual's feelings, thoughts, and actions in consideration of personal needs and the behavior of others in the environment. Behavior is generated within the individual, dependent upon the needs to be satisfied, and antecedent experiences and outside forces are not of consequence since the focal point is present experiences and the client's awareness of how better choices of behaviors can be made. That each individual and society has a set of personal standards is a basic concept recognized by proponents of reality therapy and is an important consideration when helping clients who may be working contrary to society's or their own sets of standards. Also of importance is teaching individuals to achieve more effective control of their environments and to choose more effective behaviors. In essence, reality therapy views teaching as therapeutic since the end result of therapeutic teaching should be greater fulfillment of the client's needs.

Eight basic steps are included in the practice of reality therapy. First, after establishing a relationship with the client and making friends, the counselor seeks input from the client as to what he or she is "controlling for" (i.e., what the client wants). The counselor then determines what the client is currently doing to achieve what he or she wants. The third step involves aiding the client to evaluate the effectiveness of what he or she is doing relative to achieving what is desired. This is followed by aiding the client in making a plan to achieve more effective control of the situation or environment. For the latter to work, the counselor gets a commitment from the client to follow through on the plan (step five) and then does not accept excuses from the client if the plan is not carried out (step six). Step seven concerns consequences, where possible, when a plan is not fulfilled. Involved are reasonable consequences such as temporary restrictions of freedom or temporary removal of privileges. The final (eighth) step in reality therapy is not to give up and not to allow the client to control the counselor. If a client is persistent in not following through on a plan, then the counselor helps the client attempt another plan which can be implemented, and the cycle continues until the client gains effective control of his or her life. Glasser acknowledged that gaining more effective control of one's life may take a long time. However, he believed that the process must eventually be successful because the individual controls the environment; the environment does not control the individual.

Transactional Analysis. Often referred to as TA, transactional analysis was developed by Eric Berne during the 1950s. The focal points of this theory are the child, the adult, and the parent, which are three independent and observable ego states that exist within every individual. These ego states are patterns of experiences and feelings that correspond to patterns of behavior. During the child ego state, an individual behaves like a child, emotionally, regardless of age. During the adult ego state, however, an individual reacts unemotionally to stimuli, primarily by using logic and factual data. The parent ego state involves behaviors that in essence replicate those exhibited by a parent. An individual's moral attitudes, beliefs, and values are the concern of the parent state. An individual in this state may attempt to influence, control, or evaluate the development of others.

A second important concept of TA is a transaction, or a unit of communication between individuals. Two levels of transaction are involved, the overt social level and the covert psychological level. Diagraming transactions (a counseling function within transactional analysis) provides both the counselor and the client with a pictorial illustration of the latter's interactions with significant others in the client's environment. Circles containing the letters P, A, or C to represent the respective ego states of parent, adult, and child, are connected by arrows according to the type of transaction involved. A solid-line arrow depicts a social transaction and a broken-line arrow represents a psychological transaction. In addition, three other types of transactions are utilized. During a complementary transaction (i.e., parallel arrows), an exchange is direct and overt with definite communication between individuals. When a transference transaction (i.e., crossed arrows) occurs, exchanges are covert and discussion on a specific topic ceases immediately. The final form, an ulterior transaction (i.e., a solid-line arrow is parallel to a broken-line arrow and represents a dual-level exchange), involves an exchange between individuals during which both levels of transaction are actively and simultaneously in operation. With these game-type transactions, both the social level and the psychological message need to be used during interpretation and evaluation of an individual's behavior.

According to TA principles, social interactions between persons are based upon their respective needs for recognition, presented in the form of "strokes." Strokes, which are learned and are essential for growth, range from positive (approval) to negative (disapproval) to none at all (not caring); they shape individual personalities, and vary from family to family. Individuals develop a system of stroking through their interactions with others, thus forming the basis to their acceptance of being OK or not OK and accepting others as OK or not OK. This developmental patterning is referred to as a **life script** and is illustrated with an **epogram**.

Five psychological forces are included in the epogram representing the critical-parent, nurturing-parent, adult, free-child, and adapted-child functions that comprise an individual's personality. Personalities are formed according to the differing contributions of each psychological force. The critical-parent finds fault, makes and enforces rules, and strives for individual rights. The nurturing-parent fosters growth and development. The adult is nonjudgmental, precise, and nonemotional. Spontaneity, eagerness, and creativity are some of the energies found in the free-child, whereas the adapted-child is conforming, flexible, and easy to get along with. A well-balanced energy system forms a bell-shaped epogram and is the goal of transactional analysis. Also included are the concepts of time and energy as extended in an ego state; if raised in one state, time and energy will be decreased in another state. A well-balanced energy system also exists in a bell-shaped epogram; the energy extended by the psychological forces is approximately normally distributed.

Affective Models

Approaches based on the affective model include Gestalt therapy and Existential psychotherapy. They share the belief that problems accumulate and have to be discharged before the client can think clearly again.

Gestalt Therapy. Gestalt therapy, which was developed by Fritz Perls, focuses on the process of helping individuals become increasingly aware of the effect of their immediate, current experiences upon their current behaviors. Past and future experiences or behaviors are not emphasized. The process, undertaken individually but collaboratively by the counselor and the client, emphasizes the development of the client's self-awareness. Involved are the basic concepts of phenomenology, field theory, existentialism, and dialogue. The **phenomenological perspective** systematically analyzes only that which is currently being experienced by clients, with the intent being to help them become more aware of their own degree of awareness. With the **field theory perspective**, a behavior is viewed as a function of the person's life space or field. Meaning is given to a situation based on what is currently observed, the here-and-now, which may include antecedent experiences if they affect related elements such as beliefs. The third perspective, **existentialism**, focuses on the individual who is doing the perceiving and the truth of the individual's relation to the environment. The fourth perspective stresses the importance of **dialogue and contact** with others in the environment. This perspective involves inclusion (i.e., experiencing another's situation as much as possible without losing one's own identity), presence (i.e., the counselor expressing his or her self to the client), commitment to dialogue (i.e., permitting contact to happen instead of making it happen and controlling the result), protecting the integrity of the client's experiences, and experiencing dialogue rather than talking about it.

Important to Gestalt therapy is holism and multidimensionality. Individuals exist with a clear boundary between themselves and others and therefore need to understand themselves as a function of their environment. Abnormal behavior results from problems delineating the boundaries between one's self and others in the environment. The abnormal behaviors may be confluence (an absence of distinction between self and others), isolation, withdrawal, retroflection (a split between aspects of the self), introjection (lack of discrimination or assimilation of new information gained), projection (confusion of self and others), and deflection (avoidance of contact with others). Solutions to problem behaviors are achieved by dialogue and phenomenology concerning the client's present experiences. Therefore, a strong working relationship between the counselor and client is important, with the client assuming responsibility for what is. The goals for the client are to develop complete self-awareness through direct contact with the counselor and self-regulation of a whole existence that is comprised of integral parts. Involved are the good Gestalt (i.e., the whole is clearly organized and in good form) and creative adjustment (i.e., a balance is established between self and the environment). Self-regulation, according to Gestalt therapy theory, can be achieved through (a) phenomenology or here-and-now experiences and experimenting, (b) dialogue through direct contact with the counselor, and (c) awareness of the whole-field concepts of what is done as well as how and why it is done. The client focuses upon what he or she is aware of experiencing at the present time and then experiments with changes by using imagery, body techniques, or visualization.

Existential Psychotherapy.   The focus of existential psychotherapy is for the client to find a true sense of being. Authors closely associated with this theory include Victor Frankl, Irvin Yalom, and Rollo May. The approach is concerned with feelings of love, creativity, anxiety, despair, isolation, anomie, grief, and loneliness. A basic component is the "I-Am" or ontological experience (i.e., realizing that humans are living and experiencing individuals who are able to choose their own being). When an individual's existence or values are threatened, anxiety is experienced. Therefore, existential psychotherapy emphasizes the reduction of anxiety and concentrates on aiding individuals to be tolerant of the to-be-expected anxieties normally experienced in daily being. Of major concern to the existential psychotherapist is the client's neurotic anxiety, an anxiety that is inappropriate to a given situation.

A second area of focus is the neurotic guilt experienced by a client due to fantasized transgressions, or self guilt due to an inability to live up to potentialities. As with anxiety, guilt also may take a normal form. The expectation is that individuals will experience some guilt in their daily being and therefore, need to be tolerant of this to-be-expected form of guilt.

According to existential psychotherapy theory, an individual's world is comprised of the *Unwelt*, or the biological (i.e., natural) world, also referred to as the environment, which addresses an individual's drives, needs, and instincts. The *Mitwelt*, or personal community, is concerned with interpersonal relationships. Self-awareness and self-relatedness are included in the third mode, *Eigenwelt*, which is concerned with one's relationship with self. The dimension of time is also significant in existential psychotherapy. Whether a client is able to recall important antecedent events is dependent upon his or her commitment to the present and future. Without the latter, past events have little relationship or effect upon the difficulties the person is experiencing. Relatedly, an individual's ability to transcend antecedent events to the present and future is important. Through *transcendere*, individuals are capable of continually emerging from the past to the present and the future (i.e., being able to transcend time and space because of the ontological nature of human beings).

Difficulties can arise for individuals when they experience conflicts with the ultimate concerns of existing. Essential concerns or sources of anxiety include freedom or being responsible for one's existence (e.g., actions and choices). A second concern is existential isolation: a gap between oneself and the world and others. Death constitutes a third concern, while meaninglessness is a fourth. Of particular importance with meaninglessness is the development of values that provide an individual with purposeful meaning for existing.

Existential psychotherapy counselors view their role as helping individuals to experience conflict in order to determine their unconscious anxieties and the maladaptive defense mechanisms being used, and to develop alternative strategies or mechanisms for coping with their problems. This entails identifying methods that clients use to avoid these instances when they occur, and helping clients to become aware of these situations and to make appropriate decisions for terminating a conflict for the betterment of their existence.

Family Therapy

Family therapy is a relative newcomer to the theoretical approaches used by counselors. It has both built on and differentiated itself from individual and group approaches. The movement from individual-focused thinking to marital conceptualization and a more family-centered viewpoint began to occur in the 1950s and 1960s (Sporakowski, 1995).

An approach that has become increasingly popular among practitioners is family systems therapy (Corey, 1996). Family-systems thinking currently is influencing the counseling field in important ways. Systemic counselors believe that individual behavior is better understood when it occurs within a family social system (Goldenberg & Goldenberg, 1996). Rather than concentrating on a specific person in therapy, the counselor examines the behaviors and interactions within the family. These interactions are seen as having circular causality whereby the behavior of one family member influences that of a second, which in turn affects the first person's behavior (Schilson, 1991). Thus, in order to understand fully and help make changes, the counselor must examine the processes and dynamics at work within the context of the entire family unit. A family has been defined as a natural social system with is own unique properties. These properties include an evolved set of rules of behavior, an organized power structure, strategies for negotiating and solving problems, a shared history and perceptions, and overt and covert modes of communication. Family counseling is often considered within the context of systems theory which views a family as being composed of members who interact and mutually affect one another.

Building on these basic tenets of systemic thinking, several theorists have developed a number of different approaches to family therapy such as Murray Bowen's approach of intergenerational family counseling, Virginia Satir's human validation model, Carl Whitaker's experiential/symbolic approach, the structural model of Salvador Minuchin, and the strategic approach of Jay Haley and Cloe Madanes. The salient points of these approaches are highlighted below.

Intergenerational Family Counseling.   Murray Bowen is the foremost proponent of intergenerational family counseling. The primary goal of intergenerational family counseling is to assist one or more family members to achieve greater self-differentiation (i.e., the extent to which people can separate cognitions and emotions in order to function effectively). With this approach, genograms are used to help family members understand the multigenerational transmission process and structure of at least three generations of a family. Other constructs used in this approach include triangulation (i.e., the process of involving a third person in a dyad particularly when the dyad is stressed or confronting a problem) and the nuclear family emotional system (i.e., pattern of emotional interchange among family members in a single generation).

Human Validation Counseling Model.   Virginia Satir reported that family problems are grounded in suppression of feelings, emotional and behavioral rigidity, and lack of awareness and sensitivity. The goal of her model is to increase intrafamily communication. Counselors applying this model describe family dysfunction using an individual or dyad as the unit of analysis.

Satir has describe four nonproductive roles of communication that family members may use when under stress. One role is the *placater* who agrees and tries to please. A second role is the *blamer* who dominates and finds fault. The third role is the responsible *analyzer* who remains emotionally detached and intellectualizes. The final role is that of the *distractor* who interrupts and constantly chatters about irrelevant topics.

Experiential/Symbolic Counseling Approach.   The primary goal for family counseling in using the experiential/symbolic counseling approach, as advocated by Carl Whittaker, is to increase each person's belongingness in and individuality within the family. Whittaker advocates the use of a cocounselor to prevent the counselor from becoming enmeshed in the family. He also emphasizes the use of creative and sometimes relatively radical techniques in family counseling.

Structural Family Counseling. Salvador Minuchin is generally acknowledged as the founder of structural family counseling. The primary goal of this approach is to resolve presenting problems by bringing them into the open and facilitating structural changes such as those related to organizational patterns and action sequences. Structural family counseling is action-oriented with the counselor playing an active role in the therapeutic process.

This approach is based on the idea that family functioning involves family structure, subsystems, and boundaries. Accordingly, the resolution of presenting problems typically results from or in a change in the underlying family structure (i.e., pattern of intrafamily interactions). Techniques used in this approach include *joining,* in which the counselor helps to act out the mood of the family; *enactive formulation,* whereby the counselor acts to slow down a family interaction; *challenging the communication roles of the family,* with the counselor imposing new communication for the family; *reframing,* which involves applying a positive connotation to a negative behavior; and *relabeling* whereby a negative descriptive adjective is replaced with a positive one. Other techniques with the related role of the counselor include: *challenging the structure of the family* (counselor points out ineffective patterns of behavior and/or interaction); *restructuring* (counselor intentionally modifies a family's typical way of interacting); *talk setting* (counselor gives a specific homework assignment intended to extend what has taken place during counseling); *making boundaries* (counselor helps family members establish more effective boundaries by usually placing limitations on specific behaviors); and *shaping competence* (counselor helps family members to develop and be recognized as having new competencies).

Strategic Family Counseling. Jay Haley is recognized as the foremost proponent of strategic family counseling along with Cloe Madanes who is noted for her analyses of power in the family. The primary goal of strategic family counseling is to resolve presenting problems as rapidly as possible, often through behavioral goals, by minimizing insights and using action-oriented techniques. Haley was particularly concerned with family life cycle transitions and suggested that if the family does not adapt to change or stress effectively, one or more family members will become symptomatic.

Strategic family counseling is intended to be simple, pragmatic, and focused on changing symptomatic behaviors and rigid rules. A primary technique in this approach is the use of directives or prescriptions, which are orders that the counselor gives directly or indirectly to the family to achieve compliance or rebellion. Key concepts include *the perverse triangle* (two family members at different levels of the family hierarchy align against a third member), *double bind* (a family member cannot win regardless of what the member says or does), *power in the family* (the authority to make or enforce rules or decisions), *incongruous dual hierarchy* (family member holds both a superior and inferior position of power in the family), *symptom as metaphor* (a symptom serves as a metaphor for the problem being experienced by another member of the family), *cyclical variation maintaining incongruous dual hierarchies* (symptoms come and go in cycles but the incongruous hierarchies remain), and *pretending* (one family member is instructed to pretend to have a symptom while others react to it).

☐ Summary

The desire for more autonomous and self-competent individuals in society causes professional counselors to seek the most effective counseling theory and methods available. At this time, however, no single theory has been established as the quintessential approach to professional counseling. Therefore, this chapter addresses the important concerns of individual and group counseling. Established counseling theories were reviewed, while several existing approaches were not included because they are either off-shoots of the ones presented or are highly unique.

Consultation

Jack Wooten, a social worker, recently returned from a site visit at a community mental health center located in a neighboring state. As a result of his visit, he wants to integrate new ideas into his employment setting, but he is unsure whether some of these strategies will work. Jack believes he could clarify his concerns and plans by talking with another person who shares his interest.

Martha, an employee of the telephone company, is missing more and more days, and she frequently leaves work early complaining of back trouble and headaches. At work, she becomes easily frustrated and lashes out at people. Jane Martin, Martha's supervisor, recognizes that there has been a change in Martha's work performance, that Martha is unhappy, and that something needs to be done. However, she is unsure what to do. She would like to discuss the situation with someone else who is knowledgeable about human behavior.

In each of the above vignettes, the individual can benefit from a counselor serving as a consultant. The case of Laura Gordon offers a more specific illustration.

The Case of Laura

Laura needs help. She is a first-grade teacher in an elementary school that has a traditional orientation toward educating children. Currently, Laura is experiencing some problems in her classroom for which she is unprepared. The students like her and she feels comfortable in the school environment, but she is having frequent classroom disturbances that are affecting the children's learning process. Several of the students disrupt the class by constantly talking to themselves at a level that is barely audible, but still distracting. Two other children in Laura's class move around the room at times when all the children are to be seated. The children's disorderly conduct also occurs outside the classroom in the hallways, the lunchroom, and the playground area. The principal senses that Laura is losing control of the class and believes the children are not learning. Laura, who wants to be a successful teacher, recognizes that the principal is unhappy. She has tried threats, sent children to the office, and contacted parents about their respective child's inappropriate behavior, all to no avail. As a result of the situation, Laura is having serious doubts about her choice of teaching as a career and whether she will be able to finish the academic year in her present assignment. Unhappy, fatigued, and disillusioned, she is unsure what to do. She views quitting as the only solution, but is afraid that she may be unable to obtain another teaching job because of a low evaluation she will receive from the principal.

Laura's situation has reached an intolerable level, for her, for the principal, and for the children. She is in need of assistance from someone regarding these professional matters; the person of choice is a professional counselor serving as a consultant. The professional counselor acting in a consulting role helps other professionals with possible solutions to professional problems by listening and by providing feedback, assurance, relief, and help with stress reduction. Through the consultation process, the professional counselor will help Laura deal with her problems with the children in her class. Ultimately, the focus of the process is actually on helping the children, as opposed to helping Laura personally, as would be the case in a counseling process.

☐ The Consultant's Role

Consultation involves a process for helping other professionals (i.e., individuals, groups, or agencies) to cope with their problems, and therefore to function more effectively and with greater satisfaction. Consultation may be referred to as an indirect function for professional counselors because the counselor helps others (the consultees) in working with still others (the persons or clients receiving the services provided by the consultees). The helping function of consultation can be an important part of the professional counselor's role, primarily because of the growing recognition that assisting other professionals to function more effectively is ultimately the most economical and far-reaching use of the professional counselor's skills, efforts, and time. Through the provision of consultation services, professional counselors are able to impact far more people than they could impact directly.

The consultation process is most comprehensive and effective when it is used for preventive purposes, when the counselor helps consultees help others to avoid future difficulties. Therefore, the most efficient time for consultation is when professionals (consultees) are not under excessive stress and want to explore possible alternative behaviors or discuss their ideas with someone else before they try them. The provision of consultation in these situations creates more confident professionals. In reality, however, consultants are often asked to assist with difficulties after they have already occurred. For example, in the previous vignette Laura's situation has gone beyond a point where preventive efforts can be implemented. In working with problems similar to Laura's, the professional counselor who serves as a consultant must provide an opportunity for the consultee to think aloud and to aid in reducing stress and providing relief so that the consultee can decide upon appropriate courses of action to undertake.

There are a number of reasons why understanding the nature of consultation, as it is practiced within the context of professional counseling, can be confusing. Consultation is not a specialty with a single professional identity; it is an activity practiced in almost every profession. Surprisingly, however, the literature on research in the practice of consultation is relatively scarce (Fuchs, Fuchs, Dulan, Roberts, & Fernstrom, 1991). In particular, evidence of successful consultation as a preventive intervention, other than anecdotal or descriptive analysis, is hard to locate. The nature of the consultant's role is further clouded by the numerous meanings and connotations attached to the term consultation. For example, as used by physicians, consultation means meeting with a patient to discuss the patient's medical condition, but in many businesses, the term means being engaged in work-related conversation with another person. Attorneys also use the term in reference to any meeting with a client. None of these examples, however, adequately reflects the use of the term consultation within the counseling profession.

Parsons (1996) noted that attempts at a single operational definition of consultation that can be applied in all human service fields have been relatively unsuccessful, primarily due to the variations in emphases of professionals and theorists. He highlights, however, a number of core characteristics that exist among the different forms of consultation that are practiced:

> Consultation can be characterized as a helping, problem-solving process involving a helpgiver (the consultant), a helpseeker (the consultee), and another (the client). This voluntary, triadic relationship involves mutual involvement on the part of both the consultant and consultee in an at-

tempt to solve the current work-related problem in a way that it not only stays solved, but that future problems may be avoided and or more efficiently handled (prevention). (p. 11, 13)

Parsons' operational definition of consultation is consistent with the consultation model of Gerald Caplan (1970), who is credited for pioneering the use of consultation in mental health activities, and whose model of consultation has become a standard among the mental health professions, including counseling. He wrote that consultation is a voluntary, nonsupervisory relationship between professionals for the purpose of aiding the consultee(s) to improve professional functioning. He further indicated that this may involve helping a consultee with current work problems related to a specific client or program or with anticipated future concerns. Caplan (1970) suggested that consultation can reduce areas of misunderstanding so that consultees may be able to cope more effectively with the same type of problem in the future. He also discussed consultation as a triadic relationship involving an interplay between consultant, consultee, and client.

As specified by Caplan's and Parsons' definitions, the consultee-consultant relationship is voluntary and collegial or coprofessional, and the focus of the consultation activity is professional as it relates to the consultee's client or professional problem. Viewing the consultation relationship as triadic underscores the multiple impacts that consultants' work can have, directly on the behavior and attitudes of the consultee and indirectly on the client, who benefits from the improved services provided by the consultee. Although consultation focuses on professional problems and an awareness of the consultee's coping skills and personality assets and liabilities, consultation as we know it today is much more complex as practiced by a professional counselor. The typical service provided by a professional counselor serving as a consultant, includes (a) dyadic consultations as an expert or peer to individuals, parents, families, and institutions, (b) triadic consultation as an expert or peer to clients, parents, families, or institutions, and (c) training and processing as an expert or peer. The integration of the features comprising effective counselor-consultant service delivery is illustrated in Figure 6.1 which provides a conceptual view of the components and process of consultation.

☐ Consultation Versus Counseling

Given the many misconceptions associated with consultation, it is sometimes helpful to indicate what consultation, as performed by the professional counselor, is not. Within the counseling profession, consultation is not therapy, advocacy, liaison with agencies, direct service, or adminis-

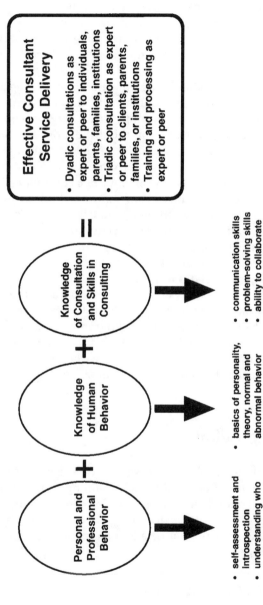

FIGURE 6.1. Features of a Professional Counselor Consultant.

trative control over the consultee. Nor is it collaborating or working with (i.e., as in cocounseling) parents and colleagues jointly to provide a direct service to their child or client, respectively. These activities are inconsistent with the construct of consultation as used in this book and as viewed by many professional counselors. For example, assisting parents in resolving problems concerning their child is providing a direct service to the parents; the parents are the target of the service (and are not professional helpers or consultees).

Many of the communication skills associated with the counseling process, such as responsive listening, reflecting, clarifying, and summarizing, are also part of the consultation process. Therefore, differences between counseling and consultation are dictated primarily by the distinctions between the theoretical framework of counseling and the model of consultation, as well as by their respective intentions. The term model is used to describe the structure of consultation because the area, unlike counseling, has not obtained a level of sufficient substance to warrant use of the term theory.

One major difference between counseling and consultation is that the consultant-consultee relationship is more objective and emotionally external than is the counselor-client relationship, which is more personal and involves disclosure of emotions. In addition, the target of consultation is problem-solving as it relates to professional functioning, whereas the target of counseling is primarily personal growth and adjustment (Parsons, 1996). It is important that professional counselors serving in a consulting role take the time to explain these differences to consultees by clarifying what should and should not be expected from the consultation process. Addressing misconceptions directly and early on can reduce the likelihood of misunderstandings and will facilitate smoother and more efficient consultation.

☐ Models of Consultation

The professional counselor's role as a consultant can be more easily understood by reviewing five often-used models: training workshops, mental health, process, behavioral, and atheoretical problem-solving consultation. Of course, in professional practice these models are often modified or combined in some way to meet more adequately the individual needs of the professional consultant.

Training Workshops Consultation

Training workshops are a type of consultation in which selected traditional and nontraditional educational methods are used to provide information and to develop skills as a basis of prevention. A distinction needs to be made between training and teaching. In contrast to teaching or educational programs wherein people are usually passive listeners, training workshops encompass a form of consultation that involves considerable experiential learning by the participants. For example, training workshops frequently involve putting participants in dyads or triads to learn and practice new skills.

To effect training workshops consultation, mental health agencies, schools, or college and university offices of student affairs often have one- or two-day retreats. More common, however, are designated periods of time (e.g., office, work, in-service, or conference days), during which clients are not seen, classes are canceled, and offices are closed, and instead, a variety of professional activities takes place in the context of a training workshop conducted by a consultant.

Approaches to training workshops and staff participation vary by setting. For example, with clinical mental health counselors, one-way mirrors can be used to permit observation of (usually simulated) counseling sessions. A professional counselor serving as a consultant conducts the sessions while other counselors observe through the one-way mirror, and consultant-led group discussions follow the sessions.

Professional counselors also often help other professional personnel (teachers, administrators, ministers, or social workers) to work with problems specific to their respective employment environments. The professional counselor's training and experience in communication skills, and knowledge of consulting models and mental health, are used to enable groups of professionals to function more effectively. For example, training workshops may involve meeting with a group of concerned teachers to discuss ways of working with children with behavior problems, incidences of substance abuse, or adolescent suicide. Yet another example could be a professional counselor working as a consultant with a group of vocational rehabilitation counselors or residence-life staff members to improve their communication skills in their work settings.

Most training workshops conducted by professional counselors have clearly defined purposes and are preventive in nature. They are usually held to enable other professionals to share here-and-now (i.e., current and immediate) problems and to get help with practical solutions. Also, these solutions may be used with problems that could be encountered in the future. If problem areas have not been determined before the counselor is called upon to run the training workshop, the professional counselor, as a consultant, typically surveys the group members to determine their concerns. The professional counselor who serves as a training workshop consultant has an extremely potent role in helping other professionals and therefore needs to be particularly knowledgeable of their specific needs.

The following example provides a typical sequence of events during a training workshop on substance abuse. A professional counselor is asked to conduct a training workshop concerning substance abuse interventions for college age students because a group of university residence-life directors believe they are insufficiently skilled to help people with problems in this area. Also, the group holds ambivalent attitudes and values concerning the topic (i.e., whether or not they should have to do something about the problem). The professional counselor surveys the group and finds that the specific concern is how to handle certain aspects of drug prevention without causing unfavorable reactions from their students. A secondary concern is that the other student-development staff members and parents feel that the directors were, at a minimum, ambivalent about the problem, if not neglectful. The professional counselor's survey further reveals an unexpected amount of ignorance about drugs and the physiological effects of substance abuse.

With this basic information, the counselor plans the training workshop to contain two parts. For the first part, a pharmacologist is engaged to give instruction on the most commonly abused drugs and their psychotropic effects. Following the more formal didactic presentation by the pharmacologist, the counselor-as-consultant divides the participants into small groups of five or six. Then, role playing is used, during which one participant assumes the helper's role and the others become the helpees. The helpees are given directions to assume the role of badgers, asking every conceivable question about drugs, such as "Is it harmful?," "What does snorting mean?," "Is 'crack' any worse than smoking pot?," or "How do you know that drug use relates to poor grades?" The helper assumes a supportive role and tries to be specifically helpful to each helpee asking a question. During the session, much anxiety is generated when the helper is not familiar with the terms used and has no well-formulated response to such questions. However, through role playing, helpers are able to practice making accurate responses to questions, without implying value judgments. Once the helpers have the opportunity to become more familiar with the often-asked questions and commonly used slang words and terms, their initial anxiety decreases and their abilities to provide effective responses increase.

Mental Health Consultation

Caplan's (1970) mental health consultation is the prototype of most consultation models used in the counseling profession. Caplan based his model on psychodynamic assumptions about human behavior and proposed that predictable deficit areas of professional behaviors include the professional's lack of skills, self-confidence, knowledge, or objectivity. The model emphasizes the process of consultation as a triadic relationship between consultant, consultee, and client. In Caplan's approach, the focus of consultation can be client-centered, consultee-centered, program-centered, or consultee-centered administrative.

Client-centered case consultation is the classic triadic approach, which involves a consultee seeking assistance from a consultant about a client. The focus is on the client, although the consultant does not have direct contact with the client; any assistance afforded a client from the consultant is effected through the consultee.

Consultee-centered consultation concentrates on the consultee's professional problem. The process and focus is usually dyadic (involving the consultant and consultee), with the target being the consultee.

Program-centered consultation involves a consultant helping with an organization's problem. This approach is also dyadic, except that the focus is on the organization.

Consultee-centered administrative consultation has as its goal either improving administrators' problem-solving skills or helping them in the broad areas of skill deficit or emotional entanglement with an issue.

An important component of and typical impetus for mental health consultation is the consultee's loss of professional objectivity. Caplan suggested that a loss of objectivity occurs when a consultee has identified with the problem (e.g., the client reminds the consultee of an event or person in their past), or it may be due to a much more severe problem (e.g., the consultee has a characterological disorder such as being paranoid, histrionic, or avoidant). Caplan described these situations as "theme interference," wherein the consultee fits the client into a previously determined unconscious category and links him or her to an inevitable outcome. To illustrate, a consultee who perceives a client as passively demanding may see the client's success in working with coworkers as doomed to failure. The syllogism linking the client to failure is unconsciously dynamic because, subconsciously, the consultee does not really believe that the counseling can be effective. To help the consultee with theme interference, Caplan suggested (a) "unlinking," or alleviating the consultee's subconscious perception, or (b) "theme-interference reduction," which involves the consultant trying to help the consultee construct other possible outcomes.

Process Consultation

The process consultation model emphasizes behavioral, group-dynamic dimensions within an organization by examining the effects of communication on each strata of the organization as it pertains to the attainment of its goals. The origin of the process consultation model, which is frequently identified with Schein (1969), rests in social psychology. It is primarily a group problem-solving approach that seeks to make people more aware of the interpersonal communications that are negatively affecting their work productivity and attitudes. Process consultation is also known as organizational development and is frequently used to improve organizational functioning by concentrating on and working with small groups of employees. The model attempts to strengthen the organizational system by using existing personnel optimally to produce and enhance a growth-oriented environment. A counselor-as-consultant using the process consultation model seeks to help members of the organization to understand the patterns of interaction that may be interfering with the goals of the organization.

Schein (1969) suggested that patterns of interaction which interfere with an organization's functioning include inconsistent decision-making styles, hidden personal agendas, poor leadership skills, inappropriate agenda setting, scapegoating, or inappropriately high levels of competition. Consultants using this approach are also sensitive to problems with the structural system and with managerial procedures within the organization.

Schein (1969) recommended the following seven interacting and overlapping steps for process consultation:

1. initial contact with the client organization
2. definition of the consultation relationship, including both the formal and psychological contracts
3. selection and setting of a method of work
4. data gathering and diagnosis
5. intervention
6. involvement reduction
7. termination

Process consultants are seldom experts within the organizations or industries for which they are providing consultation. Instead, they are usually professionals whose focus is the how of the interpersonal process within an organization. Hence, the knowledge and skill of a process consultant can be useful in a variety of organizational settings. In summary, process consultation is oriented toward manifesting and facilitating the many levels and potentially effective modes of communication that exist in an organization.

Behavioral Consultation

The behavioral model of consultation is based heavily on the assumption that changes in an environment will necessarily change the behaviors of people in that environment. This approach is particularly well suited for consulting with professionals employed in settings such as schools, prisons, hospitals, and other controlled and regulated environments.

Like the mental health consultation model, the behavioral consultation model is a problem-solving approach. It is based on social learning theory, with client and consultee problems conceptualized as having evolved from direct or vicarious previous learning. The consultant's goal is to work with the consultee to ascertain what the problem or target behavior is, determine and isolate environmental variables that foster or support the target behavior, and suggest environmental changes that will diminish the probability of the behavior continuing. Bergan and Kratochwill (1990) suggested an additional important goal of helping consultees develop their own problem-solving approach to addressing clients' needs. The consultant who employs this model utilizes the principles and traditional behavioral techniques of behavior modification (e.g., shaping, chaining, successive approximation, or modeling) to produce new behaviors. In addition, the behavioral consultation model may include other activities that facilitate learning, such as role-playing, homework assignments, and feedback.

Although behavioral consultation may be applied in any setting, the usefulness of behavioral techniques in schools is particularly well documented. Perhaps this may be, in part, because teachers feel comfortable working with techniques and interventions that are based on learning principles that are familiar to them.

Atheoretical Problem-Solving Consultation

Myrick (1977) suggested an atheoretical approach to consultation that he believed is particularly well suited for professional counselors. The approach relies heavily on communication skills described as "facilitative" (Wittmer & Myrick, 1974). Myrick's (1977) approach to consultation is a systematic set of procedures that follow seven steps. The first step focuses on identifying the consultee's problem. This is followed by the consultant clarifying both the emotional and behavioral aspects of the consultee's situation, primarily through encouraging the consultee to talk about feelings, specific behaviors that influenced the consultee's current ideas and situation, what the consultee expects to achieve, what has already been tried in attempting to correct the situation, and positive attitudes and behaviors already present in the situation. Step three involves identifying the goal(s) or desired outcome(s) for the situation. In step four, relevant behaviors associated with the situation are observed and recorded by the consultee and possibly by the consultant. Next, the consultant and consultee develop a plan of action together, with the expectation that the consultee will play the major role in carrying out the plan. Step six is the initiation of the plan by the consultee under the supervision of the consultant. Step seven is follow-up, examining what has happened to determine whether the plan is working or what changes, if any, need to be made in the plan. Myrick recommended this approach for both individuals and groups. This model is straightforward, progresses systematically, and involves many already familiar skills and behaviors. For these reasons, the model appeals to many professional counselors, particularly those working in school systems.

Myrick (1977) purported that the model is helpful with crisis, preventive, and developmental consultation. Crisis consultation is defined as assisting the consultee who is experiencing an urgent problem, such as an agency director who has a concerned board member coming in at the end of the day and is unsure how to approach the conference. Preventive consultation, the second type, is used when the consultee believes that an urgent problem is imminent. In this situation, the consultee has received signals that a problem will be developing if the situation is not handled correctly now. Finally, developmental consultation involves helping the consultee help others develop skills and behaviors that will either prevent future problems or enable them to cope effectively with such problems, should they arise. An example of developmental consultation is the school counselor who helps teachers help students develop ways to avoid involvement with substance abuse.

A variation of the model proposed by Myrick is systematic problem solving which is a functional but abridged model of consultation. The systematic problem solving model is illustrated in Figure 6.2, which provides a conceptual view of the components and process a consultant using this model would follow.

☐ An Example of Individual Consultation

Many times a professional counselor is approached for consultation in a rather informal manner. Other professionals who are in need of consultation but are uneasy about making a formal request for it, often seek out professional counselors who have established themselves as consultants, in informal atmospheres such as a staff dining room or lounge area, or at a social event. The following illustrates such an exchange. First, however, it is important to remember that confidentiality is an ethical imperative for counselors who serve as consultants. Individual clients should not be discussed in settings where confidentiality cannot be assured. Although

Intent	Purpose

1. WHAT IS THE PROBLEM OR SITUATION?

IDENTIFY THE PROBLEM

active listening	establish rapport
door opening	tentative identification of problem
	stimulate discussion
	who "owns" the problem
	ventilation

2. WHAT HAVE YOU TRIED?

CLARIFY THE CONSULTEE'S SITUATION

what has been done	gather data
feelings of consultee	elicit perceptions
specific behaviors	identify issues
consultee's expectations	what are the issues
positive attitudes and behaviors of consultee	[avoid generalizations]
	[avoid over-detailing]
	[avoid tangents]

3. WHAT ELSE COULD YOU DO?

IDENTIFY THE GOAL/DESIRED OUTCOMES

what are the options	"mutualize" reality
what are the outcomes	identify issues
what else is involved	focus on solutions
	identify outcomes of options (behaviors)
	[consider several options, not just the best]
	consultee's words

4. WHAT IS YOUR NEXT STEP?

DEVELOP A PLAN

what can be done	select viable options
how will you do it	plan change program
when will you do it	consider contingencies
	should be concrete/specific
	[how much structure is needed]
	[consider self/others]

FIGURE 6.2. Systematic Problem Solving.

consultants may be approached for feedback in informal settings, they should refrain from discussing or allowing others to discuss details about clients that may make them readily identifiable to others. This vignette is of a consultant and consultee who are alone and in a secure environment where others could not potentially overhear their conversation.

Consultee: *I hate to disturb you now with shop talk, but could I ask you about a client of mine? I don't think I am making as much progress with the case as I would like. She's immature, but I believe her behavior is a method to avoid taking responsibility for her actions. I've been seeing her weekly since October, and during our sessions she has been timid, quiet, and generally nonresponsive—the very behaviors that prompted her to see me. And, she is concerned about keeping up with her responsibilities at the insurance company where she works. She's a great person, and I don't think there's anything seriously or pathologically wrong with her. Yet, I am worried that if I continue seeing her and she doesn't make any progress, she may think that she has a serious problem that can't be helped, and she may lose her job.*

Consultant: *Yes, it's always a problem deciding if you are doing the right things with a client. What can you tell me about her?*

Consultee: *She's young—just turned 18 in May. She graduated early from a small high school—just after she reached 16.*

Consultant: *What other people are closely involved in her life? Others can sometimes play an important role in determining behavior. How about her parents or friends?*

Consultee: *I'm not too sure. I have been focusing on her situation pretty much as a job-related motivational problem.*

Consultant: *What approaches have you tried?*

Consultee: *Primarily some time-management schemes: homework-type assignments on use of time. I've also been having her practice speaking to others at work. I thought that if I got her to interact with others she might come out a bit more, be less timid and quiet, and do a better job at work.* (By this time the professional counselor has helped the consultee to formulate the problem, and has learned what has been done.)

Consultant: *What other directions might you take?*

Consultee: *I could explore with her the influence that others in her life are having on her—specifically her parents. I recognize that she is young and, you know, maybe too much pressure is on her to keep up with those older employees.*

Consultant: *Specifically, how do you think you can approach your client during your next session?*

(This question helps the consultee to think aloud about a plan of action.)

Consultee: *Well, I think I will tell her that I have been reviewing our sessions and believe that I would like to explore some new avenues which might be helpful. Also, if her parents are a dominant factor, as I now think they may be, I might suggest that we have a session or two that includes them.*

Consultant: *How do you think your client will feel about that? Sometimes parents can unwittingly make things difficult for their child, even a young adult.*

Consultee: *Oh, I don't believe there would be a problem. I somehow sense the family is close.*

Consultant: *Try it and call me. Let me know after your next session with her what's happening.*

A week later, the professional counselor received a call from the consultee indicating that the last session went well and that, indeed, her client was feeling pressured into employment and marriage by her parents. In addition, a session had been established with the client and her parents together.

This example, in which the process of consultation has been considerably abridged, shows how the professional counselor serving as a consultant and the consultee interact as coprofessionals, not as an authority and subordinate. The consultee actually made the important decisions and the professional counselor, as consultant, primarily helped to clarify and provide support for the consultee's decisions. In effective consultative relationships, consultees perceive consultants as persons who respect and understand them, and are responsive to their needs.

As a consultant, the professional counselor usually tries to respond to a consultee's presenting problem by helping the consultee to determine alternate solutions; however, consultees are not always receptive to the assistance they seem to have asked for. They may want the situation to be different, but prefer not to have to rely on others, a natural human tendency. Alternately, consultees sometimes want someone else to make the needed changes for them. This, of course, must be resisted by the consultant who, in doing so, would be leaving the role of a consultant and becoming a provider of direct services. If this happens, consultees are not allowed to further develop their own skills in order to respond more effectively in future cases.

☐ Counselors as Consultees

Professionals within a given field may vary as much as professionals from different fields. Professional counselors, for example, differ in the amount and quality of training they have received, mainly because of variations in the college and university programs from which they have graduated. They may also vary in intellectual functioning, personality characteristics, skills and abilities, and performance. In addition, even the most capable, enthusiastic, and well-trained professional counselors can find themselves incapable of handling all the problems with which they are confronted in their work setting. Situations may be encountered where a counselor lacks the skills, insight, or knowledge to work effectively with a given problem. For these reasons, counselors have much to benefit from the assistance of a consultant.

There are many other practical reasons for counselors to seek the services of a consultant, and doing so is not necessarily an indication of weak counseling skills or a lack of experience. Seasoned professional counselors know that consultation can be a valuable effort. Talking with another professional counselor about professional concerns can be an ideal way to clarify goals, sharpen skills, develop new treatment strategies, and gain insights into work-related functioning. Consulting with other professionals is also recommended in cases where legal or ethical concerns have arisen. It has been suggested that counselors who practice regular consultation in such circumstances can reduce the risk of legal difficulties (Swenson, 1996). At the very least, consulting about a problematic case demonstrates an effort to act responsibly and professionally, which can only help if legal difficulties arise.

☐ Summary

Consultation is a dynamic process. It is a problem-solving activity, inherent in which are the elements of internal change, external demands, and the interface of both. By serving as consultants, professional counselors can effect positive changes in consultees that, in turn, benefit many others with whom the consultees work. The effects of consultation can be even more far-reaching, extending beyond the consultee and client to the benefit of an organization as a whole. Blake and Mouton (1983) noted that education and consultation most likely are the two most important factors that are basic to the forward movement of society. They also suggested that consultation might be the more meaningful factor because it has an even greater potential for widespread effect. Thus, the potential of consultation as a function in professional counseling is unlimited. There will always be a need for new and better ways to solve problems, assuring that consultation will continue to be a significant and valued practice in the field of professional counseling.

Group Counseling: Working with Groups

A practical issue for professional counselors, particularly those working in institutional settings, is having adequate time to provide counseling services to all the people who desire them. For example, when school counselors decide to see students for individual counseling, they make a substantial commitment of time weekly or biweekly which thereby decreases the time they have available for counseling services for others. Thus, a school counselor has to decide whether a large portion of time is appropriately spent working with individual students. An alternative is group counseling, which evolved from individual counseling as counselors realized they were limited in the amount of time available to individually reach all persons who desire help (Kemp, 1970). However, group counseling does not have an unequivocal connotation among professionals. This situation may exist because group counseling is an outgrowth of individual counseling (Vander Kolk, 1985), resulting in many different approaches.

Graduates from most counselor education programs have been required to complete one or more courses in group counseling because of its helpfulness with diverse client populations. As Gazda (1978) indicated, through prearranged meetings that focus on a commonly agreed-upon purpose, the interaction between a collection of individuals can result in enhancing the members' personal growth or preventing or remediating difficulties they may be encountering.

Although group and individual counseling are applied in many settings, practical considerations such as time, resources, and costs make group counseling particularly suitable for schools, businesses, and some community agency settings. Group counseling can be designed in a variety of ways to serve the needs of either homogeneous or heterogeneous groups. Homogenous groups are comprised of similar individuals (e.g., adolescents, young adults, or single parents) who have a common concern (e.g., interpersonal relationship difficulties, self-development, or self-awareness). With heterogeneous groups, different individuals (e.g., older adults, adolescents, married couples, and the bereaved), with individual manifestations of their respective concerns, are brought together for discussions. The counselor facilitates the development of common goals among members of a counseling group. Thus, a feeling of safety in numbers often develops in group members along with the feeling that they and their concerns will be accepted by the group (Trotzer, 1989).

Because counseling groups consist of individuals with diverse backgrounds, interests, and life situations, each group becomes a social laboratory in which many beliefs, coping strategies, and practices are shared, compared, and examined. Through observation and experimentation under the leadership and facilitation of the group counselor, members of a group have the opportunity to learn or improve interpersonal, behavioral, and social skills (e.g., caring, challenging, intimating, and refuting) that closely approximate those in society (Corey, 1999). Also within the realm of group counseling, the group members get to experience therapeutic factors that can occur in groups such as the instillation of hope, universality, imparting information, altruism, corrective recapitulation of primary family group, development of socializing techniques, imitative behavior, interpersonal learning, group cohesiveness, and existential factors (Yalom, 1995). Therapeutic factors like these are believed to be associated with the personal change and help-giving that occurs in so many groups.

Group counseling usually permits a counselor to make more effective use of time by working with several people simultaneously. The rationale is that counselors are able to expand their sphere of influence beyond that which is possible in individual counseling by drawing upon the resources of group members and channeling them appropriately. Recognition must be made, however, that some situations or problems do not readily lend themselves to rectification through a group counseling process. In fact, individual counseling, characterized as a relationship between two people and defined by terms such as *personal* and *face-to-face*, is by far the most predominant form of counseling used by professional counselors. The major difference between group and individual counseling seems to be the number of persons (clients) being helped in a given block of time. In addition, all elements of what is thought of as counseling in groups take place within individual counseling except for interactions among group members. Individual counseling does have the advantage over group counseling of providing a setting that is perceived by many as being safer. Therefore, individual counseling may progress more quickly because the client has maximum personal contact with the professional counselor.

In summary, both individual and group counseling are very important activities for professional counselors. The effectiveness of group counseling depends on many components, including communication within the group, the group process, the model or theoretical approach followed, and legal and ethical issues. A discussion of each of these components follows.

☐ Communication within Group Counseling

Group counseling typically involves use of some of the communication skills employed in individual counseling. However, counseling several individuals simultaneously makes some elements of the group counseling process much different from those of individual counseling. Professional counselors doing group counseling must consider a number of issues that are of little or less concern when counseling a single client (e.g., selection of group members, size and composition of the group, initiation of the group, and duration of the counseling process).

Group counseling is often considered to be counseling by the group rather than counseling in the group, and that is a major difference between individual and group counseling. With group counseling, group members learn to accept responsibility for helping others within the group as well as themselves (Ohlsen, 1970). Thus, productive change can take place within individuals as a result of the behaviors of the individual, the group counselor, and the other group members. Trotzer (1989) referred to this composite phenomenon as constructive influence through harnessing the power of the peer group.

As with most small-group situations, powerful norms usually develop in the group. Group counselors strive to facilitate (rather than impose) the development of helpful norms within a group. One typically sought norm for the purpose of resolving problems is **open communication** while another is **collaboration among group members**. Thus, in group counseling, there are opportunities not only for members of the group to be helped but also for members to be helpers for others, a condition rarely present in individual counseling. As members witness others giving and receiving help, they become more willing to do both themselves. This spectator-type counseling process increasingly enhances each group member's opportunities for feedback and assistance. Group members develop the ability to think and perform for the good of others and to ask for feedback for themselves, with the group leader reinforcing the right of and necessity for members to make their own decisions (Kemp, 1970; Trotzer, 1989).

☐ Group Process

The group process is complex given the composition of a group and factors that influence what happens as the group strives to achieve its goals. Therefore, consideration needs to be given to procedures for establishing a group and to various group dynamics including size and format, length and frequency of sessions, voluntary or involuntary participation, developmental stages of groups, and roles of the various participants.

Establishing a Group

Unfortunately, the establishment of a group is often under emphasized. Yet, careful consideration needs to be given to the screening and selection of group participants. A primary criterion in determining the make-up of a group is whether the potential members will contribute to the group or be counterproductive. Thus, a pregroup interview with each prospective member is stressed by both the American Counseling Association (ACA) (1999) and American Specialists in Group Work (ASGW, 1980). Through this procedure, a counselor can identify members who might be counterproductive, such as individuals who are hostile, aggressive, self-centered, suicidal, sociopathic, or highly suspicious, or individuals who like to dominate others or who lack ego strength. A pregroup interview also provides an opportunity for potential members to become familiar with the group leader. In addition, it enables the group leader to acquaint prospective members with the group's orientation and goal(s) and their rights as a group member.

Knowing the group's expected composition is a prerequisite for the screening and selection procedures. For example, a heterogeneous group often enhances participants' perspectives and stimulates interpersonal interactions whereas homogeneous groups generally tend to be more helpful in addressing specific issues. Thus, the composition of a group is influenced by its goals. As an illustration, a group comprised of adult children of alcoholics would appear to be a homogeneous grouping. Yet, adult children of alcoholics may comprise a diverse group whose members have a range of presenting issues that involve different developmental levels in addressing their resolution. For a group of this nature, the composition is both homogeneous and heterogeneous, which is often useful in promoting social learning among members.

Group Dynamics

What happens within a group has an effect upon the group's success in meeting its goals since various group dynamics can be either beneficial or harmful to the group process. Jacobs, Harvill, and Masson (1988) identified 12 factors that affect the efficiency of a group: setting or environment, size, length of session, composition of group, members' attitudes toward each other, members' attitudes toward the leader, leader's attitude toward members, interaction patterns among members and leader, group's level of progression, levels of goodwill, degree of commitment, and extent of trust. Specific considerations concerning these group dynamics factors are discussed in the following paragraphs.

Setting or Environment. For a group to be effective, consideration needs to be given to the environment in which the group meets. A comfortable and quiet setting is needed so that members will have a sense of privacy and an opportunity to interact freely with each other.

Size. Large groups (more than 10 to 12 individuals) make the attainment of goals more difficult and somewhat impossible. Determining how many members should comprise a group depends on several factors including the purpose of the group, the leader's background and experience, age, and developmental level of group members (e.g., whether the group will be comprised of children or adults). As Corey (1995) stated, a group needs to be large enough to permit sufficient interaction but small enough to enable everyone to be an active participant and to feel a part of a group.

Format of Group. A decision that needs to be made before starting the group or during the first session is whether new members can join the group as space becomes available (this is referred to as an **open group**) or whether the group will maintain its original composition throughout its prearranged time period (**closed group**). While the latter is a means of maintaining stability and thus encouraging trust and effective interactions among members, the overall effectiveness of the group can be problematic if too many individuals terminate their association with the group prior to the prearranged conclusion date. An open group format is a means of addressing this concern, since new members can have an invigorating effect. However, as Corey, Corey, and Calanan (1988) indicated, individuals joining a preexisting group may find becoming part of the group difficult. Likewise, the trust and cohesion that has been established within a group may be disrupted by the introduction of new members.

Duration and Frequency of Groups. The duration of a group meeting and the frequency of meetings affect group dynamics. With closed groups, a termination date should be established during the first group meeting. With regard to the duration and frequency of meetings, adults usually find one and one-half or two-hour weekly meetings suitable. Adolescents and children, however, generally benefit from shorter sessions that meet more frequently.

Self-initiated or Required Participation. Another factor that can affect the dynamics of a group is whether members are required to participate or whether they are attending based on their own self-interest. While the membership in a majority of groups is voluntary, some individuals participate because a mental health center or other institution has mandated that they do so. This required membership may result in a lower degree of motivation which, as Yalom (1995) indicated, may be the most important criterion for inclusion in a group. When membership is involuntary, motivation can be enhanced through adequate preparation during the pregroup interview and by permitting ventilation of feelings about being required to attend group sessions (Corey & Corey, 1987; Corey, 1999).

Developmental Stages. Typically, groups progress through predictable stages, although each group remains unique across stages. The first stage, **orientation**, involves the formation of the group and making decisions such as the nature and structure of the group. During this stage, group members begin to get acquainted and become involved in the group. Stage one is followed by the **control** or **transition** stage during which group members become acquainted with the boundaries of the group and its leader. Members may test one another and the leader through conflict, resistance, confrontation, or attempts to dominate the group. These challenges are made in an attempt to better understand the group's structure and to address the group's goals and objectives. Stage three is known as the **work** or **action** stage. During this stage, members tend to begin working toward the goals of the group. Cohesiveness begins to form, the group's focus shifts toward taking action, and the behaviors of group members tend to change. The final stage, **termination**, is characterized by the group's moving toward conclusion. During this final stage, a variety of emotions may need to be addressed because group members are ending relationships.

Members' Roles.   Various roles assumed by group members can either impede or facilitate the group process. Generally, these roles can be divided into three groups: positive social-emotional roles that promote group building and maintenance, task roles that help facilitate the group's progress, and negative social-emotional roles. As outlined by Hanson, Warner, and Smith (1980), positive roles include being:

1. facilitators or encouragers, who ensure that everyone feels comfortable;
2. gatekeepers or expediters, who make certain that the group functions as proposed;
3. harmonizers or conciliators, who strive to reduce group conflict;
4. compromisers or neutralizers, who want to address differences through cognitive solutions;
5. group observers who provide feedback to other members by summarizing the content or process; and
6. followers, who express much agreement with the group but may be unsure of themselves.

Roles that are instrumental to the group's tasks include:

1. initiators-energizers;
2. information or opinion seekers;
3. information or opinion givers;
4. elaborators and/or coordinators;
5. orientators-evaluators; and
6. procedural technicians.

Hanson and colleagues (1980) indicated that negative or antigroup roles include:

1. aggressors, who generally disagree with others' beliefs;
2. blockers, who contradict the wishes of others;
3. playboys, whose behaviors express noninvolvement;
4. help seekers, whose dependent behaviors focus mainly on their own personal problems;
5. monopolists, whose incessant talk interferes with the sense of equality among participants;
6. recognition seekers, whose behaviors attract self-attention at the expense of others;
7. do-gooders, who are always right, particularly on moral issues, and who imply that others are wrong;

8. self-confessors, who disclose information that distracts group members from concentrating on their tasks;
9. informers, who share information about another member's behavior outside the group;
10. hostile members, who use intimidation or sarcasm as a means of self-protection; and
11. nonparticipating, withdrawn, or silent members, who avoid interactions with others.

Group Leader's Role and Characteristics.   The most important attributes accounting for any group's success are the role assumed by the leader and the leader's characteristics (Corey & Corey, 1987). As can be expected, the leader's role is partially defined by the leader's level of competency, which includes knowledge competencies as well as skill competencies. Knowledge competencies include in-depth understanding of major theories, basic principles of group dynamics, strengths and weaknesses of individual group members, ethical and professional issues, research, roles and behaviors of group members, logistical factors including appropriate time to meet and the meeting environment, group stages, group interactions, and counselor roles. Skill competencies include the ability to:

1. assess clients' readiness for group participation;
2. define group counseling;
3. diagnose group members' self-defeating behaviors and intervene appropriately;
4. model appropriate behavior;
5. interpret nonverbal behavior;
6. use skills productively;
7. employ major techniques, strategies, and procedures related to group counseling;
8. promote therapeutic factors;
9. work with a coleader;
10. conclude group sessions;
11. establish and terminate groups; and
12. employ assessment and follow-up procedures.

Within a group, the leader or facilitator has many functions that are important in order to make the group successful. A successful group leader should be caring and show empathy for group members, should provide emotional stimulation to promote direction and motivation so that the group reaches its goals, and should provide attribution of meaning to the group or individual group members to assist in making sense of the group experience. The group leader also needs to hold an executive function which helps the group maintain focus in the here-and-now and apply learning from the group to outside experiences.

Several personal features appear to be helpful to a group leader. Effective group leaders can be described as being willing to model behavior; believing in the group process; being open, nondefensive, and creative; having courage, stamina, personal power, a caring attitude, and a sense of humor; exhibiting goodwill and self-awareness; and recognizing the importance of their own leadership style. Several different leadership styles have been identified for working with groups. An authoritarian group leader makes all decisions for the group and directs how the group functions. In contrast democratic group leaders assist the group in making decisions and allows the group to function in a democratic fashion. Group leaders who incorporate a laissez faire leadership style are involved as little as possible, allowing the group members to function in their own manner and take whatever course they choose as a group. Speculative group leaders work to keep the group discussion focused on the present, especially as it relates to the behavior of the group members. Confrontive group leaders, as with speculative leaders, focus on the present but are more concerned with the impact that the group's behaviors and verbalizations are having on the members of the group. Charismatic group leaders use their personal power and personality to affect the group and lead them toward selected purposes and goals.

☐ Planning for Groups

To enable the group's work to be successful, the three stages of planning, performing, and processing need to occur. Planning, the first stage, is perhaps the most difficult and time consuming, but it can make a difference in whether a group is successful. When planning for a group, there are several important areas to consider. First and foremost, the leaders must be aware of and adhere to ethical guidelines. This involves following the ACA Code of Ethics. Also, it is important that the leader be aware of the values, norms, and morals of the local community. Second, program development is essential to group counseling and includes such factors as sessions goals, activities, leader responsibilities, process of activities, and continually evaluating and monitoring the group and the members' satisfaction levels in order to determine if the group is meeting its goals and serving its intended purposes. Third, the unique dynamics of the group must be considered. This involves such considerations as the necessity of one or two facilitators, the meeting space requirements, and attracting and screening members. All these planning factors play an integral role in a group's success.

The second stage in successful group counseling is applying the plan. In order to be effective in this phase, group leaders must:

1. know their competencies;
2. be both members of groups and leaders;
3. be able to apply successful group models even though each group evolves differently;
4. work to foster the needed therapeutic environment so that group experiences are beneficial for all members; and
5. be willing to adapt so that the intent and goals of the groups are being met.

The final stage in group counseling is processing, which involves the evaluation of the group's work to determine what occurred in each session and across the entire event. Through evaluation, group leaders determine what was successful and unsuccessful, strategies to be used, how they as leaders could change, and what they might do differently. The evaluation process enables the leaders to learn from experience in order to be prepared for future group work.

☐ Group Models

Because group counseling is an outgrowth of individual counseling, many different models exist with several attempts having been made to classify these models by types of counseling. Saltmarsh, Jenkins, and Fisher (1986) grouped the different models by nature of management and nature of group process. Their resulting four groups focus, respectively, on tasking (volunteer, mission, goal, and working groups), relating (staff development, relationship skills, theme-defined, and in-service groups), contacting (therapy, encounter, laboratory, and mutual concern groups), and acquiring (resource, discussion, discovery, and education groups).

Gazda (1989) provided an orientation which views the different models on a continuum with three main categories that include overlapping goals. The **preventive and growth engendering** category (group guidance and life-skills training groups) overlaps the **preventive-growth engendering remedial** category (i.e., group counseling, T-groups, sensitivity groups, organizational development groups, encounter groups, and structured groups including life-skills training and social-skills training groups), which in turn overlaps the **remedial** category (i.e., psychotherapy groups and life-skills [social skills] training groups).

In addition to the type of counseling provided, different models are grounded in specific theoretical frameworks. Thus, the focus and goals of each may vary depending on its affiliated theoretical constructs. Several of the models included in both the Saltmarsh and colleagues (1986) and Gazda (1989) classifications are discussed briefly here. For more detailed descriptions of these models, see Corey (1999) and Vander Kolk (1985). Also, the reader is referred to Chapter 5 for an in-depth discussion of a specific model's theoretical framework.

Encounter Groups

The term **basic encounter groups** was originally introduced by Rogers (1970) and later shortened to **encounter groups**. Members of encounter groups generally focus on personal development, emotional experiences, and awareness of the behavior of others (Eddy & Lubin, 1971; George & Dustin, 1988; Gladding, 1991). Rogers (1971) and Johnson and Johnson (1987) postulated that persons would like and understand themselves more and would allow themselves to explore ways of changing if they were provided a "safe environment" in which to discuss their problems. Encounter groups are a means of meeting this need.

Task Groups

Task groups are goal-oriented. Rather than an emphasis on changing one's behavior, task groups focus on a successful performance or a finished product resulting from the collaborative efforts of group members (George & Dustin, 1988).

T-Groups

T-groups, which originated as training groups following World War II, focus on interpersonal relationships and personal growth with an emphasis on how one is perceived by other members of the group. Thus, group members have the dual benefit of being better able to understand group process and their own style of relating to others within a group (Shaffer & Galinsky, 1989). The goals of T-groups are to foster a climate of openness and understanding, and to help group members become more cognizant of how their actions are interpreted by others.

Psychodrama Groups

An experiential approach to group counseling is provided within psychodrama groups, which involve a complex form of group role-playing (i.e., group members act out their concerns within the group context) (Moreno

& Kipper, 1968; Vander Kolk, 1985). Through personal enactment designed by the group leader, members encounter suppressed feelings or new experiences which in turn help facilitate change in or development of behaviors.

Self-Help Groups

Many types of self-help groups exist, but they all have the primary purpose of assisting members in reducing psychological stress and taking control of their lives. Ones that are established and maintained by professional organizations or individual professionals generally are referred to as support groups. Representative of this type of self-help groups are Alcoholics Anonymous, Parents Without Partners, and support groups sponsored by the American Cancer Society. Other self-help groups usually grow out of a desire by individuals in a given geographical area to address a common concern or problem (e.g., parents who have adopted children from a foreign country, or parents of children who are HIV positive).

TA (Transactional Analysis) Groups

A uniqueness of TA groups is that they originated with a group-counseling focus rather than extending an individual counseling basis to include groups. As a result, the framework for TA groups is fairly well established and structured, including specific terminology.

The emphasis of TA groups is on an open relationship and equality among members, all of whom do not have to meet a certain criteria before joining the group, and between members and the leader. Members assume responsibility for examining and reexamining their previously made decisions for the purpose of making new ones based on their own personal awareness. As part of this process, members identify specific goals, clarify how they will attempt to reach the goals, and determine how goal achievement will be determined. Within TA groups, the leader is responsible for teaching concepts and terminology to members and facilitating members' self-examination. Individuals are helped to understand cognitively their own and others' behavior through the analyses of life scripts, which include four categories: I'm OK and You're OK, I'm OK and You're Not OK, I'm Not OK and You're OK, and I'm Not OK and You're Not OK (Harris, 1967).

Rational-Emotive Behavior Therapy (REBT) Groups

REBT groups are based on rational-emotive-behavior therapy, which focuses on identifying members' basic irrational beliefs and helping them develop more rational points of view. The assumption is that members are responsible for their own problems and concerns which result from their own irrational beliefs and evaluation. Thus, the goal of REBT groups is to replace a member's irrational and self-defeating perspective with a more rational and tolerable point of view.

During group sessions, one person's problem is generally addressed at a time. The leader's responsibility is to identify the irrational or self-defeating beliefs of a member and, along with the other group members, confront, challenge, or persuade that member accordingly. Through this process, all members of the group are provided opportunities to reflect upon and compare their own beliefs that may be irrational or self-defeating.

Reality Therapy Groups

Reality therapy, as with transactional analysis, originated through work with groups. Since the assumption of this model is that an individual's choice of behaviors results from internal needs, the focus of reality-therapy groups is developing an identity of success based on realistic and responsible behavior. Members are encouraged to make value judgments about their own behaviors and to develop a plan of action for change.

The leader's role is to help members focus on the reality of their respective situations with an emphasis on selecting actions that are appropriate for attaining success and, as cited in Chapter 5, satisfying the basic needs of staying alive, reproducing, having power, being free, and having fun. These actions are achieved through eight steps that involve helping group members:

1. establish meaningful relationships;
2. focus on present behaviors;
3. determine whether their present behaviors are achieving what they want;
4. develop a positive plan to do better;
5. commit to the positive plan;
6. formulate another plan rather than make excuses if the positive plan failed;
7. learn to live with the consequences of a failed plan without punishing themselves; and
8. remain committed to the goal of change, realizing that achieving change can take time.

Gestalt Groups

Gestalt groups comprise individual counseling within a group environment with the responsibility for change resting more on the individual group member than on the group leader. The focus in Gestalt groups is on helping members increase their own awareness of how their immediate, current experiences affect their present behaviors. As a result, past and future experiences or behaviors are not emphasized.

The goal for group members is to develop complete self-awareness (through direct contact with the counselor and others in the group), which includes self-reliance, self-regulation, and self-support. Members focus upon what they are aware of experiencing at the present time and then experiment with changes through the use of various techniques such as imagery, role-playing, body techniques, or visualization.

Behavior-Therapy Groups

Within behavior-therapy groups, behavior is viewed as a function of its consequences, and members' actual behaviors, rather than cognitive processes, are of concern. As a result, the focus is on modifying observable and measurable behaviors through behavior modification techniques. Members' previous thoughts and unconscious conflicts are considered of little or no value in counseling. Rather, current causes of behavior are emphasized with treatment techniques varying according to members' needs.

The leader's role in behavior-therapy groups is to help group members change maladaptive behaviors by learning new and more effective behaviors. This process may involve the use of behavioral techniques such as stimulus control; shaping; partial, positive, and/or negative reinforcement; punishment; modeling, and extinction.

Adlerian Groups

Adlerian groups focus on exploring life-styles of members since the underlying premise is that behavior takes place in a social context; behavior exists as the process of individuals interacting with each other. The constancy of the group members' lifestyles and the alternatives confronting them affect whether their behaviors change across the life span. Thus, the focus of Adlerian groups is on becoming, which is accomplished through striving for mastery and superiority in self-selected goals.

The group leader's role is to help members recognize that through self-determinism, they have choices about goals that they can pursue. Members are encouraged to accept full responsibility for the life style they have chosen and any subsequent changes they wish to make. This involves helping members recognize their strengths and their power to change, as well as uncovering suppressed feelings associated with past events that are affecting present behaviors.

☐ Ethical and Legal Issues

All ethical and legal issues that apply to the profession of counseling, in general, are relevant to group counseling. Yet, some issues exist that are unique to group work, as outlined below.

- Because of the involvement of multiple clients, the opportunity for confidentiality to be broken is increased. That is, members within the group may not honor the confidentiality code as it applies to the group setting.
- In establishing a group, potential members need to be provided sufficient and relevant information so that they can make informed decisions about participating in the group. Included should be information concerning the group's purpose and goals, length and duration of sessions, services that can and cannot be included, the leader's qualifications, and procedures that will be followed.
- In addition to the group leader's qualifications and experience, a group's success is dependent upon the contributions of its members. Therefore, potential members need to be screened in an attempt to determine whether they will contribute to the group's purpose and goals. Sometimes, a group member can have a detrimental effect upon the group and thus limit its effectiveness. Therefore, prior to the group's establishment, it is essential that potential members who might be counterproductive to a group are identified.
- If a potential member has been receiving services from another mental-health provider, that professional needs to be informed of the potential member's plans to participate in the group.

☐ Summary

As a result of being able to meet a greater number of clients' needs, the use of group counseling has increased significantly in recent years. Because group counseling has developed as an extension of individual counseling, a variety of good counseling models are being employed. Several of these have been presented as well as the various components that need to be considered when establishing a group. The chapter has concluded with ethical and legal issues that are relevant to group counseling.

CHAPTER

Career Development and Counseling

All animal species on earth engage in work. In the so-called lower-order animal species, work is almost exclusively associated with the gathering or cultivation of food and the development and maintenance of protective habitats. Work in those contexts is physiologically and biologically necessary for the continued existence of the respective species. The same is of course true for human beings; they must work to have the food and shelter necessary for continued life. However, an additional psychosocial dynamic is associated with work for humans. Among people in most societies of the world, work has value and meaning beyond fulfillment of subsistence needs; it has the potential to fulfill psychological and social needs as well. Indeed, concern about and attention to this uniquely human psychosocial aspect of work are the bases of large portions of human social, economic, political, educational, and legal systems. Particularly pertinent here is that these needs also are the basis for a large portion of mental health. That is, for most people in most societies, the nature of a person's work is integrally related to what the person is.

Attention to work as an important part of the human experience spurred the beginning of the counseling profession and has remained a major focus in the counseling profession (Peterson, Sampson, & Reardon, 1991; Sharf, 1996; Zunker, 1997). The historical antecedents within the counseling profession, in combination with preeminent values attributed to work in contemporary society, have prompted counseling theorists, researchers, and practitioners to explore thoroughly the nature of work, its roles and functions in the human condition, and most importantly, ways

124

for people to find and attain the work that is best-suited to and most satisfying for them. For example, Peterson, Sampson, and Reardon (1991) identified four broad "lines of inquiry" that have been focused upon in the development of career counseling, including ways to help individuals to (a) acquire self-knowledge, (b) become knowledgeable of the world of work, (c) relate interests, abilities, and values to occupations, and (d) integrate self and occupational knowledge.

These types of activities and the evolution of practical applications from them are likely to continue. For example, Seligman (1994) wrote:

> Career counseling, during the 1990s and into the 21st century, almost certainly will continue to take a life span approach, focusing on the interactions of various life roles, their combination and sequence.
>
> Concurrently, emphasis on the individual seems likely to increase. So-called meaning making, people's own construction of reality, is being given increasing attention.
>
> The growing emphasis on the individual is reflected by the newest counseling theories.
>
> Understanding the interactions of development, person, and context; focusing on the whole person; and viewing people as purposive, self-organizing systems are likely frameworks to guide evolution of modern career development theory. (p. 462)

One of the by-products of the attention given to work and its place in the human condition has been the generation of a subset vocabulary within the counseling profession. Therefore, some of these terms must be clarified before the career development and counseling activities of professional counselors can be discussed further.

The world of work may be configured along a system of levels. For example, a **position**, or placement, may be defined as a set of tasks performed by one person in a workplace, while a **job** is a set of similar positions in the workplace, or more generally, a set of identifiable and specific functions for which a person is paid. Because essentially similar jobs are performed by different people in different settings, an **occupation** may be defined as similar jobs found in different work settings (Herr & Cramer, 1995). The term **vocation** is often used as synonymous with occupation, but is sometimes used to imply a psychological commitment to the occupation as well. Relatedly, because individuals usually have more than one occupation in the course of their lives, the term **career** may be defined as a lifelong sequence of occupations.

Some authorities view the definition of career as "a series of occupations" as too restrictive and therefore have broadened the definition. For example, Zunker (1997) wrote that "Career refers to the activities and positions involved in vocations, occupations, and jobs as well as related activities associated with an individual's lifetime of work" (p. 7). In a now considered classic conceptualization of career development, Super (1976) defined the concept of career as:

> The course of events which constitutes a life; the sequence of occupations and other life roles which combine to express one's commitment to work in his or her total pattern of self-development; the series of remunerated and nonremunerated positions occupied by a person from adolescence through retirement, of which occupation is only one; includes work-related roles such as those of student, employee, and pensioner together with complementary avocational, familial, and civic roles. (p. 4)

Super's definition of career is noteworthy in several regards. For one, it suggests the centrality of work in people's lives and therefore reflects values typically held in society. For another, it conveys the diversity and complexity among the many life factors associated with work. For example, leisure is a concept closely related to work. McDaniels and Gysbers (1992) provided the following integrated definitions:

> WORK—a conscious effort, other than having as its primary purposes either coping or relaxation, aimed at producing benefits for oneself and/or oneself and others.

> LEISURE—relatively self-determined activities and experiences that are available due to having discretionary income, time, and social behavior; the activity may be physical, social, intellectual, volunteer, creative, or some combination of all five.

> CAREER—the totality of work [*and leisure*] one does in a lifetime. (p. 137)

Herr and Cramer (1995), citing Super (1976), used the term **avocation**, in place of leisure, to refer to an activity pursued systematically for its own sake with an objective other than monetary gain. The term avocation reflects the centrality of work in peoples' lives and therefore has been favored by some career development theorists. However, some authors (e.g., Edwards & Bloland, 1990) have proposed that leisure exists apart from work and therefore, the term leisure is preferable over avocation. In any event, regardless of the term used, leisure is now viewed as an integral component of the term career (McDaniels & Gysbers, 1992).

In attempting to help people achieve the jobs, occupations, and careers for which they are best suited and which will be most meaningful and successful for them, professional counselors are concerned with facilitating individuals' **career development** (used here as synonymous with **occupational** or **vocational** development). Peterson, Sampson, and Reardon (1991) defined career development as, "the implementation of a series of interrelated career decisions that collectively provide a guiding purpose or direction in one's life" (p. 21). Zunker (1997) wrote that "[T]he term [career development] reflects individually developed needs and goals associated with stages of life and with tasks that affect career choices and subsequent fulfillment of purpose" (p. 7). Seligman (1994) took an even broader view in writing that "[C]areer development is viewed as a process that encompasses the total lifespan and includes all of a person's roles and positions" (p. 26). These definitions emphasize both the complexity and enormity of the task with which counselors must contend; facilitating career development amounts to life counseling.

Activities by professional counselors that facilitate career development consist primarily of fostering the positive development of one major characteristic or trait (i.e., **career maturity**) and two major skills (i.e., decision making and career management) in their clients. The characteristic, career (or vocational) maturity, may be viewed as a developmental, multidimensional construct. Peterson, Sampson, and Reardon (1991) defined **career maturity** as "the ability to make independent and responsible career decisions based on thoughtful integration of the best information available about oneself and the occupational world" (p. 9). Super (1957) presented a widely accepted set of components, or dimensions, of vocational (career) maturity, including (a) orientation toward work (attitudinal dimension), (b) planning success (competency dimension), (c) consistency of vocational preferences (consistency dimension), and (d) wisdom of vocational preferences (realistic dimension).

The first skill area, decision making, encompasses problem solving, which may be defined as the thinking process in which information about a problem is used to determine a course of action, as well as affective and other cognitive processes that allow a chosen solution to be transformed into action (Peterson, Sampson, & Reardon, 1991). The second skill area, career management, may be defined as active and conscious participation in the planning and implementation of one's career and accepting responsibility for the related actions and choices (Herr & Cramer, 1995). Taken collectively, the greater the extent to which an individual develops this characteristic and these skills, the greater the likelihood that the individual will achieve an appropriate and satisfying career.

Several terms have been used to provide descriptions of professional counselors' career development facilitation activities. The broadest term used is **career guidance**, defined by Zunker (1997) as " . . . all components of services and activities in educational institutions, agencies, and other organizations that offer counseling and career-related educational programs" (p. 7). The general set of activities that fall under the rubric of career guidance is typically subdivided into the categories **career education** and **career counseling**. As generally conceived, career education involves integrating career development concepts and activities into educational curricula or other structured learning activities. Toward that end, Peterson, Sampson, and Reardon (1991) noted that "Career education represents an ambitious effort to utilize a systems approach to facilitate change in public policies, educational institutions, public service agencies, and communities" (p. 192). Typically, the primary purpose and focus of career education is the organized and systematic provision of information about various aspects of the world of work so that individuals can make informed and therefore, theoretically, intelligent job, occupation, and career choices.

Career counseling also often includes the provision of information, but extends beyond career education in the attempt to help individuals use and act upon the information provided. For example, Zunker (1997) stated that, "Career counseling includes all counseling activities associated with career choices over a life span" (p. 7). The National Career Development Association (NCDA) Professional Standards Committee (1992) provided a comprehensive perspective:

> [C]areer counseling is defined as counseling individuals or groups of individuals about occupations, careers, life/career roles and responsibilities, career decision making, career planning, leisure planning, career pathing, and other career development activities (e.g., resume preparation, interviewing and job search techniques). . . . (p. 378)

Both career education and career counseling will be discussed later in this chapter. However, before either of them can be fully understood, the major theoretical perspectives underlying career development used in the counseling profession must be addressed.

☐ Theories of Career Development and Counseling

Sharf (1996) explained the role of theory in career development and counseling:

> Career development theory can serve as a guide for career counseling. . . . By tying together research about career choice and adjustment with ideas about these issues, career development theorists have provided a conceptual framework within which to view the types of career problems that emerge during a person's lifetime.
>
> Career development theory attempts to explain behavior that occurs over many years and is made up of reactions to thousands of experiences and situations. . . . (p. 3)

Clearly different theories of career development have different implications for career counseling. However, there is a commonality among them. McDaniels and Gysbers (1992) indicated that:

[C]areer theories provide the foundation knowledge from which counselors draw useful concepts to explain client behavior. They offer a framework within which client behaviors can be examined and hypotheses formed about the possible meanings of that behavior. (pp. 27–28)

Perspectives on career development theories vary considerably. For example, Herr (1986) described six different systems just for classifying theories of career development. All of these systems have their respective merits and limitations. Therefore, selection of a classification system is primarily a matter of personal preference, and no one classification system is necessarily better than another. Following are some illustrative examples of approaches to career development and counseling.

Trait-and-Factor Theory

Sharf (1996) succinctly captured the essence of the trait-and-factor theory when he wrote:

The trait-and-factor approach has been the most durable of all theories of career guidance. Simply stated, it means matching the individual's traits with requirements of a specific occupation, subsequently solving the career-search problem. (p. 23)

Developed initially by Parsons and developed further and popularized by Williamson, the trait-and-factor approach was easily the most widely used approach during the first several decades of the counseling profession (Sharf, 1996).

The trait portion of the trait-and-factor approach refers to client characteristics; in order to use this approach effectively, counselors must have extensive and valid information about their clients' characteristics. The factor portion refers to characteristics of various jobs; in order to use this approach effectively, counselors also must have extensive knowledge of the world of work and the requirements for specific jobs or occupations. Accordingly, trait-and-factor career counseling has been referred to colloquially as the "know the client, know the job" approach.

A significant question within this approach is what information about clients needs to be known by professional counselors? Herr and Cramer (1995) identified 10 major types of client attribute information usually sought by professional counselors, paraphrased here as follows:

Abilities—clients' general intelligence and specific aptitudes. Cognitive abilities are important to the types of work clients are able to perform, the education and/or training for which they are eligible and in which they are likely to succeed, and their potential levels of success and attainment in various occupations.

Needs and Interests—clients' psychological needs and vocational interests. Psychological needs are important in that appropriate work must fulfill some, and probably many, of clients' needs. Similarly, clients are not likely to find their work attractive, enjoyable, and satisfying if their jobs are not consistent with their vocational interests.

Stereotypes and Expectations—clients' perceptions of the natures of particular jobs and occupations. Clients often act upon stereotypic perceptions and expectations about jobs regardless of the accuracy of their perceptions and expectations (unless presented with information which corrects their perceptions and expectations).

Significant Others—people in clients' lives who are viewed as important and valued and/or who serve as role models. Clients' significant others potentially have strong influences on clients' training, occupational choices, and career aspirations.

Values—clients' internalized beliefs about the worth of various aspects of life in general, and work in particular. Clients' values also are potentially strong influences on their occupational choices and aspirations.

Residence—clients' living situations and lifestyles. The realm of clients' environments, lifestyles, and experiences in part determines their educational and occupational possibilities and their perceptions of the world of work.

Family—persons perceived as closely related to a client. Family members typically exert strong influences on clients' values, lifestyles, experiences, and personal characteristics, and therefore on the courses of their careers.

Adjustment—clients' levels of adaptation in the world. Clients who are not personally well-adjusted in the world are not able to make effective work-related decisions or to perform occupational activities effectively.

Risk-taking—clients' abilities and desires to engage in probability-based decision-making. Clients' risk-taking abilities are influential in determining career opportunities potentially available to them.

Aspirations—clients' vocational and personal goals. Aspirations are viewed as primary determinants of clients' achievement and success motivations.

This list is extensive, but not exhaustive. However, it does illustrate the comprehensiveness of the information sought within this approach.

In order to obtain the desired comprehensive information about clients efficiently and effectively, professional counselors using the trait-and-factor approach to career counseling use tests and inventories extensively. Historically, the early development of trait-and-factor career counseling was a primary impetus for the development and use of tests throughout the counseling profession. The tests and inventories that have been developed are typically subdivided into five general categories: intelligence, aptitude, achievement, personality, and interest. Purist trait-and-factor career counselors use tests or inventories from each of these categories in their career counseling activities. More typically, however, professional counselors following this approach only use tests or inventories to obtain information which cannot be obtained expeditiously from other sources (e.g., the client, academic or employment records, or counselor observation).

A second significant question within this approach is what information about jobs needs to be known by counselors? Responses to this question have resulted in a plethora of job/occupation/career information systems and of activities related to the use of the systems, some of which will be discussed later in this chapter. In general, these systems at least provide information on the activities specific to a job, preparation and/or training necessary for entry to the job, the nature of the work involved (e.g., levels of involvement with data, people, or things), and future trends and possibilities in the career of which the job is a part. More sophisticated systems also provide information about characteristics and abilities of people who have been successful in and are satisfied with the job and suggest methods for determining suitability for the job. Sharf (1996) identified three aspects of occupational information to be considered for use within the context of trait-and-factor career counseling: (a) type of information (e.g., description of work functions, conditions, and salary), (b) classification system (i.e., how is the information organized), and (c) occupational requirements (e.g., what are the characteristics and attributes of persons in the occupations). The provision of occupational information within the context of trait-and-factor career counseling is viewed as essential not only to the client's understanding of the world of work, but also to the counseling process itself.

The trait-and-factor approach to career counseling in the manner proposed by Williamson and others is not particularly popular among counselors today. This decline in popularity is attributable to widely held perceptions that trait-and-factor career counseling is based on a static model of career choice, too directive, overly dependent on test data, and difficult to use because of the increasing complexities of the world of work, occupational information systems, and society. It has been sometimes (negatively) characterized as simply the "test-and-tell" approach to career counseling (Peterson, Sampson, & Reardon, 1991). However, Chartrand (1991) poignantly argued that these stereotypic perceptions of trait-and-factor counseling are ill-founded, ill-conceived, and generally erroneous. Chartrand (1991) explained that trait-and-factor career counseling is now more accurately characterized as a dynamic process of attempting to achieve a person-by-environment (P × E) "fit." Acknowledged within this newer conceptualization is that congruence between personal characteristics, including cognitive, behavioral, and affective attributes, and environmental characteristics must be achieved before trait-and-factor career counseling is successful. Thus, while many of the components from previous conceptualizations of trait-and-factor career counseling have been retained, far greater attention is given to human and environmental congruence, and therefore to human sensitivities, in the P × E trait-and-factor approach to career counseling.

Person-Environment-Correspondence

"Work adjustment theory differs from the general trait and factor theory in that it makes use of clearly defined concepts and follows an articulated theoretical model" (Sharf, 1996, p. 63). The theory of work adjustment has long been a part of the career development literature. However, in the early 1990s, Lofquist and Dawis (1991) broadened it to include differences between personality structure and personality style and between personality style and adjustment style, and broadened the name to person-environment-correspondence (PEC) (Dawis, 1996). In summarizing this theory, Zunker (1997) wrote that:

> According to Dawis and Lofquist, individuals bring their requirements to the work environment, and the work environment makes requirements of the individual. To survive, the individual and the work environment must achieve some degree of congruence (correspondence).
>
> To achieve this consonance, or agreement, the individual must successfully meet the job requirements, and the work environment must fulfill the requirements of the individual.
>
> The process of achieving and maintaining correspondence with a work environment is referred to as *work adjustment*. (p. 25)

Work adjustment in this theory is indicated primarily by tenure (i.e., length of time on the job). However, job performance is also an important component of work adjustment, which is what distinguishes PEC from most other career development theories (Sharf, 1996).

The two major components of work adjustment are job or work satisfaction and satisfactoriness. Sharf (1996) wrote:

> [S]atisfaction refers to the extent to which an individual's needs and requirements are fulfilled by the work that he or she does. Satisfactoriness concerns the appraisal of others, usually supervisors, of the extent to which an individual adequately completes the work that is assigned to him or her.... (pp. 62–63)

Note that it is possible that a person could feel satisfied with a job but not fulfill the satisfactoriness requirement, and therefore likely not achieve job tenure or work adjustment.

Within the PEC perspective, effective career development and counseling (i.e., achievement of work adjustment) requires attention to at least six variables:

Personality Structure—the relatively stable characteristics of an individual's personality.

Personality Style—the individual's characteristic ways of interacting with and in the work environment.

Abilities—the individual's work-related acquired skills and predicted skills (i.e., aptitudes).

Values—the individual's personal needs (e.g., need for recognition, achievement, or status).

Interests—the individual's wants and desires relative to the work situation.

Environmental Structure—the characteristics and abilities of the people in the work situation.

The PEC approach to career counseling often includes extensive use of tests and other assessments to allow for evaluation of these variables. However, because of the complexities of PEC-based career counseling, it is much more than a test-and-tell approach to counseling.

Decision Approaches

In contrast to the trait-and-factor approach, decision approaches to career development and counseling focus on the process of how career-related decisions are made. The major supposition in these approaches is that people will have effective career development only if they are able to make decisions effectively. Two fundamental assumptions underlie this supposition. The first is that people strive to maximize gains and minimize losses through the work-related decisions they make. In this context, gains and losses are not necessarily monetary; they may be in terms of life-style, success, prestige, happiness, security, or any of a variety of other psychosocial and environmental factors or conditions. The second assumption is that at any choice-point, people have several alternatives available to them. One alternative is, of course, to do nothing. Another is to do something, and this assumes that several "some-things" always exist. In a broad sense, then, the purposes of decision approaches to career counseling are to help people to (a) understand their

own decision-making styles, (b) identify choice-points and options, and (c) enhance their decision-making skills and abilities.
Sharf (1996) indicated that:

Although there are many approaches to career decision-making, the models or theories can be divided into two categories: descriptive and prescriptive. Descriptive theories are ones that describe or explain the choices that an individual makes when deciding upon a career or some aspect of a career. In contrast, prescriptive decision-making theories focus upon an ideal approach to decision making. (p. 302)

Although both descriptive and prescriptive career decision-making theories are presented in the professional literature, the former are far more common, primarily because they are more in concert with the realities of counseling. Therefore, only descriptive theories are addressed here.

Herr (1986) noted that three major personal factors are relative to an individual's decision-making behaviors. The first is **risk-taking style**, the degree to which an individual is willing to live with ambiguity and uncertainty of outcomes. The second is **investment**, the monetary and/or psychosocial capital the person uses to either create a choice or enhance the probability of the success of a choice. The third is **personal values**, the things, ideas, and perspectives the individual identifies as having personal worth. Each of these factors need to be considered individually and collectively in order for individuals to make work-related decisions effectively (Herr & Cramer, 1988).

Two major theoretical perspectives underlie decision approaches. The first is expectancy theory, which has as its basic premise that motivational force is a product of expectancy multiplied by value. Any specific decision-making event involves consideration of a combination of the individual's perception of personal capability to achieve the potential outcome and the value the individual attributes to the outcome. Thus, expectancy theory holds that a person makes a decision toward an outcome the person believes can be achieved and that the person values. Career counseling based on this theory therefore incorporates, in part, clarification of the client's (typically self-perceived) capabilities and values.

The second major perspective is self-efficacy theory. Bandura (1977) proposed that an individual makes decisions primarily on the basis of the belief that a specific behavior can be performed; that is, that the individual can be self-efficacious. The level and strength of the person's beliefs determine whether a specific behavior will be initiated as well as the amount and duration of effort that will be expended in the behavior. Expectations about behavioral self-efficacy are derived from four sources: personal accomplishments, vicarious experiences, emotional arousal, and verbal persuasion. Thus, many career counseling approaches use this theory to incorporate examination of the client's previous experiences and feelings about various aspects of work, and to persuade the client to consider various alternatives.

A considerable number of decision-making paradigms presented for use in the context of career counseling have been developed from these two theoretical perspectives, and most of them approximate conceptualizations of scientific analysis. For example, Bergland (1974) stated that career-related decision making involves (a) defining the problem, (b) generating alternatives, (c) gathering information, (d) processing information, (e) identifying goals and making plans, and (f) implementing and evaluating activities. Relatedly, Pitz and Harren (1980) stated that any decision problem can be examined in terms of four sets of elements: objectives sought, available choices, possible outcomes, and attributes of the outcomes. More recently, Peterson, Sampson, and Reardon (1991) related an information processing paradigm to career decision-making, including the following components:

1. Information is received which signals that a problem exists. One then queries oneself and the world to locate the gap [i.e., difference between existing and ideal states of affairs] that is the problem. (*Communication*)
2. The causes of the problem are identified and the relationships among them are placed in a conceptual framework. (*Analysis*)
3. Possible courses of action are formulated. (*Synthesis*)
4. Each course of action is prioritized according to its likelihood of success or failure and its probable impact on self or others. (*Valuing*)
5. Once a course of action has been selected, a strategy is formulated to carry it out. (*Execution*) (p. 28)

This CASVE model, as well as others, synthesizes the components of decision-making into an action plan for career counseling.

Although some authors classify Tiedeman and O'Hara's career counseling model as a developmental approach, most authors view it as decision-making paradigm. Tiedeman and O'Hara's (1963) approach focuses upon the intersection of processes for the anticipation of occupational choices and adjusting to a choice. The anticipation process includes the exploration, crystallization, choice, and clarification phases, wherein occupational alternatives are identified and explored. Adjusting to a choice is a process that includes induction, reformation, and integration phases, wherein the individual develops an understanding of the occupation chosen within both personal and social contexts. Although the anticipation and adjusting processes are sequential, the respective phases within them are not always sequential; thus the focus on decision-making rather than stage progression (Sharf, 1996).

Tiedeman and O'Hara also proposed that career development is a continuing process of differentiating ego identity, and used Erikson's (1963) model of psychosocial crises at seven developmental stages as a means to explain differences in career development. They also stressed the interaction of the self-concept with the concept of career as both develop over time. Later, Peatling and Tiedeman (1977) emphasized the individual's competence, autonomy, and agency as major factors in the career development process.

In recent years Miller-Tiedeman and Tiedeman (1990) have reformulated Tiedeman and O'Hara's conceptualizations into what they refer to as the individualistic perspective (Sharf, 1996). While retaining most of Tiedeman and Ohara's (1963) original premises and constructs, their individualistic perspective incorporates greater attention to ego development and valuing in the career development process (Sharf, 1996). Miller-Tiedeman and Tiedeman (1990) noted that:

> Our approach to career decision making is a response to the need we perceive to expand the horizons of previously mapped dimensions of career development. In past years, career theorists have presented theories of how individuals end up in particular occupations, jobs, or careers. But career theorists have often neglected the essence of the individual's life processes in career development, particularly those of growth, choice, willingness and capacity to adapt and change, and continued self-exploration and self-renewal. (p. 308)

Thus, Miller-Tiedeman and Tiedeman's individualistic perspective, at least philosophically, purports to address a wide variety of human characteristics to explain career development.

Peterson, Sampson, and Reardon (1991) presented a cognitive information processing (CIP) approach to career development based on the CASVE process described previously. They listed 10 assumptions underlying the CIP paradigm:

1. Career choice results from an interaction of cognitive and affective processes.
2. Making career choices is a problem-solving activity.
3. The capabilities of career problem solvers depend on the availability of cognitive operations as well as knowledge.
4. Career problem solving is a high-memory-load task.
5. Motivation [must be present for career development].
6. Career development involves continual growth and change in knowledge structures.
7. Career identity depends on self-knowledge.
8. Career maturity depends on one's ability to solve career problems.
9. The ultimate goal of career counseling is achieved by facilitating the growth of information processing skills.
10. The ultimate aim of career counseling is to enhance the client's capabilities as a career problem solver and decision maker. (pp. 8–9)

The CIP model incorporates many constructs and concepts from other career development theories, but couches them in an information processing perspective. Thus, the CIP model is, in essence, a reframing of established career development ideas into a newer paradigm. The advantage of the CIP model is that it is consistent with much of what counselors do in many other types of counseling, that is, helping clients think about things in new, presumably more effective, ways.

Sociological/Economic Approaches

Sociological, sometimes called situational, approaches to career development and counseling evolved from the belief that other, primarily psychological, approaches placed too little emphasis on the context in which career development takes place. Herr (1986) stated that:

> Situational or sociological approaches to career development accentuate the reality that one's environment both provides the kinds of choices from which one can choose and also shapes the likelihood that persons holding membership in different groups are likely to make certain choices and not others. A sociological or situational view of career development suggests that the narrowness or the breadth of the individual's cultural or social class boundaries has much to do with the choices the person is likely to consider, make, or implement. (p. 182)

In general, psychological career development models presume that individuals have considerable control over their own lives, particularly in regard to impacting their own career developments. Comparatively, sociological/economic career development models presume that life circumstances have much impact on individuals' lives, and therefore that individuals can control the directions of their lives only to certain extents.

Given that sociological/economic factors influence individuals' career developments, the question becomes which factors are most important and therefore merit the most attention? Unfortunately, a simple answer to this question is unavailable, and in fact, a multitude of factors have been suggested as being important. However, only a few of them can be briefly discussed here.

Culture and social class boundaries have been identified as major, usually restricting, factors in career development (Drummond & Ryan, 1995; Peterson, Sampson, & Reardon, 1991; Seligman, 1994). In general, although career progression is generally viewed as a primary means to rise above one's station in life, such progression is not always easily achieved, particularly for those in lower socioeconomic strata (Sharf, 1996). The extant conditions in those strata often inhibit and obstruct career upward mobility because of limited economic and other resources, deemphasis on education and training, conflicting values, and lack of role models.

Chance is viewed as a significant factor in career development within sociological/economic perspectives on career development (but not in traditional psychological perspectives). Bandura (1982) described two major classifications of chance encounters affecting career development. The first is an individual's chance encounters with people who directly or indirectly exert strong subsequent influence on the individual's career-related decisions. The second is chance encounters with events: those happenings to which an individual is accidently exposed which also subsequently influence the individual's career-related decisions. Chance encounters are viewed as significant components of career development because of the roles they may play in changing, either positively or negatively, an individual's career motivations and aspirations. Cabral and Salamone (1990) noted that the individual's level of self-concept and sense of internal locus of control are important determinants of how an individual copes with chance encounters relevant to career development.

Social structures also are an important factor in career development, primarily because of the influences they exert on personality development. Because humans tend to be adaptive, they are responsive to the social structures in which they are enmeshed. When their social structures change, their personalities attempt to adapt to the changes. Regardless of the outcome of the attempt at adaptation, the change itself affects the individual's personality, and therefore affects the individual's existing career development pattern.

Only three sociological/economic theories of career development have received much attention in the counseling literature (Sharf, 1996). **Accident theory** holds that much of career development is the result of either positive or negative accidents (i.e., chance encounters). For example, an adolescent's career development might be changed significantly, either positively or negatively, by an accidental encounter with a particular school teacher or counselor. **Status attainment theory** takes into account the roles of social status and achievement in explanation of an individual's career development. For example, a child's current family social status is a good predictor of a child's eventual social status (including a status-appropriate career), unless the child has status-inappropriate higher or lower achievement motivation. **Human capital theory** holds that individuals invest in their own education and training so that they can achieve the highest possible lifetime earnings. While this perspective is valued by educated individuals, it is valued far less by individuals in lower economic strata.

Sociological or situational approaches to career development are helpful because they identify many factors not usually considered in narrower (i.e., psychological) approaches. However, because of the complexities and expansiveness of the concepts and factors involved in sociological/

economic approaches, career counseling based on such approaches is much less defined or distinct. Typically, professional counselors incorporate sociological/economic considerations into other career development and counseling approaches.

Personality Approaches

Approaches to career counseling and development in this category are distinctive in that they focus almost exclusively on an individual's personal characteristics, and give little attention to external factors such as job characteristics or sociological/economic conditions. Moreover, whereas the trait-and-factor approaches tend to focus on relatively easily-identifiable traits and abilities, personality approaches often involve inferred characteristics. Thus, personality approaches to career development and counseling are closely aligned with (aspects of) theories of personality, and attempt to relate those theories to occupational and career development behavior.

Psychodynamic theories of personality have served as the basis for some approaches to career development and counseling. For example, Bordin, Nachmann, and Segal (1963) constructed a theoretical framework for career development based on a set of eight propositions:

1. Human development is continuous; early (i.e., in infancy) psychological and physiological activities are associated with those in adult life.
2. Sources of gratification are the same for children and adults; only the form of gratification differs.
3. The individual's pattern of needs develops early in life, usually during the first six years.
4. The occupation sought is related to the individual's needs.
5. The theory applies to all types of people and work, except where external (e.g., cultural or financial) factors preclude its application.
6. Work may be conceived of as the sublimation of infantile impulses into socially acceptable forms.
7. Either emotional blocking or a severe lack of information can inhibit fulfillment of occupational expectations.
8. A number of psychic dimensions and/or body zones can be gratified in any job. (p. 42)

According to Bordin et al. (1963), the eighth proposition covers the following psychoanalytic dimensions: (a) nuturant, including feeling and fostering; (b) oral aggressive, including cutting, biting, and devouring; (c) manipulative, including physical and psychological control; (d) sensual, including sight, sound, and touch; (e) anal, including acquiring and time-ordering; (f) genital, including erection, penetration, impregnation, and producing; (g) exploration; (h) flowing and quenching; (i) exhibiting; and (k) rhythmic movement.

More recently, Bordin (1990) updated his conceptualizations, including acknowledgement of the importance of play in people's lives in general and their career developments in particular. Bordin (1990) also presented seven newer propositions underlying his theory:

1. This sense of wholeness [achieved through play], this experience of joy, is sought by all persons, preferably in all aspects of life, including work.
2. The degree of fusion of work and play is a function of an individual's developmental history regarding compulsion and effort.
3. A person's life can be seen as a string of career decisions reflecting an individual's groping for an ideal fit between self and work.
4. The most useful system of mapping occupations for intrinsic motives will be one that captures life-styles or character styles and simulates or is receptive to developmental conceptions.
5. The roots of the personal aspects of career development are to be found throughout the early development of the individual, sometimes in the earliest years.
6. Each individual seeks to build a personal identity that incorporates aspects of father and mother yet retains elements unique to the self.
7. One source of perplexity and paralysis at career decision points will be found in doubts in and dissatisfactions with current resolutions of self. (p. 105 ff)

Bordin and others have presented some research to support the notion that these propositions can be used to explain career behavior. However, the psychoanalytic approach to career development has not been employed extensively for several reasons. First, psychoanalytic personality theory has not been widely used in the counseling profession, and it follows that a career counseling approach based on it also would not be widely used. Second, this approach implies use of psychoanalytic interviewing techniques which are typically too time consuming for effective use by most professional counselors. Finally, the measurement of important constructs and dynamics in the approach is at best difficult, and therefore also not suited to the circumstances of most professional counselors.

Although, in general, psychodynamic-based career development theories have not been used widely, one such theory has been, and that one is not even a true career development theory. Jung's **theory of psychological type** has become viewed as a basis of career counseling because of the widespread use and popularity of the Myers-Briggs Type Indicator, which is based upon Jung's theory, by career (and many other) counselors (Sharf, 1996). In brief, the Myers-Briggs typology encompasses two basic, bipolar concepts: perception-judgment and extraversion-introversion.

The Myers-Briggs' perspective is based first on the ways individuals perceive their world (Sharf, 1996). Individuals obtain information from the world through their perceptions, and once they have their perceptions, they make judgments about them. Myers-Briggs' theory postulates that there are two ways of perceiving: sensing, which includes visual, auditory, and other sensory inputs, and intuition, which includes inputs from the unconscious that add to external perceptions. This theory also postulates that there are two ways of judging: thinking, which includes analyzing and being objective about an idea or event, and feeling, which includes subjective reactions usually related to personally held values. These possibilities lead to four possible combinations of ways of perceiving and judging: sensing and thinking, sensing and feeling, intuition and feeling, and intuition and thinking.

In Myers-Briggs' theory, as opposed to more colloquial connotations, introversion refers to making perceptions and judgments based on personal interests whereas extraversion refers to using perceptions and judgments from external sources. The inner world of thoughts and ideas is most important for the introvert while the outer world of people and objects is most important for the extravert.

In the Myers-Briggs' typology, 16 combinations of "preferences" are possible. The Myers-Briggs Type Indicator is designed to assess preferences for each of these combinations. However, typically, the results are identified by primary preference in each of four areas: extravert-introvert, sensing-intuition, thinking-feeling, and judgment-perception (e.g., INFP or ESTJ).

The popularity of the Myers-Briggs Type Inventory notwithstanding, use of the Myers-Briggs' typology as a singular basis for career counseling is ineffective at best, and perhaps unethical. There are many, many other factors and variables that have to be considered and evaluated before individuals can make effective career choices. Fortunately, most counselors only use the Myers-Briggs Type Inventory as part of a more comprehensive approach to career counseling.

An historically popular personality approach to career development is the one developed by Roe (1956). Her approach involves synthesis of several perspectives on personality. One of the primary ones is Maslow's (1954) theory of prepotent needs. Maslow proposed that human needs may be arranged in a hierarchy of low-order to high-order needs:

1. Physiological.
2. Safety.
3. Belongingness and love.
4. Self-esteem, respect, and independence.
5. Information.

6. Understanding.
7. Beauty.
8. Self-actualization.

According to Maslow (1954), people must fulfill lower-order needs (e.g., physiological or safety) before they can strive to fulfill higher-order needs (e.g., self-actualization). Roe used Maslow's conceptualizations to suggest that, in general, vocational behavior is the individual's attempt to fulfill certain needs and that the particular level of needs for which gratification is sought in part determines the nature of the behaviors used.

Roe also emphasized the importance of using the child-rearing practices to which the individual had been exposed to help explain the individual's vocational behaviors. She described three general types of child-rearing practices. The first, emotional concentration on the child, includes the extremes of overprotection and overdemand on the child. Children raised under these conditions tend to have their lower-order physiological and safety needs met relatively quickly, but not their higher-order needs such as those for belongingness, love, and self-esteem. Therefore, the prediction would be that they would seek fulfillment of these needs through their occupations. The second type is avoidance of the child. The supposition in this condition is that neither the physiological nor emotional needs of children raised under these conditions are fulfilled, and therefore individuals seek things and limited contact with other persons in their occupation. The third type, acceptance of the child, involves the child being accepted as an integral part of a democratic family unit, wherein many of the child's needs are met. Therefore, an individual raised in this condition would seek fulfillment of the highest needs in an occupation.

A third major component in Roe's approach is attention to genetic endowments. In general, Roe suggested that genetic endowments, such as intelligence or physical ability, are mitigating factors in the manifestations of previous child-rearing practices and need fulfillment behaviors. That is, the specific vocational behaviors exhibited by an individual are influenced by the individual's genetic endowments. Roe also noted that sociological/economic factors, interests, and attitudes influenced career-related decisions, but that genetic endowment could be used to overcome these factors (Sharf, 1996).

Roe (1956) developed a "fields and levels" occupational classification scheme to facilitate understanding of her approach. In her schema, the fields are classified by interest and the primary focus of the occupations while the levels are classified by degrees of responsibility, capacity, and skill. The fields identified by Roe are (1) Service, (2) Business Contact, (3) Organizations, (4) Technology, (5) Outdoor, (6) Science, (7) General Culture, and (8) Arts and Entertainment. The levels identified are: (1) Professional and Managerial, higher; (2) Professional and Managerial, regular; (3) Semiprofessional and Small Business; (4) Skilled; (5) Semiskilled; and (6) Unskilled. When these fields and levels are configured as an eight-by-six matrix, any occupation (theoretically) can be placed in a cell representing the appropriate combination. More commonly, however, Roe's career development conceptualization is presented as a set of concentric circles where sectors represent the fields and the rings represent the levels.

The theoretical base of Roe's approach is well-developed, but career counseling methods derived from it are not widely used by counselors. This is perhaps because of the difficulties in gathering some of the needed information (e.g., that pertaining to early child-rearing practices and their effects), but more likely because other approaches (e.g., Holland's and Super's) have become much more popular among counselors.

The basic premise of Holland's (1966, 1985) approach to career development and counseling is that an individual is the product of heredity and environment; thus, career choice and adjustment are an extension of personality (Sharf, 1996). In general, early genetic endowments develop under the influences of various environmental factors so that an individual develops preferred modes and methods for coping and dealing with social and environmental tasks. The most typical way a person responds to his or her environment is known as the person's **modal personal orientation**. Holland proposed six general classifications of modal personal orientations (i.e., personality types): realistic, investigative, artistic, social, enterprising, and conventional. Holland further proposed that these same six classifications are appropriate for characterizing work environments. In Holland's view, people search for those work environments which allow them to use their skills and abilities and to express their attitudes and values, and which contain agreeable tasks and problems, in other words, which match their personality types. Accordingly, vocational behavior is a result of the interaction between the personality and environmental characteristics, and effective career development is the result of an effective matching of personality and environmental characteristics. Because Holland described personality characteristics and work environments in the same terms, he emphasized a perspective that has a long history in society in general and in the counseling profession in particular; specifically, that work is a way of life.

Because of the centrality of the personal orientation/work environment classification system in Holland's theory, the categories are summarized here.

Realistic—activities that require explicit, ordered, or systematic manipulation of objects, tools, machines, or animals, and that reflect aversion to education or therapy.

Investigative—activities that involve observational, symbolic, systematic, and creative investigation of biological, physical, and cultural phenomena toward the goal of understanding and control, and that reflect an aversion to socializing, repetitiveness, or persuasion.

Artistic—activities that are ambiguous, imaginative, free, and unsystematic toward the manipulation of physical, verbal, or human material to create art forms and products and that reflect an aversion to explicit, systematic, and organized experiences.

Social—activities that involve manipulation of others to inform, train, develop, cure, or enlighten and that reflect an aversion to ordered and systematic use of machines, tools, or materials.

Enterprising—activities that require manipulation of others to achieve monetary gain or organizational goals and that reflect an aversion to observational, symbolic, or systematic experiences.

Conventional—activities that involve systematic, ordered, and explicit manipulation of data and that reflect an aversion to ambiguous, exploratory, or unsystematic experiences.

These Holland personality/environment types are usually referred to by the first letter of each word; hence, the name RIASEC model. This model is usually configured as a hexagon, as shown in Figure 7.1. Adjacent types are presumed to have more in common than diagonally opposite types. That is, the Realistic type is more similar to either the Investigative or Conventional types than it is to the Social, Enterprising, or Artistic types. Further, because people rarely fit within a single type, they are usually assigned a three-letter code. For example, a person assigned the code SEC would be presumed to be most like the Social type, next most like the Enterprising type, and next most like the Conventional type.

Holland's approach has found great favor among counseling researchers and practitioners. For example, well over 500 research studies have been completed on various aspects of Holland's theory. Relatedly, numerous assessment instruments and approaches have been developed in the context of Holland's theoretical propositions, and more recently, other existing instruments have been modified so that their results can be interpreted within the context of those propositions. One reason for the extensiveness of these efforts is that, in the context of Holland's theory, a vocational interest inventory is also a personality inventory, a situation which expands the potential interpretations of any research effort. However, also acknowledged is that Holland and his associates have done much to spur interest. For example, Holland developed the Vocational Preference Inventory and the Self-Directed Search, two widely used vocational interest inventories, based on his theory. Three-letter codes, based on the RIASEC model, for thousands of occupations have also been developed (Zunker, 1998). This latter effort in particular has made his approach popu-

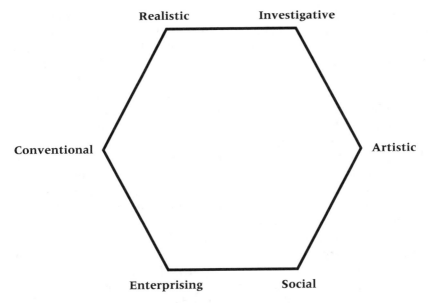

FIGURE 7.1. Holland's Hexagonal Model.

lar because of the ease with which the system can be used by both counselors and clients.

Developmental Approaches

These approaches differ from the previous ones in that they view occupational choice much more as an on-going process than as isolated acts. Occupational choice in this context also is not restricted to a certain period in life, but rather is a set of recurring events throughout the life cycle. Thus, career development may be viewed as an evolutionary process which is flexible, and in which individuals adapt their occupational choices to changing conditions in their lives.

Ginzberg, Ginsburg, Axelrod, and Herma (1951) indicated that the developmental process of occupational decision-making "is not a single decision but a series of decisions made over a period of years" (p. 185). They proposed that this process is divided into a set of phases. The first, from birth to approximately age 11, is called the Fantasy stage. In it, individuals have idealistic and typically unrealistic conceptualizations of the jobs they would like to assume. The second phase, Tentative, lasts from approximately ages 11 to 17, and contains the subperiods of interest, capacity, value, and transition. Individuals gather information about various occupations and make extremely tentative occupational decisions during this phase. The last phase, Realistic, lasts from approximately ages 17 to young adulthood, and contains the subperiods of exploration and crystallization. Individuals engage in initial work activities and make final occupational decisions during this phase.

In the early formulations, Ginzberg and associates postulated that occupational choices are a series of compromises among various influencing factors and that choices are relatively final after individuals reach their early twenties. However, Ginzberg (1972) later revised these propositions, and then used the term optimization, rather than compromise, to imply that occupational choice is the result of the individual's attempt to maximize the benefits of any occupational decision. He also suggested that occupational decision-making continues throughout life rather than being finalized in young adulthood.

Ginzberg's efforts were significant, at the time of their initial presentation, because they represented a very different view of career development. However, although Ginzberg spurred interest in developmental approaches to career development and counseling, his and his associates' work was overshadowed by that of other developmental theorists. Thus, it is given little recognition today, and few counselors do career counseling based directly on it.

Super's work on a theory of career development began shortly after Ginzberg's and, in part, was a reaction to what he perceived as deficiencies in Ginzberg's approach. Briefly, Super believed that Ginzberg failed to provide an effective definition of occupational choice and that the distinction between choice and adjustment was not as sharp as Ginzberg proposed (Herr & Cramer, 1995). Super initially described it as a differential-developmental social-phenomenological psychology (Super, 1969). Super (1990) later described it as a "segmental theory," one which borrows concepts from many different theories for specific application to career development. Today, Super's conceptualizations are usually referred to as the "life-span, life-space" approach to career development (Zunker, 1997). Four components of Super's work have received the most attention: life stages and their associated developmental tasks, life roles, and self-concept as related to occupational choice and career maturity.

Life Stages.   Super proposed that five major life stages are present, each incorporating different developmental tasks that can be used to understand career development. The first stage, **Growth**, lasts from birth to approximately age 14. Historically, it included the substages of fantasy (ages 4–10), interest (ages 11–12), and capacity (ages 13–14). The important developmental tasks in this stage are developing a self-concept and establishing an orientation toward the world of work. **Exploration**, the second stage, covers approximately ages 14–24, with the substage, tentative, existing approximately from ages 15–17. The primary developmental tasks in the Exploration stage are crystallizing a vocational preference, specifying the preference, and implementing the preference. The third stage, **Establishment**, lasts from approximately ages 24 to 44 and includes the substages of stabilization (ages 25–30) and advancement (ages 30–44). The major developmental tasks in this stage are stabilizing the vocational preference and advancing in occupations. **Maintenance**, the fourth stage, lasts from approximately ages 44–64. The major developmental task in this stage is preserving achieved status and gains. In the final stage, **Decline**, lasting from approximately age 64 on, there are two substages: deceleration (ages 64–70) and retirement (age 70 on). The major developmental tasks in this stage are *decelerating* occupational activities, and *disengaging* and *retiring* from occupational activities.

More recently, Super (1990) reiterated the applicability of the main sequential stages but blurred the age boundaries for them, perhaps in reaction to increasing longevity. In addition, in his later writings Super gave emphasis to the concepts of cycling and recycling in the regard to the various developmental tasks. That is, he proposed that individuals engage in a process of reencountering various developmental tasks across various life stages. The result of this emphasis was clarification of Super's belief that age-related tasks and transitions were flexible across the lifespan, and did not necessarily occur in a well-ordered sequence (Zunker, 1997).

Life Roles.   Central to Super's lifespan, life space conceptualization are the life roles that people have over the course of their lives: child, student, leisurite, citizen, worker, spouse, homemaker, parent, and pensioner. Although individuals have more or less involvement in each of these roles throughout their lives, in combination they constitute a life career. Super used the term *role salience* to indicate the relative importance of each life role at any point in a person's life. He created the "Life-Career Rainbow" to depict approximations of role salience across the life span. Zunker (1997) described this model succinctly:

> This two-dimensional graphic schema presents a longitudinal dimension of the lifespan, referred to as a "maxicycle," and corresponding major life stages, labeled "minicycles." A second dimension is the "life space," or the roles played by individuals as they progress through the developmental stages, such as child, student, "leisurite," citizen, worker, spouse, homemaker, parent, and pensioner. These roles are experienced in the following theaters: home, community, school (college and university), and workplace. (p. 36)

The Life-Career Rainbow is a set of concentric semicircles in which the bands represent the life roles, and career development stages are indicated on the outer semicircle. Relative degrees of role salience are indicated by differentially shaded sections of the bands.

At the end of his professional career, Super created the "archway model" to illustrate the changing diversity of life roles that individuals experience over the life span. This model serves to clarify how combinations of personal, psychological, environmental, and socioeconomic factors come together to influence career development.

Vocational Self-Concept.   Another component in Super's approach is the development and implementation of the vocational self-concept. A person's vocational self-concept is presumed to be a substantial and integral part of his/her total self-concept. Zunker (1997) stated that "the research has indicated that the vocational self-concept develops through physical and mental growth, observations of work, identification with working adults, general environment, and general experiences" (p. 31). The theory assumes that individuals choose occupations that are consistent with and allow expression of their vocational self-concepts. Thus, an individual's vocational self-concept is a major determinant of what work (i.e., occupations) will be appropriate and satisfying for the individual.

Career Maturity.   The concept of career maturity (sometimes referred to as vocational maturity) plays an important role in Super's approach. Super (1990) indicated that:

> Career maturity is defined as the individual's readiness to cope with the developmental tasks with which he or she is confronted because of his or her biological and social developments and because of society's expectations of people who have reached that stage of development. (p. 213)

Thus, the concept implies that specific behaviors are indicative of an individual's mastery of various developmental tasks. Different authors have proposed different components of career maturity, such as career exploration ability, decision-making ability, career planning ability, knowledge of the world of work, and knowledge of preferred occupations. Super, Thompson, Lindeman, Jordaan, and Myers (1979) proposed specific career development skills while Crites (1973) proposed that attitudes toward involvement in the choice process, orientation toward work, independence in decision making, preference for choice factors, and conceptions of the choice process are important components of career maturity.

A basic assumption in Super's developmental stage approach is that the individual must master tasks appropriate for a career development stage before the individual can complete subsequent stages successfully. Therefore, measurement of career maturity is important because it allows inference about an individual's career development stage. Relatedly, conceptualizations of desired levels of career maturity at various career development stages are frequently used as the bases for establishing goals and objectives for various career guidance, education, and counseling activities.

The work of Super and of others who have based their work on his has been widely accepted within the counseling profession. In fact, Holland's and Super's approaches are preeminent to the extent that the vast majority of current career development and counseling activities can be traced directly to one of these two approaches.

☐ Career Guidance, Education, and Counseling

Hoyt (1972) presented a definition of career education that is still frequently used and quoted today:

> Career education is the total effort of public education and the community aimed at helping all individuals to become familiar with the values of a work-oriented society, to integrate those values into their personal value systems, and to integrate those values into their lives. . . . (p. 1)

In general, career education involves communication of information about jobs, the world of work, and career development concepts and approaches in the environments in which people exist. Two basic premises underlay career education. The first is that, left to their own devices, people will not have sufficient opportunities or resources to obtain comprehensive information about a variety of jobs and careers. The second is that such comprehensive information is essential for effective occupational and career decision-making, and therefore career development. Traditionally, career-education activities have taken place primarily within educational systems and institutions. However, they have recently been extended into other situations such as business and industry, government, and the military.

Hoyt (1974) presented a summary of conditions formulated by the United States Office of Education (USOE) that serve as the basis of the need for career education. These include the following situations: (1) too many students leaving educational systems are deficient in basic academic skills necessary for effective adjustment in society and the world of work; (2) too few students are able to relate what they learn in school to the world of work; (3) the American educational system is considerably less pertinent to non-college-bound students than it is to college bound students; (4) the American educational system does not adequately serve the vocational needs of ethnic minorities, women, or the disadvantaged; and (5) too many students leaving educational systems are deficient in vocational skills, self-understanding and career decision-making skills, and work attitudes necessary for successful transition from school to work (Hoyt, 1974). In sum, educational systems were viewed as not doing as much as they should or could to prepare people for the world of work. This situation prompted a national impetus for career education in the 1970s. Unfortunately, these same conditions still seem to exist.

The USOE's attention to career education in the 1970s resulted in the development of four national models for career education. The first is the **school-based** or **comprehensive career-education** model. This model was originally proposed as a method for revitalizing schools from within by infusing ideas, experiences, and skills (related to work and careers) not typically found in them. The general goals for this model included development of students' career awareness, self-awareness, positive appreciations and attitudes toward work, decision-making skills, economic awareness, skill awareness and beginning competence, educational awareness, and educational identities. However, over 1000 other specific goals were developed in the construction of activities designed to implement these general goals (Herr & Cramer, 1995).

The second model, **employer-based** or **experienced-based**, was designed to meet the needs of students who did not do well in traditional learning environments. This model had goals similar to those for the first model, but the natures of the learning experiences involved are quite different. In this model, a significant portion of education occurs through direct involvement in on-going work activities. Thus, under this model, students learn by doing, through placements at actual employer sites in the community.

The third model is called the **home/community-based** model. This model was developed to be useful to adults, and has goals such as the development of educational delivery systems in the home and community, new placement systems, new career education programs (specifically for adults), and more competent workers. The model makes extensive use of television and other mass media, referral sources, and community resources to facilitate learning among out-of-school adults.

Rural/residential, the fourth model, was developed to help entire disadvantaged, rural families improve their economic and social situations through intensive programs at residential centers. This model was implemented on a very limited basis, but the results of those efforts were generally favorable.

Prominent attention to career education and guidance currently falls under the general rubric of school-to-work transition programs. This work-based initiative is the result of the combined efforts of the United States Departments of Education and of Labor. Every school-to-work program implemented in local school systems must incorporate (1) school-based learning, (2) work-based learning, and (3) connecting activities (Zunker,

1997). These programs are designed to bring together multiple facets of students' school and life situations to facilitate their learning about the world of work, opportunities for work, and how work relates to other aspects of their current and future lives.

Because the conveyance of information is a primary (but certainly not the only) purpose of career education, a considerable number of resources about the world of work have been developed. Relatedly, a multitude of sources exists from which counselors can obtain such information for use in their respective settings and with their respective clients. Therefore, because of the large numbers involved, only a few representative examples can be presented here.

Until relatively recently, almost all occupational and career resources were in the form of printed material. These materials ranged from occupational briefs to the far more complete *Dictionary of Occupational Titles* and the *Occupational Outlook Handbook*, from biographies of workers to stories in magazine form, and from brochures to newspapers. Relatedly, public, private, governmental, and religious agencies as well as companies, corporations, and not-for-profit organizations all offer many different types of materials that are potentially suitable for an equally diverse array of audiences. Thus, counselors have the wide-ranging flexibility to either purchase a complete career information system or to develop a home grown system. That's the good news. The bad news is that such systems require considerable storage space, frequently require sophisticated filing systems, and rapidly go out-of-date in regard to the information presented.

More recently, a variety of visual media have become available. These resources include film-strips, multimedia presentation packages, films, and videotapes. These media have the advantage of a presentation format that is more interesting than that of printed materials, but many of the disadvantages of printed materials are also applicable to visual media.

One form of information conveyance that has found favor with many counselors is the direct contact approach. Generally, four types of activities are subsumed under this heading. First are simulations, typically in the form of role-playing, in which clients interact with persons who have particular types of work or career knowledge. Second are interviews, in which clients interact with persons actually occupying particular jobs or involved in careers in which clients are potentially interested. Third are field trips, wherein clients visit a particular employment setting for a limited time period to observe the work being done and talk with various employees. Finally there are apprenticeships, which involve clients working in particular jobs, usually for pay, for reasonable time periods so that they can gain an understanding of the work involved in the occupation. While these activities are popular with clients, they necessitate considerable time investments by counselors to arrange and coordinate them.

McDaniels and Gysbers (1992), in discussing improvements in career information delivery systems, noted that:

> The trend toward more effective career information resources received a boost in 1976, when congress authorized the National Occupational Information Coordinating Committee (NOICC) as a federal interagency committee that promotes the development and use of educational, occupational, labor market information. NOICC's primary mission is to improve coordination and communication among developers and users of career information and to help states meet the occupational information needs of various groups and individuals. (p. 240)

Congress also created state occupational information coordinating committees (SOICCs) in 1976 so that there would be an extensive, coordinated network of occupational information dissemination. Thus, governmental and private organizations work together through the NOICC and SOICC systems so that current career information is readily available to both counselors engaged in career counseling and their clients.

The most recent advancement in occupational and career information systems is the use of computer-based technology. Among the most widely known systems available specifically for stand-alone use are the *System of Interactive Guidance and Information* (SIGI PLUS), *Career Information System* (CIS), *Coordinate Occupational Information Network* (COIN), DISCOVER, *Guidance Information System* (GIS), and CHOICES (McDaniels & Gysbers, 1992). Some of these systems allow integration of career information provided through the NOICC and SOICC systems. Each of these systems, and others like them, allow the client to interact with the computer both to gain information and to explore occupational and career possibilities. The advent of microcomputer versions of some of these systems has made them particularly attractive for career education because of reduced costs and the opportunity for clients to use them without substantial investments of the professional counselors' time. However, Peterson, Sampson, and Reardon (1991) have noted that such systems should never be used to replace career education or counseling by a professional counselor because of the limitations of such systems as well as ethical considerations. In addition, use of systems such as SIGI PLUS, DISCOVER, CHOICES, and the like merely for career education purposes is under-utilization of their respective capabilities. That is, while these systems do, in fact, present much valuable career information, they are designed for use in computer-assisted career guidance (CACG) activities that involve much more than communication of information.

With its relatively recent explosion of personal and professional use, it is likely that the Internet will be "the latest step in the evolution of guidance" (Sampson, 1999). Sampson suggested that the Internet is ideal for providing distance guidance, an expansion of services delivered in the past via telephone. Because it is a "pointcast" medium (i.e., one that allows the user to choose exactly what information is delivered), the Internet reduces the counselor's need to anticipate the needs of the user (Stevens & Lundberg, 1998). The ever-increasing storage capacities and transfer rates of modern computers and computer networks also reduce the amount of physical space needed to house resources. It is entirely likely that many CACG systems may also become available over the Internet to users who pay a fee (Sampson, 1999). Because the Internet's current use is a mere fraction of its future potential, Stevens and Lundberg (1998) suggested that counselors' competency and comfort in using and integrating Internet resources into career guidance will become increasingly important in years to come.

Career education is one of the major components under the broad rubric of career guidance; career counseling is the other. Career counseling quite obviously focuses on the facilitation of clients' decision-making and career development activities and is similar to other types of counseling in that it may be conducted individually or in groups. Sharf (1996) wrote that, "the two most common goals of career counseling are the selection of an occupation and the adjustment to an occupation" (p. 17). In both individual and group career counseling, the counseling process begins with the establishment of rapport between the professional counselor and the client. In the next step, the professional counselor, typically in collaboration with the client, determines whether career counseling is merited or the client needs some other type of counseling. If career counseling is indicated, the professional counselor proceeds to implement strategies consistent with a theoretical orientation.

Herr and Cramer (1995) identified eight assumptions underlying career counseling intervention strategies:

1. many factors beyond control of the client will influence the client's decision-making;
2. clients are not able to obtain or process all information relevant to decision-making;
3. during counseling, clients are only able to make decisions that will allow them to achieve some of their objectives;
4. clients' decisions are typically evaluated in terms of the process used to reach them rather than on the basis of outcomes;
5. clients can be taught how to make decisions;
6. sometimes factors unknown to either the counselor or the client defeat the purposes of career counseling;
7. the importance of various factors in clients' decision-making varies across clients and the reasons for the variations are often unknown; and

8. career counseling presumes client motivation, but appropriate client motivation is not always present in the career counseling process.

Although these assumptions may seem negative, they are not intended to be. Rather, they describe some of the obstacles with which career counselors must contend and they therefore provide a realistic perspective on the conditions under which career counseling is usually conducted.

One of the ways to maintain positive perspectives within career counseling is to do it in the context of the practitioner-scientist perspective presented in Chapter 1. That is, if career counselors, like other counselors, keep a focus on the conceptual and empirical aspects of good counseling practice, then career counseling is very likely to be effective and successful for clients. In addition, career counseling within the practitioner-scientist perspective also serves to benefit counselors in general and the counseling profession as a whole.

☐ Summary

Today, career education and career counseling are infrequently conducted as distinct activities; more typically they are included as parts of comprehensive career guidance programs (Drummond & Ryan, 1995). Historically, such programs usually have been conducted in educational systems such as elementary, middle or junior high, or secondary schools, and colleges and universities, primarily because they were initiated by professional counselors or educators affiliated with those systems. More recently, comprehensive career guidance programs have become available in other settings as well because there is an evident need for them. In general, career guidance programs are now available to a large majority of people in society, and the number of programs continues to increase.

The broad goal of career guidance and counseling programming is the facilitation of individuals' career development through the provision of services and activities that can be responsive to any of the variety of career development needs of the individuals for whom the programs were established. This is indeed a lofty goal, but effectively planned and implemented comprehensive career-guidance programs, and effective career education and career counseling within them, are able to achieve it.

CHAPTER

Assessment and Measurement

The essential goal of assessment is to quantify a client's behavior and characteristics so that the professional counselor can understand and help the client. Professional counselors, however, have given much less attention to assessment than they have to other professional issues in counseling. Nevertheless, data obtained through assessment to quantify a client's behavior is important in helping a professional counselor make calculated decisions. For this important reason, an understanding of assessment is necessary for effective counseling.

A starting point for an introductory discussion of assessment is terminology. Accordingly, definitions of often-used terms are presented here.

Measurement is the process of assigning numbers to human attributes or characteristics.

Assessment is the use of methods and processes to gather data about, or evidence of human behavior. Assessment is a preferred term because it (merely) connotes the collection of data concerning the present state of human behavior whereas terms such as "diagnosis" often connote determination of the degree of abnormality.

Interpretation is the act of stating the meaning and/or usefulness of behavioral data.

Evaluation is the process of applying judgments to or making decisions based on the results of measurement. An evaluation program is a program test designed to measure and assess an individual's growth, adjustment, or achievement, or a program's effectiveness.

Appraisal is a term used synonymously with evaluation.

Also, included with an introductory discussion of assessment are a variety of statistical concepts that are important to know and understand. These terms are provided from Vacc (1999).

Frequency Distribution. A tabulation of scores in numerical order showing the number of persons who obtain each score or group of scores.

Normal Distribution. A bell-shaped curve derived from the assumption that variations from the mean are by chance, as determined through repeated occurrences in the frequency distribution sets of measurements of human characteristics in the behavioral sciences. Scores are symmetrically distributed above and below the mean, with the percentage of scores decreasing in equal amounts (standard deviation units) as the scores progress away from the mean.

Skewness. The degree to which a distribution curve with one mode departs horizontally from symmetry, resulting in a positively or negatively skewed curve.

Positive Skew. When the "tail" of the curve is on the right and the "hump" is on the left.

Negative Skew. When the "tail" of the curve is on the left and the "hump" is on the right.

Percentiles. Result from dividing the (normal) distribution into one hundred linearly equal parts.

Percentile Rank. The proportion of scores that fall below a particular score. Two different percentiles may represent vastly different numbers of people in the normal distribution, depending on where the percentiles are in the distribution.

Stanines. A system for assigning a score of one through nine for any particular score. Stanines are derived from a distribution having a mean of five and a standard deviation of two.

Error of Measurement. The discrepancy between the value of the observed score and the value of the corresponding theoretical true score.

Standard Error of Measurement. An indicator of how closely an observed score compares to a true score. This statistic is derived by computing the standard deviation of the distribution of errors for the given set of scores.

Confidence Interval. The interval between two points on a scale, within which a score of interest lies, based on a certain level of probability.

The goal of assessment in counseling is rather simple: to help the counselor and client. However, this goal becomes tremendously difficult to attain if the data gathered are misused or misinterpreted. Incorrect interpretation or inappropriately used data result in wrong decisions, which adversely affects clients and limits their opportunities. Further, many counselors-in-training mistakenly view assessment merely as paper-and-pencil testing, but assessment in counseling is a multidimensional process of which paper-and-pencil testing is only one component. The professional counselor needs to be interested in the results of a client's performance in a given situation in relation to the client's total functioning. Therefore, effective assessment procedures take into consideration not only the client's performance, but also the client's history, behavior, and environment. Because of this, assessment can be undertaken apart from the formal counseling process (e.g., through observations made by parents, loved ones, teachers, or employer).

Because good assessment is multidimensional, many areas within the process overlap. Yet, a dichotomy of functions exists: those that are involved within conventional assessment and those that are part of the assessment process which we shall refer to as empirical counseling. The discussion that follows is presented according to this dichotomy.

☐ Traditional Assessment in Counseling

The process of conventional assessment, which is based in the medical model, is diagnostic and evaluative in nature. The purposes of conventional assessment include diagnosis of traits and factors, assessment of strengths and weaknesses, classification, and selection for placement.

The outcome of conventional assessment leads to prescription, which unfortunately tends to have as its focus the determination of what is wrong with a client. Its use in counseling dates back to the late 1930s, when the conventional-assessment model being used by psychologists was adopted with modifications by professional counselors (Williamson, 1939). The resulting model is referred to, in this text, as traditional assessment in counseling. In traditional assessment, the professional counselor assesses and focuses on classifying or selecting people for training, educational, or vocational placement. Clients are expected to participate in assessment by reacting to the test results and the professional counselor's appraisal of their characteristics. However, a very highly skilled professional is needed to enable a client to be an active participant in the assessment process. Thus, a common concern with this model is that it often leads to prescription only, as mentioned earlier. The process of conventional assessment too often provides answers, solutions, and advice rather than encouraging clients to take charge of their lives. When properly utilized, the traditional assessment model is an important element in professional counseling. Therefore, the essential components of this assessment process and their use are presented in the following material.

Purposes

In the traditional assessment model, tests are administered by professional counselors for a variety of purposes, but primarily because they provide information to assist the counselor and client in making decisions. The specific reasons for giving tests vary, depending on the setting in which the professional counselor is working. The following four reasons have been described by Cronbach (1990).

Prediction or Planning. Tests are often given for the purpose of assisting professional counselors, clients, or administrators with decisions concerning future performance (e.g., the planning of an educational program for an individual or a group in business, industry, or school). Tests designed for this purpose provide measures of ability, achievement, or other human characteristics, and are used for making decisions.

Selection or Screening. A familiar use of tests involves the selection process employed by colleges and universities whereby individuals are accepted or rejected by an institution based, in part, on their performance on a standardized test. Tests also are used by many employers as a means of selecting individuals to fill vacancies in their work force. In a school setting, tests often are administered for the purpose of screening students with superior academic abilities, social problems, or academic difficulties.

Classification or Placement. Most states have laws that specify criteria for certain educational programs. For example, standardized tests provide measures to be used for placing students in selective educational programs such as the academically gifted or beginning resource rooms and self-contained classrooms for students with specific learning problems. Also, tests are frequently used by the military or government for selecting individuals to participate or become eligible for benefits. In addition, tests can be used to classify students for individual or group counseling.

Many problems are apparent in the use of tests to make classification or placement decisions, including problems with validity and reliability. Reliability is the degree to which an individual would obtain the same score on a test if it were readministered to the individual with no intervening learning or practice effects. Validity is the extent to which a given test measures or predicts what it purports to measure or predict. Validity is also application specific, not a generalized concept. That is, a test is not in and of itself valid, but rather is valid for use for a specific purpose for a specific group of people in a specific situation. This explains why most governmental regulations concerning people in public schools, the military, or agencies require that classification and placement decisions be based on test results.

Program Evaluation.   In traditional assessment, a program, method, or treatment, rather than an individual, is being assessed. Suppose, for example, that High Point Hall, a drug rehabilitation center, decides to try an experimental aerobics program to help recovering substance abusers or substance users. Data would be needed concerning the effect(s) that the experimental program might have on the center's clients. The traditional treatment program would have to be evaluated, followed by the implementation and evaluation of the experimental aerobics program. Typically, tests would be administered to each client before and after the traditional treatment program and the same pre-post testing procedure would be used during the experimental program. Clients' progress during the traditional program could then be compared with their progress during the experimental program for the purpose of evaluating each program's relative effectiveness.

Assessment of Individual Progress.   An important use of tests not mentioned by Cronbach (1990) is the examination of client (or student) change or progress. Professional counselors' and clients' conclusions that progress is being made can sometimes be verified by the administration of standardized tests.

Standardized Tests

A standardized test is one in which testing conditions are the same for all examinees, including directions, scoring procedures, test use, data on reliability and validity, and adequately determined norms. Professional counselors are required to administer, score, and interpret a multitude of standardized tests throughout their career. Because they also receive test information from colleagues and from a variety of other professionals outside the field of counseling, for professional counselors to have a working knowledge of standardized tests is important.

Even though most standardized tests are very similar, there are alternate forms of standardized tests. These forms include parallel forms, which have identical content and psychometric properties, equivalent forms, which sample the same content areas and are considered equivalent in regard to derived scores, and comparable forms, which have similar content areas but do not share statistical similarity. Having this knowledge is important for counselors to consider when determining which test procedure to use.

No one basic standardized test exists for counselors to use in assessment. Instead, they rely on a potpourri of instruments that can be classified into three categories of measurement: aptitude or general ability; achievement; and personality, vocational-interest, vocational-maturity, and attitude inventories. Certain types of tests are used more extensively by professional counselors in given professional settings. For example, tests purporting to yield information about vocational interest and maturity, personality, and attitude are more frequently used by the professional counselor who works with adolescents and adults.

The common characteristic of standardized tests is that they expose a person to a particular set of questions or tasks in order to obtain a performance that can be compared with that of individuals in a normative population. Norms are statistics that describe the performance of individuals of various ages and grade levels, who comprise the standardization group for the test. Also, local norms which may be a set of scores obtained from a specific sample that are not considered generalizable to a population beyond the sample will be used for testing of specific groups. Another characteristic of standardized tests is their major strength of permitting tasks and questions to be presented in the same way to each person tested. Further, the responses are scored in a predetermined and consistent manner, thus permitting the performances of several individual test takers to be compared. This standardized sample is the group of people from which a sample was used to establish norms for a given test. This is done in an attempt to determine the different success levels specific to the test.

The actual scores achieved on a test are referred to as quantitative data (e.g., scoring at the 84th percentile on the verbal section of the Graduate Record Exam or earning an IQ score of 125). In addition to quantitative data, qualitative information can be derived from the administration of a standardized test. This information consists of nonsystematic observations made while a client is taking a test or while the counselor is discussing the results of the test with the client.

Standardized tests used in traditional assessment can be classified into two principal categories, those assessing the cognitive domain and those assessing the affective domain. The major testing subcategories of the cognitive domain will be presented first.

Assessing the Cognitive Domain

The presentation of cognitive-domain assessment is divided into subcategories according to general ability measures, tests of general intelligence, aptitude tests, and standardized achievement tests.

General Ability Measures. Dictionary definitions of intelligence include the ability to learn and understand or the ability to cope with new situations. Mehrens and Lehmann (1991) reported that definitions of intelligence also include the capacity to learn, think abstractly, integrate new experiences, and adapt to new situations. Intelligence also has been used interchangeably with aptitude. Some test specialists, however, suggest that subtle shades of meaning distinguish these two terms. They consider intelligence to be a general mental ability and aptitude to be a specific ability factor. To illustrate this difference, the Stanford-Binet Intelligence Test would be considered a general measure of intelligence, whereas the Seashore Musical Aptitude Test would be viewed as a specific measure of aptitude. Historically, intelligence tests were assumed to measure innate characteristics that are not subject to change. As Mehrens and Lehmann (1984) reported, this assumption is invalid, and many test authors, in an attempt to avoid the implication of innateness, have instead adopted the term aptitude.

A helpful scheme for understanding aptitude tests is to categorize them as (1) individually administered instruments that provide a general measure of intelligence, (2) group administered tests that provide a general measure of intelligence, (3) group administered, multifactor aptitude tests that provide multiple measures, and (4) group administered aptitude instruments that provide a specific measure.

Individual Tests of General Intelligence.   Although most schools, colleges, businesses, and industries use group tests of intelligence, having clinical information which can be gained most effectively through the administration of individual intelligence tests can be helpful in some situations. For example, sometimes it is desirable for the examiner to have an opportunity to observe the test taker's approach to problem solving, the amount of stress exhibited by the client during the test administration, and the client's test-taking behaviors.

The individual intelligence test has been considered the psychologist's basic tool (Bardon & Bennett, 1974). When correctly administered, individual intelligence tests provide a more reliable measure and a better understanding of the test-taker's behavior than do group intelligence tests. Correct administration, an important factor in obtaining a reliable measure, requires considerable training. In fact, many states mandate certain licensure, usually that of a psychologist, in order to use individual intelligence scores in any way that may affect a person's future. Instruments that require special qualifications to administer are referred to as restricted, and they include tests such as the Stanford-Binet and the various Wechsler tests (Wechsler Intelligence Scale for Children Revised, WISC-R, ages 6 through 16; Wechsler Pre-school and Primary Scale of Intelligence, WPPSI, ages 4 through 6-1/2; and the Wechsler Adult Intelligence Scale-Revised, WAIS).

Group Tests of General Intelligence.   As graduates of American schools and colleges know, group intelligence tests are very much a part of an individual's educational life. For example, two tests widely used in predicting college success are the College Entrance Examination Board

Scholastic Assessment Test (SAT) and the American College Testing Program (ACT). At the graduate school level, widely used tests are the Graduate Record Examination Aptitude Test (GRE) and the Miller Analogies Test (MAT). Many can recall those times when they carefully and completely filled appropriate bubbles on an answer sheet with a heavy dark mark using a soft-lead pencil, for one of these tests. However, with the increasing popularity of the computer, a shift has occurred toward the computerization of testing. Computer-based testing uses instruments like the bubble answer sheets that are presented on and responded to through use of a computer. Because of the speed and accuracy of computerized testing, computer-generated interpretative reports are also being used. The computer is capable of analyzing complex data sets and intricate patterns of data. However, computer-generated reports are only as good as the programming underlying them, and never as good as when used in conjunction with sound clinical judgement.

Group intelligence tests are used much more frequently in educational settings than are individually administered tests, perhaps by a ratio as large as 20 to 1. Group intelligence tests are less expensive to administer because they can be given to a large number of individuals at one time. Also, they are not restricted tests and, therefore, are designed to be administered by nonlicensed individuals. Their value and wide use, however, result generally from the fact that the data derived from them are comparable to those derived from the more time-consuming individual tests. Many group tests of general intelligence report two subscores such as verbal and quantitative ability.

Although most group tests can be scored by hand, they are more often scored by a machine that produces raw scores, scaled scores, and percentile ranks. Scaled scores are a unit in a system of equated scores established for the raw scores of a test. Related to the scaled score are the standard score and the "true score." The standard score is a type of score that indicates the extent to which a score deviates from the mean, and a true score is the mean score of the theoretical distribution of scores that would be obtained by the individual test taker on an unlimited number of identical administrations of the same test. When used with group intelligence tests these scores can be extremely informative to the professional counselor, particularly when assessing the client's overall functioning. But the results of group testing always should be used with caution. A case in point concerns the cultural fairness of intelligence tests. People of different national origins and people in various diverse groups in America place different values upon verbal fluency and speed, factors which are important for performing well on intelligence tests. Also, educationally disadvantaged persons typically will be handicapped when intelligence tests are used to describe their functioning. No one intelligence test is best for all uses; care must be taken to select the correct test for a particular situation and population.

Multifactor Aptitude Tests. As mentioned earlier, differences of opinion are found on the value of multifactor aptitude tests in comparison to general intelligence measures. Supporters of multifactor aptitude tests believe that intelligence is composed of many specific abilities. Therefore, some professional counselors use multifactor aptitude tests for the practical reason that they facilitate vocational and educational counseling. They believe that differential descriptions of test results are helpful when discussing strengths and weaknesses with respective clients although, as Mehrens and Lehmann (1991) indicated, little data exist that support differential predictive validity.

Group Administered (Specific) Aptitude Tests. Specific aptitude tests usually measure the capacity to acquire proficiency in a specified activity. This type of test is typically used by professional counselors to help clients make vocational and educational selection decisions, and by institutions for placement decisions.

Standardized Achievement Measures. Professional counselors working in school settings are frequently involved with schoolwide achievement testing programs. They make arrangements for teacher administration and computer scoring, and they are often requested by other school personnel to assist with selecting tests. The latter function usually involves a decision made by a committee comprised of teachers, administrators, school psychologists, and professional counselors. The professional counselor who is involved with any test selection process should make certain that the instruments selected are valid for their respective purposes and possess other necessary psychometric properties.

Achievement tests are designed to measure an individual's progress or current knowledge as a result of education or training. How well does Mary read? Does Burt know the definitions for a list of words? After reading a paragraph, is Nancy able to recall its content? These are examples of questions that can be answered using data derived from achievement tests. Standardized achievement tests are seldom used by professional counselors working in noneducational settings with the exception of using achievement tests for purposes of screening or placement (e.g., typing, shorthand, computer proficiency, and similar knowledge or skill-based tests).

Assessing an individual's achievement level is useful because it enables the professional counselor to help plan successful experiences for others in learning or training. This is particularly important with students and clients concerned with career and educational planning. A professional counselor can assist these individuals with identifying their cumulative achievement, determining their strengths and weaknesses in academic performance areas, and comparing their achievement level with their ability or intelligence level.

Many standardized achievement tests are available, ranging from assessments of general information (i.e., survey achievement tests) to assessments of a specific knowledge area (i.e., diagnostic tests). However, the current trend in educational settings is less emphasis on survey achievement tests and greater emphasis on those that assess specific kinds of functioning related to school achievement.

Survey Achievement Tests. Survey achievement test batteries consist of a group of tests, each assessing performance in a different content area. All tests in a survey battery are standardized on the same population, thus permitting meaningful comparisons of the results in the various content areas.

A general survey achievement battery (e.g., Stanford Achievement Tests or Iowa Tests of Basic Skills) is used when school personnel are interested in a student's academic progress in all subject areas because comparative information will be available (e.g., whether the student is better in mathematics, spelling, or reading). However, if school personnel are interested in a student's specific strengths or weaknesses in a single-subject area, then a diagnostic test would be used.

Diagnostic Tests. This type of standardized achievement test is designed to identify a student's specific strengths and weaknesses in a particular academic area. Examples of standardized diagnostic tests are the Stanford Diagnostic Reading Test (SDRT), Diagnostic Tests and Self-Helps in Arithmetic, Metropolitan Readiness Tests, and Gates-MacGinitie Reading Test. The belief is that specific data enable teachers, principals, professional counselors, and school psychologists to decide what kinds of classroom activities will be most effective in helping a student learn, and to plan and organize future learning tasks that are appropriate for a student's developmental level.

In general, the age of the test taker and the kind of information desired determine the achievement test to be used.

Assessing the Affective Domain

This section is concerned with standardized noncognitive group inventories. The following addresses tests that are concerned with individuals' interests, personality, attitudes, and the affective domain.

The primary characteristics of standardized noncognitive tests are uniform administration and objective scoring. Most of the tests also have normative information that enables a professional counselor to make comparisons between a client and other individuals. With standardized noncognitive group tests, professional counselors can help answer questions such as what are Bill's interests? How does Ruth compare with other women concerning her interest in engineering? Is Tom abnormally aggressive? and Is Alice's concern about others atypical?

Many children and adults have difficulty with age-appropriate behaviors because emotional, interest, or attitude factors interfere with their cognitive functioning. In this regard, standardized noncognitive tests can help ascertain important information that can be of value during counseling. In addition, professional counselors occasionally use standardized noncognitive tests to identify clients for group counseling (e.g., establishing group counseling for clients who show similar characteristics of high anxiety).

A number of standardized noncognitive instruments are available, making it possible for the professional counselor to assess noncognitive functioning in a variety of ways. However, disadvantages do exist in using group tests in this domain. In comparison to cognitive measures, noncognitive instruments are not well documented concerning their predictive validity (i.e., the ability to foretell what a person's behaviors will be in the future). Also, a client's responses can be affected by the influence of social desirability. Professional counselors need to be sensitive to the fact that most people are unwilling to provide, on paper-and-pencil tests, responses which are presumed to be different from the norm.

Another problem associated with all standardized noncognitive group tests is their susceptibility to client response sets (i.e., the tendency to reply in a particular direction, almost independent of the questions asked). For example, clients may be predisposed to remain in the middle of the road if a five-point, agree-disagree continuum is used, or they may have the tendency to select true for true-false items. Other problems with this type of test include (1) a reading level that may be above the client's reading achievement level, making the test beyond his or her ability; (2) a tendency for clients to guess in order to provide a response; and (3) the sacrifice of speed for accuracy, or vice versa.

As imprecise as standardized noncognitive group tests are, they do provide professional counselors with valuable information to use in helping clients. It must be remembered, however, that while this information is helpful, it certainly is not definitive. In addition, most standardized noncognitive group tests can also be used with an individual. In fact, noncognitive tests are frequently administered to groups, but interpreted on an individual basis.

In summary, knowledge about a client's interests, personality, and attitudes is important in helping a professional counselor to communicate effectively during counseling and with other professionals. However, the use of these tests is not without limitations.

Personality Assessment. Personality assessment can be either a structured or unstructured self-report. Structured personality tests consist of questions that can be interpreted in relatively the same way by all clients. Unstructured personality tests, referred to as projective tests (e.g., Rorschach Inkblots Test), consist of ambiguous pictures or items to which clients respond according to their interpretation of the stimulus.

A variety of structured, self-report personality tests is widely used by professional counselors in numerous ways; the counselor is usually not dependent upon a single personality test. The vast majority of these tests are intended for use with adults. However, some can be administered to elementary or secondary school aged students if the students' reading ability is adequate. The general public appears opposed to the general use of personality tests in schools, and therefore, they are rarely used in school settings with groups of students. However, in some instances they may be used with a few select students with whom the professional counselor is doing individual counseling. Perhaps the ones most widely used across age levels are problem checklists and adjustment tests.

Attitude Assessment. Individual behavior is influenced by numerous confounding variables, many of which are extraneous to the person, but affect attitude. As research has demonstrated, individuals' attitudes are related to their behavior; they influence an individual's behavior concerning other people, activities, and objects. For example, if a group of students has an unfavorable attitude toward education, little learning will take place in the classroom. Accordingly, in order to know why Jim is behind in his college assignments and what can be done to help him improve his performance, or to know whether Jim is prejudiced, the professional counselor must develop an understanding of Jim's attitudes.

An important concern is that professional counselors understand that attitudes, which are not directly observable, are inferred from a person's verbal and nonverbal behaviors. To illustrate, prejudice cannot be seen as an object, but it can be observed, over a period of time, in the behavior of someone who is prejudiced.

Attitudes, which are learned, result from socialization and tend to be changeable, particularly with young people. The key to changing an attitude is to have knowledge of its status. This needed information can be gained through assessment using an attitude test or scale. As with all tests, the usefulness of any attitude scale depends upon its reliability, validity, and norms; the ease with which it can be administered and scored; and the meanings that can be derived from the data. However, perhaps more so than any other noncognitive assessment instrument, attitude scales have problems with psychometric properties. Typically, research correlations obtained between scores obtained using an attitude scale and observed behaviors are low. None the less, the information that a professional counselor and client can acquire from the client's performance on attitude tests makes them useful during counseling.

☐ Assessment within Empirical Counseling

The term empirical counseling, as used in this book, connotes the use of assessment for the purpose of determining goals, strategies, and effectiveness during the counseling process. Structured clinical interviews define what is asked and how it is asked, thus influencing client responses through the choice of a particular line of inquiry. In comparing structured interviews with unstructured interviews, Spitzer, Endicott, and Robins (1978) indicated that unstructured interviews are susceptible to information variance due to differences in the quantity and quality of information that is obtained from the same client by different counselors. Structured interviews are trustworthy assessment procedures. Many counselors formulate decisions early in the interview process, with negative information about a client seeming to weigh more heavily than positive information (Perloff, Craft, & Perloff, 1984; Siassi, 1984). Also, visual clues during both structured and unstructured clinical interviews play a larger role than do verbal clues (Perloff et al., 1984). Thus, structured clinical interviews can reduce the error variance in the information elicited from the client, helping to mitigate low reliability in the assessment and diagnostic process. For professional counselors to make decisions about a client's progress or services is becoming increasingly unpopular unless objective, systematically collected data can be amassed that bear directly upon those decisions. Collecting data at regular intervals during the counseling process provides direct information about the client's progress, the essence of assessment in empirical counseling. The following presents the goals of assessment in empirical counseling: improvement of counseling and accountability.

Improvement of Counseling.   Through assessment, the professional can determine whether the counseling procedures being used are producing desired results and can facilitate the revision of unproductive counseling procedures. Accordingly, professional counselors can determine whether they are wasting a client's or their own time on ineffective counseling procedures. If counseling is producing desired results, the professional counselor can, with confidence, continue the counseling process.

Accountability. The second reason for professional counselors collecting quantified measures of their clients' progress is to respond to requirements for accountability. Within a school setting, for example, the professional counselor may have to demonstrate to the pupil-personnel director, principal, or board of education that counseling processes are actually helping students. In student development in higher education, a similar situation exists with the professional counselor needing accountability data for his or her supervisor or the institution's vice president for student affairs. Or, a business or industry may want to compare several methods of communication-skill training workshops if it is concerned about which method will do the best job. Accountability data for the professional counselor in community or agency settings are needed for insurance companies and third-party payers as well as for supervisors. For example, counselors who want to receive payments from a health organization or insurance company may be required to submit a report after 8, 24, 40, and 60 sessions. The report asks for information about the client's problem, the provider's goals and planned interventions, and an estimate of progress. The latter is related to the specific treatment goals and typically derived from assessment data.

Professional counselors have always had to justify their existence, but now the necessity of establishing indices of progress requires a scientific approach to being accountable.

Assessment Process

The process of assessment during counseling helps the professional counselor know what the target problem is, who defines it as a problem, when and where its occurrence is visible and perceived as a problem, and how well counseling is progressing.

A self-coaching model for assessment in empirical counseling is presented in Figure 9.1. The components of the model are discussed separately here.

Step 1: Determine the Focus or Problem. At the beginning of the counseling process, the professional counselor needs to establish a cooperative and mutually respectful relationship with the client. First, the professional counselor verbally and behaviorally conveys that he or she wants to help the client and values the relationship with the client. Next, the professional counselor makes an inventory of the spectrum of concerns as seen by the client, and perhaps by others if the client is seeking help as a result of a referral. However, much of today's counseling will be through self-choice rather than the medical model of finding the problem and making a referral to a specialist.

STEP 1: DETERMINE THE FOCUS OF COUNSELING. Establish a relationship with the client and identify issues and concerns to be addressed during counseling.

Establish relationship.
Identify spectrum of issues and concerns.

STEP 2: CLARIFY THE SITUATION. In cooperation with the client, the professional counselor clarifies the priority of issues and concerns for counseling and the target attributes or specific behaviors needing intervention. This step includes identifying the conditions and circumstances of the target issues and concerns occurrence.

Narrow list of target issues and concerns.
Determine expected attainment from counseling (goals).
Gather data on specific issue and concern behaviors.

STEP 3: IDENTIFY THE COUNSELING ACTIVITIES. Determine concrete, detailed information on what will be done, how and when it will be done, and duration. Within this step, plans are made for measuring the client's target behavior(s) several times during the counseling process.

Determine procedures for counseling.
Determine procedures for assessment.

STEP 4: INITIATE PLAN. Implement Step 3 and derive meaning by analyzing and interpreting data from the assessment. Utilize the results from the data analysis and, if necessary, make revisions in the counseling process.

FIGURE 9.1. Self-Coaching Model for Assessment.

Completion of this phase varies depending on the setting in which the professional counselor is working. For example, if the counselor is in private practice and a physician makes a referral (medical model), the referral will probably describe a specific concern the physician has about the client. The physician has most likely spent time with the client (e.g., perhaps a series of visits over several months), and the client has agreed that assistance is needed. However, the information conveyed by the physician to the professional counselor (i.e., the reason for referral) may not include the particular information necessary for the counselor to be of help to the client. Therefore, the professional counselor, by carefully interviewing and assessing the client, can acquire accurate information on the nature of the client's problem.

If the professional counselor is in a school setting, the referral may be a teacher's request for assistance. For example, the teacher might ask the counselor to help Tammy adjust to the classroom because she is disrupting the other students. Of course, many reasons are possible for Tammy's behavior. The professional counselor's task, in this situation, is to help Tammy while at the same time assisting Tammy's teacher. Again, the professional counselor must first identify the spectrum of issues.

In contrast to the example of the physician's referral, Tammy's teacher has more than likely spent considerable time with the class and is likely to know much about Tammy and the other students. The teacher, however, may not be able to convey to the professional counselor the type of information necessary for helping Tammy. The counselor may need to obtain additional information by carefully interviewing the teacher, and exacting specific data concerning Tammy's behaviors.

Step 2: Clarify the Situation.   Usually the professional counselor's second step in individual assessment is to focus upon the primary concern(s) of the client. For a professional counselor to be presented with a spectrum of issues and concerns (e.g., inadequate social skills, marital difficulties, and uncertain vocational goals) is not infrequent. At times, establishing multiple goals for counseling is feasible, and measurement of each is necessary. On other occasions, and when possible, several different issues can be rank ordered when they are not of comparable importance to the client. In most situations, the professional counselor is likely to have identified several, if not a host, of target behaviors. Therefore, the counselor may have difficulty determining the priority of help needed and the associated specific, operational goals. This requires determining the priority of target concerns for counseling. Sundel and Sundel (1999) suggested the following general principles as a guide for the professional counselor (and, if possible, the client) when selecting a priority concern.

1. Select the concern with which the client or significant other is immediately concerned.
2. Select the concern which if continued will have the most aversive consequences for the client, significant others, or society, thus minimizing the amount of pain inflicted on the client or others.
3. Select the concern with which the client would have immediate success, thus providing the client with increased motivation and trust in the professional counselor and the counseling process.
4. Select the concern that needs attention before any other problem can be resolved.

During the clarifying stage of the assessment model, the professional counselor, in cooperation with the client, determines goals and objectives for counseling by gathering information about specific behaviors that the client considers important to the counseling outcome. Among these behaviors might be speaking up more frequently in class or reaching a decision about the behavior of one's spouse.

The professional counselor identifies the focus of counseling within the larger situational context of its occurrence. To return to Tammy, the professional counselor would specify other elements related to her target concern(s). This might involve, but not be limited to, spending a period of time in Tammy's classroom to observe her reactions to the academic material, the teacher, and other children; her behavior when assignments are made; and her responses or reactions when called upon. Also, the counselor wants to obtain detailed information on the methods that have been tried by the teacher to help Tammy adjust to the classroom. In addition, the counselor may decide that more information is necessary from other significant people in Tammy's life, such as the school nurse, personnel director, and parents. Again, the professional counselor, through careful interviewing, can provide information, in exact detail, concerning which of Tammy's behaviors are of concern and what has taken place. The professional counselor is interested in the who and where of the target concern.

Finally in Step 2, the professional counselor gathers data about specific behaviors. In all cases, specific and concrete information needs to be obtained.

Step 3: Identify Counseling Activities.   In Step 3 of the self-coaching model, the professional counselor describes in some detail the procedures to be used when working with a client (i.e., develops a counseling plan). Needed is information on what is to be done, how it will be done, and when it will be done (i.e., timing and duration). Basically, the components of the counseling process that the counselor has reason to believe are important to the counseling outcome need to be determined. Only when counseling procedures are planned are they modified or adapted to a new situation. Identifying counseling activities is necessary and important if the counselor is to improve counseling procedures and to help others.

Step 4: Initiate Plan.   The professional counselor next begins to implement the activities identified in Step 3. Through an analysis of data, meaning is derived for the purposes of evaluating the client's progress and, if necessary, making revisions in the counseling process.

By being able to collect data early in the counseling process, the professional counselor is able to develop a substantial baseline for viewing progress. Baseline refers to measures of the specific behavior prior to, or at the beginning of, counseling. An attempt should be made, initially, to collect data on as large a number of measures of a client's behavior(s) as possible. As counseling proceeds, nonimportant or unhelpful measures can be abandoned and helpful measures retained.

☐ Summary

This chapter focuses on the purpose and use of assessment with an emphasis on the counseling process. Understanding the need for assessment in effective counseling is stressed. Discussed are standardized tests, inventories, informal assessments, traditional assessment, assessment with empirical counseling, and a model for the counselor to employ when assessing clients.

Emphasized in this chapter is that assessment can be viewed as part of the larger process known as empirical counseling. When professional counselors assess clients during empirical counseling, they consider (1) the way their client performs and reacts to a variety of tasks in a variety of settings or contexts, (2) the meaning of a client's performances in view of the total functioning of the client, and (3) possible explanations for the client's performances during counseling.

Although clients can be assessed ad infinitum, increased emphasis has been on the study of observable, operationally defined behavior and a decrease in emphasis on unobservable thoughts, motives, drives, traits, and general functioning as measured through assessment. Mental health practitioners, who have been required to defend their activities when working with individual clients, have had considerable difficulty defending the psychometric adequacy of using normative measures to assess some hypothetical norm, and the relevance of the information provided by the instruments. Professional counselors must work with clients using standardized and empirical assessment approaches concurrently. They must take into consideration assessment data designed to discover laws or rules that apply to people in general (i.e., nomethetic data), and they must attempt to obtain information about particular event(s) and respective conditions (i.e., idiographic data).

Assessment is helpful because it enables the professional counselor to plan counseling and to assist the client. But an assessment procedure should be selected on the basis of its appropriateness for counseling with a particular client. Initially, the professional counselor's selection of assessment methods will be guided by the type and intensity of counseling to be provided. The underlying theme of this chapter is that better quality counseling is provided when assessment information is utilized than when no assessment information is employed. The professional counselor can use a wide variety of assessment approaches within both conventional and empirical counseling, as long as the selection is suitable for helping clients realize their respective goals.

CHAPTER

Research in Professional Counseling

Professional counselors typically view themselves primarily as practitioners of applied behavioral sciences; their work is to help clients to resolve problems or to prevent future problems. Thus, the need for counselors' time to be devoted to the direct service of helping others is usually viewed as urgent by supervisors, administrators, managers, clients, colleagues, and sometimes by counselors themselves. In contrast, conducting research is rarely viewed as urgent. However, research is extremely important for counselors. For one thing, research helps the entire counseling profession. Hadley and Mitchell (1995) wrote that:

> Counseling exists as a profession partly because of the work of individuals who are recognized as both great researchers and great counselors. For example, we know of Carl Rogers, Donald Super, John Holland, and Virginia Satir not from their counseling activities alone but because they conducted research and published their findings. In the process, they changed the course of our profession. (p. 4)

Research is, however, also extremely important to and for each professional counselor. Heppner, Kivlighan, and Wampold (1998) wrote:

> We as professionals assume responsibility for not only promoting the welfare of the people who seek our services, but also protecting clients from harm. Thus, as professionals we need to continually update and extend our knowledge about human nature and the field of counseling as well as evaluate our services, especially because the applied nature of our work affects the daily existence of thousands of people. (p. 3)

In the context of the practitioner-scientist model espoused in this book, professional counselors have two important responsibilities in regard to research: they must be both effective consumers of research and effective producers of research. In clarifying the difference between research producers and research consumers, Hittleman and Simon (1997) wrote that, "Like research producers, research consumers are interested in answering educational [counseling] related questions; however, they do so by reading and applying research producers' results, rather than by conducting research" (p. 2–3). In order for counselors to fulfill each of these responsibilities effectively, they must have good research knowledge and skills (Hadley & Mitchell, 1995; Heppner, Kivlighan, & Wampold, 1998; Houser, 1998; Wilkinson & McNeil, 1996).

The counselor's role as scientist includes the effective use of research because research is the basic method of science. More formally, "research is the formal, systematic application of the scientific method. . . . " (Gay, 1996, p. 6). Houser (1998) delineated eight steps to the scientific method:

1. Identify a problem;
2. Define the problem operationally;
3. Develop hypotheses or research questions;
4. Develop and/or identify techniques or instruments that can be used to gain knowledge about the identified problem;
5. Collect data;
6. Analyze the data collected;
7. Generate conclusions about the data; and
8. Report the data in a public arena such as a professional journal or presentation. (p. 11)

Houser subsequently related these steps to the components of a typical journal article:

Introduction:	Steps 1, 2, and 3
Methods:	Steps 4 and 5
Results:	Step 6
Discussion:	Steps 7 and 8

In relating the steps of the scientific method to the sections of a journal article, Houser demonstrates how knowing and understanding the scientific method (i.e., knowing and understanding research method) relates to both the research producer and consumer roles counselors should fulfill.

Professional counselors are sometimes dismayed to find that their colleagues and clients fail to share the value they place on research. In fact, in some work settings research is viewed with suspicion and disdain. Such behavior can be attributed partially to the fact that many counseling service settings are beset by so many pressures and problems that they focus only on addressing the immediate counseling concerns with which they are confronted. In such settings, research is not viewed as an integral part of good practice, but rather as a luxury to be conducted only if time is available for it. The appropriate situation is somewhere between the extremes. Professional counselors should devote most of their time to counseling activities. However, research is an appropriate and an important part of good professional counseling practice, and some time should be devoted to it.

Inherent in the view that research and scientific inquiry are synonymous with drawing valid conclusions and making decisions effectively is the need to perceive research from a much broader perspective than typically has been true among professional counselors. The core of this view is that professional counselors must habitually inquire and maintain a critical (but not negative) attitude about their professional work. Respect for objectivity and unbiased conclusions is integral to a counselor's professional training and practical functioning. Thus, research should be equated with good inquiry and not just with traditional methods of data gathering and analyses.

Successful and effective counselors are continually engaged in careful, scientific review of all their activities, although some of that research may not be structurally well-designed. For example, in many work places, the procedures needed for rigorous, carefully controlled research studies admittedly are difficult, if not sometimes impossible, to carry out. Also, counselors do not ordinarily initiate studies that are far removed from their immediate work and current clients. That is, most of their research is directed toward current situations and not toward general problems in the field of counseling. The former can be described as research that addresses immediate concerns of a counseling situation (e.g., answering questions such as "What progress is being made during counseling?" and "What techniques are most effective with the client?"). The latter addresses issues that are more theoretical and general such as the why and how of counseling. Although the distinction between these different forms of research is forced, it illustrates that research on what happens during counseling sessions usually focuses upon specific client situations where client progress is of immediate concern to the counselor. That is, it concentrates on information to help the client. Research about the why and how of counseling, however, is broader and concerned with generalizable inferences about the process of counseling and other interventions; it is not necessarily specific to an individual client or group of clients. However, research on the effect counseling is having on a client not only affects that client, but affects all other clients as well. For example, if a professional counselor answers questions about one client's progress in counseling, the resulting information can be used to adjust how other clients are counseled.

Scientific inquiry, or research, is essentially a systematic and controlled extension of common sense. Built into this extension is the development of theoretical structures and concepts that are continuously being tested and evaluated. Central to scientific inquiry is the research process with its basic components of reasoning and logic. The former can be divided into inductive and deductive reasoning. Inductive reasoning is inferential and progresses from the specific to the general; if a specific behavior is (consistently) observable, then a general idea or theory may be true. In deductive reasoning, however, the logical progression is from the general to the specific; that is, if a general idea or theory is true across situations, then a specific behavior may be observable in any given situation. These basic differences in ways of thinking are reflected as the two main, broad categories of research done by counselors: qualitative and quantitative.

☐ Qualitative Research

The nature of qualitative research was captured succinctly by Rafuls (1997), who wrote:

> Qualitative research as a field of inquiry transcends many disciplines and subject matters. It is multi-method in focus and involves interpretive, naturalistic, and descriptive approaches to study phenomena. Essentially, qualitative research focuses on understanding and illuminating meaning with an emphasis on discovery and description through open, reflexive, and interpretive methods. Interviewing, observation, document analysis, and visual methods, which may be used alone or in combination, are typical qualitative methods. (p. 65)

Qualitative research is inductive, and its primary goal is to promote greater understanding by explaining how and why people behave the way they do. Qualitative researchers seek to find holistic, in-depth understanding of the phenomenon observed. Qualitative research methodologies are grounded in the belief that behavior is significantly influenced by the environment in which it occurs. Therefore, typically, qualitative research is conducted in settings in which subjects can feel natural (i.e., comfortable). In general, then, qualitative research involves collection of extensive, but relatively subjective, data on many variables over an extended period of time in a naturalistic setting.

Measurement, data collection, analysis, interpretation techniques, research design, and method in qualitative research are flexible and evolve as the research process proceeds. A distinguishing characteristic of qualitative research is that the actual methodology used can not be determined *a priori*; the methodology emerges quite literally during the process. Qualitative research may involve interactive strategies, such as participant observation, or noninteractive strategies, such as review of documents.

Qualitative research usually involves purposeful sampling, as opposed to probabilistic sampling, to ensure that the right person(s) or situation(s) are examined. Generalizability of results is not a major concern in qualitative research, and in fact usually generalizability is very restricted in qualitative research. Sampling methods typically used in qualitative research include:

Comprehensive sampling, in which all members of an entire group are selected as the units of study.

Maximum variation sampling, in which objects of observation are selected because they represent disparate examples of the phenomenon being studied.

Critical case sampling, in which a unit is selected for study because it represents a dramatic example of the phenomenon being studied.

Network (sometimes known as **snowball**) **sampling**, in which future successive participants are identified by prior participants.

A qualitative research case study design involves focus on one phenomenon, such as a person, concept, process, group, or program. Qualitative case study designs are often used to describe and analyze a situation, event, or process; develop a concept or model; evaluate a program; investigate social and cultural beliefs; or serve as a prelude to quantitative research.

Ethnographic research is sometimes considered synonymous with qualitative research and sometimes viewed as a subtype of qualitative research. In the latter perspective, ethnographic research is usually interpreted to mean the study of a culture. In this context, a culture is any group of people who regularly associate with one another and who develop characteristic ways of behaving and thinking.

Other key concepts in qualitative research include:

Participant observation, in which the researcher literally becomes a participant in a situation and makes research observations while participating.

Observer effect, in which the presence of the participant observer alters the nature of the situation.

Observer bias, in which the participant observer makes inaccurate or invalid interpretations of the phenomenon being observed.

Fieldnotes, which are the actual data resulting from the participant observation process.

Grounded theory, which is theory (or components of theory) developed from the data collected in real world settings.

Peer debriefer, which is a colleague who works with the primary researcher to generate meaning from the data collected.

Auditability, which is the process of maintaining a record of data management techniques that document the decision trail used.

Key informant, which is a person other than the researcher who provides information (data) about the phenomenon being studied.

Low inference descriptors, which are concrete, precise, and almost literal descriptions of phenomena.

Negative case/discrepant data, in which a unit is not behaving within the parameters of the emerging pattern.

This brief synopsis of qualitative research may suggest that it is somehow not as accepted as quantitative research. However, that is not the case. In fact, use of qualitative research methodologies is increasing rapidly in the social sciences in general and in the helping professions in particular. But like most trends, this increase is not without its drawbacks. Gay (1996) noted that:

> A current problem with qualitative research is not the fault of the approach, but rather the way in which it is being used. As more and more people have gotten into the qualitative act, some with little or no related training, there has been an increase in the number of poorly conducted, allegedly qualitative studies. (p. 230)

Qualitative research is certainly accepted as a viable and valid method of scientific inquiry if it is conducted appropriately. Nonetheless, the fact remains that there is much more quantitative research being conducted than there is qualitative research. Therefore, it merits greater coverage.

☐ Quantitative Research

There are many approaches to research that fit under the general rubric of quantitative research, and no one organizational schema for the different approaches has found significant favor in the professional literature. For purposes here, it is convenient to simply divide them into descriptive and experimental research. The distinguishing feature in this differentiation is the intentional manipulation of one or more variables: descriptive research does not involve the intentional manipulation of variables whereas experimental research does involve intentional manipulation of one or more variables.

Descriptive Research

Descriptive research is the attempt to characterize the nature of a situation without influencing any of the variables inherent in the situation at the time of characterization. That is, presumably the conduct of the descriptive research does not alter the situation being studied in any way.

Descriptive research methods include historical, case study, field study, survey, developmental, causal comparative, and correlational research.

Historical research. The systematic search for facts relating to questions about the past and the interpretation of those facts is historical research. It involves specific definition of the time period addressed within the research and encompasses use of primary and secondary sources. Primary sources are first-hand accounts or original source documents whereas secondary sources involve interpretations of existing primary source data or information.

Case study research. The study of a single individual for a specified period of time is case study research. Such research involves assessment of a variety of variables that potentially contribute to the person's current situation. Case study research also may be conducted through use of a qualitiative research paradigm.

Field study research. The simultaneous study of a small number of people is field study research. This research is sometimes conceived of as a multiple case study, but it includes consideration of the members' interactions. Field study research also may be conducted through use of a qualitative research paradigm.

Survey research. Collecting data from members of a population to determine the current status of the population with respect to one or more variables is survey research. It is often a precursor to other types of research, most commonly correlational or experimental research. Survey research typically includes self-reported data. Survey research methods often include use of questionnaires, surveys, observations, interviews, or sociometry.

Developmental research. This is the study of one or more variables in a relatively homogenous group of people over a relatively long period of time (i.e., long enough for potential developmental changes to occur). Developmental research is sometimes considered synonymous with the term longitudinal research, however, developmental research may be either *cross-sectional* or *longitudinal* in nature. Cross-sectional research involves studying cross sections (i.e., subgroups) of a population presumed to be at different developmental levels to determine if developmental patterns or trends exist as predicted. Longitudinal research involves studying the same group of people over a relatively long period of time to determine if developmental patterns or trends exist as predicted.

Other types of developmental research include (a) trend studies, in which a given general population is sampled at each data-collection point in time; (b) cohort studies, in which a specifically defined population is followed over time; and (c) panel studies, in which the same, presumably representative, panel (i.e., relatively small group) is assessed periodically.

Causal comparative research. Usually considered synonymous with the term ex post facto research, causal comparative research is an attempt to attribute causation without experimental manipulation of a variable. It is based on the premise that both the effect and the alleged cause exist at the time the research is conducted.

Correlational research. This includes studies having as their purpose the determination of relationships between or among variables through the use of correlational statistics. It has the advantage of allowing study of many variables simultaneously. Correlational research is probably the most common type of research in the counseling and development professions.

Experimental Research

Experimental research is conducted to determine if differences result from the interjection of some phenomenon into peoples' lives. In other words, the researcher does something in the subjects' lives that would not have otherwise occurred just to be able to examine the result. The researcher's interjection is, in effect, the manipulation of a variable; thus, experimental research always involves intentional manipulation of one or more variables. Experimental research also typically involves comparing conditions under various stages of the treatment (e.g., pre-post) and systematic manipulation of experimental conditions in which extraneous influences are controlled or eliminated.

Technically, the goal of experimental research is to be able to explain the variance, or lack of it, that results from manipulation of one or more variables in the subjects' lives. In other words, the researcher is trying to determine what, if anything, is different as a result of experimental manipulation of the variable(s). In order to make valid conclusions about the results of experiments, Kerlinger (1986) admonished researchers to apply the MAXMINCON principle:

Maximize the independent variable's effects on the dependent variable (i.e., maximize treatment variance).
Minimize error factors and/or variance.
Control extraneous variance.

Although there is a variety of ways to classify approaches to experimental research, four types are commonly cited in the professional literature.

True experimental research. In true experimental research, the researcher (theoretically) has control over all the relevant variables. In order to achieve high levels of control over the relevant variables, this type of research often is conducted in laboratory or other highly controlled settings. True experimental research is relatively rare in the counseling and development professions because of the extensive control required.

Quasi-experimental research. This type of research approximates true experimental research, but in it the researcher has control over many (usually most) but not all relevant variables. Quasi-experimental research is usually differentiated from true experimental research by the inability to assign subjects to groups randomly (e.g., intact groups are used) or lack of a control group.

Single-subject experimental research. Such research involves studying an individual in both treatment and nontreatment conditions and evaluating performance on the dependent variable in both conditions. It is sometimes confused with a case study, but it should not be. Single-subject research involves manipulation of one or more variables in the subject's life whereas (either qualitative or quantitative) case study research does not involve manipulation of variables.

Action research. This is an attempt to solve a specific, immediate, and concrete problem in a local setting. Action research is not concerned with generalization to any significant degree, but rather often is used to test the effectiveness of new skills or methods. Action research often lacks general credibility because of vague definitions and controls.

☐ Experimental Research Designs

The plans used by researchers to conduct experimental research are known as research designs. There are many, many different research designs in the professional literature. However, the reality appears to be that a few of the more basic designs are used for the vast majority of experimental research studies in the counseling profession, with the other, more complex research designs used only rarely. Therefore, the focus here is on only the most commonly used research designs.

In general, experimental research designs can be divided into two types, depending upon the nature of the comparison or type of effect to be evaluated. Between Groups designs involve comparison of the variable(s) across (i.e., between) two or more tightly-controlled conditions (e.g., experimental or control). Conversely, Within Groups designs involve each subject being exposed to each treatment condition, but under a randomly assigned sequence of treatment presentations (i.e., each subject is his or her own control). Because within groups designs, such as the crossover, counter-balanced, and Latin Squares designs, are used relatively rarely, the focus here will be on the between groups designs.

Between groups experimental research designs may be divided into three categories based on the degree of control over extraneous variance, i.e., the degree to which a difference can be attributed solely to the treatment: (a) Pre-Experimental, (b) Quasi-Experimental, and (c) True Experimental designs. The following notation conventions are commonly used in diagraming experimental research designs:

R   = random assignment of subjects to groups
NR = nonrandom assignment of subjects to groups
E   = experimental group
C   = control group
X   = experimental intervention, also known as the treatment
O   = observation (i.e., measurement)

Note that in the diagraming of research designs, X is used to indicate the treatment or intervention, and O is used to indicate the result on measurement, whereas in the literature on assessment, X is used to indicate a score on a test. Care should be taken to understand the notational differences for capital X in these two different contexts.

Pre-Experimental Designs

The **One-Group Posttest-Only Design**, also known as the **One-Shot Case-Study Design**, involves a single group receiving some sort of intervention followed by some measurement of something:

Group	Subject Assignment	Pretest	Treatment	Posttest
E	NR		X	O

This design is substantially lacking in credibility because there are numerous potential sources of invalidity for the results. However, it may have some (little) use as a means to suggest some variables that might warrant further investigation.

The **One-Group Pretest-Posttest Design** is a minor variation of the preceding one in that a pretest is added to the basic plan:

Group	Subject Assignment	Pretest	Treatment	Posttest
E	NR	O	X	O

At first glance, this design appears to allow attribution of any difference in the pre- and posttreatment group means to the intervention. However, there remain a considerable number of alternative explanations for any differences found, and therefore, this is not a particularly strong research design either.

The **Nonequivalent Groups Posttest Only Design**, sometimes called the **Static Group Design**, is intended to allow posttreatment comparisons of group means for two different groups that received two different treatments, one of which often is considered unusual or unique:

Group	Subject Assignment	Pretest	Treatment	Posttest
E_1	NR		X_1	O
E_2	NR		X_2	O

Unfortunately, there also are multiple sources of potential invalidity in this design. For example, if a posttest difference is found, is it attributable to the differences in the groups, differences in the treatments, or some combination of both?

Quasi-Experimental Designs

The **Nonequivalent Groups Pretest-Posttest Design**, sometimes known as the **Nonequivalent Control Group Design**, is close to a generally acceptable research design, one for which there can be confidence that the results are attributable only to the intervention:

Group	Subject Assignment	Pretest	Treatment	Posttest
E	NR	O	X	O
C	NR	O		O

However, the primary source of invalidity for this design is initial differences between the groups. Because the groups are not composed of persons randomly assigned to the respective groups, it is likely that there would be differences (on important variables) between the two groups even before the treatment was conducted. Thus, any posttreatment differences would not necessarily be attributable to the treatment even though both groups received the same treatment.

The **Single-Group Interrupted Time Series Design** is actually a modification of the One-Group Pretest-Posttest Design, except that there are multiple pretests and multiple posttests:

Group	Subject Assignment	Pretest	Treatment	Posttest
E	NR	$O_1 O_2 O_3 O_4$	X	$O_5 O_6 O_7 O_8$

The significant advantage of this design is of course that it shows the pattern of values of the variable(s) being investigated both before and after treatment. However, there are three primary limitations to this design. First, subjects may react adversely to the many assessments necessary. Second, this design often is costly to use because of the large number of assessments that must be made. Third, because there is no control group in this design, it is not possible to attribute causation solely to the treatment; other factors unique to the group or the experience of the group may have caused the posttreatment difference. The **Control-Group Interrupted Time Series Design**, which simply adds a control to the preceding design, was developed to address this last concern:

Group	Subject Assignment	Pretest	Treatment	Posttest
E	NR	$O_1 O_2 O_3 O_4$	X	$O_5 O_6 O_7 O_8$
C	NR	$O_1 O_2 O_3 O_4$		$O_5 O_6 O_7 O_8$

True Experimental Designs

The **Pretest-Posttest Control Group Design** is generally recognized as the fundamental experimental research design:

Group	Subject Assignment	Pretest	Treatment	Posttest
E	R	O	X	O
C	R	O		O

Basically, this is the design that most people think of when they think of a social science research study, before and after measurements with one group that gets the treatment and another that doesn't. There are many benefits to this design. However, one limitation of this design is that the pretest may sensitize participants to what is forthcoming, or more generally, to react to the experimental situation in other than normal ways.

One simple way to remove the potential pretest sensitization effect is to remove the pretest, which yields the **Posttest-Only Control Group Design**:

Group	Subject Assignment	Pretest	Treatment	Posttest
E	R		X	O
C	R			O

This is a very strong experimental research design because it controls for most sources of invalidity. However, it only works in situations where subjects can be randomly assigned to groups and there is high confidence that the random assignment has lead to initial equivalence of the experimental and control groups.

The **Solomon Four-Group Design** can be used when there is some doubt about the initial equivalence of the experimental and control groups because this design facilitates comparisons of conditions that will allow valid evaluation of initial equivalence:

Group	Subject Assignment	Pretest	Treatment	Posttest
E_1	R	O	X	O
C_1	R	O		O
E_2	R		X	O
C_2	R			O

Careful observation reveals that this design is actually just a combination of the two preceding it. The major advantage of this design is that it allows control over or explanation of the majority of sources of invalidity in experimental research. The major disadvantage is that this design requires relatively large numbers of participants and substantial control over the research situation.

Factorial Designs

Each of the preceding research designs is appropriate for use when there is one (e.g., pre-post assessments) or two (pre-post assessments and experimental and control groups) independent variables. By contrast, factorial experimental designs are appropriate for use when there are more than two independent variables.

In the language of factorial designs (which should not be confused with the statistical process of factor analysis, covered later in this chapter), a factor is an independent variable. Each factor in factorial design has at least two levels, which, in this context, are synonymous with categories. Use of the term levels in this context is really a poor choice of words because no hierarchal order of categories in the variable is implied or necessary. For example, the variable "gender" in a factorial design has two levels (male and female), but clearly no hierarchy exists in these categories.

The notation for a factorial design is a set of numbers that identifies how many independent variables are involved and the number of levels in each of the variables. For example, an experiment in which the independent variables are group (experimental or control), gender (male or female), and secondary school class level (9, 10, 11, or 12) would be denoted as a: 2 × 2 × 4 factorial design. (Note: read × as "by.") Thus, in this notation, the number of numbers is the number of factors and the numbers themselves are the number of levels in each of the respective factors. In the 2 × 2 × 4 factorial design example presented, there are three factors (independent variables of group, gender, and class level), the first factor has two levels (the categories of experimental or control), the second factor has two levels (male or female), and the third factor has four levels (9, 10, 11, or 12).

The order of the factors is not important in this notation as long as the appropriate number of levels is correctly associated with the corresponding factors; the order of the numbers is not fixed by any rule. The example presented could have been denoted as a 2 × 4 × 2 factorial design, in which the first factor was gender, the second was grade level, and the third was group.

Threats to Internal and External Experimental Design Validity

The threats to experimental design validity are potential sources of invalidity in the results of an experimental study. Internal threats to design validity have to do with procedures or methodology whereas external threats have to do with generalizability of the results. Internal Threats to Experimental Design Validity include the following:

Contemporary History is invalidation resulting from events that occur during the course of the experiment (e.g., exposure to media events, life situation changes, or random personal activities).

Maturation is invalidation resulting from changes in the subjects during the course (i.e., time period) of the experiment (e.g., developmental change, fatigue, or hunger).

Testing (sometimes called **Pretest Sensitivity**) is invalidation resulting from changes in subjects' scores on a subsequent test due to having taken the test on a previous occasion (i.e., changes due to test content familiarity or recall).

Statistical Regression is invalidation resulting from the natural regression to the mean among persons initially at an extreme (e.g., inclination to homeostasis).

Selection is invalidation resulting from initial differences between subjects in the various groups (e.g., selection bias).

Attrition (sometimes called **Experimental Mortality**) is invalidation resulting from subjects systematically dropping out of participation in a study (e.g., differential attrition across groups).

Instrumentation is invalidation resulting from changes in the measurement instruments or procedures (e.g., calibration, accuracy, interpretation, or experience).

Interactions Among Factors is invalidation resulting from either confounding (canceling) or compounding (summative) combinations of the preceding seven threats.

Compensatory Equalization of Treatments is invalidation resulting from compensation (e.g., special treatment) being provided to a control group presumed not to be receiving the treatment.

Resentful Demoralizing of Subjects in Less Desirable Treatment Conditions is invalidation resulting from subjects in one (e.g., alternative treatment or control) group giving up on performing appropriately.

Compensatory Rivalry by Subjects Receiving Less Desirable Treatments is invalidation resulting from members of the control group attempting to outperform the experimental group (e.g., to demonstrate equivalent competence).

Diffusion or Imitation of Treatments is invalidation resulting from intra- or intergroup communication among subjects (e.g., helping one another during the course of an experiment).

External Threats to Experimental Design Validity include the following:

Reactive Effects of Testing are generalizability limitations resulting from the difference between the experimental and real life situations (e.g., pretest sensitization is not present in real life situations).

Interaction of Selection and Treatment is a generalizability limitation resulting from experimental subjects being particularly susceptible to the treatment (e.g., volunteers may be particularly motivated to change).

Reactive Effects of Experimental Arrangements are generalizability limitations resulting from lack of comparability between the experimental (e.g., laboratory) and real world setting.

Multiple-treatment Interference is a generalizability limitation resulting from simultaneous application of multiple interventions or treatments, some of which may be unintentional applications.

Single-Subject Designs

Single-subject experimental designs are sometimes known as **N=1** or as **Intra-Subject Designs**. They are usually used to assess effectiveness in changing a specific behavior of a specific individual. Following are common features of single-subject designs.

• Clear specification of the treatment goal, usually presented as a behavioral goal (e.g., change in a targeted behavior).
• A focus on changing only one variable at a time during the treatment phase(s).
• Repeated measurement of the target variable throughout the experiment.
• Consistency and stability of baseline and treatment conditions.
• Diligent description of all the conditions under which the target behavior is observed (i.e., measured).

The commonly used notations for single-subject designs include:

A designates the **baseline** condition, and
B designates the **treatment** condition.

The **A-B Design** is the simplest, but least interpretable, of the single-subject designs. The premise of the A-B design is that after the baseline is established, the condition (i.e., behavior) would have continued in the same pattern had not the treatment been introduced. The intervention is initiated after the baseline behavior achieves a level of stability that provides a satisfactory estimate of pretreatment performance. The criterion for satisfactory stability is defined by the counselor. With this design, the assumption is made that any change in behavior is a (direct) result of intervention. However, with only two phases, it is difficult to be certain that this assumption is accurate or valid. Extraneous factors occurring simultaneously with the commencement of intervention also could influence outcomes.

The **A-B-A Design** is sometimes known as the **reversal** or **withdrawal** design. This design allows a strong causal inference if the target behavior returns to the baseline level after the treatment is terminated. However, because this design ends with the treatment not in effect, it may be unethical to use this design for some counseling situations.

The **A-B-A-B Design** affords the strongest causal inference about the effect of the treatment. This design has the advantage of ending the experiment with the treatment in effect (which may be desirable for ethical reasons). This design extends the A-B format to include a sequential replication of the two phases (i.e., A and B). If the pattern of behavior observed during the first two phases is replicated during the last two phases (i.e., the pretreatment baseline contingencies are reestablished during the third phase and the intervention contingencies of phase two are reestablished during phase four), it can be assumed that the changes in behavior are accounted for by the intervention.

Although this design eliminates the problem of uncertainty of effect encountered with the A-B design, in many situations in counseling the A-B-A-B format would be detrimental to the client. For example, if an intervention technique introduced during the second phase was found to be effective in helping a client with acting-out aggressions toward his or her peers, a reversal to the baseline to reestablish aggressive behaviors would not be desirable. In situations of this nature, a multiple-baseline design is an effective alternative.

The **Randomized A-B Design** involves a randomized presentation of the A and B (i.e., baseline and treatment) conditions over time. Because of the random presentation of conditions, parametric statistical analyses can be applied to the resultant data. This design also can be used to analyze carryover effects of the treatment.

Multiple-Baseline Designs employ the A-B design logic, but allow collection of data on two or more actions, subjects, situations, or combinations thereof. In **Multiple-Baselines Across Behavior** designs, baselines are established for two or more independent behaviors for one subject. The (same) treatment is first applied to one behavior, then to the next, and so on in sequence using the same time interval for each application of the treatment. In **Multiple-Baselines Across Situations** designs, the same behavior is targeted across situations (e.g., settings). The A-B design is replicated (i.e., same intervention and time periods) across situations and then the results are compared. In **Multiple-Baselines Across Individuals** designs, the behavior and the situation are held constant. The establishment of a baseline and subsequent application of the treatment proceed sequentially across individuals.

In multiple baseline designs, multiple target behaviors are recorded simultaneously and the respective baselines for the different behaviors are staggered. The assumption is made that subsequent behaviors serve as a means of control for the preceding behavior. Although deliberately oversimplified, the following illustration demonstrates the use of a multiple-baseline design in counseling.

The Jacksons, who worked for different accounting firms, had been married for seven years and sought the help of a professional counselor due to marital problems focused primarily on lack of communication with each other. They worked with the professional counselor over a period of five weeks for three communication problem areas: use of obscenities, shouting, and negative statements. Using a multiple-baseline design to examine counseling effectiveness, the professional counselor divided the measurement of effectiveness into five phases, each of which lasted one week. During each phase, data were collected by recording the frequency with which each of the communication problems occurred. The data gathered during phase one became the baseline data against which the frequency counts for the remaining phases were compared. During phase two (second week), the Jacksons went to separate rooms whenever either individual used an obscenity. During phase three (third week), the Jacksons continued with the procedure introduced during phase two but also went to different rooms whenever there was shouting. With phase four (fourth week), the Jacksons focused on negative statements, again going to separate rooms when this behavior occurred. They also continued largely on their own with the procedures introduced in phases two and three. The three procedures used in phase four were continued in phase five (fifth week) for purposes of follow-up data collection.

To recap the illustration using the Jacksons, after baseline conditions have been established for three behaviors, phase two is introduced; it consists of initiating intervention for the first behavior and continuing with the baseline conditions for the remaining two behaviors. In changing to the third phase, intervention is introduced for the second behavior and the baseline condition is continued for the third behavior only. Finally, during the fourth phase, the intervention is used with all behaviors. A change in performance for all behaviors upon initiation of the intervention confirms that the results are due to the treatment effect only.

☐ Legal Aspects of Research

There are actually relatively few legal aspects to the conduct of research in the counseling profession (or in the social sciences in general). However, the few considerations that exist are especially important ones because they are focused on human rights and responsibilities. The general legal principles for research include that subjects have the right to freedom from invasion of privacy and subjects' participation in research always is voluntary. Assuming these two principles are upheld, any type of research is permitted if appropriate procedures are followed.

The Family Educational Rights and Privacy Act (FERPA) of 1974, also known as the Buckley Amendment, has important implications for research in counseling, particularly school counseling, because it provides guidelines for researcher access to information in records. Among other things, the FERPA stipulates that written parental permission is required for access to students' records and person-data linkages should be avoided (i.e., data should remain anonymous whenever possible). Although the

FERPA applies specifically to educational systems, its principles have been extended to other situations as well.

The FERPA stipulates that the written request for data about a student must include an exact specification of the data requested, an explanation of how the data are to be used, and an explanation of to whom the data will be disclosed and how it will be disseminated. It is important to note that the data obtained can be used only for the purpose for which the request was made. That is, the researcher cannot obtain data under the auspices of one request and then later use the data (or part of it) for a purpose that was not specifically identified in the original request.

The National Research Act (NRA) of 1974 is another statute that has very significant implications for research in the counseling profession. It applies to all persons associated with any institution or agency that receives any federal funds. Within the counseling profession, therefore, about the only professionals exempt from the requirements of the NRA of 1974 are those in private practice.

The NRA of 1974 established the requirements for informed consent procedures in research. Institutional Review Boards (IRBs), also known as human subjects committees, were established to ensure that the provisions of the NRA are implemented effectively and legally. Among other things, IRBs are charged with ensuring that researchers use a legally appropriate informed consent form. It is important to note that there is no single informed consent form; rather, an informed consent form is created by the researcher(s) for each research project. A valid informed consent form must communicate the following clearly.

- That participation in a research activity is being requested.
- The duration (and/or frequency of occurrence) of the participation requested.
- An explanation of the nature of the participation requested in language that the person receiving the letter can reasonably be expected to understand.
- A (brief) description of the research procedures.
- Specific identification of any procedures that are experimental.
- A description of any potential risks or discomfort resulting from participation.
- A description of any benefits of participation, specifically including whether there will or will not be monetary compensation.
- A statement of the extent of confidentiality or anonymity to be accorded to participants.
- Sources of assistance should harm or discomfort occur during or as a result of participation.

- The name and contact information to which to direct questions or inquiries about the research.
- A statement that participation is completely voluntary.
- A statement that discontinuing participation at any time will NOT result in any form of harm, recourse, or loss of benefits to the participant.

Each subject must be given a copy of the informed consent form (separate from the one retained by the researcher).

☐ Ethical Aspects of Research

Ethics as applicable to the counseling profession in general are discussed at length in the next chapter. Of importance here are those ethical principles specifically associated with the conduct of research by professional counselors. The following four general ethical principles serve as a framework upon which all other ethical standards in the counseling profession are based.

> **Nonmaleficence**—do no harm.
> **Beneficence**—do as much good as possible.
> **Justice**—equality for all.
> **Fidelity**—fulfill all obligations.

Specific applications of these general ethical principles may be made in regard to how they are applied to the work of researchers or the participation of subjects. The following two subsections present some of the more important ethical principles associated with these research applications found in the ACA and NBCC *Codes of Ethics.*

Ethics Related to Scholarly Work

The information derived from a research study should promote the welfare of members of society (Beneficence).

The principal researcher has responsibility for all aspects of execution of the study, including the behaviors of all research participants (Beneficence and Fidelity).

The results of research must be reported accurately, honestly, and fairly (Beneficence and Nonmaleficence).

Credit for all contributions to the research must be given accurately and adequately (Justice).

Acknowledgment must be given to original contributions or scholarly insights of others and distinguished clearly from those of the author(s) researcher(s); plagiarism is always unethical (Justice).

Ethics Related to Subjects

Researchers must strive to minimize harm or risk to subjects (Nonmaleficence).

Researchers must strive to maintain or improve subjects' welfare and dignity (Beneficience).

Researchers must use informed consent procedures that are to the subjects' benefit (Beneficience and Fidelity).

Researchers must respect subjects' privacy by maintaining confidentiality or anonymity (Fidelity).

Researchers must fulfill all treatment obligations and responsibilities offered to subjects (Fidelity).

Researchers must be extremely careful to protect subjects' welfare and dignity in the conduct of experiments involving deception (Nonmaleficence and Fidelity).

Researchers must provide subject debriefing, including dehoaxing or desensitization, for any research involving deception (Beneficence and Fidelity).

Researchers must avoid use of any form of pressure to coerce subject participation (Nonmaleficence).

Researchers are obligated to attempt to countermand any negative consequence(s) of participation in the research (Beneficence and Fidelity).

☐ Computers and Research

Computers serve three major functions in regard to research in the counseling profession: data management, document production, and Internet transversal. The data management functions include uses for data gathering, storage, and manipulation. Historically, the data gathering function involved manually entering data into a computer file via a keyboard. However, the data gathering functions now often include use of optical scanners and computer-based assessments to enter data directly. The data storage functions may include data-entry and retrieval as well as storage. For example, data storage is also data entry if the data stored are imported directly from another program. The data storage functions are facilitated primarily through the use of spreadsheet and database programs. Spreadsheet programs are designed to make data entry and understanding as easy as possible by using a row-column format whereas database programs are designed to make data-entry and reporting functions as easy as possible through free format procedures. The data manipulation functions include data analyses and other procedures to clarify the nature of the data.

The document production functions primarily include using word processing, graphics, and desktop publishing programs to develop manuscripts or electronic forms for communication of research. The most important word processing functions include formatting, spell-checking, and grammar-checking. Increasing sophistication in document production capabilities is allowing some researchers to disseminate (written) results directly to interested consumers and outside of regular (e.g., journal) publication outlets.

A highly significant, current trend in dissemination of research documents is publication on the Internet. The Internet also serves four other primary functions in regard to research: aiding collaboration among researchers, simplifying information gathering, facilitating data collection, and fostering professional discourse.

☐ Variables

A variable is something that can have different values (as opposed to a constant which always has the same value). The variables examined in a research study are generally referred to as the dependent or independent variables. The dependent variable is the one that (presumably) changes as a function of the different conditions (i.e., values, levels, or categories) for the independent variable. It must be logically related to the attribute or behavior being studied. In addition, it needs to be specific and measurable. Because measurement of the dependent variable provides an indication of the amount of a characteristic that the subject actually possesses or a subject's actual level of performance, it is always appropriate to use the most sensitive measure available in order to maximize the precision of results.

The independent variable is the variable that is manipulated (i.e., allowed to have different values). An independent variable can have two or more levels. Remember that, in this context, a level is a category and no hierarchy is implied or presented. For example, if three methods of counseling were being compared (e.g., individual, group, and family counseling), the dependent variable might be counseling effectiveness and the independent variable (i.e., counseling methods) would be divided into three levels, each representing one of the counseling methods.

Theoretically, it is possible to have a very large number of dependent or independent variables or both in any particular study. However, typically no more than three dependent variables and no more than five independent variables are included in any particular study because the results of studies having more than these numbers are extremely difficult to interpret.

☐ Selecting Subjects

Three primary factors need to be considered in the subject-selection process—appropriateness, representativeness, and number of subjects.

Appropriateness

The subjects in a study need to fit the definition for the given population. As Houser (1998) indicated, a population consists of all elements of any well-defined class of people, events, or objects being investigated. In addition, a population may be generally defined as the group of people to whom the results of a research study will be applied (Houser, 1998). Consideration needs to be given to units or restrictions in the population as they relate to the topic being studied. Failure to give this careful consideration may result in selective inclusion or exclusion of particular potential subjects.

Representativeness

Subjects are the people who participate in the research. The subjects selected for a study (the sample) need to be representative of the population if the research results are to be generalizable to the given set of individuals, events, or objects. The important concept is representativeness. Good and effective sampling is evaluated in terms of the result, not the sampling method used. In other words, the important point is whether the (resultant) sample obtained is an accurate representation of the population to which the results of the study are supposed to apply. No particular sampling procedure guarantees or restricts representativeness; good or bad (i.e., not representative) samples can be obtained from any particular subject-selection procedure.

Sampling is the procedure used to identify and enlist the subjects. Good sampling starts with effective description of the population. Description of the population includes consideration of the population's demographic and psychosocial characteristics. Demography is the statistical study of populations (i.e., identifiable groups of people) and demographic information typically comes from statistical summaries (aka, statistical abstracts).

Psychosocial characteristics are those attributes, behaviors, and characteristics typically associated with an identifiable group of people. Psychosocial information typically comes from the professional literature. Generally, effective sampling works as follows.

1. The population for the study is identified, usually using colloquial descriptors.
2. The primary (or major) demographic characteristics of interest are selected.
3. Demographic information about the population is found from some statistical resource.
4. The psychosocial characteristics of the population are identified from the professional literature.
5. Sampling is conducted based on demographic characteristics (e.g., proportions of males and females, etc.).
6. It is *assumed* that the psychosocial characteristics of the sample equal those of the population.

There are two categories of approaches to sampling: probability and nonprobability.

Probability sampling. In this category of sampling, subjects are drawn from the population in such a way that the probability of selecting each member of the population is known. Probability sampling methods include:

Random Sampling, in which each person has an equal likelihood of being selected and the selection of one does not affect the selection of another.

Systematic Sampling, in which every n^{th} person from a list of all persons in the population is selected.

Stratified Sampling, in which each person who is a member of the stratum (i.e., category) is eligible to be selected and selection is made through a first encounter process.

Stratified Random Sampling, in which each member of a stratum has an equal likelihood of being selected, selection of one within the stratum does not affect the selection of another in the stratum, and the number of subjects drawn within strata may be either proportional or nonproportional to the population.

Cluster Sampling, in which naturally occurring groups or units are the population (e.g., classes or neighborhoods), clusters of groups or units are randomly selected from the population of groups or units, and individuals are randomly selected from the clusters selected.

In all probability methods, representativeness is assumed to be achieved if the laws of probability are effectively operationalized.

Nonprobability sampling. In this category of sampling, subjects are drawn from the population in a logical way so that representativeness can be reasonably assumed. Nonprobability sampling methods include:

> **Convenience Sampling**, in which an intact group of people is used as the subjects based simply on ease of access to them.
>
> **Purposeful Sampling** (sometimes called **judgmental sampling**), in which specific persons are selected from the population because they are judged to be representative or informative about the topic being studied.
>
> **Quota Sampling**, which is used when a probability sampling method cannot be used, but subjects are able to be selected to represent identified characteristics of the population. Quota sampling procedures typically include use of a sampling framework, which is a diagram of the proportionate relationships among the variables upon which the sampling is based.

Number of Subjects

No set sample size is required under all conditions; therefore, the number of subjects necessary for a given study is unclear (at least initially). However, because an at-least-adequate sample needs to be obtained for each study, an at-least-adequate sample size must be established for each study. There are two basic ways to determine the minimum sample size needed. If a quota (or sampling frame) approach is used, effective fulfillment of the various cell entries is the minimum total needed to represent the population effectively. If a probability sampling approach is used, statistical power (which is the probability that a given statistical technique will result in failure to reject a false null hypothesis) should be computed. For a given level of statistical significance, a statistical power formula can be used to provide an estimate of the needed minimum sample size for that significance level. However, it should be noted that statistical power is always enhanced by a large sample size. Other important factors to consider in sampling include the following.

> **Type of research**—correlational research requires larger samples than does experimental research.
>
> **Research Hypotheses**—expectation of smaller differences requires larger samples.

Cost—what is the largest possible sample size that can be achieved with available resources.

Importance of Results—the greater the implications, the larger should be the sample.

Number of Variables—the greater the number of variables, the larger the sample needed.

Data Collection Methods—larger samples are needed if there is considerable measurement error.

Accuracy Needed—the greater the accuracy needed, the larger the sample needed.

Size of Population—the larger the population, the smaller the percentage needed to represent it.

☐ Research Questions and Hypotheses

The reason that research is conducted is to find out something that is unknown. In the context of a research study, presenting what is unknown (i.e., what is being studied) is done through the use of questions or hypotheses. The decision of whether to use a research question, null hypothesis, or directional hypothesis is made on the basis of what is known about the topic being studied. By convention, research studies use all research questions, all null hypotheses, or all directional hypotheses. Because the decision about which to use is based on the available information about the topic as a general entity, these are not mixed in a particular study.

Research Questions

It is appropriate to use research questions when relatively little is known about the topic, that is, when there is very little basis for making a conjecture about what the results might be. Research questions typically are in the form: "What (is)/(are) the (differences)/(relationships) (between)/ (among)....?" The "is" or "are" and "between" or "among" decisions are made simply to achieve correct grammatical structure.

The decision of whether to use "relationships" or "differences" is made based on the types of variables involved. In general, variables studied in research can be classified as either "discrete" or "continuous." A discrete variable may be thought of as having categories whereas a continuous variable may be thought of as having scores (i.e., a full range of values). Typical examples of discrete variables include gender, marital status, grade or class level, state of residence, or diagnostic classification. Typical examples of continuous variables include age, years of work experience, annual income in dollars, scores on a test, or frequency of a particular behavior. The word *relationship* is used if all the variables involved are continuous. The word *difference* is used if at least one of the variables involved is discrete. Here are some examples of research questions.

What is the relationship between levels of assertiveness and stress among adult, working women?

What are the differences among married and divorced males' and females' attitudes toward divorce?

What is the difference in college seniors' GRE scores following participation in a test preparation workshop?

Directional Hypotheses

If a great deal is known about a topic and there is ample support for the belief that the results will be of a particular form, then directional hypotheses should be used. The general form of a directional hypothesis is a declarative sentence. An effective directional hypothesis should specify both the nature and direction of the relationship or difference expected. Here are some examples of a directional hypothesis.

Males engage in abusive verbal behavior more frequently than females.

The "test buster" activity is effective in reducing students' test anxiety.

There is a positive relationship between frequencies of use of alcoholic beverages and cigarettes.

Null Hypotheses

In between the extremes of knowing a great deal or very little about a topic is the much more common middle area wherein some information is available, but it is mixed information about the topic. That is, the situation is that the topic has been studied fairly extensively, but there is no definitive pattern in the results of research on the topic. It is in this middle area where the use of null hypotheses is appropriate.

In order for any general statement to be true, it must hold as specified for all occasions. If any occasion is an exception to the general statement, then the statement is not true (i.e., one exception disproves the rule). Therefore, hypotheses are often stated in *null form* because researchers study only one occasion at a time and thus cannot prove but can only disprove a null statement.

There are two commonly used forms of null hypotheses, the traditional form and the modern form. Here is an example of a traditional null hypothesis.

H_0: There will be no significant relationship between counselor trainees' personality needs as measured by the Personality Research Form and their counseling effectiveness as measured by the Counselor Evaluation Rating Scale.

The modern form is written in the present tense, does not use the word significant, and does not indicate the measurement tools. Here is an example of the modern form of the previous hypothesis.

H_0: There is no relationship between counselor trainees' personality needs and their counseling effectiveness.

A study of differences in academic performance on the basis of gender and residence classification would have two major hypotheses:

H_1: There is no difference in academic performance based on gender.

H_2: There is no difference in academic performance based on residence classification.

But there are the combinations that need to be considered. Therefore, subhypotheses would need to be added to each primary hypothesis.

H_1: There is no difference in academic performance based on gender.

H_{1a}: There is no difference in academic performance among males based on residence classification.

H_{1b}: There is no difference in academic performance among females based on residence classification.

There is also the possibility that the two variables, gender and residence classification, may somehow interact with each other to yield a unique result. Therefore, in such situations an interaction hypothesis should also be presented:

H_{1c}: There is no gender by residence classification interaction for academic performance.

Evaluating Research Questions or Hypotheses

The evaluation response to a research question is a declarative statement that provides a direct answer to the question posed. For example, if the research question is in the form, "What is the difference in Variable A as a function of Variable B?," the evaluation response should be in the form, "The difference in Variable A as a function of Variable B is. . . . "

There are only two possible evaluation responses for either a direct or a null hypothesis: "reject" or "fail to reject." A null hypothesis is never accepted because one study cannot *prove* the universal truth of a direct or null hypothesis. It also is inappropriate to *partially* reject an hypothesis, even if the hypothesis is multifaceted (i.e., encompasses several variables in a single statement).

There are two types of errors that can be made in evaluating hypotheses.

A **Type I Error** occurs when the researcher rejects the null hypothesis when it is in fact true.

A **Type II Error** occurs when the null hypothesis is not rejected when it should have been rejected.

The evaluation possibilities look like this:

	Null Hypothesis is TRUE	Null Hypothesis is FALSE
Reject the Null Hypothesis	**Type I Error**	Correct Decision
Fail to Reject the Null Hypothesis	Correct Decision	**Type II Error**

☐ Basic Statistics

An important component in research is determination of which statistical procedures will be used to analyze the data collected. Decisions concerning data analyses are made when designing the study because the statistical tools used are dependent upon the purpose of the research undertaken and the type of data derived.

Types of Data

Nominal data, also referred to as discrete, classification, or categorical data, are information in the form of mutually exclusive groups or categories. Each category is presumably distinct from the other categories, with the data serving only as labels of identification. Examples of nominal data include year in school, occupation, and yes or no responses to a question.

Ordinal data are characterized by rank-order measurements and an underlying continuum, which in turn allows relationships of "more than" or "less than" among the data. Measurements using Likert-type scales exemplify this data type.

The properties of identity and order of difference, found in nominal and ordinal data, respectively, are extended to include magnitude of difference for interval data. Also characteristic of this type of data is an arbitrary zero point. Examples of interval data include the Celsius and Fahrenheit temperature scales as well as calendar time. The last type of data, ratio, includes all the properties of interval data, except the zero point is not arbitrary. A score of zero represents total absence of the variable being measured. Examples of ratio data include response time, weight, and height. Both interval and ratio data also fall under the general rubric of continuous data.

Descriptive Statistics

Descriptive statistics are used when the researcher is interested only in describing the group(s) being studied. Descriptive statistics can be divided into two general categories: central tendency and dispersion or variance. The most common measures of central tendency are the mean, median, and mode.

The mean, also referred to as the arithmetic average, of a distribution of scores is derived by summing all the scores in a distribution and dividing the sum by the number of scores in the set. Although this statistic is not used with nominal or ordinal data, it is the most frequently used measure of central tendency. It is more stable than the other measures of central tendency and is amenable to additional manipulation, making it useful in inferential statistics. However, the mean is affected by extreme, or outlying, scores. Therefore, if a distribution has a few extreme scores and accuracy of measurement is important, the median will be a more appropriate measure of central tendency. The median represents the middle point in a distribution of scores, or the point above or below which half of the scores fall. The median is used with all types of data except nominal data. The mode is the most frequently occurring score or interval in a distribution. This statistic is the only measure of central tendency to use with nominal data, but it may also be used with the other three types.

The second category of descriptive statistics includes measures of dispersion (i.e., indications of the degree to which scores vary from a measure of central tendency). Statistics in this category are the range, semi-interquartile range, and standard deviation. The range, which provides a quick but limited index of the amount of variability in a distribution, is determined by subtracting the lowest from the highest score in the distribution, and adding 1.

Any distribution can be divided into four equal parts separated by points referred to as quartiles. Thus, 50 percent of the scores in a distribution fall between the first quartile (Q1) and the third quartile (Q3). The difference between Q1 and Q3 divided by 2 constitutes the semi-interquartile range. Because this statistic uses more of the scores in a distribution than does the range, it provides a more stable and more representative picture of the score dispersion.

The standard deviation is not so easy to calculate as the other measures of variability, but it is used far more often. The standard deviation, which provides a standardized measure of a score's deviation above or below the mean, is limited to use with interval and ratio data. The major advantages of this statistic are that it is used in many more complex statistics and it is considerably less effected by extreme scores.

☐ Statistical Analyses

Clearly it is not possible to present a comprehensive review of all statistics here. Therefore, what follows is a very general overview of major statistical analysis procedures. It is extremely important to note that there are technical exceptions to (or variations of) most of what is presented. However, the information provided here is adequate for understanding most of the statistical analyses used in research in the counseling profession.

Parametic Statistics

Use of so-called parametric statistics is based on assumptions including that:

- The data represent population characteristics that are continuous and symmetrical.
- The variable(s) has (have) a distribution that is essentially normal in the population.
- The sample statistic provides an estimate of the population parameter.

It should be recalled that variables typically involved in research can be divided into the categories of discrete or continuous. Based on this distinction, (in general) all statistical analyses can be divided into (a) analyses of relationships among variables or (b) analyses of differences based on variables. *In the context of this general (inexact) overview, all of the variables involved in analyses of relationships are continuous. Similarly, for analyses of differences, at least one variable must be continuous and at least one variable must be discrete.*

Analyses of Relationships

The simplest (statistical) relationship involves only two (continuous) variables and the relationship between two variables is expressed as a **correlation coefficient**. Calculation of the correlation coefficient allows us to address the question, "What do we know (or can we predict) about Y given that we know X?". More technically, the correlation coefficient is used to indicate the relationship between two variables, known more formally as the Pearson Product-Moment Correlation Coefficient, designated by a lower case r, and ranges in values from -1.00 through 0.00 to $+1.00$.

When $r = -1.00$, there is a perfect negative, or inverse, relationship between the two variables. This means that as one variable is changing, the associated variable is changing in the opposite direction in a proportional manner. When $r = +1.00$, there is a perfect positive, or direct, relationship between the two variables. This means that as one variable is changing, the associated variable is changing in the same direction in a proportional manner. When $r = 0.00$, there is a zero-order relationship between the two variables. This means that change in one variable is unrelated to change in the associated variable.

An important question is, "How do we know if the correlation coefficient calculated is any good?" In general, there are two major ways to evaluate a correlation coefficient. One is in regard to statistical significance. Statistical significance has to do with the probability (likelihood) that a result occurred strictly as a function of chance. Statistical analysis result evaluation based in probability is like a game of chance. The researcher decides whether it will be a high stakes or a low stakes situation, depending on the implications of being wrong. The results of the decision are operationalized in the alpha level selected for the study. In the language of statistics, the alpha level (e.g., .01 or .05), sometimes called the level of significance, represents the (proportionate) chance that the researcher will be wrong in rejecting the null hypothesis. That is, the alpha level is the probability of making a Type I Error. The p value is the exact probability of obtaining the particular result for some statistical analysis. Technically, the p value is compared to the alpha level to determine statistical significance; if p is less than the alpha, the result is reported as statistically significant. Most statistical analysis programs generate p values (i.e., exact probabilities) from statistical analyses. However, most journal articles report results as comparisons of p values to alpha levels; that is, they report, for example, $p < .05$, rather than, for example, $p = .0471$.

There is at least one prominent limitation in the evaluation of a correlation coefficient based on statistical significance. This limitation is related to the conditions under which the statistical significance of the correlation coefficient is evaluated. The **critical value** is the value of the correlation coefficient necessary for it to be statistically significant at a given alpha level and for a given sample size. In statistics, sample size is usually expressed in regard to **degrees of freedom**. For the correlation coefficient, there is an inverse relationship between the critical values and degrees of freedom; as the degrees of freedom (i.e., sample size) increase, the critical values (needed for statistical significance) decrease. This means that a very small correlation coefficient can be statistically significant if the data are from a very large sample. Thus, the statistical significance of a correlation coefficient cannot be evaluated as good or bad in an absolute sense; consideration must be given to the sample size from which the data were derived.

Another way to evaluate a correlation coefficient is in terms of **percentage of shared variance**. Consider two variables: A and B. By definition, if A is a variable, it has variance (i.e., not every person receives the same score on measure A). All (i.e., 100%) of the variance of A can be represented by a circle. Similarly, because B is a variable, it has variance, and all (i.e., 100%) of the variance of B can be represented by a circle. Together, A and B as circles present a Venn diagram. Of interest is how much variance variables A and B share, that is, the intersection of circles A and B.

The percentage of shared variance is equal to r^2 times 100. In this formula, the term r^2 is known as the **coefficient of determination**. The percentage of shared variance is how much of the variance of variable A is common to variable B, and vice versa. Another way to think of it is that the percentage of shared variance is the amount of the same thing measured by (or reflected in) both variables.

The good news is that the shared variance method as a basis for evaluating a correlation coefficient is not dependent upon sample size. The bad news is that there is no way to determine what is an acceptable level of shared variance. Ultimately, the researcher and/or research consumer has to be the judge of what is a good correlation coefficient.

The correlation coefficient can be used to predict one variable from another. That is, it can be incorporated into a formula that will allow prediction of the value of one variable given the known value of the other variable (e.g., using SAT scores to predict freshman year grade point averages). That is helpful, but has limited application because only two variables are involved. Suppose we know of the relationships between variable Z and several other variables. The statistical technique known as **multiple correlation** allows one variable to be predicted from a set of other variables. The variable being predicted is known as the **criterion variable** and the variables in the set are known as the **predictor variables**. The capital letter R is used to indicate the relationship between the set of predictor variables and the criterion variable being predicted. In computing R, the most desirable situation is what is known as the Daisy Pattern. In the hypothetical best possible Daisy Pattern, each predictor has a relatively high correlation with the criterion variable, and each of the predictor variables has a relatively low correlation with each of the other predictor variables. The multiple correlation computational procedures lead to a weighted combination of (some of) the predictor variables and a specific correlation between the weighted combination and the criterion variable.

The same two methods used to evaluate a Pearson Product-Moment Correlation Coefficient can be used to evaluate a multiple correlation coefficient. That is, the methods of evaluating R include:

Statistical significance, although the sample size limitation concern is less problematic if the sample is sufficient for the computations; and

Percentage of shared variance, where the expression $R^2 \times 100$ represents the sum of the intersections of the predictors with the criterion variable.

A **canonical correlation** (R_c) extends this pattern and represents the relationship between a set of predictor variables and a set of criterion variables. A canonical correlation is usually expressed as a lambda coefficient, often Wilks Lambda, which is the result of the statistical computations. The statistical significance of the lambda coefficient can be readily determined. The percentage of shared variance also can be calculated. However, because the lambda coefficient can have values greater than one, the calculation of the shared variance involves more than just squaring the lambda coefficient.

Factor analysis, a special type of analysis of relationships, is a general family of data reduction techniques. It is used to reduce the redundancy in a set of correlated variables and to represent the variables with a smaller set of derived variables (aka, factors). Factor analyses may be computed within either of two contexts: exploratory or confirmatory. The former is used when the researcher has no predetermined expectation for the nature of the results, whereas the latter is used when the researcher uses theory, previous research findings, or some other basis to establish a prediction of the results.

Factor analysis starts with the input of raw data. Next, an intervariable correlation matrix is generated from the input data. Then, using sophisticated matrix algebra, an **initial factor loading matrix** is derived from the correlation matrix. There are three major components to the factor loading matrix:

The first is the set of item numbers, usually arranged in sequence and in hierarchal order.

The second is the factor identifications, usually represented by Roman numerals.

The third is the actual factor loadings, usually provided as hundreths (with or without decimal points).

An important question is, "How many factors should be retained?" In factor analysis, theoretically, there can be as many factors as items. However, usually one or some combination of three methods is used to decide how many factors are retained (i.e., actually used). An eigenvalue is the sum of the squared factor loadings for a particular factor. One common method is to retain factors having eigenvalues greater than one, which is known as applying the Kaiser Criterion. A second method is application of the scree test, which is actually a visual inspection of a plot of the eigenvalues. A third method is to retain factors to achieve a percentage of the total variance. The total variance, equal to the number of items, is the sum of the eigenvalues. Thus, if a percentage is desired, factor eigenvalues can be added until that percentage is achieved.

Another important question is, "How are the relationships among factors to be conceptualized?" A factor is two things. Conceptually, a factor is a construct, and mathematically, a factor is a vector in n-dimensional space (which is a hypothetical, but mathematically possible, situation in which more than three lines can be perpendicular to one another at a single point in space). Factors as constructs may be separate and entirely distinct from one another or separate but conceptually related to one another. Factors as vectors reflect these possibilities by being positioned in n-dimensional space as either perpendicular to one another or as having an acute angle between them. The initial factor loading matrix is rotated in n-dimensional space to achieve the best mathematical representation and clarity among the constructs. If the factors are assumed to be distinct (i.e., independent) from one another, the rotation is said to be orthogonal. An orthogonal rotation is one in which the angles between factors are maintained as right angles during and after the rotation. The most common orthogonal rotation is the Varimax procedure. If the factors are assumed to be related (i.e., dependent) to one another, the rotation is said to be oblique. An oblique rotation is one in which the angles between factors are maintained as less than right angles during and after the rotation. The most common oblique rotation is the Oblimin procedure.

After the final factor structure has been determined, a name that encompasses whatever is reflected in the items having their highest factor loadings on the factor is assigned to each factor. This process is relatively arbitrary. Therefore, caution should be exercised not to just assume that the factor name assigned is an accurate reflection of the content of the factor.

There are a few things to be remembered about factor analysis. First, a valid factor analysis requires lots of subjects, usually a minimum of 10 times as many subjects as items. Second, even though factor analysis is a sophisticated data analysis technique, quite a few relatively arbitrary decisions are made by the researcher in the process. For example, selection of the context and type of factor analysis to be used, determination of the number of factors to retain, and naming of the factors are just a few of the decisions to be made. And finally, just because a research study contains a factor analysis doesn't necessarily mean that it is good research; the validity and appropriateness of the factor analysis must be evaluated in order to evaluate the worth of the research.

Analyses of Differences

Recall that for purposes here, an analysis of difference involves at least one continuous variable and at least one discrete variable. In this context, the variable that is continuous is sometimes called the dependent variable and the variable that is discrete is sometimes called the independent variable. In this framework, the purpose of the analysis of differences is to investigate differences in the continuous variable as a function of the categories in the discrete variable.

Imagine that the same test was given to a group of people on many occasions, but on each occasion the test was administered, they had not taken the test previously. Next, imagine that the mean for the test was computed for each occasion it was administered. If a graph was made of the various means for the group against the frequency of occurrence of the respective means, the result would be a normal distribution of the means (because the various factors affecting test performance would come together in different ways on different occasions). This very special distribution is known as the theoretical distribution of sampling means.

The theoretical distribution of sampling means represents 100 percent (all) of the possible means that the group might achieve on any occasion. In other words, there is 100 percent probability that the mean would fall between the endpoints of this distribution. Because the theoretical distribution of sampling means is a normal distribution, all of its mathematical properties are known. For example, it is symmetric about the mean, and standard area percentages under the curve are known.

This theoretical distribution can be grounded in reality if one assumption is accepted: that an observed mean (i.e., one from an actually administered test or measurement) is the mean of the theoretical distribution of sampling means. Generally, this assumption is presumed valid unless there is specific information that the assessment situation or the respondent sample was something other than normal. Once the test is given, the areas under the curve can be related to any mean if the value of the standard error of the mean is known. Fortunately, the standard error of the mean is easy to calculate once the test has been administered. There is approximately a two-thirds chance (about 68%) that the mean for the group will fall between ± one standard error of the mean on any occasion. Similarly, the probability, or likelihood, of the mean falling between ± two standard errors of the mean on any occasion is approximately 96%, and so on. Two of the more useful statements that can be made based on this information are:

There is a 95% probability that the mean will fall between ± 1.96 standard errors of the mean on any occasion.

There is a 99% probability that the mean will fall between ± 2.58 standard errors of the mean on any occasion.

Now assume a situation in which the same thing is measured (i.e., using the same test or measure) on two different occasions for the same group (a la pre-post testing). If the group did not have exactly the same mean for each testing occasion, there was a difference between the means. That difference happened either because something caused the difference or because of chance. The important question is, "What is the likelihood (i.e., probability) that the difference happened simply by chance?" Another way to pose the same question is, "Is the post mean inside or outside of the 95% confidence limits for the pre mean?"

The (**Student's**) **t-test** is a statistical significance test that covers this situation. It is used to determine if there is a statistically significant difference between two means. The t-test is appropriate for use when data from 30 or fewer subjects are being analyzed.

There are two types of t-tests. A dependent, or correlated, t-test is used when the difference between the means of the same group assessed on two occasions is being evaluated (e.g., pre-post). An independent, or uncorrelated, t-test is used when the difference between the means of two separate groups is being evaluated (e.g., males and females).

A t-test yields a statistic called a t-value. Computer programs generating the t-value also present the (exact) probability of obtaining a t-value of that magnitude. The exact probability calculated for the t-value is then compared to the predetermined alpha level for the analysis.

For the t-test, it was noted that the discrete variable (i.e., the one that has categories) is sometimes called the independent variable. The discrete variable is sometimes also known as a factor. It is important to remember that this is a different and distinct use from factor analysis, which was a type of analysis of relationships. In the context of analyses of differences, a factor is a variable that is discrete (i.e., has categories) and is sometimes called the independent variable. The categories of this factor are called levels. Again, this is a poor choice of words because levels implies some type of hierarchy, but that is not really what it means in this context. For example, suppose that gender as a (discrete or independent) variable is included in a study. In the study, gender would be a factor having two levels (i.e., male and female). Remember that levels are categories; no hierarchy is necessarily applicable.

A *t*-test would be the appropriate analysis for a study having only one factor that has two levels. The levels (categories) of the factor may be uncorrelated (e.g., gender) or correlated (e.g., pre-post). Instead of correlated, the phrase *repeated measures* is used to indicate that the levels of a factor are actually two or more measurements on the same group of people as part of a single research study.

Now suppose that instead of viewing gender as either male or female, it was considered sex-role orientation. The possible categories might then be male, female, and androgynous, which would be the three levels of the sex-role orientation factor. Then suppose a measure of counseling effectiveness could be obtained for everyone in each of the three groups. One question might then be, "Are there statistically significant differences among the counseling effectiveness means of the three groups?" The appropriate analysis for this situation is a **one-way analysis of variance**. It is called one-way because there is only one factor involved. This is one of several types of analyses of variance, all of which are abbreviated **ANOVA**.

A one-way ANOVA is appropriate when there is one factor in the study and the factor has three or more levels. The levels may be either uncorrelated (e.g., three categories of sex-role orientation) or correlated (e.g., pre-post-follow-up for an experimental study).

A one-way ANOVA yields an F statistic (or as it is more commonly known, an **F value**). Computer programs generate an exact probability for the F value, which can then be compared to the alpha level. A statistically significant F value means that there is at least one statistically significant difference among one or more pairs of means. However, a statistically significant F value does not indicate which means are significantly different from one another. Therefore, a **multiple comparison** is the statistical procedure used to determine which means are statistically significantly different from another. Note that a multiple comparison is only appropriate following a statistically significant F value.

There are different types of multiple comparison procedures and they range on a continuum of liberal to conservative. The more liberal the procedure, the smaller the difference needed to be considered statistically significantly different. More conservative procedures reduce the chance for Type I error, but make it more difficult to achieve a statistically significant difference. Some of the multiple comparison methods are:

Pairwise Comparisions (i.e., *t*-tests)
Fisher's LSD procedure
Duncan Multiple Range Test
(Student) Newman-Keuls
Tukey HSD procedure
Scheffe's procedure

A **factorial analysis of variance** (ANOVA) is appropriate when there are two or more factors, each of which has at least two levels. Suppose the research question for a study was, "What are the differences in graduate-level academic aptitude as a function of gender and race?" The variables for this study could be as follows.

The dependent variable is GRE Total Score.
One factor is gender, and it has two levels: male (M) and female (F).
Another factor is race, and it has three levels: African-American (AA), Hispanic-American (HA), and Caucasian-American (CA).

One F value would be obtained for each factor (F_{gender} and F_{race}). These are known as the **main effects** F values. These F values are independent; the statistical significance of one is unrelated to the statistical significance of the other. An **interaction F value** also would be obtained ($F_{gender \times race}$). An interaction F value allows evaluation of whether the effects of one variable are consistent for all levels of the other variable. The interaction F value is independent of the other two.

Now suppose another factor is added, such as academic degree (Master's, Specialist, or Doctorate). There will be one F value for each factor (main effects): F_{gender}, F_{race}, and F_{degree}. These F values are all independent of one another. If either the F_{race} or F_{degree} is statistically significant, a multiple comparison would be needed to determine the pattern of significant differences.

There also would be three two-way interactions: $F_{gender \times race}$, $F_{race \times degree}$, and $F_{degree \times gender}$. There also would be one three-way interaction, which represents the combination of variables three at a time: $F_{gender \times race \times degree}$. These F values also are independent of all the others.

The *t*-test, one-way ANOVA, and factorial ANOVA are known as **univariate analyses** because only one dependent variable is involved. If a second (or more) dependent variable is added, the appropriate analysis is a **multivariate analysis of variance** (MANOVA). A MANOVA also yields an F value. If the multivariate F value is *not* significant, it means that there are no significant differences anywhere among the sets of means.

If the F multivariate is statistically significant, appropriate univariate analyses must be computed to determine which means are significantly different from one another.

Nonparametic Statistics

So-called nonparametric statistics are used when the data are nominal or ordinal, or when the data are interval but the assumption of a normal distribution of the variable cannot be met. In general, there are nonparametric statistical analyses that parallel most parametric statistical analyses. The following are commonly used nonparametric correlational techniques because most are actually derived from the Pearson Product-Moment Correlation Coefficient.

Spearman's Rho is a correlation coefficient appropriate when the data being correlated are ranks (i.e., ordinal data).

A **Point Biserial Correlation** is appropriate when one of the variables is continuous and the other is dichotomous.

A **Bisterial Correlation** is appropriate when both variables are actually continuous, but one is being treated as a dichotomous variable.

A **Tetrachoric Correlation** is appropriate when both variables are actually continuous but both are being treated as dichotomous.

A **Phi Coefficient** is appropriate when both variables are actually dichotomous.

A **Coefficient of Contingency** is appropriate when one or both of the (nominal) variables has three or more categories.

The following are commonly used nonparametric tests of differences.

The **Median Test** is appropriate to use to test the significance of difference between the medians of two independent samples.

A **Sign Test** is appropriate to use to test the significance of difference between two or more sets of paired observations (i.e., measurements).

The **Wilcoxon Rank Sum Test** is appropriate to use to test the significance of difference when the data from two independent samples can be assigned ranks.

The **Mann-Whitney U Test** is essentially the same as the Wilcoxon Rank Sum Test, but is often used with smaller samples.

The **Kruskal-Wallis** is essentially a one-way analysis of variance appropriate to use to test the significance of difference among three or more sets of ranks.

The **Chi Square Test**, which is the most commonly used nonparametric statistic, is a test of the magnitude of discrepancy between observed (i.e., measured) and expected distribution frequencies. The Chi

Square Test is used either as a **"goodness of fit"** test or as a **test of independence**. The Chi Square goodness of fit test is usually used to test the degree of independence between observed and (theoretically) expected frequencies for a single variable. The Chi Square Test as a test of independence is used to test the degree of independence between the observed and expected frequencies for two variables.

Because the distributions to which the various nonparametric statistics are applied vary considerably, methods to evaluate the statistical significance of the various statistics generated are unique to the respective techniques. However, similar to most parametric statistics, the resultant nonparametric statistical value is evaluated against its probability as a chance occurrence.

☐ Needs Assessment and Program Evaluation

In the vast majority of cases, counseling services are provided within a counseling program. In other words, for other than perhaps private practice situations, professional counselors provide counseling services in the context of a broader counseling service delivery program. Therefore, a fundamental question in the counseling professions is, "How can we integrate good needs assessment and program evaluation practices to yield an effective and comprehensive understanding of a service delivery system?" Any response falls under the general rubric of program evaluation, which may be defined as the collection of information about a counseling program so as to be able to evaluate its quality and make decisions about how it can be improved (Loesch, in press).

There are many program evaluation models that can be used for counseling program evaluation. However, one of the more widely recognized approaches is Stufflebeam's **CIPP** model, in which CIPP is an acronym for:

Context evaluation,
Input evaluation,
Process evaluation, and
Product evaluation.

Within the CIPP model, context evaluation is essentially equal to needs assessment. A needs assessment is a way of determining what the potential counseling service clientele want from the program (i.e., what services are desired and what delivery modes are preferred). An effective context evaluation (needs assessment) necessitates clear specification of potential service recipients, involves gathering data directly from potential service recipients, and should point to program goals and objectives.

Primary context evaluation methods include use of surveys or interviews or both. Effective context evaluation provides answers to questions such as:

What is the diversity of the needs expressed among the potential service recipients?

What are the priorities among the various categories of needs expressed?

Do the needs expressed reflect current or future circumstances?

Which of the expressed needs are in concert with program activities?

The input evaluation component of the CIPP model is intended to identify both available resources and constraints for a service delivery program. Input evaluation follows directly from a context evaluation (i.e., needs assessment) and should yield the parameters within which the program can and should be conducted. Effective input evaluation will provide answers to questions such as:

What is the environment (i.e., physical space and material resources) available for the program?

What are the fiscal resources available for the program?

What are the human or personnel resources available for the program?

What rules (and/or entities) govern the conduct of the program?

Together, the results of context and input evaluations determine the nature of the accountability for the program and for the program participants. That is, they allow determination of who will be accountable to whom, how, and for what.

Process evaluation, in the CIPP model, is concerned with the effectiveness of the day-to-day operation of the program. Process evaluation is often used interchangeably with the term "formative" evaluation. It provides data upon which to base service delivery program decisions while the program is in operation. Effective process evaluation will provide answers to questions such as:

What is the efficiency level of the service delivery program?

What factors influence the expenditure of funds within the service delivery program?

How efficient is the service delivery program?

How efficient is the service delivery program schedule?

What factors influence decision-making processes in the service delivery program?

The last component of the CIPP model is product evaluation, which is intended to allow determination of the actual outcomes of the service delivery program. Product evaluation is often used interchangeably with the term "summative" evaluation. For most counseling programs, product evaluation is considered the bottom line in accountability processes. That is, because it is focused on final outcomes, it gives indication of the ultimate results of the program activities. Effective product evaluation provides answers to questions such as:

To what extent are the service delivery program's goals and objectives being met?

What are the service delivery program's impacts in terms of identifiable changes?

What is the service delivery program's cost-benefit ratio?

What are the "lost opportunity" costs attributable to intraprogram changes?

The CIPP model and accountability are integrally linked because any service delivery program should be held accountable for what it is attempting to accomplish (content evaluation), what resources it uses (input evaluation), how resources are used (process evaluation), and what happens as a result of the program (product evaluation).

The CIPP model is only one program evaluation approach among many that could be used effectively for counseling program evaluation purposes (Houser, 1998; Loesch, in press). However, it is the most frequently cited in the professional counseling literature (Hadley & Mitchell, 1995). Presumably, one of the reasons for the apparent popularity of the CIPP model in the counseling profession is that it allows a variety of data collection techniques to be used within its general framework. In this regard, three techniques are receiving attention recently: the focus group interview, the nominal group technique, and the Delphi technique.

A **focus group interview** (FGI) is an information-gathering technique used to determine group members' perceptions and feelings about a topic, such as a counseling program. The FGI is not designed to facilitate decision making. Rather, the FGI is usually used to develop ideas for subsequent, more systematic data collection, to identify potential problems, or to provide understandings of program functioning.

Focus groups (e.g., persons who had received services from a counseling program) are helpful in providing feedback and reactions quickly, and at relatively little cost. They also allow more complex and complete responses to questions and concerns as each participant keys off the comments of others. The short-coming of the FGI is that the information obtained is complex owing to the open-ended questions asked.

In contrast to the focus group interview, the **nominal group technique** (NGT) is intended to facilitate decision making. The word nominal here refers to the fact that the participants are a group in name only; the participants usually are disparate in regard to personal characteristics and situations, their association with the program being evaluated, and their vested interest in the results. In the NGT, each person's input is as valuable as any other's, which allows for considerable diversity among opinions expressed. The NGT is usually used to address a single question, although the question often is broad in form to allow diverse responses. The result of use of a NGT process is a prioritized list of suggested changes and improvements. The disadvantage of the NGT is that some responses may lack quality or relevance.

The **Delphi technique** is also used to facilitate group decision making. It can be used to identify program problem areas or to set goals and objectives. Typically, the Delphi technique involves three rounds of contact with respondents. In the first round, respondents evaluate a broad and comprehensive list of items, often generated by various persons associated with the counseling program. For the second round, the list is reduced by systematic application of some criterion indicative of greater agreement (e.g., eliminating items having response standard deviations above some value) and then redistributed to the same evaluators. The process is repeated for a third and final round. The results of the third round are usually considered the final consensus among the group of respondents.

The Delphi technique is most appropriate when respondents otherwise would be unlikely to have opportunity to be able to provide input. Electronic communication capabilities have greatly increased use of the Delphi technique. Thus, an advantage of the Delphi technique is that it allows participants to respond at times when they can focus their attention fully on the task. Another is that it avoids problems attributable to social desirability in responding. However, the implementation time period may be long if traditional mailing methods are used.

It is likely that one of the major reasons that professional counselors rarely engage in program evaluation activities is that they (erroneously) consider program evaluation as synonymous with accountability. However, they are not the same thing. Gredler (1996) clarified the distinction succinctly:

> The major difference between [counseling program] evaluation and accountability is that the purpose of accountability systems typically is to assign responsibility for outcomes among a program's operators. Accountability is thus a measure of control. This perspective is a restricted view of the reasons for program success or failure. (p. 15)

No wonder counselors avoid accountability! Nonetheless, accountability is a commonly featured topic in the professional counseling literature, so much so that seven types of accountability have been identified.

Service delivery accountability addresses the question, "To what extent does the program deliver the services it promises to deliver?"

Ethical accountability addresses the question, "To what extent are services delivered within the parameters of acceptable ethical practice?"

Legal accountability addresses the question, "To what extent are services delivered within the parameters of legal constraints?"

Coverage accountability addresses the question, "To what extent does the service delivery program serve all of the people it purports to serve?"

Efficiency accountability addresses the question, "To what extent is time used efficiently in delivery of the service program?"

Fiscal accountability addresses the question, "To what extent are available fiscal resources used in a manner which maximizes the likelihood of positive program outcomes?"

Impact accountability addresses the question, "To what extent does the service delivery program actually make positive changes in peoples' lives?"

Just as program evaluation and accountability are not synonymous, neither is research synonymous with either of these terms. However, they are related in that program evaluation and accountability activities often use some of the same techniques that are used in research, have the same or similar ethical standards, and yield results that can be of benefit to individuals as well as the counseling profession. Thus, research knowledge and skills are as essential for program evaluation and accountability activities as they are for specific research activities.

☐ A Concluding Opinion

Although professional counselors often apply scientific inquiry as the basis for helping others (vis-à-vis the practitioner-scientist perspective), typically they have done little to integrate science into counseling through traditional research. It is likely that there are several reasons for this situation. However, the major problem appears to be that using traditional research techniques that emphasize data collection using relatively large groups of subjects and analyses based on aggregate group data poses immense practical difficulties for practicing counselors. Thus, they either use other methodologies, or more likely, avoid doing research altogether.

The conduct of traditional research in applied (counseling) settings requires, among other things, access to a large number of relatively homogeneous clients in a relatively short period of time. Consider for example a professional counselor who is interested in studying the effectiveness of two treatment approaches for adolescents who are concerned about substance use behavior. Using a traditional approach, the counselor would need approximately 30 clients matched on relevant background variables (e.g., age, gender, severity of problem, and history of previous treatment) who ideally would need to receive counseling within approximately the same time period. This in itself would be a daunting task considering the type of clients and the time allocation required. However, using even a simple experimental design of a treatment group and no-treatment control group format to examine effects due to treatment would impose nearly impossible demands on the counselor. Of course, this illustration has been deliberately oversimplified. However, it does demonstrate the problems encountered in conducting research using a traditional experimental design in an applied setting.

Another possible effect upon the professional counselor's use of traditional research methodology has to do with the ethical issues and considerations involved in establishing control groups by withholding treatment from clients. This, of course, should not be done without careful consideration of the risks involved for the untreated group. An interesting argument on this subject, advanced by Barlow, Hayes, and Nelson (1984), is that

> [I]n most instances there is no evidence that the treatment works in the first place, which forms the basis for conducting research on its effectiveness. Therefore, one could argue that withholding an unproven treatment for a control group might be less of a risk than applying this treatment to the experimental group. (p. 26)

Traditional research methodology of working with large groups and determining average results, with associated general disregard for individual applications, has limited relevance in contributing to improvements for specific clients. Therefore, traditional research methodology has had little influence in affecting the professional counselor's practice or self-evaluation.

An alternative is to use single-subject designs for measuring and demonstrating the effect(s) of counseling. This type of design adapts the traditional experimental research approach to fit the practice of counseling. Single-subject methods can be generalized across settings and situations because the techniques can vary depending on the particular circumstances and goals of each client. Also, the methods are not dependent upon any particular theoretical orientation, but rather reflect a way of thinking. The basic elements of single-subject research consist of measuring change, relating this change to a particular aspect of counseling, and basing future professional actions on the observations. Thus, single-subject research methodologies can serve professional counselors well in their responsibility to conduct research.

Are we suggesting that single-subject research is more important and necessarily better than traditional research? Certainly not. What we are suggesting is that single-subject methods have been underutilized and undervalued in the counseling profession, despite the fact that they have strong potential to be a pragmatic means by which counselors can integrate research into their professional practices effectively and efficiently. Thus, single-subject methodologies can serve counselors quite well. However, we also suggest that professional counselors engage in more traditional research because such methodologies typically yield results that have greater generalizability for the counseling profession. The most effective professional counselors do both types of research.

It should be emphasized that regardless of the type of research conducted, professional counselors must be careful about how they integrate research activities into their professional practices. In particular, professional counselors who do research at their work places must not give their clients or others the impression that research is more important than the direct practice of helping. Otherwise, clients and other personnel can easily perceive themselves as mere subjects in some type of laboratory experiment being directed by the counselor. Professional counselors avoid these problems by carefully explaining the value of the research activity and how it may help the client and others in return.

Professional counselors of course should devote most of their time to direct-service counseling activities. However, research also is an appropriate and important part of good professional practice for counselors. Effective research is required if professional counselors are to be able to evaluate counseling effectively, determine which human factors are important in the counseling profession and how, examine the counseling profession (as well as preparation for it) objectively and systematically, and have a substantive basis upon which to build future improvements in the profession. Thus, research is one of the essential roles that truly professional counselors fulfill effectively.

Evolution of the Counseling Profession

It would be nice to relate that the counseling profession has a long and storied history. Alas, such is not the case. In fact, developments that have had the most significance in regard to enhancing the competence of professional counselors in general and extending the recognition and acceptance of counseling as a true profession have occurred within approximately the last two decades. Nonetheless, some understanding of the history of the counseling profession is necessary if its current status and future are to be understood effectively. The question is, how can the history of an entire profession be explained? One possibility, and the one of choice here, is to review the history of an organization that has long served as a representative of a profession. In the current context, the American Counseling Association (ACA), formerly known as the American Association for Counseling and Development (AACD) prior to 1992, and known even earlier as the American Personnel and Guidance Association (APGA) prior to 1983, is such an organization.

Counseling professionals who view themselves solely as therapists might suggest that the history of the counseling profession dates at least to Sigmund Freud and probably farther back to the earliest psychological healers. However, that view is parochial and inconsistent with the perspective of the counseling profession taken here. More typically, the history of the counseling profession traces its beginnings to approximately the turn of the twentieth century. That was when education professionals began to realize that young people in society needed help in making effective vocational decisions. The visionary efforts of professionals such as Frank Parsons and Mrs. Quincy Adams Shaw were particularly notable. In 1909, Parsons wrote *Choosing a Vocation*, which is generally considered the first counseling text. More importantly, about that time these individuals and their colleagues began a series of significant activities designed to enable teachers to help students with vocational planning and decision making. The significance was twofold. First, their activities marked the first attempt at formally providing psychologically-based services for normal people (i.e., the use of psychological services for persons without severe mental illness). Second, through the Vocational Bureau of Boston, they sought to train a new professional with the title counselor (Jones, 1994). Thus, they associated the title counselor with the provision of helping or counseling services for people who were not suffering from serious psychological disturbance.

As interest and activities in vocational counseling grew during the early 1900s, those involved soon recognized that a national organization would be beneficial for sharing a common professional interest. Therefore, the National Vocational Guidance Association (NVGA) was formed in 1913, primarily as a result of the efforts of Jesse B. Davis who served as the first NVGA secretary. NVGA retained its original name until 1985 when it became the National Career Development Association (NCDA).

Other professionals did not lag far behind those interested in vocational counseling in deciding that normal people had needs other than for educational or psychotherapeutic assistance. For example, the needs of students on college and university campuses, and those of the professionals who addressed college students' needs, were recognized in the second decade of the twentieth century. Female university administrators were the first to organize to be more responsive to college students' needs. Thus, the National Association of Deans of Women (NADW) was formed in 1913. Then, the National Association of Student Personnel Administrators (NASPA) was formed in 1916. Soon after, college and university placement officers, then called appointment secretaries, determined that their particular professional needs and interests were not being met fully by NVGA and that their work represented a broader professional perspective than that reflected in either NADW or NASPA (Johnson, 1985). Therefore, they established the National Association of Appointment Secretaries (NAAS) in 1924. NAAS continued to broaden its professional scope, and eventually evolved into the National Association of Placement and Personnel Officers (NAPPO) in 1929, and then to the American College Personnel Association (ACPA) in 1931. In the late 1980s, the duality of ACPA's interests (i.e., student personnel/development administration and counseling) prompted division within the organization. Thus, the American College Counseling Association (ACCA) was formed in 1992 for those specifically interested in counseling activities for college students (Dean & Meadows, 1995).

The early historical association between counseling and education also has been reflected in other ways. For example, the Teachers College Personnel Association (TCPA) was established in 1931, with the intent of focusing on testing and research activities. This focus, however, was not unanimously agreed upon within the organization and TCPA existed both as a separate organization and as an affiliate division of the American Association for Colleges of Teacher Education (AACTE) during its first 20 years. In 1951, TCPA changed its name to the Student Personnel Association for Teacher Education (SPATE). One year later it separated from AACTE. In 1974, SPATE restructured its professional perspective and became the Association for Humanistic Education and Development (AHEAD) (Sheeley, 1992).

The value and importance of effective counselor preparation and supervision also has been evident throughout the history of the counseling profession. This importance was first formally recognized with the founding of the National Association of Guidance Supervisors (NAGS) in 1940. Although NAGS was originally composed exclusively of counselor supervisors, it soon attracted counselor trainers (now commonly referred to as counselor educators). Thus, in 1952 the name was changed to the National Association of Guidance Supervisors and Counselor Trainers (NAGSCT). Nine years later, NAGSCT changed its name to the Association for Counselor Education and Supervision (ACES).

"Strength through unity" was a common theme in the United States in the early 1950s and this theme was reflected in the relationships among the various organizations with interests in the counseling professions. Thus, NVGA (now NCDA), ACPA (now ACCA), NAGSCT (now ACES), and SPATE (now AHEAD) joined together in 1952 to form the American Personnel and Guidance Association (next AACD and now ACA). Herr (1985) aptly summarized the nature of this founding:

> The intent of these four associations was to create a unified structure that would have the collective strength to pursue goals impossible to achieve for smaller, special interest groups, as were the founding divisions at the time.
>
> In creating the confederation known as the American Personnel and Guidance Association, however, it was apparent that the founders were not ready to completely surrender the autonomy of their individual associations. . . . They sought common cause within the larger association umbrella, but did so with an intent to retain the capability to advance the special interests of their divisions. (p. 396)

The common bond but individual identity theme remained evident as APGA (AACD; ACA) grew in terms of both members and divisions.

Vocational guidance continued as the major focus of counseling services in American schools for approximately four decades prior to World War II. However, the post World War II era fostered an awareness that traditional vocational counseling services were not the most appropriate for a growing segment of the school population: students planning to attend college. During the late 1940s, therefore, a large number of school counselors turned their attention to college-bound students. This schism in the professional focus of counselors working in schools prompted the need for a professional organization better suited to counselors who were less oriented toward vocational counseling in schools (Paisley & Borders, 1995). The result was the formation in 1953 of the fifth APGA (ACA) division, the American School Counselor Association (ASCA) (Minkoff & Terres, 1985). ASCA soon became the ACA division having the largest membership. However, it is unknown as to whether that status remains true today because ASCA now accepts members who need not belong to ACA.

Recognition of the counseling needs of persons with disabilities also increased in the post World War II era and incited the passage of the (Federal) Vocational Rehabilitation Act (VRA) in 1954. The VRA not only symbolized the importance of the needs of persons with disabilities, it also provided funds for training counselors to assist with those needs. At about the same time, a growing number of members within APGA (ACA) were becoming involved in rehabilitation counseling activities. These factors melded together during the early 1950s and led to the formation of the Division of Rehabilitation (DRC) within APGA (ACA) in 1958. In 1962, the DRC became the American Rehabilitation Counseling Association (ARCA) (DiMichael & Thomas, 1985).

Although what might be referred to as a "subliminal affection for empiricism" had long been present in the APGA (ACA) membership, it did not fully emerge until the mid-1960s. A number of professionals, most of whom were already APGA (ACA) members, then moved to form a division specifically for professionals with interests in measurement and evaluation. Their efforts resulted in the 1965 origination of the Association for Measurement and Evaluation in Guidance (AMEG), the seventh APGA (ACA) division. However, formal incorporation of this division did not occur until 1968 (Thompson, 1992). In 1984 AMEG changed its name to the Association for Measurement and Evaluation in Counseling and Development (AMECD) to be consistent with the name change of the parent organization. In 1992, AMECD changed its name to the Association for Assessment in Counseling (AAC) to reflect more accurately its place in the counseling profession.

The recurrent vocational counseling emphasis in APGA (ACA) reemerged with a new focus in 1966 with the formation of the National Employment Counselors Association (NECA). The new focus was on employment counseling as a specialty area within the more general field of vocational counseling. Similar to AAC (AMEG; AMECD), most of the original members of NECA were already members of other existing APGA (ACA) divisions (Meyer, Helwig, Gjernes, & Chickering, 1985). In 1992, the organizational name was changed slightly to the National Employment Counseling Association (NECA) to be consistent with the name change of the parent organization (i.e., ACA).

The late 1960s and the early 1970s were times of social consciousness raising in the American society and APGA (ACA) was not untouched by this movement. A large number of professionals within the association believed a need existed to recognize specifically the needs and talents of ethnic minority persons. However, opinions differed considerably about how the recognition should be manifested within a professional organization. Eventually, in 1972, the disparate ideas came together in the formation of the Association for Non-White Concerns in Personnel and Guidance (ANWC) (McFadden & Lipscomb, 1985). ANWC changed its name in 1985 to the Association for Multicultural Counseling and Development (AMCD) in order to reflect more accurately the prevalent orientation in APGA (ACA) and to create a more positive representation for AMCD (Parker & Myers, 1991).

Although the Association for Spiritual, Ethical, and Religious Values in Counseling (ASERVIC) traces its history in APGA (ACA) to 1973, the seminal activities for the division began in 1951 with the formation of the Catholic Guidance Council in the Archdiocese of New York (Bartlett, Lee, & Doyle, 1985). That beginning led to the 1961 formation of the National Catholic Guidance Conference (NCGC) by members of APGA (ACA). The evolution from National Catholic Guidance Conference (NCGC) to the Association for Religious Values in Counseling (ARVIC) reflected change in the nature and purposes of the division. The division made another name change in 1993 to the Association for Spiritual, Ethical, and Religious Values in Counseling (ASERVIC) to extend the mission of the organization. More recently, the name was changed to the Association for Spiritual, Religious, and Ethical Value Issues in Counseling (ASREVIC) to clarify further the focus and mission of the organization.

Throughout most of the early history of the counseling profession, the emphasis was on one-to-one counseling interaction between the counselor and client. However, maturation of the profession brought with it a realization that group counseling and other professional work with groups is not only effective but also economical and efficient. This realization prompted APGA (ACA) professionals who were interested in all facets of group dynamics and processes (including counseling) to form the Association for Specialists in Group Work (ASGW). It became an APGA (ACA) division in 1973 (Carroll & Levo, 1985).

A unique example of the counseling profession's responsiveness to the multifaceted needs of society is found in the Public Offender Counselors Association (POCA), which officially became an APGA (ACA) division in 1974. POCA was created to be responsive to the specific professional needs and interests of counselors who work with public offenders (Page, 1985). In the 1980s, interest grew among POCA members to broaden its focus and purposes, and therefore POCA became the International Association of Addictions and Offenders Counselors (IAAOC) in 1990.

The rapid growth of the American Mental Health Counselors Association (AMHCA), which officially became an APGA (ACA) division in 1978, perhaps knows no equal in the history of professional organizations. From its beginnings in 1976, AMHCA expanded exceptionally rapidly in the early 1980s, at one point having the largest divisional membership in ACA (Smith & Robinson, 1995; Weikel, 1985). Similar to ASCA, however, the current membership rank of AMHCA is unknown because of changes in ACA membership requirements. AMHCA's growth reflected the fact that a considerable number of professional counselors now work in other than educational settings.

The Military Educators and Counselors Association (MECA) was formed first as an organizational affiliate of ACA in 1984. MECA was created to be responsive to the professional needs and interests of counselors who work with military service personnel and veterans, their dependents, and civilian employees of the military services (Cox, 1985). In 1994, MECA was renamed the Association for Counselors and Educators in Government to include the needs of all employees of the government.

The graying of America was, and is, a phenomenon that substantially impacted professional counselors as they increasingly worked with older persons (Myers, 1995). Greater attention to the counseling needs of and services for older persons was accompanied by recognition of the need to attend to the circumstances and needs of adults of all ages. Thus, the Association for Adult Development and Aging (AADA) was formed as an AACD (ACA) division in 1986 and is comprised of members who have as their primary professional interest counseling persons at all stages of adult development. However, the greatest emphases are given to midlife, preretirement, and gerontological counseling specializations.

Concerns about the demise of the traditional American family have been voiced for several decades, and those concerns have not gone unnoticed by professional counselors. Commencing in the early 1980s, provision of marriage and family counseling services has become a major movement in the counseling profession. This professional movement became formalized within AACD (ACA) in 1989 with the formation of the International Association of Marriage and Family Counselors (IAMFC) (Smith, Carlson, Stevens-Smith, & Dennison, 1995). While professional counselors in this group focus on the nuclear family, their interests and counseling services extend to marital and sibling problems, family subsystems, external societal influences affecting family systems, and other circumstances that may cause difficulties for and within families.

In response to the growing interest in gay, lesbian, bisexual, and transgender issues, ACA's newest division, the Association for Gay, Lesbian, and Bisexual Issues in Counseling (AGLBIC) was formed in 1997 (Association for Gay, Lesbian, and Bisexual Issues in Counseling, 1999). The goal of this division is to provide education regarding sexual orientation and gender identity that will enable counselors to help their clients develop effectively regardless of lifestyle orientation. In addition, AGLBIC advocates for a nonthreatening counseling atmosphere by advocating for reduced intolerance among counselors.

In 1983, APGA changed its name to the American Association for Counseling and Development (AACD). The change was symbolic of the evolving professional orientation among AACD (ACA) members, and indeed within the counseling profession. As Herr (1985) stated:

> [T]he overriding issue was that the term guidance was essentially used only in elementary and secondary school settings and was becoming an archaic and vague term even there. Although such a perception of the term guidance is questionable, the primary argument for the name change was that association members were increasingly being found in settings other than education and that what these persons did was *counseling*, not *guidance*. (p. 395)

However, the desire for clarity of professional definition did not end in 1983. Members of ACPA involved with student personnel/development administration activities became increasingly disenchanted with the counseling emphasis in AACD in the 1980s, and moved to withdraw from the parent organization in the late 1980s. Consequently, the withdrawal of ACPA from AACD, the formation of ACCA, and change of name from AACD to the American Counseling Association (ACA) became official in July, 1992. Dr. Ted Remley, ACA Executive Director in 1992, hailed the name change in stating:

> This is significant, particularly as it relates to the public outside of the profession. The new name is easy to remember and more narrowly focused and descriptive of what our members do. It also more clearly defines which profession the association represents. (quoted in Sacks, 1992, p. 10)

The evolving history of APGA to AACD to ACA thus exemplifies the broadening scope of the counseling profession as well as the continuing quest among professional counselors for distinct identity within the helping professions. In 1999, ACA membership exceeded 51,000, which is a small decrease over recent years. However, this change in membership may be due in part to ACA's recent by-laws amendment allowing for members to join ACA without joining a division, and vice versa for some ACA divisions, cases. Literally every facet of the counseling profession and all types of professional counselors are represented within it. The following list of the 1999 ACA divisions is ordered by original organizational founding date.

1952 Association for Humanistic Education and Development (AHEAD)

1953 American College Counseling Association (ACCA)

1953 Association for Counselor Education and Supervision (ACES)

1953 National Career Development Association (NCDA)

1953 American School Counselor Association (ASCA)

1958 American Rehabilitation Counseling Association (ARCA)

1965 Association for Assessment in Counseling (AAC)

1966 National Employment Counseling Association (NECA)

1972 Association for Multicultural Counseling and Development (AMCD)

1974 Association for Spiritual, Religious, and Ethical Value Issues in Counseling (ASREVIC)

1974 Association for Specialists in Group Work (ASGW)

1974 International Association for Addictions and Offender Counselors (IAAOC)

1978 American Mental Health Counselors Association (AMHCA)

1984 Association for Counselors and Educators in Government (ACEG)

1986 Association for Adult Development and Aging (AADA)

1989 International Association of Marriage and Family Counselors (IAMFC)

1997 Association for Gay, Lesbian, and Bisexual Issues in Counseling (AGLBIC)

☐ Lessons from History

Clearly the history of ACA is not a complete history of the counseling profession. Nonetheless, as a professional organization whose members are counseling professionals, its history reflects the issues and trends within the counseling profession. Therefore, a number of inferences about the counseling profession can be drawn from the history of ACA. As Oliver Wendell Holmes, Jr. noted, "A page of history is worth a volume of logic."

Lesson 1. Professional counselors are identifiable and unique

Unfortunately for professionals who refer to themselves as counselors, the title counselor has been used in a wide variety of contexts in the

American society. The media are replete with references to legal counselors, real estate counselors, financial counselors, travel counselors, and the like. Overexposure to the title counselor has served to desensitize the public to the title in general and to its application to a type of mental health professional in particular. However, regardless of the overuse of the title, a group of professionals exists who may be accurately and validly referred to as counselors.

Application of this title is more than self-anointment by those who refer to themselves as counselors. In 1999, at least 45 states have licensure (or similar credential) laws for professional counselors (or corresponding titles that include the word counselor), and in all states and the District of Columbia, school counseling is regulated by state-level departments of education (American Counseling Association, 1999). Thus, the use of the title counselor to refer to a particular type of mental health professional is, and continues to be, grounded in law. Relatedly, although this specific use of the term counselor has not yet become fully understood by the general public in the same way as it is in the counseling profession, such understanding is rapidly increasing.

Professional counselors are also uniquely identifiable within the counseling profession. Of course, there are a variety of different types of professionals who do counseling (e.g., clinical and counseling psychologists, clinical social workers, psychoanalysts, marriage and family therapists, and psychiatrists). However, professional counselors are not mini-psychologists, closet psychoanalysts, imitation social workers, or pseudo-shrinks. Nor are they people who only give advice, tell students what courses to take, or tell people which jobs to pursue. They are, simply, professionals whose primary vocational activity is the provision of counseling and closely related mental health services.

Lesson 2. Counseling professionals may be differentiated in a variety of ways

Why is differentiation necessary or appropriate? An effective answer must encompass two components, one theoretical and one pragmatic. With regard to the former, there are those in the counseling profession who have alleged that "counseling is counseling is counseling" regardless of the natures of the persons receiving the counseling services, persons providing the services, locations of services, and how or with which set of techniques the services are being provided. Unfortunately, this perspective belies the complexities of people in society and in the counseling profession, as well as the widely varying places and circumstances in which counseling services are rendered. In an age of specialization, the needs for and benefits of specialization within the counseling profession are readily evident. To suggest that counseling is an activity that is applicable regardless of clientele, location, or type of service provider is to deny the effectiveness gained from years of research and development of specialized counseling activities.

With regard to the second component, the simple fact of the matter is that counseling professionals work in relatively easily differentiated settings (e.g., educational systems or institutions, private practice, business and industry, or community agencies) and with relatively easily differentiated clients (e.g., students, persons with disabilities, or couples and families). It follows, then, that professional counselors can maximize their effectiveness by developing specialized skills specifically applicable in the settings in which they work and to the clients with whom they work. Thus, to differentiate among counseling professionals is prudent for both the public and counseling professionals because it facilitates effectiveness and efficiency in counseling service delivery.

There are several ways to differentiate. One is on the basis of title, as alluded to in Chapter 1. Others include on the basis of type of setting in which counseling services are provided, type of counseling service provided, or type of primary professional interests and activities. By relating this to the ACA history presented previously, it can be noted that the various ACA divisions also may be clustered along three dimensions. For example, ASCA and ACCA clearly relate to particular settings. Similarly, ARCA, NCDA, NECA, ASGW, IAAOC, AMHCA, ACEG, IAMFC, and AGLBIC relate to types of counseling service, while ACES, AHEAD, AMECD, AMCD, and ASREVIC relate to primary professional interests and activities.

Unfortunately, neither these differentiations nor the ACA divisional titles listed are sufficient to differentiate completely among counseling professionals because complete differentiation actually is not possible. For example, school counselors quite obviously engage in and are concerned with vocational counseling and working with people of varying ethnicities. Similarly, other professional counselors are involved with and concerned about matters and activities beyond their primary professional activities. Thus, professional counselors tend to be multifaceted in terms of professional concerns and involvements. Nonetheless, to differentiate among them often is expedient for purposes of communication clarity.

Lesson 3. Professional counselors fulfill societal needs not fulfilled by other professionals

One example of the validity of this statement is reflected in the membership of POCA (now IAAOC). Page (1985) stated that, "POCA is unique because it emphasizes the importance of providing counseling services to public offenders. . . . Other professional associations such as the American Correctional Association place emphasis on correctional concerns rather than on rehabilitation concerns" (p. 455). Other examples are also readily available. School counselors, as represented by ASCA, are the primary (and in many cases the only) providers of mental health services to students in schools (e.g., Keys, Bemak, & Lockhart, 1998). And finally, rehabilitation counselors, as represented by ARCA, are the primary providers of counseling services to persons with disabilities.

Lesson 4. Professional counselors fulfill societal needs also being fulfilled by other professionals

The provision of many counseling services is not restricted to professional counselors. For example, marriage and family counseling services are provided by marriage and family counselors, as represented by IAMFC, but are also provided by professionals such as social workers, counseling and clinical psychologists, mental health counselors, and marriage and family therapists (Goldenberg & Goldenberg, 1996). Similarly, ACCA members provide counseling services to college and university students, but so do other professionals such as counseling and clinical psychologists, and psychiatrists. Thus, many of the professional activities performed by professional counselors are also offered by other professionals (as was illustrated with the case of Keith presented in Chapter 1). This overlap helps to associate and involve counselors with other professional specializations and allows them to benefit from the knowledge gained from the work experiences and research of other professionals.

Lesson 5. The counseling profession reflects needs and trends in society

The beginning of the counseling profession, vis-à-vis the earliest vocational counseling activities, is testimony to this lesson. The counseling profession literally came into existence because of societal needs which were not being met in other ways. If young people had not had a need for assistance with vocational concerns, or if such a need had been fulfilled through other means, Parsons and others would not have found it necessary to act as they did to begin the counseling profession.

Current examples also are obvious. The formation and rapid growth of both AMHCA and IAMFC reflect the widespread and dramatically increasing need for mental health and for marriage and family counseling services for (other than seriously disturbed) people in society. Problems such as those relating to interpersonal and family relations, stress management, life style management and development, and vocational and personal adjustments are common to normal people. Counselors help people with the various manifestations of these problems and professional concern about these problems is reflected in the professional activities of counselors and their professional organizations.

The counseling profession's efforts to meet the needs of society also are reflected in the many new settings and situations in which counselors now work. For example, there has been tremendous growth in the numbers of counselors working in private practice, business and industry settings, residential facilities (e.g., for youth or for older persons), abused person shelters, medical facilities, and various other places where, historically, counselors have not worked. Perhaps most importantly, because of the counseling profession's responsiveness to the needs of society, the expansion of the number of settings and situations in which counselors work continues to increase.

Lesson 6. The counseling profession sometimes seems to act in opposition to trends in society

Concerns about the rights and responsibilities of and respect for individuals have a long history in the American society. However, in the so-called modern era, these concerns were most evident in society during the 1960s and early 1970s. In general, those were times in which attention was given to individuality as the essence of the human condition. Relatedly, they were times when empiricism, as applied to human characteristics, traits, and behaviors, was decried in society at large. However, during the same times, there was a resurgence of interest in empiricism in the counseling profession. This phenomenon was reflected in the formation of ACC (AMEG) in the mid-1960s. Another fact to be considered is that AAC had its largest membership during the late 1960s and early 1970s, but as society's emphasis on individuality ebbed, so did AAC's membership.

This situation was not the paradox it seemed to be; rather, it was an example of a professional response to current conditions in society. As society harkened to individuality, counseling professionals sought to understand better both individuals and individuals within society. The counseling profession sought to gain this understanding through application of proven scientific methods. Such methods incorporate, and indeed emphasize, empiricism. Therefore, although the counseling profession appeared to be antithetical to the trend in society, it was in fact attempting to be effectively responsive to that trend. Those activities in turn lead to development of many empirical methods and resources for understanding individuals. As those methods and resources became available and

common, ostensible interest in empiricism among counseling professionals waned.

Lesson 7. The counseling profession has a flirtatious relationship with empiricism

Throughout its history, the counseling profession has wavered between
being enamored with empiricism (vis-à-vis rigorous psychodiagnosis,
assessment, research, and evaluation) and being disenchanted with empiricism (vis-à-vis almost totally unstructured approaches to counseling).
The history of AHEAD (formerly TCPA and SPATE) is a classic example.
Originally conceived as an organization dedicated to research and evaluation, it evolved into an organization for counselors primarily interested
in humanistic perspectives. Humanism and empiricism are certainly not
totally separate, but just as certainly empiricism is not a major focus within
humanistic perspectives.

Other evidence of the fluctuating relationship between the counseling
profession and empiricism can be found through a review of the contents
of professional counseling journals. For example, the contents of ACA's
Journal of Counseling and Development (the *Personnel and Guidance Journal*
prior to 1983) show that the journal, at times, was almost completely
devoted to research but at other times almost totally devoid of research.

In more recent times, the counseling profession has sought a balanced
relationship with empiricism. On one hand, the counseling profession
has acknowledged the need for and benefits of empiricism, an acknowledgment reflected, for example, in professional preparation and ethical
standards adopted within the profession. On the other hand, the counseling profession has not mandated that empirical perspectives be adopted
within the profession and indeed has gone to some lengths to ensure that
it is not considered mandatory (as reflected in the professional preparation and ethical standards). In general, the counseling profession seems
to have taken the position that empiricism is important, but only within
limited contexts.

☐ The Counseling Profession Today

A rapidly growing understanding of, and demand for, positive mental
health is evident in the American society in a number of ways. For example, self-help mental health books are setting sales records, businesses
and industries are allocating substantial fiscal and physical resources to
employee well-being and efficacy, communities are acting to alleviate

various types of physical and mental abuse, prominent campaigns have been launched against drug and alcohol abuse, and wellness activities are being sought by millions of people. Collectively, these and other activities similar to them signify society's realization that positive mental health is desirable, and more importantly, achievable. And positive mental health is supposed to be the result of effective delivery of counseling services.

☐ Counseling and Mental Health

Society's concern with mental health is reflected in the counseling profession; reciprocal impacts exist between the parallel mental health movements in society and in the counseling profession. For example, these movements have fostered the realization that in order for positive mental health to be achieved, it must be present within, across, and throughout people's lives. That is, both people in society and professional counselors have come to understand that positive mental health cannot be attained in one aspect of life without being achieved in other aspects of life as well, and also that positive mental health should be achieved at all age levels. This realization has in turn created demand for counseling services that relate to many different facets of people's lives. The direct effect on the counseling profession has been a greatly increased need for more, and more diverse, professional counseling services, and relatedly for professional counselors.

The counseling profession has impacted the positive mental health movement in society by literally providing more services than are sought. Many counseling services are provided simply to help people with existing problems, the typical view of the purpose of counseling. The counseling profession, however, takes a much broader purview of the situation and seeks to foster and promote positive mental health in a number of other important ways. For example, professional counselors engage in many developmental and preventive activities intended to help people cope with certain types of problems before they occur. Additionally, professional counselors frequently provide consultation services to help people helping other people with problems and concerns. And finally, the counseling profession has extended its service provision settings to many places where people would not typically expect to find them (e.g., health care centers, government agencies, or religious institutions).

These mutual impacts have resulted in the counseling profession having a rapidly growing recognition and appreciation in society. Most counselors readily acknowledge, however, that the counseling profession has not yet achieved a complete or fully recognized place in society. The counseling profession is therefore acting within itself to enhance its identity within society. These activities include trends such as development of new counseling theoretical bases and techniques, increased use of technology, promotion of professional standards, improvement of training methods, expansion of political involvements, extension of service areas, promotion of public awareness of the counseling profession, and increased attention to accountability.

☐ Counseling and Its Theoretical Bases

The counseling profession has long been grounded in a relatively few basic counseling theories (e.g., client-centered, existential, behavioral, rational-emotive, or gestalt) and has worked diligently to establish effective techniques based on those theories. However, the counseling profession also has been receptive to new theoretical perspectives (e.g., cognitive-behavioral, social learning, and systemic theories, solution-focused counseling, and developmental counseling and therapy) that have evolved from the fields of counseling, psychology, sociology, education, and other related disciplines. True to the history of the profession, it is also working hard, through research, professional discourse, and experimentation, to develop effective new techniques based on these newer theories. As a result, professional counselors have before them ever expanding sets of theoretical perspectives and techniques upon which to base their counseling activities. These trends have added to the identity of the counseling profession by allowing professional counselors to provide more and better services to increasing numbers of people.

☐ Counseling and Computer-Based Technologies

The counseling profession also has begun to capitalize on modern technological advancements (Harris-Bowlsbey, Dikel, & Sampson, 1998; Sampson, Kolodinsky, & Greeno, 1997). This trend is perhaps most evident in the area of vocational counseling where a number of relatively sophisticated computer-based systems are regularly used to enhance vocational development and counseling activities. However, integration of technology also is evident in other parts of the counseling profession. For example, more and more counselors are using computers for data and information management in their normal counseling activities. Unfortunately, the use of technology to assist counseling processes and activities is by no means universally accepted or practiced. Sampson, Kolodinsky, and Greeno (1997) aptly summarized the situation:

The delivery of counseling services over the information highway may (a) improve client access to counseling in remote areas; (b) improve client orientation to the counseling process; (c) facilitate completion of assessment instruments and homework assignments; (d) enhance record keeping and monitoring of client progress; (e) enhance counseling referrals; (f) expand access to assessments and support for test interpretation; (g) reduce scheduling complications in couples and family counseling; (h) encourage individuals to seek counseling via self-help resources; (i) increase options for supervision and case conferencing; and (j) enhance the collection of research data. However, without careful design, use, and evaluation, counseling services offered via the information highway may (a) limit the confidentiality of the counseling relationship; (b) deliver invalid information; (c) lack necessary counselor intervention; (d) be misused by inadequately trained or overworked counselors; (e) limit counselor awareness of important location-specific counseling variables; (f) restrict equality of access to counseling resources; (g) limit needed privacy for counseling; and (h) encourage service delivery by counselors without appropriate credentials. (p. 211)

The use of computers and other so-called modern technology contributes to the identity of the counseling profession primarily by expediting the work of counselors; fostering communication among counselors via e-mail, list-servers, and chat-rooms; and providing information on web pages and in electronic newsletters. In addition, computer-based technology is now being used to prepare counselors via online supervision and classes. All of these applications have allowed counselors to provide better services to more people.

☐ Counseling and Ethical Standards

Two major types of professional standards are currently being emphasized within the counseling profession. One is ethical standards, that is, standards of behavior voluntarily adopted by the members of a profession to ensure the welfare of service recipients. The primary ethical standards for professional counselors are those developed and maintained by ACA. ACA's *Ethical Standards* and *Standards of Practice* were developed by the membership over a period of approximately 40 years and are periodically updated to reflect new needs and circumstances. Adherence to ethical standards is voluntary because they have no basis in law. However, the vast majority of professional counselors diligently strive to adhere to them because such behavior enhances society's view of the counseling profession as one which cares deeply about the welfare of its service recipients.

☐ Counseling and Counselor Preparation

The other set of standards currently receiving considerable emphasis within the counseling profession is that related to preparation practices. These Standards of Preparation are discussed at greater length subsequently. The important points as they apply to this discussion are that counselor professional preparation standards exist and that they are widely implemented within the counseling profession. Well over 400 counselor preparation programs exist in the United States and its territorial possessions. Standards of preparation are necessary to ensure that counselor trainees receive appropriate and effective preparation regardless of the preparation program in which they participate (Hollis, 1998). The implementation of standards of preparation also is particularly important in a mobile society where both counselors and clients frequently relocate; standardized counselor preparation helps to ensure effective counseling services regardless of location. Such standardization also helps to enhance society's perception of the counseling profession as one that carefully monitors its own activities.

In addition to the implementation of standards of preparation, the counseling profession continually seeks other ways to improve counselor preparation. For example, professional journals focusing on counselor preparation are replete with research on current training practices as well as innovative ideas for new training methods. Professional meetings for counselors also emphasize new approaches to counselor preparation. Collectively, these are indicators that the counseling profession is striving, in many different ways, to improve the effectiveness of counselor preparation. This effort is being put forth because the counseling profession realizes that effective preparation has a direct result in effective services and an indirect result in enhancement of society's perceptions of the profession.

☐ Counseling and Political Involvement

Another major thrust in the counseling profession is increased involvement in political systems. The most obvious example of this phenomenon is the widespread passage of state-level counselor licensure laws. However, professional counselors also are becoming active in other political arenas. For example, state and national counselor organizations frequently employ lobbyists to promote legislation that benefits not only the counseling profession but also the people who receive counseling services. The situation was effectively summarized by Solomon (1982), who wrote that:

Counselors and other human service providers are in a pivotal position to effectively communicate the concerns of people they serve to policy makers at local, state, and national levels of government. They are in an even better position to shape legislative initiatives, bills, and laws to more appropriately address counseling issues that directly impact the counseling profession as well as the people they serve. Most of the political successes that affect the counseling profession will depend largely on counselors themselves. (p. 580)

Political awareness and sophistication are rapidly increasing within the counseling profession, with one result being an enhanced public perception of the profession. In addition, politically involved counselors enable the counseling profession to take a collective outlook in terms of improving society as a whole (McClure & Russo, 1996).

☐ Counseling and Public Relations

Counseling professionals have realized that effective public relations are important parts of promoting positive mental health in society (as well as in establishing a favorable professional identity), and therefore they are increasingly engaged in public relations activities. Professional counselors' public relations activities take many forms, the most common of which are providing assistance for development of public service announcements and other media presentations, donating time to charitable causes, and developing mental health facilitation media which can be used without counselor intervention. In addition, increasing numbers of counselors are providing pro bono (i.e., free) services on a regular basis. Some professional organizations (e.g., AMHCA) have even suggested that pro bono work for a limited proportion of the counselor's clientele is an ethical and professional obligation.

☐ Counseling and Marketing

Historically, counselors and other mental health professionals were relatively low key in promoting the counseling profession. In fact, advertising is specifically prohibited in most ethical standards applicable to professional counselors. However, more recently a distinction has been made between advertising, presumably for a counselor's personal gain, and marketing, presumably for enhancement of the counseling profession in general. Ritchie (1989) noted that, "Marketing essentially is an exchange of goods or services. School counselors offer guidance and counseling services in exchange for public support" (p. 54). Obviously this perspective can be readily generalized from school counseling to other types of counseling.

Gilchrist and Stringer (1992) delineated the potential benefits of marketing in the counseling profession when they indicated that:

> Effective marketing may benefit counselors in three ways. First, marketing may help counselors maintain their position as service providers.
>   A second benefit of marketing is that it may help enhance the image of counseling services.
>   Third, the marketing process may help meet increasing demands for counselor accountability. (p.156)

Relatedly, Wittman (1988) wrote that:

> [T]he challenge is for the counseling profession to perfect those skills necessary to remain highly responsive to the needs and demands of its clients. The health care and business professions are turning to the use of marketing skills for this purpose. It is now time for the counseling field to discover how it can benefit from the lessons learned from marketing. (pp. 308–309)

Yet while marketing is receiving increasing attention, it is by no means universally endorsed in the counseling profession; significant controversy remains. Fong-Beyette (1988) noted that community-based assessment and evaluation techniques and strategies developed for use by counselors already exist and have been proven effective, and therefore that there is little need for counselors to adopt marketing techniques more suitable to business and industry. Gilchrist and Stringer (1992) perhaps provided the comment that should serve as a guideline for counselors: "Counselors need the benefits of effective marketing programs, but marketing must not jeopardize professional or ethical conduct" (p. 156).

☐ Counseling and Accountability

Awareness of the need to be accountable is increasing in the counseling profession as professional counselors realize that the benefits of their activities are not self-evident to persons outside the profession. Counseling is, for most people, a very private matter. Even those who benefit greatly from counseling services are not likely to share their experiences with others because of the (perceived) stigma of having had a need for counseling. Thus, few people outside the counseling profession are singing the praises of counselors. Professional counselors are aware that their responsibility is to prove that what they do is helpful, effective, and desirable; therefore, they have intensified their efforts to be accountable. A major thrust is being made to show that counseling results in behavior change among counseling service recipients. Clearly this thrust is consistent with the practitioner-scientist perspective presented in Chapter 1. More generally, however, it reflects the fact that demonstrating an ability to produce behavior change provides the strongest basis for the positive identity of the counseling profession within society.

☐ Summary

Over the last five decades the counseling profession has evolved from an amorphous collection of disparate professionals with vaguely defined similarities to be represented now by professionals with focused and specialized preparation in a variety of counseling skills who have a relatively singular purpose: provision of effective counseling services. The evolutionary process has been both reflective of and responsive to societal, educational, legal, and political trends. Significant obstacles have been encountered and overcome. Thus, identity as a professional counselor is now more meaningful than at any point in history.

Even in light of the substantial accomplishments and advancements in the counseling profession, more remains to be achieved before professional counselors enjoy a clear, distinct, and fully respected identity. Fortunately, mechanisms already exist through which such an identity can be achieved. Continuing emphasis on standardized, effective counselor preparation, credentialing, and accountability will enable the noble goal to be reached.

CHAPTER

Legal Concerns in Counseling

The stature of the counseling profession has improved dramatically in recent years. This has been due to, among other things, implementation of credentialing processes, expansion of counseling service realms, increased counseling effectiveness, and more focused conceptualizations of who counselors are and what they do. However, these gains have not been, and further gains will not be, achieved without difficulties. As counselors' professional identity advances, they and their activities are subject to increased scrutiny by their clients, the general public, and other audiences. Thus, there are more reasons than ever for professional counselors to be mindful of the implications of their behaviors, and to be attuned to pertinent ethical and legal considerations. Remley (1988) wrote:

> Ethical and legal considerations are important to us [i.e., counselors], but not because we need help in protecting ourselves from suits filed by the clients we serve. Instead, adherence to ethical and legal standards are vital if we are to take our place as full partners in the practice of mental health counseling. (p. 167)

Professional legal and ethical issues are quite frequently intertwined, and it is often difficult to separate them in examining the potential inappropriateness of any particular counselor's behavior. However, they are separated here for the sake of clarity of presentation. It would help to understand the nature of the U.S. legal system. According to Fischer and Sorenson (1996):

> The legal system of the United States is based primarily on *case* (i.e., decided by a court) law, and thus is referred to as a *common law* system. In

240

such a system legislative bodies may create (statutory) laws, but judicial processes determine the validities and appropriate applications of those laws. Judicial decisions have the "force of law" because they determine the conditions under and manners in which statutory laws will be applied. Judicial decisions, within the context of a *common law* system, reflect "the common thought and experience of a people." (p. 2)

There are two primary implications from the use of a *common law* system. One is that the legal system of the United States is by no means static; "the common thought and experience of a people" change over time, and interpretations of law change accordingly. A classic example is the Prohibition era; consumption of alcoholic beverages which had been legal, was made illegal, and then made legal again. The second implication is that interpretations of law are often situationally contingent. This is why seemingly self-evident laws are continually tested in the courts based upon the nuances of the circumstances in which the laws are being applied.

The common law system and the implications of its use are of significant importance to counselors. They necessitate that counselors be particularly cognizant of the local (usually state) laws and legal issues (which may vary greatly from region to region) that are applicable to their counseling activities and situations. Counselors also must be aware and knowledgeable of the laws and legal issues for their clients. Therefore, for the sake of clarity, the legal aspects of counseling of which counselors should be aware are addressed separately, first those for counselors and then those for clients.

☐ Legal Concerns for Counselors

Following are some of the legal topics and issues of which counselors should be aware and with which they frequently have to contend. The topics presented here were selected either for their prominence or because they are issues counselors frequently overlook. However, they are by no means the only ones which could have been presented. Effective professional counselors are always on the lookout for legal concerns about which they should be knowledgeable.

Informed Consent

How easy it is to begin counseling. A client comes to the counselor for help and the counselor begins. This, although a common scenario, belies a potentially significant legal issue for counselors. A counseling relationship is only one of several types of (verbal or other) relationships that two, or a small group of, people may have. Counselors are well-aware of what's involved in a counseling relationship. They have a conceptualization of what constitutes counseling. But most people in society are not. Thus, there exists potential for misunderstanding about the nature and method of provision of the "help." If the difference in perspective is great enough, there may be grounds for legal recourse by the client.

The best way for counselors to avoid misunderstandings about the nature and methods of provision of counseling services is for them to obtain informed consent for counseling from prospective clients (Anderson, 1996). Technically, the client gives informed consent (permission) to the counselor in order to be counseled. Robinson (1991) provided three criteria for informed consent for counseling. These may be paraphrased as follows:

1. The client (or in the case of a minor, the child's parent or legal guardian) must be capable of engaging in rational thought to a sufficient degree to make competent decisions, including initiating participation in a counseling process.
2. The client must receive relevant information about counseling as the counselor perceives it in a manner that the client understands. That is, it is the counselor's responsibility to ensure that the client understands counseling as the counselor will conduct it.
3. The client (or in the case of a minor, the child's parent or legal guardian) must give the consent voluntarily.

Crawford (1994) noted that informed consent may be either implied (behavioral) or expressed (written or verbal with witness). Implied consent for counseling is given when clients engage in behaviors that reasonable people would interpret as informed choice. For example, when clients voluntarily seek counseling services with the expectation to pay for services rendered from a counselor in private practice, informed consent usually would be implied. Expressed consent for counseling is given when clients have received an explanation of counseling from the counselor and either acknowledge consent in the presence of a witness or sign a document (informed consent form) indicating consent.

The obvious key to informed consent for counseling is the explanation given to the client. Rinas and Clyne-Jackson (1988) indicated that:

It is generally accepted that the description given to the client should consist of the following elements: diagnosis of the client's presenting problem(s), a description of the recommended treatment approach, benefits that should result as well as probability of such benefits, possible adverse effects that could follow the intervention with an estimation of their likelihood, [and] alternative treatment approaches with their incumbent risks and benefits. (p. 76)

Thus, in a colloquial sense, clients should be told what they are getting into and the alternatives available to them in a manner and language they understand.

Informed consent is a term that counselors usually associate with the research or data gathering processes, but it is equally applicable to counseling practice. It is always good professional practice for counselors to obtain informed consent for counseling, and in some cases it is imperative (e.g., when information obtained from counseling will be disclosed to persons not involved in the counseling process). In addition to reducing the risk of malpractice charges due to breach of contract (Swenson, 1996), informed consent procedures also may have a positive impact on the counseling relationship. Research suggests that clients who are provided with detailed information about the counseling process in advance are more likely to view their counselor as trustworthy (Walter & Handelsman, 1996). Counselors should obtain expressed, written consent whenever there is any doubt as to whether implied consent can be defended.

Duty to Warn

As professionals with specialized training and skills, counselors are expected to be able to interpret and predict human behavior effectively. Usually, such interpretations and predictions are about relatively innocuous behaviors—but not always. Among the most difficult decisions counselors have to make are those about the seriousness of clients' stated intentions to harm others or themselves. All ethical standards call for counselors to divulge such information when they believe a client will carry out a stated intention to harm, so there is a professional basis for such disclosure. However, there also is a legal basis for such disclosure, a responsibility known as *duty to warn*.

The legal bases for counselors' duty to warn evolve primarily from the case of *Tarasoff v. Regents of the University of California* (1974). In the Fall of 1969, Posenjit Poddar was a student at the University of California at Berkeley and a client at a university mental health facility. He informed his psychiatrist that he harbored anger at Tatiana Tarasoff and that he intended to kill her. The psychiatrist notified the campus police who detained Poddar for a short time, but later released him. On October 27, 1969, Poddar killed Tarasoff. Thereafter, Tarasoff's parents sued the psychiatrist and his employer (as well as a supervising psychiatrist and the university's police department). Tarasoff's parents claimed that, among other things, the psychiatrist had been negligent by not informing their daughter of Poddar's stated intention. A lower court ruled in favor of the defendants, but the California Supreme Court subsequently ruled in favor of the parents. The court held that:

> [W]hen a therapist determines, or pursuant to the standards of his profession should determine, that his patient presents a serious danger of violence to another, he incurs an obligation to use reasonable care to protect the intended victim against such danger. (p. 34; cited in Kagel & Kopels, 1994, p. 48)

A critical element of the *Tarasoff* ruling was that although the psychiatrist had informed the campus police, he had not gone far enough in his duty to warn; he should also have informed the intended victim.

In subsequent cases, the courts broadened the interpretation of counselors' duty to warn to include situations even where there is not a specifically identifiable intended victim. For example, *Lipari v. Sears, Roebuck, & Co.* (1980) involved a patient who had been receiving inpatient, and then outpatient, treatment at a Veteran's Administration (VA) hospital. The patient purchased a shotgun just prior to terminating treatment, a termination that his psychiatrist opposed. Later, he entered a nightclub and began shooting, killing Dennis Lapiri and seriously injuring Lapiri's wife. The court held that the psychiatrist had a *duty to warn* even though there was not a specific intended victim. In regard to this case, Herlihy and Sheeley (1988) noted that, "The court stated that there were ways other than alerting the victim to act on the duty to warn, such as attempting to detain the patient" (p. 147). Thus, counselors' duty to warn extends, at least potentially, to far-reaching situations.

In summarizing results and implications from several cases related to duty to warn, Hummel, Talbutt, and Alexander (1985) concluded:

> These cases clearly indicate that therapists have a duty to warn victims; that the facts must be clear enough for the therapist to know the intended victims; and that there is a duty to warn even when victims are not named if their identities are clear. Although these court cases deal with therapists, counselors should assume that the same standards apply to them. (pp. 74–75)

The nature of counselors' duty to warn is complicated also in situations where a client indicates intent to do harm to self, including physical injury or suicide. The boundaries for counselor liability in this regard are vague at best. For example, Sheeley and Herlihy (1989) offered the opinion that school counselors likely would be immune from liability for a student suicide outside of the school setting. However, there is some legal precedent for counselors to incur liability in the case of a student's suicide. For example, in 1991 the Maryland Supreme Court upheld a case in which a school counselor was held responsible for a student's suicide because (allegedly) the school counselor was aware of the student's intent, but did not notify the student's parents (Pate, 1992).

The ruling described by Pate (1992) may portend a trend of holding school counselors liable in cases of student/client suicide. Whether duty to warn in cases of potential suicide extends to other types of counselors is unknown. However, there is a tendency to treat all mental health service providers as if they had equal skills and competence (Sheeley & Herlihy, 1989). Furthermore, courts often fail to specify which professionals are included under specific rulings, making use of broad terms such as "therapist," which may be applied to a variety of mental health professionals (Isaacs, 1997; Rosenhan, Teitelbaum, Teitelbaum, & Davidson, 1993). Therefore, it is likely that counselors' duty to warn in cases of potential suicide will encompass all counselors.

It is obvious that if a counselor becomes aware of a client's intention to harm someone, including self, the counselor is required to inform appropriate persons (Costa & Altekruse, 1994; Rosenbaum, Teitelbaum, Teitelbaum, & Davidson, 1993). At issue is Who are appropriate persons? Unfortunately, only general guidelines can be given. If a specific intended victim is identified, that person (or a parent/legal guardian) should be told. In the specific case of potential suicide, effort should be made to ensure that the client is monitored or restrained by others (e.g., family members). If an identifiable group of people are identified, they should be told. If no specific intended victims are identified, attempts should be made to obtain legal restraint of the client. And in any case, the law enforcement authorities should be told. A counselor also would be well-advised to consult with other professionals, including attorneys, about who should be informed. It is likely that such actions will damage, if not terminate, the counselor's counseling relationship with the client. However, preventing injury must be the highest priority.

Disclosure

In situations where a counselor's duty to warn is applicable, there is a relatively clear legal mandate that the counselor must disclose information received from a client without the client's permission. There are other situations in which counselors are admonished to disclose information from clients, but the legal bases for such disclosures are not always as clear.

Another situation which necessitates disclosure by counselors is suspected child abuse or neglect. Kalichman (1993) provided the definition of child abuse contained in the 1974 National Child Abuse Prevention and Treatment Act (PL 93-247):

> Physical or mental injury, sexual abuse or exploitation, negligent treatment, or maltreatment of a child under the age of eighteen or the age

specified by the child protection law of the state in question, by a person who is responsible for the child's welfare, under circumstances which indicate that the child's health or welfare is harmed or threatened thereby. (p. 12)

Because child abuse is not a crime under federal law, each state has created a definition of child abuse for use in its child protection legislation (Yell, 1996). Most of the state definitions, however, contain most of the elements of the definition in PL 93-247.

All states and the District of Columbia have enacted legislation which make it legally mandatory for school counselors to report suspected child abuse (Davis & Ritchie, 1993; Fischer & Sorenson, 1995; Isaacs, 1997; Kalichman, 1993). Moreover, it appears that the legal responsibility for reporting suspected child abuse has been extended to other types of counselors in most states (Kalichman, 1993). Thus, as a general rule, counselors have legal responsibility to report suspected child abuse.

It is important to understand that counselors are required to report suspected child abuse, but are not required to prove child abuse. Counselors do not have to provide substantive evidence of child abuse; they just have to have good reason to suspect it. However, upon reporting suspected child abuse, it is likely that counselors will be asked to at least explain the basis of their allegation. Sandberg, Crabbs, and Crabbs (1988) suggested that the best basis for supporting an allegation of child abuse is good record keeping, particularly in notation of child behaviors (including verbalizations) and in regard to observation of physical abuse symptoms.

It also is important to note that state child abuse reporting laws offer legal protection for persons who report suspected child abuse, and therefore state laws provide encouragement to report suspected child abuse. Indeed, counselors may be subject to civil or criminal legal action if they fail to report suspected child abuse (Kalichman, 1993). In effect, suspected child abuse situations provide legally mandated and protected reason for counselors to disclose information obtained from clients without their permission.

The situation may seem more complicated for counselors when they suspect child neglect or psychological abuse. However, it is not necessary for counselors to distinguish clearly between physical (including sexual) abuse and neglect or psychological abuse (Fischer & Sorenson, 1995). Again, counselors are required to report child neglect or psychological abuse *suspected from their professional judgments and interpretations of child behaviors, verbalizations, or psychological states* (Fischer & Sorenson, 1995; Yell, 1996).

There are many other situations in which a counselor's legal obligation to disclose information without a client's permission is far less clear cut.

For example, having knowledge of clients' criminal or substance abuse activities poses complicated legal (as well as ethical) dilemmas for counselors. Another unclear circumstance can arise when a client makes a counselor aware of his or her intention to destroy the property of another. Some states have given professionals the right (but not duty) to disclose this type of information (Swenson, 1996). Another situation with which counselors are increasingly confronted is working with clients who are HIV-positive or who have Acquired Immune Deficiency Syndrome (AIDS) and who are sexually active with one or more partners who are unaware of the clients' medical conditions. There has been much speculation and debate in recent years about the legal and ethical implications of working with clients who are HIV-positive or have AIDS and who pose risk of infection to others (Costa & Altekruse, 1994; Erickson, 1993; Schlossberger & Hecker, 1996; Stanard & Hazler, 1995). Unfortunately, definitive legal precedents, requirements, or guidelines for disclosure in such situations have not been established. Therefore, counselors involved in such situations are advised to seek legal consultation immediately upon finding themselves confronted with legally complicated disclosure circumstances.

Record Keeping

The very real limitations of human memory in combination with large case loads highlight the need for counselors to keep accurate notes and records about their clients. Unfortunately, such record keeping presents potential difficulties for professional counselors, and there are only a few circumstances in which clear guidelines are available.

Concerns about the nature of educational records kept and about who had legitimate access to those records lead to passage of the Family Educational Rights and Privacy Act of 1974 (FERPA), also known as the Buckley Amendment. The FERPA was enacted to regulate (among other things) who had legitimate access to the educational records of students in public schools. In general, the FERPA stipulates that school personnel (i.e., school system employees) have legitimate access to information in students' records to facilitate educational or learning activities. More importantly, the FERPA stipulates that parents or legal guardians have access to the information kept in their child's records and that the information must be made available to them in a manner in which they can understand. Thus, test data, teachers' notes, demographic information, and any other information kept in students' records must be accessible to students' parents or legal guardians.

Employed school counselors have legitimate access to information in students' records when they use the information to facilitate students' educational processes and progress, and similarly, they can add information to students' records for such purposes. However, complications arise when school counselors maintain case notes for counseling purposes. If school counselors maintain such case notes in students' records, the provisions of the FERPA clearly apply, and parents or legal guardians and other school personnel presumably have legitimate access to those notes (Arthur & Swanson, 1993; Bullis, 1993; Fischer & Sorenson, 1995; Hopkins & Anderson, 1996). However, whether school counselors' case notes that are maintained in their own personal files are subject to the provisions of the FERPA and accessible by others (e.g., by subpoena) has not been clearly determined.

Legal standards and practices in regard to record keeping by counselors in other professional settings are even less clear. In general, school and other counselors' professional records (e.g., case notes) are considered a form of communication between counselors and their clients, and so are subject to laws related to privileged communication (to be covered subsequently). Therefore, counselors' professional records are protected (i.e., need not be disclosed without client permission) only in situations in which clients are receiving counseling in circumstances where they have a right to privileged communication, and those circumstances are relatively rare.

Because counselors only infrequently provide counseling in situations in which their professional records or case notes are not subject to access (e.g., by subpoena), the best advice that can be given is that counselors should maintain professional records and case notes as if they will be reviewed by others. This does not mean that such records and case notes cannot contain professional judgments, but it does mean that the bases for such judgments should be clearly indicated in the records or case notes. According to Remley (1992a):

> Attorneys who are asked to defend counseling actions taken, or to explain actions not taken, are delighted if the counselor has extensive written materials that help prove his or her version of the controversy. Notes are extremely good evidence that attorneys can use to help counselors substantiate their positions. (p. 31)

Thus, counselors who maintain records and case notes should keep comprehensive, accurate, and exact notes that allow for detailed clarifications or explanations of counselors' or clients' behaviors, including their respective verbal behaviors.

☐ Criminal and Civil Liability

Counselors may be held liable for their professional actions and behaviors within either of two legal regards. The first is in regard to criminal liability, which arises when a counselor is charged with participation in or aiding and abetting criminal activity. In general, criminal liability involves a counselor's participation in a crime against society, as opposed to against an individual, and it includes acts that are prosecuted by the government rather than private individuals (Anderson, 1996; Swenson, 1996). The most common examples of situations in which counselors are at risk for criminal liability include: being an accessory to a crime such as theft, assault, or fraud; civil disobedience; and contributing to the delinquency of a minor (Anderson, 1996; Fischer & Sorenson, 1995; Gladding, 1988; Hopkins & Anderson, 1996). Fortunately, criminal liability prosecution of counselors is relatively rare.

The second regard in which counselors may be held liable is civil liability. In general, civil liability involves a crime against an individual (Anderson, 1996; Fischer & Sorenson, 1995). Civil liability is rooted in the concept of tort, "a wrong that legal action is designed to set right" (Hopkins & Anderson, 1996). According to Hummel, Talbutt, and Alexander (1985):

> The basic concept of tort . . . is that each individual has a legal and social obligation to protect other individuals in society. If one person breaches or twists the relationship and someone is injured, then the injured party may sue and be compensated for the injury. The injured party has been diminished; and the only means we have, as a society, to make the person whole again is through a monetary settlement. (p. 68)

Although there are a number of facets of civil liability in which counselors could become involved, most frequently counselors' involvements are in regard to malpractice. Hummel, Talbutt, and Alexander (1985) wrote that, "*Malpractice in counseling* can be defined as harm to a client resulting from professional negligence, with *negligence* defined as departure from acceptable professional standards" (p. 70).

Anderson (1996), Talbutt and Hummel (1982), and Slimak and Berkowitz (1983) identified the following areas, among others, of potential malpractice for counselors:

1. Making a faulty diagnosis, such as attribution of a physically-based problem to a psychological condition.
2. Failing to take action when someone other than the client is in danger.
3. Improperly certifying in a commitment proceeding.
4. Engaging in behavior inappropriate to accepted standards of the profession, such as unethical behavior.
5. Failing to take adequate precautions for a suicidal client.
6. Providing services for which competence has not been demonstrated, established, or proven.
7. Breaching confidentiality.
8. Promising a "cure."

9. Taking advantage of the counseling relationship for personal gain, monetary or otherwise.
10. Failing to use a technique that would have been more helpful.
11. Failing to provide informed consent.

Among these various possibilities, the most common one for which malpractice suits are brought against counselors is the category "taking advantage" of the counseling relationship. Within this category, the most frequently presented basis for malpractice suits against counselors is sexual harassment or misconduct. Indeed, this is the single most common type of malpractice suit brought against counselors. In some states, sexual misconduct by a therapist with a client is considered a criminal offense (Anderson, 1996). Further, counselors may be found guilty of malpractice for having a sexual relationship with a former client if it can be established that the basis for the sexual relationship initiated during the counseling relationship (Hummel, Talbutt, & Alexander, 1985). Therefore, it is imperative that counselors refrain from sexual relationships with current, or recent former, clients if they are to avoid this type of malpractice suit (Crawford, 1994).

Provision of Services

There are two other aspects of law in regard to the provision of services in which counselors may become entangled. The first is contract law, and in particular breach of contract. Counselor and client contracts for provision of counseling services may be either expressed or implied (analogous to the situation for informed consent) (Anderson, 1996; Bullis, 1993). An expressed contract is one that is written, verbal, and/or witnessed by a person not involved in the counseling relationship. An implied contract is one that is situationally evident from the client's and counselor's behaviors or verbalizations. Hopkins and Anderson (1990) noted the possible subtleties of establishment of a contract, such as when counselors rather casually communicate to clients that they will provide treatment for a certain number of counseling sessions, a certain number of hours, or a particular fee, or that they will use particular techniques. If counselors fail to provide counseling services as presented to clients, they can be held liable for breach of contract. In general, then, counselors who wish to avoid suits for breach of contract must provide counseling services of the nature and under conditions as presented to clients (Swenson, 1996).

The second aspect of law relative to provision of services is what has sometimes been legally construed as fraud. Because of the relative recency of professional counselor credentialing procedures such as licensures or certifications, counselors frequently have not been recognized by health insurance companies as eligible for direct (i.e., third-party) payments. In order to be paid by insurance companies for their counseling services, some counselors have provided their services under the supervision of professionals eligible for third-party payments. According to Coven (1992) wrote that:

> An accepted standard of practice which has prevailed within the mental health provider community for many years has been for services to be actually rendered by a "lesser" trained provider such as a counselor; to be "supervised" by a "better qualified" provider such as a psychologist or psychiatrist; and for the health care or insurance forms to be "signed off, on, by" the supervising "more qualified" provider. Frequently the supervising provider had no face-to-face contact with the patient. (p. 1)

Although the practice may have been common, it is unlikely to continue. Coven (1992) indicated that, "Since 1983 some health care providers and insurance companies have challenged the standard of 'nonapproved' providers collecting monies under the supervision and signature of the supervisor, even an approved provider" (p. 3). The basis of the challenge is that the collection of monies for the provision of counseling services by persons other than those who actually provided the services is fraud. Scant legal precedent exists to support this challenge at present. However, it seems likely that such precedents will accumulate rapidly. Thus, counselors should be cautious in entering into arrangements in which payments for services rendered are not made directly to them.

Expert Witness Testimony

An increasing number of counselors are being called upon to provide expert witness testimony, a new and relatively lucrative activity for professional counselors. Weikel and Hughes (1993) cited a number of advantages to being involved as an expert witness, including financial benefits and a chance "to make a difference." According to Remley (1992b):

> An expert witness is an objective and unbiased person with specialized knowledge, skills, and/or information, who can assist a judge or jury in reaching an appropriate legal decision. (p. 33)

Unfortunately, many counselors believe they have "specialized knowledge, skills, and information" simply because they have graduate-level training or experience in counseling. This naive perspective belies the intricacies and complexities of forensic psychology. Ill-prepared, unskilled, or uninformed or misinformed counselors who become involved in provision of expert testimony are at risk at least for embarrassment and at worst for legal repercussions. Rinas and Clyne-Jackson (1988) summarize the common scenario succinctly:

When involved in a court situation, the mental health professional is typically in a foreign arena. In court settings, for example, the consultant [i.e., expert witness] is frequently confused as to what constitutes a "mental health" opinion versus a legal conclusion. In cases of criminal responsibility the mental health expert may be asked "whether individuals have acted with appreciation of the nature of their acts or with free will to avoid violations of the law if they so choose." Such legalistic terms have no real meaning to the mental health professional who unsuccessfully struggles with trying to translate these terms into language he or she understands, for example, what does the legal profession mean by the expressions "appreciation," "nature of the act," and "free will." (p. 119)

Thus, counselors who provide expert witness testimony must have highly specialized knowledge (e.g., of psychopathology, personality assessment, or both), specialized skills (e.g., for working with persons known to have a particular mental disorder), and extensive relevant professional experience.

Some counselors also believe that they have specialized skills, knowledge, and information about their clients, and therefore would be good expert witnesses on behalf of those clients, because they have provided counseling services. However, Remley (1992b) points out:

After a witness has been recognized by a judge as an expert . . . the witness is given the opportunity to state an opinion about the matter before the court. . . . The attorney for the side that is harmed by the expert's testimony is given the opportunity to discredit the expert's testimony.

One of the most effective methods of overcoming the damaging effect of an expert witness opinion is to convince the court that the expert is biased and, therefore, his or her opinion cannot be trusted. (p. 33)

It is highly unlikely that counselors can serve as unbiased expert witnesses for their clients, and so they should not participate as expert witnesses for their clients.

In general, only counselors who have documented evidence of specialized knowledge, skills, and information, as well as substantial relevant experience, should provide expert witness testimony. Counselors who choose to develop such expertise should realize that it most likely will significantly limit the scope of their other professional activities.

Marketing and Advertising

A variety of definitions have been provided for the concept of marketing as applied to the counseling profession. For example, Ambrose and Lenox (1988) defined marketing as "the process of identifying client beliefs and attitudes and structuring programs to meet client needs" (p. 5; cited in

Gilchrist & Stringer, 1992), while Ritchie (1989, p. 54) defined it as "essentially . . . an exchange of goods for services," noting that counselors exchange counseling services for public support. In general, marketing involves the promotion of counseling services to the public with the intent that the public subsequently will partake of those counseling services more frequently and to a greater extent. Advertising (along with selling and public relations) are the primary communication methods of marketing (Wittman, 1988).

For the sake of discussion here, and to cast it in a positive perspective, marketing may be defined as those activities intended to promote the counseling profession as a whole. Marketing within this context would be used not to benefit particular counselors, but rather to enhance the image of the counseling profession as well as of counselors in general. Similarly, advertising can be conceived of as a process intended to achieve gain for particular counselors. Clearly these are not technically correct definitions or distinctions. However, they do allow the generality that marketing counseling is good, advertising counseling is not.

Gilchrist and Stringer (1992) identified three potential benefits of marketing counseling: (a) maintenance of counselors' positions as service providers, (b) enhancement of the image of counseling services, and (c) fulfillment of demands for counselor accountability. Obviously, achievement of goals such as these would greatly increase and improve the professional identity of the counseling profession. Therefore, movement toward these goals is being pushed by the leadership of the counseling profession. According to Beverly O'Bryant, 1992–1993 ACA President:

> It is our responsibility to change the present. It is our responsibility to represent the future and make the discipline of counseling understood, recognized, and appreciated among the mental health professions and laymen as well.
>
> Each of us must provide accurate information about all of our specialties to a multitude of publics. We must publicize our services more and participate in government relations initiatives locally and nationally. (O'Bryant, 1992, p. 36)

In order to be responsive to O'Bryant's charge, counselors will have to market the counseling profession through effective public relations and promotional activities.

Advertising, at least within the perspective presented previously, is quite another matter. Advertising has been viewed with disdain within the counseling and related professions. Indeed, most professional organizations for counseling service providers have policy statements that place severe restrictions on advertising of professional services (Swenson, 1996). Rinas and Clyne-Jackson (1988) summarized current allowable practices:

[P]rofessionals are prohibited from soliciting clients directly. They are entitled to send out announcement cards to potential referral sources but, even in doing this, restrictions are imposed. In general, the private practitioner must limit the information on the card to such items as name, address and phone number, highest level of education achieved in field of practice, office hours, type of clientele serviced (e.g., adolescents), and a brief description of the services available (e.g., family therapy, diagnostic assessments).

In addition to sending out announcement cards, the new practitioner is also allowed to be *appropriately* listed in the telephone directory. . . . (p. 12)

Many state counselor credentialing laws also provide specific regulations for advertising by credentialed counselors. Thus, counselors are well-advised to be conservative in regard to advertising, and to verify locally allowable practices before engaging in advertising. Bullis (1993) recommends that counselors who choose to advertise services take the following precautions.

- Check state regulations.
- Check ethical standards.
- Do not make quality claims that require verification.
- Make all information accurate and truthful.
- All advertisements should be reviewed and cleared by an attorney.

Defamation (Libel and Slander)

Counselors have access to personal information about clients by virtue of the very nature of the counseling process. They also necessarily form opinions about their clients, some of which are based on emotional reactions such as surprise, anger, or frustration. If counselors disclose information or opinions inappropriately, they could be subject to charges of defamation. According to Hummel, Talbutt, and Alexander (1985):

Counselors, because of the nature of their work, have many opportunities for defamation that could result in litigation. They are privy to conversations, records, and personal information and they communicate with a range of individuals who may pressure them to reveal confidential information. (p. 85)

In the legal sense, there are two types of defamation, libel and slander. Libel is defamation expressed in a written form and slander is defamation expressed in a verbal form (Anderson, 1996; Talbutt, 1988). In either case, in order for a counselor to be found guilty of defamation, it must be shown that written or verbal statements made by the counselor were: (a) false; (b) brought hatred, disgrace, ridicule, or contempt to another person; and (c) resulted in damages (Hummel, Talbutt, & Alexander, 1985). In other words, it must be proven that the communication was malicious. It is important to recognize that a communication may be judged malicious even though there was no intention to be malicious. The plaintiff in a defamation case does not (necessarily) have to prove that a communication was intended to be malicious, but merely that it was malicious in regard to the three criteria. It is also important to note that in some states even truthful statements which are communicated without a legitimate professional purpose can result in charges of defamation (Anderson, 1996).

The pressure on counselors to disclose information inappropriately are sometimes social, sometimes professional, and sometimes both. For example, if a teacher refers a student to a school counselor because the student is misbehaving or otherwise having difficulties in class, the teacher reasonably might later ask the school counselor, "What's wrong with the student?" A school counselor responding to such a question would be well-advised to avoid describing the student in terms of perceptions of the student's characteristics. Counselors also sometimes just talk about their clients in social or informal professional situations. Such talk could become the basis for a defamation suit against the counselor.

Talbutt (1988) provided four guidelines for counselors to follow to avoid allegations of defamation.

1. Always act in good faith and keep all communications free from malice.
2. Report behavior objectively and factually, and avoid use of psychological jargon that could be misconstrued.
3. Communicate about clients only in response to requests and only when a duty to respond exists.
4. Communicate only what is believed to be true and supported by facts.

These guidelines reflect a basic tenet of good professional practice: counselors should communicate about clients only in professional manners and only in professional contexts.

These, then, are the major legal concerns with which counselors should be familiar and for which they are specifically accountable. However, they are not the only legal concerns of which counselors should be aware. Counselors also should be aware of the legal concerns particularly applicable to their clients.

☐ Legal Concerns for Clients

Clients usually have all the legal rights of other members of society, perhaps the only exception being those clients who are convicted felons.

Clients also sometimes have additional, specific legal rights by virtue of being clients. Following are some of the major legal concerns for clients applicable to counseling situations.

Right to Treatment

Clients' legal right to treatment actually encompasses several different legal rights: (a) right to treatment, (b) right to least intrusive (or least restrictive) treatment, and (c) right to adequate treatment. Although these client rights are often interrelated, they are presented here separately for discussion clarity.

Increasing numbers of counselors are working in residential mental health facilities, particularly those operated and managed as state or other government agencies. Typically, government-operated residential mental health treatment facilities have large populations, few professional staff, and minimal operating budgets. Thus, unfortunately, people in such facilities often have been "warehoused" (i.e., provided custodial care only in terms of basic physical needs) because of the extant conditions. It is in regard to clients in such residential facilities that clients' right to treatment has been most frequently challenged in the courts.

Most right to treatment cases have been brought before courts for three major groups of people, including those with (a) diminished intellectual capacity, (b) severe psychological disturbances, and (c) physical disabilities. In general, the courts have held that all these types of clients have legal right to psychotherapeutic/counseling services (Rinas & Clyne-Jackson, 1988). That is, the courts have ruled that these potential clients cannot just be ignored; they must receive treatment/services in regard to their psychological conditions or situations (e.g., in residential facilities). Unfortunately, although court rulings generally have been in favor of such persons, provision of counseling and related psychological services for them continue to be withheld from many (Robinson, 1991). What progress has been made for underserved clientele has been primarily for persons (particularly students) with physical disabilities (Brown & Srebalus, 1988).

The courts have generally held that clients have the right to the least intrusive treatment that will alleviate the condition for which treatment was sought. The least intrusive treatment (i.e., counseling intervention) is that which will achieve treatment goals with the least number of associated undesirable or negative side effects. For example, use of psychotropic drugs is obviously more intrusive than use of a verbal-interaction counseling treatment. An example that may be more relevant to the professional counselor is that family counseling might be considered more intrusive if individual counseling is deemed sufficient to achieve desired treatment goals. In commenting on evaluation of treatment intrusiveness, Rinas and Clyne-Jackson (1988) noted:

In determining the degree of intrusiveness of a particular intervention, the professional should take into consideration a number of different factors. First of all, the therapist should consider the permanence of any change that could result from a particular procedure. . . . Another characteristic to consider is the "foreignness" of the change to the client, that is, the degree to which the modified behavior differs from the behaviors typically manifested by that client. The therapist should also consider the scope of the behaviors that could possibly be changed as a result of the intervention, the speed with which changes are likely to occur, the duration of the change, and the client's ability to resist such change. (p. 88)

Perhaps the most significant aspect of clients' right to treatment for counselors is clients' right to adequate treatment. At issue is professional competence. A substantial number of court cases have been brought against counselors in which the primary allegation was incompetence on the part of the counselor (Rinas & Clyne-Jackson, 1988). In general, alleged in these cases was that the counselor attempted to use therapeutic or counseling interventions for which the counselor could not demonstrate or verify professional competence. Interestingly, such challenges have been brought both from within and outside of the counseling profession. For example, in the mid-1990s, state-level associations for psychologists brought suits against licensed mental-health counselors in several states in which it was alleged that the counselors were using tests that the counselors were not qualified to administer and interpret. There is no clear trend in the outcomes of such cases. However, the important point here is that some counselors have been found guilty of attempting to use interventions for which they were unqualified.

Counselors should never use interventions beyond the limits of their competence (Crawford, 1994). Unfortunately, it is not always easy to make the determination of limits of competence. For example, is a counselor who was trained specifically in marriage and family counseling necessarily competent to do individual or small group counseling? Probably not. Conversely, counselors specifically trained to do small group counseling are not necessarily competent to do family counseling. According to Robinson (1991):

If you are not qualified to treat a certain client problem, what should you do ethically? Your first choice is to refer the client to someone who is more qualified to help him or her. If there is no one available (which would be the exception rather than the rule), then it is incumbent on you [i.e., the counselor] to get continuing education, to devour library books and articles on the presenting problem, and to seek supervision. You do not just proceed as if what you know can generalize to every client problem. You are responsible for the welfare of that client, and it is your professional and ethical responsibility to find for that client the best services possible—be it from you or from someone else. (pp. 452–453)

Robinson's advice to counselors is good from professional and ethical perspectives. However, probably only her first recommendation (i.e., make a referral) is valid legally. That is, once counseling has begun and the counselor has made a (personal) judgment of professional competence insufficiency, it is highly unlikely that a counselor could garner needed knowledge and skills rapidly enough to present a defensible position in a court of law. While counselors generally are well-advised to continue to increase their professional knowledge and skills, attempting such improvements during a counseling process for a client who has a problem exceeding the counselor's current competence is not advisable from a legal perspective.

Access to Records

The legalities of clients' rights to access to records kept on them are, at the very least, complicated and confusing. There is some degree of clarity in regard to clients' access to educational (i.e., academic) records, but the situation is particularly convoluted for other types of clients' records. In regard to the former, the FERPA continues to serve as the basis of laws covering clients' right to access. Again, the FERPA stipulates that parents of school children have legal right to the information maintained in their children's educational records. However, parents of children generally do not have legal right to access to personal notes or records maintained by school counselors for their counseling activities with children (Fischer & Sorenson, 1995). But when do personal notes and records become part of educational records, thereby permitting parental access to them? It appears that personal records become educational records when a (school or other) counselor shares his or her personal notes or records with other school personnel (Fischer & Sorenson, 1995). Thus, the act of sharing (a counselor's) personal information, either in writing or verbally, negates the counselor's strictly personal use of those notes or records, and makes them accessible to parents.

Conditions of the FERPA also generally apply to college students. If they are more than 18 years of age, they (not their parents) have right to access to their educational records. However, there are several access restrictions in the FERPA specific to college students. For example, they do not have right of access to parental or familial financial information maintained by the postsecondary institution. In regard to letters of reference,

students have the right to waive access to those letters. Potential contributors of reference letters must be informed of whether the student for
whom the letter is to be written has waived the right to access before the
letter is submitted. If right to access is waived, students cannot subsequently review those letters, except in cases where the letters are later
used for other than the originally intended purpose (Hummel, Talbutt, &
Alexander, 1985). School and other counselors asked to submit letters of
reference should take note of waiver of right of access status, and adjust
the content of their letters accordingly.

Rinas and Clyne-Jackson (1988), in discussing other than student clients, indicated that, generally, counseling clients are believed to have right
to access to their records. However, they also noted that most counseling
facilities attempt to discourage clients from accessing their counselors'
records. They further noted that there is considerable professional and
legal argument over whether clients have right to access to their counseling records if the information in the records is potentially harmful to the
clients. At issue is what is harmful to clients and, more importantly, who
decides what is harmful. Unfortunately, although legislation has been
passed in some states which gives clients right to access to their records,
there is substantial variation in that legislation. In addition, there have
been very few judicial decisions regarding clients' right to access to their
records in other than educational settings. Counselors should review carefully client-right-to-access legislation in the states in which they practice
in order not impinge upon or violate clients' right to access.

Right to Due Process

As citizens, students and other clients cannot have their rights denied,
withheld, or restricted arbitrarily or capriciously under the auspices of
the United States Constitution. This means that counselors in schools or
in other circumstances cannot act capriciously to deny clients' rights such
as freedom of speech, assembly, or association. However, clients' rights
may be restricted or denied under certain circumstances. In such circumstances, in order for clients' rights to be denied or restricted due process
procedures have to be followed.

In the case of *Tinker v. Des Moines* (1969), the United States Supreme
Court held that students had the same fundamental rights as other citizens and that they could express those rights in a variety of ways as long
as the methods did not "materially or substantively" interfere with the
rights of others or educational processes (Fischer & Sorenson, 1995). For
example, students have the right to express their opinions (i.e., have freedom of speech), but they cannot use expression of those opinions as a

means to block other students' access to classes. Similarly, although the United States Constitution gives citizens the right to bear arms, students may be prohibited from bringing weapons to schools because those weapons constitute a significant potential danger to others.

Hummel, Talbutt, and Alexander (1985) list the basic elements of due process for a person. These are summarized as follows.

1. The person must be given notice; in other words, the person must be apprised that a behavior is prohibited before procedures are instituted against the person.
2. A hearing must be held in which the person has the opportunity to refute the charges made.
3. An impartial person or persons must preside at the hearing.
4. The person has the right to counsel. For students, the counsel may be any adult, not necessarily an attorney.
5. The person has the right to question witnesses and/or to bring forth witnesses.
6. Any decision must be made on the basis of evidence presented and not on the basis of factors extraneous to the case at hand.

It is obvious that counselors could be involved in due process procedures in any of several capacities and therefore should be knowledgeable of the due process requirements for the circumstances in which they work.

Sexual Misconduct

Allegations of sexual misconduct against counselors, and lawsuits based on those allegations, have increased dramatically in recent years and account for a large percentage of legal actions taken against counselors (Anderson, 1996; Coleman & Schaefer; 1988; Nelson, 1992). Sexual misconduct may be overt and direct, such as in the case of sexual intimacy between counselor and client during or as a result of counseling, or covert and indirect, such as in the case of verbal harassment or sexual hugs and fondling. Counselors' sexual misconduct in either form has long been considered ethically and professionally inappropriate (Coleman & Schaefer, 1988). However, more recently the trend is for it to be illegal as well. For example, an increasing number of states are passing legislation specifically prohibiting sexual intimacies between counselors and their clients during or after counseling relationships (Anderson, 1996). Further, an increasing number of state counselor licensure boards are incorporating statutes against counselor and client sexual intimacy, with the penalty being revocation of licensure (Coleman & Schaefer, 1988).

Advice for counselors contemplating sexual intimacy with clients is really very simple: don't! Sexual intimacy with clients is at least unethical and unprofessional, and most likely illegal.

Privileged Communication

Privileged communication is usually (and erroneously) thought of as the legal counterpart to confidentiality. That is, counselors frequently speak or write about privileged communication as their legal right not to disclose information obtained from clients during a counseling relationship. However, contrary to this commonly held perception, "...privileged communication is a legal term that indicates that the client's communications cannot be disclosed in a court of law without the client's consent. The privilege belongs to the client, not the counselor . . . " (Robinson, 1991, p. 455). Fisher and Sorenson (1995) distinguished between confidentiality and privileged communication.

> While *confidentiality* applies to all communications between counselor and client, *privileged communication* applies to communications protected from disclosure even in judicial proceedings.
>
> Such privilege refers to the right of a person in a "special relationship" to prevent the disclosure in legal proceedings of information given in confidence in the special relationship (p. 18)

More simply, " . . . standards on confidentiality have evolved to protect the client's communications outside the courtroom whereas privileged communication protects the client from having private information divulged within the courtroom" (Rinas & Clyne-Jackson, 1988, p. 56). In the vast majority of circumstances, clients do not have the right to privileged communication because the counselor-client relationship is not legally recognized as being special.

Various authors (e.g., Fischer & Sorenson, 1995; Hopkins & Anderson, 1990) list the four legal criteria typically used to determine whether communications should be considered privileged:

1. The communications must have originated with the assumption of both parties that the communications would be held in confidence.
2. Confidentiality of communications between the two parties must be viewed as essential to maintenance of an effective relationship between the parties.
3. The type of relationship must be one which is valued by members of the community and society.
4. The damage done to the relationship by disclosure of the information communicated under the assumption of confidentiality must be judged to be greater than the benefit derived for the litigation process.

The first two criteria are clearly reflected in the ethical standards of the counseling profession. The applicability of the third and fourth criteria clearly increases with improvements in the professional identity of the counseling profession.

In the few states where counselors' clients do have the right to privileged communication, counselors involved in clients' litigation do not have to decide whether the right to privileged communication should be invoked in a court of law. Rather, that right, and responsibility for decisions related to it, belong to the client. Indeed, with the exception of circumstances in which counselors' duty to warn or requirement to report child abuse or neglect come into play, counselors are legally prohibited from disclosing counselor-client communications without clients' express permission. If clients release counselors to disclose counselor-client communications in a court of law, counselors can, and probably must, respond to inquiries about counselor-client communications (Arthur & Swanson, 1993; Fischer & Sorenson, 1995; Anderson, 1996). In general, in legal proceedings counselors are responsive to clients' decisions about right to privileged communication; they do not make decisions about that right.

Even in states where counseling clients have the right to privileged communication, there are at least two circumstances in which that right cannot be applied directly. The first is counseling children and the second is group and/or marriage and family counseling. In regard to counseling children (i.e., persons under the age of 18), the client's right to privileged communication passes to the parent(s) or legal guardian. Thus, the parent(s) or legal guardian make decisions about disclosure in courts of the child's communications during counseling (Rinas & Clyne-Jackson, 1988). In regard to group and/or marriage and family counseling, Fischer and Sorenson (1995) wrote that:

> The historical view of the courts has been that if more than two people are involved in the conversation, the privilege is lost to all, since there is no confidentiality intended. Although this view makes little sense in group counseling or therapy, counselors should realize that there is a significant lag between developments in their professional techniques and law. (p. 26)

Thus, the presence of a third party is in and of itself sufficient to negate the right to privileged communication in any counseling context (Arthur & Swanson, 1993). In general, then, where it exists, privileged communication may be assumed to apply only to communications between a professional and one other adult.

Although not many states give clients the right to privileged communication in their counseling relationships with counselors, a recent ruling by the U.S. Supreme Court held that clients' communications with psychotherapists is considered privileged in federal courtrooms (*Jaffee v. Redmond*, as cited in Remley, Herlihy, & Herlihy, 1997). This landmark decision likely will have repercussions in state and other courtrooms as well and is a significant step towards the expansion of privileged communication rights to all citizens of the United States.

The goal of counseling clients having the right to privileged communication throughout the United States is a frequently espoused and noble one because such a situation would do much to enhance the credibility of the counseling profession. However, counselors should be aware that, even if that goal were achieved, there would remain significant legal intricacies in various privileged communication statutes, and counselors would not have a carte blanche right not to disclose counselor-client communications. Therefore, counselors should make every effort to understand fully the nuances of clients' privileged communication statutes in the locations where they practice.

☐ Legal Resources for Counselors

Increasing legal complexities for counselors and for their clients necessitate that counselors be proactive in regard to legal concerns. That is, counselors must act in ways that will avoid legal problems and enable them to be knowledgeable of legal concerns before they occur. Arthur and Swanson (1993), Remley (1992a, 1992b), and Hopkins and Anderson (1996), among others, all have indicated that the best way to avoid legal problems is to act in accord with accepted professional standards (i.e., to act ethically). Certainly that is good advice. However, following that advice may not be fully sufficient to prevent counselors from becoming embroiled in legal matters because it is based on the assumptions that ethical standards cover all legal situations and that counselors know what the accepted standards of the profession are. The former assumption may not be true in general and the latter may not be true in regard to legal concerns.

In addition to acting ethically, there are at least two behaviors that counselors can engage in to avoid legal problems, each facilitated by membership in a professional organization such as ACA. The first is to increase their knowledge of legal concerns, issues, and practices. ACA makes available a wide variety of resources (including books, visual media, and professional development activities) designed to increase counselors' knowledge of the law. The second is to obtain professional liability insurance, which is frequently made available at reasonable costs through professional organizations such as ACA. Good counselors strive continually to improve their knowledge of the legal aspects of their profession. Even better counselors know that no matter what they do, they may be subject to legal involvements, and so they act to protect themselves as much as possible.

☐ Summary

Legal concerns for counselors and their clients encompass many aspects of law and almost all human interactions, conditions, and situations. When the counseling profession in general and counselors in particular were less well known, the likelihood of counselors' involvements in legal matters was far less than it is now. Increased recognition brings with it increased scrutiny and increased responsibility. Thus, counselors need to devote substantial time and effort to becoming knowledgeable of the legal concerns, issues, and intricacies applicable to their work with clients. They also must make concerted efforts to act in ways that are ethically, professionally, and legally defensible. The extent to which these goals are achieved is exactly the extent to which counselors will not have legal problems.

CHAPTER

Ethical Concerns in Counseling

The legal considerations for the counseling profession not withstanding, counseling is essentially a self-regulating profession. That is, although the number of litigations in which counselors are involved is increasing, the fact remains that a relatively small proportion of counselors are ever involved in litigation. Thus, while counseling activities must be conducted within applicable legal standards, counselors far more frequently look to professional rather than legal guidelines for their counseling activities. The professional guidelines which serve as the basis for counseling activities are known as ethical standards.

☐ The Need for Ethical Standards

A publicly professed, self-imposed set of behavioral guidelines is one of the characteristics of a profession. This criterion is not applied capriciously. It reflects the complex nature of the counseling profession and of the society in which that profession is practiced. More simply, no amount of training, preparation, or personal wisdom will enable counselors to know what is the right thing to do in every situation they will encounter. Therefore, ethical standards are needed to facilitate counselors' decision making in those situations. However, ethical standards are only guidelines. According Van Hoose (1986):

> All the psychological helping professions have ethical standards in one form or another. These standards reflect professional concerns and define basic

265

principles that should guide the professional activity of the practitioner. Ethical codes help to clarify a counselor's responsibilities to clients, and they are an aid in ethical decision making.

Ethical codes are quite helpful, indeed essential, but they do not answer all ethical questions. (p. 168)

Thus, ultimately, counselors have at least some personal responsibility for their decisions about appropriate behavior.

In general, a set of ethical standards is a reflection of the collective values and belief system of the members of a profession. Ethical standards are created, in part, to reduce the need for counselors to have sole responsibility for their professional decisions, i.e., to minimize personal responsibility for decision making. However, according to Mabe and Rollin (1986):

A responsible member of the counseling profession must look to various sources for guidance. We fear that many professions may see a code of ethics as the sole basis for explicating responsibility for its members. The code is clearly a central part, but only a part, of the basis for explication of professional responsibility. A professional code is necessary but not sufficient for the exercise of professional responsibility. (p. 294)

Thus, codes of ethics do not provide absolute rules which will absolve counselors of decision-making responsibility in every situation. For example, Mabe and Rollin (1986) provided six problem areas in which ethical standards may not provide clear guidelines for decisions: (a) sometimes counselor personal values issues cannot be handled within the context of a code of ethics, (b) sometimes aspects of a code of ethics are difficult to enforce, (c) in some circumstances, the interests of all affected persons (e.g., counselors, clients, and representatives of agencies or institutions) cannot be represented effectively in a code of ethics, (d) there is a limited number of topics that can be covered in a code of ethics, (e) there may be multiple (e.g., professional versus legal) forums in which topics need to be addressed, and (f) different codes of ethics may conflict with one another. However, even in situations where a set of ethical standards does not provide explicit guidelines for decision making, it may provide implicit guidelines by virtue of the value orientation inherent in them.

In addressing the limitations of attempting to make decisions simply on the basis of ethical standards, Van Hoose (1986) differentiated between ethical standards and ethical principles.

Counselors who are unable to find direction in ethical codes may find answers to ticklish questions in some fundamental principles of helping. Ethical principles provide a more solid framework for decision making than do ethical codes or statutes. The fundamental principles of counseling include autonomy, beneficence, nonmaleficence, justice, and fidelity. (p. 168)

Autonomy is used in this context to mean that clients' right to make their own decisions should be respected (except in certain very specific situations, such as suicidal tendency). Beneficence means that counselors should always attempt to act in the best interests of their clients. Nonmaleficence means that counselors also should make every effort to avoid doing harm to their clients. Justice means that counselors should treat people as equals (i.e., not discriminate on the bases of gender, race, economic situation, or other personal characteristics). Fidelity means that counselors have loyalty to their clients. In essence, Van Hoose was describing a moral reasoning orientation that counselors should use to make decisions, an orientation reflected in many sets of ethical standards but which may not be explicitly stated.

Although ethical standards do not absolve counselors of personal responsibility in making professional decisions, they do reflect the prevailing ethical sentiment of the profession and in so doing suggest the professional standards to which counselors should adhere. Therefore, ethical standards set the course for professional behavior while allowing, and from the profession's perspective, requiring, that counselors be integrally involved in making specific decisions about how to follow the course.

☐ Professional Preparation for Ethical Practice

Although it can be inferred that many counselor education students value the five "fundamental principles of counseling" described by Van Hoose by virtue of their selection of a potential profession, the extent to which they adhere to those principles is unknown. Therefore, it is incumbent upon counselor education programs to instill or enhance those principles in counselor education students. In addition, it is incumbent upon counselor education programs to ensure that counselor education students have thorough knowledge of applicable ethical standards. These goals are widely recognized and accepted as appropriate. For example, Engels, Wilborn, and Schneider (1990) indicated that "Because circumstances requiring moral and ethical choice pervade our increasingly complex society, it is clear that ethics needs to be overtly and deliberately taught in any counselor education program" (p. 111). At issue is how they should be taught.

In discussing ethical practice training for counselor education students, Engels, Wilborn, and Schneider (1990) provided six curricular goals, including:

> (1) to facilitate student self-awareness, with attention to personal assumptions, values, biases, strengths, and limitations; (2) to facilitate student awareness of the pervasive nature of ethical issues in life and society . . . ;

(3) to foster commitment to personal and professional ethical action and responsibility for action; (4) to facilitate broad ethical knowledge and reasoning skills . . . ; (5) to heighten student appreciation for the complexity and ambiguity of ethical principles and standards; and (6) to foster sensitivity to cultural and other issues [in ethical practice]. . . . (pp. 113–114)

Kitchener (1986) proposed that ethical behavior is essentially a type of morality, and therefore that ethical practice preparation for counselor education students should give them abilities to (a) interpret potential ethical dilemma situations as moral ones, (b) formulate a moral course of action, (c) be able to decide what to do, and (d) implement a course of action. These comments suggest that in order for counselor education students to become ethical practitioners, they must become knowledgeable of their own ethical principles, pertinent ethical standards, and the interaction between them, and have effective ethical decision-making skills.

Tennyson and Strom (1986) indicated that counselors must move beyond mere understanding of ethical standards to development of professional *responsibleness*. According to them, "Counseling is a moral enterprise requiring responsibleness; that is, action should be based on careful, reflective thought about which professional response is right in a particular situation" (p. 298). Perhaps most importantly, they emphasized that development of professional responsibleness (in regard to ethical practice) should not stop with the end of a counselor preparation program; such development should continue throughout each counseling professional's career. They advocated use of professional development activities involving discourse among professionals about ethical issues and concerns, such as workshops and convention programs, as the best means to foster continued development of professional responsibleness.

☐ Overview of the 1995 ACA Ethical Standards

Ethical standards applicable to professional counselors have been created by large professional associations such as the ACA as well as by counselor certification agencies such as the NBCC. A number of the divisions of the ACA (e.g., ASCA and NCDA) also have created sets of ethical standards specific to their respective professional interest areas. Thus, there are quite a few sets of ethical standards to which counselors should adhere. However, because the ACA *Code of Ethics* and *Standards of Practice* and NBCC *Code of Ethics* are the ones most commonly espoused by professional counselors and because they are typical of sets of ethical standards, they are the ones addressed here.

Members of the ACA have always advocated adherence to professional ethical standards. However, surprisingly, the ACA (then APGA) did not publish its own ethical standards until 1959 (Engels, Wilborn, & Schneider, 1990). Prior to that year, the ACA recommended adherence to other sets of ethical standards, particularly those of the APA. The then APGA (and then AACD) *Ethical Standards* and now the ACA *Code of Ethics* and *Standards of Practice* have been revised several times since their original publication. The complete text of the current (1995) ACA *Code of Ethics* can be found at the ACA website. The large number of specific statements in the ACA code of ethics precludes comment upon each one. Therefore, following are some general comments on the eight subsections.

Part of the *Preamble* of the *ACA Code of Ethics and Standards of Practice* explains why the code of ethics was created:

> The specification of ethical standards enables the association to clarify to present and future members and to those served by members, the nature of ethical responsibilities held in common by its members. As the code of ethics of the association, this document establishes principles that define the ethical behavior of association members.

Again, by definition, ethical standards reflect value, moral, social, and professional judgments. Thus, they are intended to communicate to counselors, clients, and other publics the value judgments made by professional counselors about how counselors should behave and how counseling should be practiced. Note also that the ethical standards presented reflect principles of ethical behavior; the document is not intended to encompass all possible situations.

Section A: The Counseling Relationship.   This section of the *ACA Code of Ethics and Standards of Practice* addresses many different aspects of counseling and provides guidelines for the conduct of counseling in general. Important considerations for topics such as client and counselor characteristics, diversity and multiculturalism, counselor-client relationship dynamics, counseling process phenomena, and counseling and technology are covered in this section.

Section B: Confidentiality.   This section covers all important aspects of confidentiality, including topics such as counselor and client rights and responsibilities, counseling context considerations, record keeping, and research situations. Although disparate topics are addressed in this section, it brings together all standards pertinent to confidentiality, and in so doing emphasizes its importance in and to the profession. It also reduces the redundant statements about confidentiality inherent in previous versions of the ethical standards.

Section C: Professional Responsibility. This section serves to clarify responsibilities specifically applicable to counselors and helps to differentiate them from client responsibilities. Topics addressed in this section include the counselor's responsibilities in regard to competence, preparation, continuing professional development, presentation of (professional) self, and respect for differing professional practices.

Section D: Relationships with Other Professionals. This section further elaborates the nature of professional relationships counselors have with other professionals. Employment considerations, relationships with professional peers and colleagues, and practices relative to compensation for services rendered are covered in this section.

Section E: Evaluation, Assessment, and Interpretation. This section presents guidelines related to assessments and evaluations based on them, both important aspects of counseling. Guidelines for competent selection, administration, and interpretations of assessments and disclosure of results, as well as guidelines for client orientation and counseling in regard to assessments, are presented in this section.

Section F: Teaching, Training, and Supervision. This section contains new statements for guiding the counselor preparation process, with particular emphasis on counselor educator-student relationship dynamics. This section also gives greater emphasis to the importance of effective and ethical supervision of counselor trainees.

Section G: Research and Publication. This section presents guidelines for the conduct of research by professional counselors, including the need to protect the rights and privacy of individuals participating in research processes. Also addressed in this section are ethical standards relative to publication processes, including specific guidelines for multiple-author and multiple-submission situations.

Section H: Resolving Ethical Issues. The ACA *Code of Ethics* concludes with this section, which was added to provide more specific guidance for professional counselors about how to proceed if they become aware of unethical behavior by a counselor or about the procedure should they be accused of unethical behavior.

The *Code of Ethics* is followed immediately by the *Standards of Practice*, which represent minimal behavior statements of the *Code of Ethics*. Members should refer to the *Code of Ethics* for further interpretation and amplification of the applicable Standard of Practice. Thus, the *Standards of Practice* are in effect a quick list of appropriate professional behavior for professional counselors; they are not intended to be free-standing, separate guidelines for ethical behavior.

The *ACA Code of Ethics* and *Standards of Practice* are intended to provide guidelines for the ethical practice of counseling in general. Therefore, although they were created by, and for specific application to, ACA members, presumably they are applicable to all who identify themselves as professional counselors. More importantly, however, they provide guidelines for ethical decision making. Therefore, all professional counselors are well-advised to review periodically the *ACA Code of Ethics* and *Standards of Practice* so that they can make ethical decisions effectively, and thereby provide the best professional counseling services for clients.

Processing Complaints of Ethical Violations

In 1997, the ACA Governing Council approved a new document for release to the profession and to the public. This document, entitled *Policies and Procedures for Processing Complaints of Ethical Violations*, was created to explain further and more simply the processes used by ACA to address complaints of ethical violations against members. It explains all aspects of the process, including the composition and responsibilities of the ethics (complaint review) committee, rights and responsibilities of both charged members and those bringing forth complaints, procedural regulations, and possible outcomes of the process. This document is important to professional counselors because it clarifies how allegations of ethical misconduct are handled. The document is available at the ACA website.

☐ The NBCC Code of Ethics

Whereas the ACA *Code of Ethics* and *Standards of Practice* are intended for specific application to ACA members in particular and professional counselors in general, the NBCC *Code of Ethics* is intended for application specifically to the subset of professional counselors who are National Certified Counselors (NCCs) or who hold a specialty certification from the NBCC for which NCC status is a prerequisite. Indeed, indicating formally (vis-à-vis signature) agreement to abide by the NBCC *Code of Ethics* is a prerequisite to becoming an NCC. The currently approved version of the NBCC *Code of Ethics* is available at the NBCC website.

The similarity of the philosophical and professional orientations between ACA and NBCC is reflected in their respective sets of ethical standards. The NBCC *Code of Ethics* was developed originally from the 1981 ACA (then APGA) *Ethical Standards*, has evolved to address most of the same topics, and has sections similar to the previous (1988) version of the ACA ethical standards. The current sections of the NBCC *Code of Ethics* include:

Preamble
Section A: General
Section B: Counseling Relationship
Section C: Measurement and Evaluation
Section D: Research and Publication
Section E: Consulting
Appendix: Certification Examination

Emphasized in the appendix is that NBCC certification applicants must have fulfilled all stipulated eligibility requirements and are responsible for the accuracy and validity of all application information.

The NBCC has also developed additional ethical standards statements for specific facets of work in the helping professions. For example, the NBCC created its *Standards for the Ethical Practice of Clinical Supervision* to clarify and provide guidelines for the clinical supervision process. The NBCC has also taken an advance step by creating its *Standards for the Ethical Practice of WebCounseling*. In creating these standards, the NBCC bypassed the rather substantial professional debate as to whether counseling services should be available over the Internet and moved directly to acknowledgment that webcounseling was already actually happening, regardless of professional debate about it. Thus, these standards are at the forefront of the interface between technology and counseling.

Both the NBCC clinical supervision and webcounseling ethical standards are presented as supplemental to the NBCC *Code of Ethics*. They are available at the NBCC website.

The ACA and NBCC codes of ethics differ primarily in regard to configuration or groupings of the elements. However, there are some elements unique to each set. For example, the ACA *Code of Ethics* does not address a particular examination (e.g., the NBCC certification examination) and the NBCC *Code of Ethics* does not address counselor preparation.

Because of the similarity of the ACA and NBCC codes of ethics, the following discussions of areas of ethical concerns for counselors are presented in reference to both sets of ethical standards in general and to the NBCC *Code of Ethics* in particular for citations. Therefore, counselors are advised to review periodically both the ACA and NBCC codes of ethics in order to keep abreast of pertinent ethical considerations and practices and to provide effective counseling services.

Although literally any counseling activity can result in an ethical dilemma for counselors, some areas of counseling practice have been identified as being common sources of ethical concern or areas in which ethical decision making is particularly difficult. These areas merit further attention.

Clients Intending to Harm Others

Maintenance of confidentiality by counselors with regard to information gained from clients is generally considered to be the primary ethical principle underlying the professional counseling ethical standards. Given the preeminence of the principle of confidentiality, it is not surprising that perhaps the most widely known ethical standard is the one which allows *exception* to the principle of confidentiality: When a client's condition indicates that there is clear and imminent danger to the client or others, the certified counselor must take reasonable action to inform potential victims, responsible authorities or both. This standard must be considered in relation to the one which holds that the primary obligation of the certified counselors is to respect the integrity and promote the welfare of the client. With regard to a client's potential danger to others, one complexity that arises in mutual application of these two ethical standards is in deciding when the welfare of members of society must supersede the welfare of the client. According to Gross and Robinson (1987):

> Definitions of client welfare are not included in the ethical standards, which is perhaps understandable when one views the existing codes as guidelines, not laws or statutes directing the behavior of individuals. Legal definitions of client welfare also do not exist but must be extrapolated from the various laws and statutes that have been established in each state. (p. 340)

Similarly, there are no ethical, legal, or statutory definitions of the welfare of members of society. Presumably, the welfare of members of society at least includes protection from physical injury or death. However, members of society also can be harmed psychologically or socially. Therefore, when a client indicates intention to harm other members of society, which also has significant implications for the client's welfare, the counselor must somehow define the welfare of both the client and of members of society. This is by no means an easy task, but it must be accomplished effectively in order to decide the appropriate priority (the welfare of the client or of members of society).

A second, and integrally related, complexity lies in deciding upon the seriousness of the client's stated intention. Gross and Robinson (1987) wrote that, "assessment of clear and imminent danger . . . lacks definition and seems to be based on the assumption that the mental health professional is able, because of his or her education, training, or experience, to make this determination" (p. 341). The assumption that counselors can make this determination effectively is tenuous at best because most counselors simply have not been trained to assess what may be called a client's lethality potential, that is, the seriousness of the client's stated intention to cause harm to others.

What should a counselor do if a client makes even a veiled threat to others? First, the counselor must take seriously any statement of intention to harm others. Next, in accord with the ACA and NBCC codes of ethics, the counselor must seek appropriate consultation with other professionals, such as other counselors, law enforcement officials, or attorneys. Consultation with regard to determining and using effective methods to evaluate the seriousness of the client's stated intention is crucial. Finally, in accord with the ACA and NBCC codes of ethics and the legal principle of *duty to warn*, the counselor must inform appropriate persons, such as potential victims and law enforcement officials, that the client has indicated intention to harm others.

Clients Intending to Harm Themselves

The ethical (and legal) issues, dynamics, and decisions to be made that arise in situations where a client indicates intention to harm self are similar to those for situations in which a client indicates intention to harm others. In brief, the counselor must evaluate the seriousness of the stated intention and then act accordingly.

Evaluating the seriousness (i.e., lethality potential) of a client's intention to harm self involves consideration of at least 10 factors, paraphrased here from Fujimara, Weis, and Cochran (1985):

1. *Previous suicide attempts.* The best indicator of a person's intention to harm self.
2. *Sleep disruption.* Disrupted sleep patterns are associated with greater seriousness.
3. *Definitiveness of plan.* Having a specific plan of how to harm self is more serious than having a vague plan.
4. *Reversibility of plan.* Intention to use an "irreversible" method, such as a gun or jumping from a high place, is more serious than intended use of a "reversible" method, such as taking pills.
5. *Proximity of others.* Intention to harm self in relative isolation is more serious than intention to harm self in proximity of others.
6. *Giving possessions away.* Having discarded personal possessions and having "arranged one's affairs" is indicative of serious intention.
7. *History of severe alcohol or drug abuse.* Greater use/abuse is associated with greater seriousness.

8. *History of previous psychiatric treatment or hospitalization.* Previous treatment for intention to harm self is associated with greater seriousness.
9. *Availability of resource or support systems.* Feelings of lack of personal and social support are associated with greater seriousness.
10. *Willingness to use resource and support systems.* Unwillingness to get help from support systems is associated with greater seriousness.

Although counselors may be aware of factors such as these, awareness is insufficient for effective evaluation. Again, most counselors simply do not have the training or experience to make lethality potential evaluations effectively. Thus, again, counselors are well-advised to seek professional assistance when the need to make such an evaluation arises.

If a client indicates any intention to harm self, the counselor must act, and act quickly, to attempt to prevent the client from self-inflicted harm, for both ethical and legal reasons. Fujimara, Weis, and Cochran (1985) indicated:

> When applying legal and ethical concerns in working with the suicidal client, the counselor needs to take action to prevent suicide. This is the case when the counselor can reasonably anticipate the situation in the counseling relationship. Liability generally arises as a result of the counselor either (a) failing to act in a way to prevent the suicide (e.g., being negligent in the diagnosis of the client's mental and emotional state) or (b) doing something (e.g., breaching a damaging confidence) that directly contributes to the client's suicide. (p. 615)

Again, counselors confronted with such situations should consult with other professionals such as other counselors and law enforcement officials. Consultation with and use of the services of professionals from local crisis intervention agencies is particularly recommended.

Clients Who are HIV-Positive or Who Have AIDS

No other situation in the history of the counseling profession has raised so complex and complicated ethical and legal issues as has counseling persons who are HIV-positive or who have AIDS (Erickson, 1993). Persons with AIDS (PWAs; used here also to include persons who are HIV-positive) are confronted with a terminal illness, but one which does not always follow a predictable course of progression because ostensible debilities from the infection may not manifest for many years after the infection is contracted initially. Thus, many PWAs do not exhibit observable physical symptoms, and so are free to lead relatively normal lives, including sexual activity. However, knowledge of being HIV-positive or having AIDS is of course difficult for PWAs, and many seek counseling services for help in coping with the psychological stress associated with their condition. This counseling situation raises significant ethical and legal issues for counselors, particularly in counseling interactions with PWAs who are sexually active with partners who are unaware of the client's medical condition.

At issue in situations where a counselor becomes aware that a PWA is sexually active with an unknowing partner is whether the counselor has responsibility to break confidentiality and inform the unknowing partner so as to protect the welfare of members of society. Again, this is the ethical counterpart to the legal concept of duty to warn. Unfortunately, there does not exist clear legal precedent to suggest appropriate ethical behavior. That is, although there have been a few legal challenges to the need for disclosure of knowledge of AIDS for medical doctors and some other professionals, no clear pattern of judicial decisions has arisen. Rather, cases apparently have been decided upon the idiosyncracies of each case, and no trend in the results of such cases is evident. Thus, there is no clear legal basis or example from which to develop corresponding ethical standards or recommended ethical behaviors.

Thoughtful and substantive arguments have been presented in the professional literature about when confidentiality should be broken (i.e., disclosure should be made) in regard to counseling clients who are PWAs and sexually active with unknowing clients. For example, Kain (1988) presented the case for caution in making such disclosures for two primary reasons. First, not all sexual activity permits transmission of the AIDS virus; therefore, counselors need to be aware of the specific sexual behaviors in which the client is engaging before considering disclosure. Second, not all clients who may be thought to have AIDS actually have it; therefore, counselors should have medical evidence and/or confirmation from the client that the client actually is infected before considering disclosure.

The cautions provided by Kain (1988) are appropriate and always should be considered in considering whether to disclose a client's medical status to an unknowing sexual partner and others. However, assuming that the counselor knows that the client has AIDS (or is HIV-positive) and is engaging in at-risk behaviors for transmission of the disease, almost all authorities and authors advocate disclosure to unknowing partners and appropriate others. For example, Cohen (1990) provided a cogent philosophical argument that disclosure under such circumstances is necessary for the protection and welfare of members of society. Gray and Harding (1988) advocated that counselors implement a program including education, consultation, and active support for the client to attempt to get the client to disclose to partners before the counselor is forced to disclose to partners. Finally, Erickson (1990) provided guidelines for decision making in regard to disclosure under such circumstances. An important recommendation in her guidelines is that the state public health agency should be informed in circumstances where unknowing sexual partners of clients who are PWAs cannot be identified specifically.

Clearly favored in the professional literature is that counselors with clients known to be PWAs and sexually active with unknowing partners should disclose the information to the partners and appropriate others. It is certainly becoming the accepted standard of practice. Thus, we too advocate that counselors should disclose, vis-à-vis breaking confidentiality, if clients who are PWAs and sexually active with unknowing partners cannot be persuaded to disclose by themselves.

Other Than Dyadic Counseling

The increasing evidence for the effectiveness and efficiency of group counseling for many client concerns in conjunction with the rapidly increasing use of couples or family counseling methods have resulted in increasing numbers of situations in which counselors have other than dyadic (i.e., one-to-one) counseling relationships with their clients. With regard to group counseling, in any interaction between the counselor and a client in a group counseling session, there is always at least one third party to the counselor-client interaction. The presence of a third party to the interaction has significant implications for the application of ethical standards to the group counseling process, particularly in regard to confidentiality issues.

In general, the legal right to privileged communication does not apply to clients in group counseling even in those states where clients have the right to privileged communication in individual counseling (Hopkins & Anderson, 1996). This legal situation exists primarily because of the recognized difficulty in maintaining privileged communication in other than dyadic interactions. If confidentiality is viewed as the ethical counterpart of privileged communication, similar difficulty exists in regard to it. That is, it is difficult to hold one client responsible for confidentiality in regard to information learned about another client during group counseling.

How does a counselor handle confidentiality issues in group counseling? Unfortunately, there is no precise answer. The ACA and NBCC codes of ethics advocate that a group counselor is to set a norm of confidentiality regarding all client disclosures. Thus, counselors should at least explain carefully the principles of confidentiality in group counseling and encourage them to abide by those principles. However, it also is incumbent upon counselors to explain that confidentiality in the traditional sense cannot be guaranteed (even within legal limits) as it can be in dyadic counseling situations. In effect, group counselors should not promise confidentiality to group members, but they should encourage them to maintain confidentiality in the best interests of the counseling process. Of course, counselors should maintain confidentiality regardless of whether the group members do.

Couples or marriage and family counseling encompass the same confidentiality issues as group counseling, but include other issues as well. Corey, Corey, and Callanan (1993) noted that most couples or marriage and family counselors engage in individual counseling sessions with couple or family members before or concurrent with couples or marriage and family counseling. Assuming that couple or marriage and family counseling is the intended primary counseling modality in such situations, at issue is whether information garnered during the dyadic counseling sessions with an individual family member should be disclosed by the counselor during couple or marriage and family counseling sessions. Strict adherence to the ethical standards for confidentiality would imply that the counselor should not disclose information obtained during the individual sessions. However, if such information is deemed by the counselor to be crucial to the effectiveness of the couple or marriage and family counseling process, then withholding the information violates the ethical standards related to provision of the best possible counseling services for clients. Again, there is no precise guideline or clearly established practice. Some couples or marriage and family counselors maintain confidentiality about information obtained during individual counseling sessions conducted in conjunction with couple or family counseling sessions, and some do not, choosing instead to inform clients prior to individual counseling that any information obtained may be discussed subsequently in couple or family counseling. Corey, Corey, and Callanan (1993) advocated the latter approach, with the caveat that the counselor inform the client that the information will be disclosed by the counselor during couple or family counseling only if the counselor deems it in the best interest of all concerned.

Strein and Hershenson (1991) indicated that counseling, even when there is ostensibly only a counselor and client directly involved, is often other than dyadic in another sense. Even in cases where there is a not a third party within the actual counseling sessions, there often are third parties to the counseling *process*, that is, others who potentially have legitimate right to know what is happening in the sessions. According to Strein and Hershenson (1991) "much of the thinking underlying counselor-client confidentiality is rooted in the implicit assumption that counseling consists of an individual relationship between two parties, each acting singly" (p. 312). They then noted examples of situations in which that assumption is not valid.

The practice of counseling encompasses a number of roles and functions in which the view of counseling as a relationship between two single-acting individuals clearly does not apply. Among these nondyadic relationships are: (a) counseling done as an integral part of a multidisciplinary team approach to treatment, in which the counselor may function as a case coordinator or simply as one member of the team; (b) coordination of services, referral, and placement; (c) mandated evaluations or services; (d) clinical or administrative supervision that requires the sharing of case material; and (e) advocacy on behalf of a client to a group of noncounselors. (Strein & Hershenson, 1991, p. 312)

In situations where third party individuals have legitimate need for and access to information from counseling sessions, counselors cannot provide the usual guarantees of confidentiality. Instead, they must inform clients of the limitations of confidentiality at the beginning of counseling. Strein and Hershenson (1991) noted that although counselors may feel awkward presenting conditions for disclosure (i.e., breaking confidentiality) to clients, it has been found through research that such conditional confidentiality generally has little impact on subsequent counseling effectiveness. Strein and Hershenson (1991) wrote:

A variety of creative methods exist to reduce the awkwardness of this disclosure, including use of written handouts, a separate precounseling session led by either the counselor or an associate, or a discussion of the client's expectations about and need for confidentiality as part of the counseling process. In summary, honesty about the limits of confidentiality, more than absolute confidentiality itself, seems to be the ethical imperative. (p. 315)

The recommendation that clients be given honest and accurate precounseling information about the limits or conditions for confidentiality would seem to be appropriate for any other than dyadic counseling situation. Presentation of limits or conditions may allow clients to decide whether counseling should proceed or at least what to divulge to counselors, and therefore generally absolves counselors of the need to make difficult decisions about whether to violate confidentiality.

Computer-Assisted Counseling

Sampson (1990) indicated that "Computer technology is now a common resource that counselors and clients use to collect, process, and disseminate information" (p. 170). Computer applications in counseling are increasingly varied, and range from counselors' rather simplistic uses of word processing software, to electronic gathering, storage, manipulation, and transfer of client data, and to emulation of counselor functioning through interactive computer programs. The diversity of potential computer applications in counseling is associated with an equally diverse set of potential ethical concerns. Unfortunately, because of that diversity, only major categories of potential ethical concerns can be covered here.

Sampson (1990) identified seven major areas of potential ethical concerns related to computer applications in counseling. Following are brief summaries of those areas.

Confidentiality.   A primary advantage of the use of computers is the capability to store incredibly large amounts of information in incredibly small storage areas (e.g., on diskettes or hard drives). However, this capability also can be a disadvantage because it is difficult at best to control access to data stored electronically. Counselors using electronic storage of client data must be concerned about access to what and by whom.

Counselor interventions.   The increasing use of computer-assisted counseling interventions necessitates that counselors (a) prescreen clients' suitability for computer use, (b) properly orient and instruct clients, and (c) follow up with clients so that clients use the technology and interpret the results correctly. Computer software used for counseling purposes should never be the sole counseling intervention; such programs are intended to assist the counseling process, not replace it. Invalid or inappropriate use of computerized assistance for counseling is unethical.

Assessment.   The primary ethical concerns in this area are use of not-fully-validated computerized assessments and overdependence on computer-based test interpretation systems. As with any type of assessment, the counselor has an ethical responsibility to use only validated techniques and to provide fully effective interpretations of assessment data.

Quality of computer-based information.   Clients quite frequently seek specific information from counselors and then make important decisions based on the information provided. Counselors now use computers for information storage and/or retrieval for clients' purposes. As has been true historically, counselors are ethically responsible for the accuracy of the information given to clients.

Use of computer-assisted instruction.   Counselors have an ethical responsibility to ensure that clients are not mislead by unreasonable expectations and that they not become overdependent upon computers in lieu of more effective professional interventions.

Equality of access to computer applications.   Access to the potential benefits of computer-assisted counseling and other applications of counseling should not be denied to special client populations. Counselors have an ethical responsibility to ensure that all clients have equal access to effective counseling, including all possible counseling aids.

Counselor training. Computer applications in counseling can be used effectively only if counselors have the knowledge and skills appropriate to those applications. Similar to any counseling activity, it is unethical for counselors to use computer applications in ways for which they are not competent or qualified.

Computer applications for counseling will continue to increase, probably at a rate faster than ethical standards can be developed to guide use of those applications. Therefore, it is incumbent upon counselors to consider carefully and thoroughly the possible ethical implications of computer applications. Determination of analogies between computer applications and other processes extant in counseling may be particularly helpful for ethical decision making.

Multicultural Counseling

A fundamental precept of the ACA and NBCC codes of ethics is that counselors have responsibility to respect the diversity of their clients and to be nondiscriminatory in all their activities. In a complex, culturally diverse society, this means that counselors must be sensitive to the particular situations and characteristics of culturally different persons and provide counseling services built upon such cultural sensitivity (Axelson, 1998; Ivey, Ivey, & Simek-Morgan, 1996; Patterson, 1996). Burn (1992) aptly summarized the situation surrounding ethical concerns and multicultural counseling.

> The professional literature contains an abundant supply of strategies and proposals for defining specific ethical principles in regard to serving culturally unique clients. If the counseling profession truly aspires to meeting the needs of the heterogeneous groups that constitute "society," it must institute principles that facilitate thorough counselor training, thus maximizing the capacity to serve effectively.
>
> The development and implementation of clear and specific cross-cultural ethical guidelines would be a significant step forward. (p. 582)

In response to professional concerns such as these, both the ACA and NBCC codes of ethics now contain more statements relative to multicultural and diversity issues. However, neither contains what might be deemed extensive attention to potential multicultural ethical issues in counseling. Because of the extensive nature of the issues involved and the lengthy recommendations made for how to address them, other documents focused on multiculturalism issues in counseling have been created. For example, a set of multicultural counseling competencies has been developed by the ACA's Association for Multicultural Counseling and Development division and is progressing through a series of adoptions and endorsements by various professional counseling organizations. Although these multicultural counseling competencies are not ethical standards in the traditional sense, they do provide very specific information about what is necessary to provide culturally sensitive counseling.

Clinical Supervision

Clinical supervision in counseling involves one counseling professional, a supervisor, who presumably has greater counseling expertise and experience, working with another (or aspiring) counseling professional, the supervisee, who presumably has lesser expertise and experience, to facilitate development and enhancement of the supervisee's counseling knowledge, skills, and abilities. Clinical supervision in counseling is typically provided in one of two contexts: (a) for counselor education students during practica or internships in counseling preparation programs or (b) for counselors who have achieved minimum credentials (e.g., an academic degree in counseling) but who need additional supervised experience to achieve a professional credential such as certification or licensure.

The necessarily close working relationship between supervisor and supervisee, in conjunction with the supervisor's third-party status in the supervisee's counseling processes, gives rise to a number of different ethical concerns. For example, ethical concerns in regard to supervisor's qualifications and competence, informed consent, confidentiality, dual relationships, evaluation, client welfare, and payment for services have been addressed in the professional literature (e.g., Borders & Leddick, 1987; Bernard, in Borders & Leddick, 1987; Corey, Corey, & Callanan, 1993; Kurpius, Gibson, Lewis, & Corbet, 1991). These and many other important ethical concerns in clinical supervision merit attention and understanding by counselors and counselor trainees. However, only two ethical concerns inherent in the supervisor-supervisee relationship can be covered here: (a) responsibility for client welfare and (b) provision of counseling to supervisees.

In the typical clinical supervision situation, supervisees have clients with whom they are working and discuss that work with clients during supervision sessions with their supervisors. It also is typical for supervisees to share audio- or videotape recordings of their counseling activities with their supervisors to facilitate discussions and allow for specific suggestions. In this typical situation, the supervisor is a third party who has at least indirect, and often direct (vis-à-vis tape recordings), access to psychological, emotional, and other information about the client. Therefore, inherent in the clinical supervision process is assumption of the client's welfare by the supervisor.

Corey, Corey, and Callanan (1993) indicated that "Supervisors are ultimately responsible, both ethically and legally, for the actions of their trainees [i.e., supervisees]" (p. 195). Similalry, Welfel (1998) wrote that "Supervisors have ultimate legal and ethical responsibility for the welfare of their supervisees' clients" (p. 271). However, Bernard (1987) noted that, legally, although supervisors may incur liability if they fail to make recommendations (e.g., in the case of a client intending to harm others) because they are unaware of the client's intentions, they probably would not incur liability for making incorrect recommendations. The law does not require infallibility, only awareness and action (Bernard, 1987).

It is important to acknowledge that although supervisors have ultimate responsibility for the welfare of their supervisees' clients, supervisees are not absolved of responsibility. Indeed, supervisees, like other counselors, have responsibility for their clients' welfare, and for all ethical standards attendant thereto. In addition, supervisees have the additional ethical responsibility to keep their supervisors fully apprised of important client information so as to preclude ethical and legal problems for their supervisors.

Borders and Leddick (1987) suggested that the supervisor-supervisee relationship is similar to the counselor-client relationship in that both require a close working relationship in which personal dynamics come into play. Historically, a few models of supervision have been proposed in which counseling for the supervisee is an integral part of the supervision process, based on the assumption that development of the supervisee's personal sensitivity and insight is essential to the development of effective counseling skills. However, more recently, the generally accepted recommendation is that supervisees should not be counseled, either during supervision or otherwise, by supervisors. Unfortunately, as Whiston and Emerson (1989) noted:

> [I]n practice, there are few guidelines for supervisors to ensure that promoting insight, sensitivity, and personal growth in trainees [i.e., supervisees] does not become counseling. This becomes particularly difficult when the supervisor suspects that trainees' [i.e., supervisees'] personal problems are the cause of their ineffectiveness with clients. (p. 321)

Nonetheless, it is now considered unethical for supervisors to counsel supervisees as a part of the supervision process (Corey, Corey, & Callanan, 1993; Davenport, 1992; Whiston & Emerson, 1989). This ethical principle is based upon the fact that supervision necessarily involves an evaluation function, and counselors, including supervisors, are ethically pro-

hibited from counseling persons about whom they must make evaluations.

Sexual/Intimate Relationships with Clients

This one is simple: Counselors should never have sexual relationships
with their clients. The ethical standards of all major professional organizations and associations for counselors, as well as those of all major counselor credentialing agencies, specifically stipulate that counselors should not
engage in sexual intimacies with their clients. However, this is a commonly violated ethical standard (Vasquez & Kitchener, 1988; Welfel, 1998).
Why is this the case? Perhaps it is because the nature of counseling is
such that the step from compassion to passion is often a very small one.
Vasquez and Kitchener (1988) wrote:

> The counselor-client relationship is typically a highly intimate and special
> one. Counselors often experience a natural sense of emotional satisfaction
> from their role in the counseling experience. The natural caring, warmth,
> and regard for clients may evolve into more erotic feelings. Indeed, attrac-
> tion to clients is pervasive. (p. 214)

Clearly clients can become entrapped in a similar way. Kitchener and
Harding (1990) write:

> Clients entrust their vulnerabilities, pain, inner thoughts, feelings, and hopes
> to a presumably wise and healing counselor or therapist. The therapeutic
> relationship is one of support, warmth, and trust. It creates a natural inti-
> macy that may evolve into sexual feelings. (pp. 148–149)

Thus, both counselors and clients are susceptible to feelings of sexual attraction as an outgrowth of a counseling relationship which is highly personal. However, establishment of the limits of psychological and behavioral boundaries, including refraining from sexual intimacy, clearly lies
with the counselor.

Counselor-client sexual intimacy can only lead to negative consequences
for clients, regardless of whether it evolves from a natural attraction between the counselor and client or it is instigated under the pretense of
therapeutic benefit for the client (Welfel, 1998). Pope (1988) identified
potential negative consequences for the client including: feelings of guilt;
a sense of emptiness and isolation; sexual confusion; impaired ability to
trust; identity, boundary, and role confusion; emotional liability; suppressed
rage; increased suicidal risk; and cognitive dysfunction. Obviously, there
are many and significant negative repercussions for clients from sexual
intimacies with counselors.

There are also significant potential negative repercussions for counselors. Welfel (1998) wrote:

If the counselor is found guilty, the probability of disciplinary action is substantial, as is the risk of malpractice suit. . . . Counselors employed by agencies may lose their jobs. Licenses are often suspended, or conditions placed on future practice. The option to continue practice without oversight is gone. Moreover, the professional liability insurers write policies to limit the amount they will cover for such claims, so the burden of payment falls largely on the individual. Even if they manage to stay in practice, they may find their liability insurance canceled and other insurers unwilling to offer coverage. In some states, criminal penalties have been added to civil and professional liability so therapists [counselors] may be charged with a crime. (p. 143)

Thus, counselors must refrain from sexual intimacies with clients for their own welfare as well as that of their clients. Kitchener (1988) emphasized that counselors not only must be aware of the potential for these negative repercussions, but also must act intentionally to avoid situations in which they might arise.

It is not uncommon for clients who have been victimized through sexual intimacy with a counselor to seek help from another counselor to cope with the negative consequences from the sexual interaction with the previous counselor. In addition to providing counseling help, the subsequent counselor should inform such clients of the options available to them with regard to the previous counselor (although the subsequent counselor should not endorse or criticize any particular option). Hotelling (1988) listed three major types of redress available to such clients: (a) ethical, including filing charges of unethical conduct with professional organizations against the previous counselor, (b) administrative, including filing grievances with pertinent certification and/or licensing agencies and with the previous counselor's employer, and (c) legal, including filing a civil or criminal lawsuit against the previous counselor.

Vasquez (1988) noted that facilitating counselors' abilities to refrain from sexual intimacies with clients must begin in counselor preparation programs. She wrote that:

Educational programs must provide a climate in which students can acknowledge, explore, and discuss . . . feelings of sexual attraction [to clients]. Teachers who are critical or rejecting of such feelings will undermine the potential for effective education. A successful training program will provide a safe environment in which the value of honest and forthright discussions of sexuality and sexual attraction, sexual socialization issues, and other relevant topics may be explored. (p. 240)

Extension of Vasquez's recommendations to professional association activities is obvious. If the frequency of counselor-client sexual intimacy, and the resultant ethical, legal, and professional difficulties, are to be reduced, then the entire profession must be open to effective dialogue about the issues and circumstances involved.

Counselor Competence and Impairment

The concept of counselor competence encompasses a variety of ethical standards and practices related to ways that counselors can be less than appropriately effective. For example, in a general sense, a counselor who violates any ethical standard can be considered less than fully competent. However, typically the term counselor competence is used to refer qualifications, the level of a counselor's knowledge, skills, and abilities to perform a particular type of counseling effectively. Both the ACA and NBCC codes of ethics specifically prohibit counselors from engaging in counseling activities which they are not qualified to perform.

Common examples of areas in which counselors may attempt counseling activities exceeding their basic qualifications include use of projective assessment methods, counseling abused persons, evaluation of suicide lethality, substance abuse counseling, use of art therapy techniques, marriage and family counseling, counseling culturally different persons, or counseling individuals exhibiting severe psychopathology. Indeed, literally any specialized counseling activity could have been listed. Attempting to implement counseling activities such as these without specific training and supervised experience in their use is unethical.

Unfortunately, counselors often attempt to use counseling activities for which they are unqualified from a sense of compassion for their clients. However, according to Gilbert (1992):

> It is misguided kindness, as well as being ethically unwise and legally risky, to attempt to carry out a treatment mission with inadequate resources [i.e., competence] out of compassion for the client. (p. 698)

Counselors must be ever mindful of the limits of their qualifications and refrain from attempting to exceed those qualifications.

Counselor impairment is a concept closely related to counselor competence. Counselors are impaired when they are experiencing emotional, psychological, or physical symptoms which prohibit them from performing a counseling activity effectively even though they may have the requisite qualifications to perform the activity. The most commonly cited types of counselor impairment result from physical and emotional handicaps (e.g., stress reactions to divorce or death of a significant other), alcohol and chemical dependencies, sexual intimacies with clients, mental illness, and suicidal orientation (Stadler, Willing, Eberhage, & Ward, 1988).

Stadler (1990) provided a poignant comment on the results of counselor impairment:

It would be the rare counselor who never experienced a frustrating day, a difficult client, or an emotional overload. But counselors who are functioning well can put these experiences into perspective; their skills remain intact and their personalities remain stable. On the other hand, impaired counselors have lost the capacity to transcend stressful events. They no longer function as well as they once did. The therapeutic skills of impaired counselors have diminished or deteriorated. (p. 178)

Clearly, impaired professionals cannot provide effective counseling services. Unfortunately, however, they often continue to provide services because they are not cognizant of their own impairment. They may even rationalize that work (i.e., providing counseling services) is therapeutic for them and will help them overcome their impairment.

Counselor impairment raises complex ethical issues, both for the impaired professional and for professional peers. According to Stadler, Willing, Eberhage, and Ward (1988):

The injunction to do no harm to clients, their families, society, the profession, and the impaired practitioner is an ethical obligation.

Pitted against this concern for the welfare of others is the autonomy of the impaired professional—the professional's capacity to determine his or her own course of action. When counselors become impaired and threaten the welfare of others, their autonomy—their capacity to determine their professional practices—should be questioned. (p. 259)

Implicit in this quote is that counselors have an ethical obligation to monitor their professional peers and to attempt to prevent impaired professionals from practicing. The decision to attempt to curtail a peer practitioner's counseling activities is by no means made easily. However, given that beneficence and nonmaleficence are the two primary ethical principles of the counseling profession, counselors are ethically obligated to do something about impaired counseling practitioners.

Future Directions in Ethical Standards for Counselors

Promotion of ethical practice remains, and will remain, a prominent thrust in the counseling profession. This emphasis reflects not only a noble professional orientation, but also the reality of increasing numbers of allegations of unethical behavior by counselors. Indeed, the numbers of charges of ethical violations by counselors has increased dramatically in recent years (Welfel, 1998). In addition, a consistent point in the research on counselors' understanding of applications of ethical standards is the fact that while most counselors do have good understanding of ethical practices, a substantial proportion apparently do not (Fuqua & Newman, 1989). Improvements in ethical practices in counseling will result from more and better ethics research, ethics education for counselors, and revision of ethical standards.

Fuqua and Newman (1989) addressed the status of ethics research in the counseling profession and concluded that most existing ethics research has resulted from surveys of adherence to ethical standards or applications of ethical standards in hypothetical situations. Fuqua and Newman (1989) noted that "Adherence by professionals to ethical guidelines is, and should continue to be, a fundamental concern of the profession. But this kind of information reveals little, if anything, about why ethical and unethical behavior occurs" (p. 86). They contend:

> It is fundamental and necessary to strive toward an understanding of *why* professionals behave as they do in various situations or *how* they arrive at their decisions to respond to situations in particular ways. The answers to questions such as these have significant implications for promoting the ethical development of counseling professionals. (Fuqua & Newman, 1989, p. 85)

The points made by Fuqua and Newman were important when they were written and they remain important today. Knowing counselors' relative abilities to apply ethical standards does facilitate understanding of professional practices. However, such data are not in and of themselves sufficient to suggest how counselors should be prepared for ethical practice or how ethical standards can be made more relevant to counselors' ethical decision-making processes. Research clarifying the why and how of counselors' ethical decision making is needed for fully effective counselor preparation and ethical standards revision.

Robinson and Gross (1989) investigated practicing counselors' abilities to determine whether ethical violations had occurred or which ethical standards were applicable in a series of hypothetical situations. One of the independent variables in their study was whether the respondents had had formal (i.e., academic course) preparation in professional ethics. Robinson and Gross (1989) wrote that:

> Perhaps the most relevant finding was that having a course in ethics significantly improves practitioners' ability to recognize which ethical standard is being violated and to suggest appropriate ethical behaviors to correct those situations. Having a course in ethics, however, did not increase the ability to recognize whether a situation involved a violation of professional standards. (p. 295)

This conclusion suggests that while counselors' academic preparation in professional ethics certainly enhances ethical behavior, it has focused upon ethical standards at the expense of considerations in ethical decision making. Thus, while counselors' preparation in professional ethics should include applications of ethical standards, it also should facilitate development of counselors' ethical principles, such as those described by Van Hoose (1986), and responsibleness, as described by Tennyson and Strom (1986).

☐ Summary

Ethical practice in counseling is paramount because it is only through strict adherence to and effective application of ethical principles and standards that counselors will command the professional respect to which they are entitled. Although there are numerous complexities and idiosyncratic considerations in understanding and effectively applying professional ethics, it is incumbent upon counselors to devote the time and energy necessary to become extremely proficient in these regards. To do anything less is to demean the counseling profession and to do disservice to those who could benefit from counseling. Counseling in accord with high ethical standards is not necessarily good counseling, but good counseling necessarily involves adherence to ethical standards.

14

CHAPTER

Professionalism in Counseling

Emener and Cottone (1989) reviewed models of professionalism and concluded that the four primary characteristics of a profession are (a) a body
of specialized knowledge and theory-driven research, (b) professional
preparation and review, (c) a code of ethics, and (d) professional identification and practice control. Similarly, Wittmer and Loesch (1986) indicated that, "A profession is typically defined as a vocational activity having (1) an underlying body of theoretical and research knowledge, (2) an
identifiable set of effective skills and activities, and (3) a publicly professed, voluntarily self-imposed set of behavioral guidelines" (p. 301).
Support for the belief that counseling is a profession is provided throughout this book. For example, professional preparation for counselors and
legal and ethical guidelines for counseling practice have been addressed.
Yet, while support can be garnered for the proposition that counseling is
a profession according to commonly applied criteria, those criteria do not
encompass perhaps the most important part of a profession—specifically,
that professionals have a distinctive orientation toward their work. This
orientation is what differentiates professional counselors from others (e.g.,
lay-person "listeners," faith healers, palmists, advisors, or spiritualists) who
purport to provide counseling services.

Professional orientation is a rather esoteric term that defies exact definition. VanZandt (1990) addressed the counseling profession specifically:

> Professionalism is a complex attribute, and there may not be total agree-
> ment on its definition. Based on my reading of the literature, however, I
> would offer the following working definition. Professionalism is:

290

1. the way in which a person relies upon a personal high standard of competence in providing professional services
2. the means by which a person promotes or maintains the image of the profession
3. a person's willingness to pursue professional development opportunities that will continue to improve skills within the profession
4. the pursuit of quality and ideals within the profession
5. a person's sense of pride about the profession. (p. 244)

In general, then, professional orientation encompasses counselors' beliefs about and attitudes toward their work. Inherent in these beliefs and attitudes is the supposition that, ultimately, all of a counselor's behaviors should be beneficial to clients served, the counseling profession, and society, regardless of the personal advantages accrued or disadvantages endured from the behaviors. Thus, professional counselors engage in some behaviors (e.g., provision of pro bono counseling services, joining professional organizations, or attaining professional credentials) neither for altruistic nor material personal gain, but rather because it is the *professional* thing to do. Above all else, counselors having and adhering to a professional orientation is what makes counseling a true profession.

Counselors most frequently manifest a professional orientation through demonstration of respect for the dignity of their clients and the professional colleagues with whom they work in their daily activities. However, counselors also manifest a professional orientation in other ways, including becoming members of professional organizations and associations, obtaining professional credentials, participating in professional self-development activities, and making contributions to the theoretical and knowledge bases of the counseling profession.

☐ Professional Organizations for Counselors

Counselors with a good professional orientation are members of professional organizations (used here as synonymous with professional associations) for three primary reasons. First, professional organizations provide the major information and activity resources that counselors can use to improve their counseling knowledge, skills, and performance. Second, professional organizations are a primary means for counselors to interact with one another. Third, professional organizations provide the most effective means for counselors to facilitate improvement of the counseling profession. Therefore, reciprocal benefits are present for counselors and the counseling profession from counselors' memberships in professional organizations. Simply put, professional organizations are the media through which the counseling profession benefits individual counselors, and vice versa.

A number of professional organizations exist to which professionally oriented counselors may belong. Many counselors are members of the American Psychological Association (APA), particularly Division 17, Counseling Psychology; American Association for Marriage and Family Therapy (AAMFT); American Educational Research Association (AERA), particularly Division H: Counseling and Human Development; and/or the American Vocational Association (AVA). However, the American Counseling Association (ACA) is the professional organization with which professional counselors primarily affiliate. ACA has an organizational and functional structure typical of many professional organizations and therefore is described here in some detail as an illustrative example.

The ACA headquarters building is located just outside Washington, D.C. in Alexandria, Virginia. The headquarters houses the professional staff who are paid employees of the association, the ACA library, and resource and meeting rooms for association activities. The headquarters staff members are divided among several functional areas such as association administration and management, budget and finance, convention coordination, membership services, and professional media and publications. In general, the headquarters staff is responsible for implementation of ACA's ongoing activities. Thus, the headquarters staff is a primary contributor to continuity within the association and the counseling profession.

In 1999, ACA membership exceeded 55,000 people located in the United States and approximately 50 foreign countries. Four types of ACA membership are possible: (1) *Professional,* for counseling practitioners who have graduated from counselor preparation programs (i.e., who hold a master's or doctoral degree in counseling or a closely related field), (2) *Student,* for persons currently enrolled in counselor preparation programs, (3) *Regular,* for persons who are not students but who are working toward fulfillment of criteria for Professional membership, and (4) *Associate,* for professionals who are indirectly associated with the counseling profession, such as test and book company representatives, program administrators, and supervisors. Professional members comprise the largest group, followed in order by student, associate, and regular members. Regardless of category, memberships and associated dues are on an annual basis, with unlimited renewals except in rare cases where membership is revoked because of ethical or legal misconduct. ACA has an open enrollment system which allows new members to join at any time.

In order to be responsive to the many different interests, needs, and circumstances of members, the ACA membership is partitioned in two different ways. One is a divisional structure, including the following 17 divisions and 1 organizational affiliate:

American College Counseling Association (ACCA)
Association for Counselor Education and Supervision (ACES)
National Career Development Association (NCDA)
Association for Humanistic Education and Development (AHEAD)
American School Counselor Association (ASCA)
American Rehabilitation Counseling Association (ARCA)
Association for Assessment in Counseling (AAC)
National Employment Counseling Association (NECA)
Association for Multicultural Counseling and Development (AMCD)
Association for Spiritual, Religious, and Ethical Value Issues in Counseling (ASREVIC)
Association for Specialists in Group Work (ASGW)
International Association of Addictions and Offenders Counseling (IAAOC)
American Mental Health Counselors Association (AMHCA)
Association for Counselors and Educators in Government (ACEG)
Association for Adult Development and Aging (AADA)
International Association for Marriage and Family Counselors (IAMFC)
Association for Gay, Lesbian and Bisexual Issues in Counseling (AGLBIC)
Military Educators and Counselors Association (MECA) (organizational affiliate)

With regard to benefits received (e.g., newsletters and journals) and annual dues, membership in ACA may be separate from or conjoint with membership in an ACA division.

The second partitioning is by geographic regions. ACA's regional components are referred to as "branch assemblies" because they are composed of the branches (e.g., state-level counterparts) of ACA. The four ACA Regional Branch Assemblies (RBAs) are Southern, North Atlantic, Midwestern, and Western. Technically, ACA members are not members of one of its RBAs, and there are no separate dues for the RBA. Rather, the RBA structure simply allows for representation of ACA members by geographic region. Thus, while the RBAs have individual governance structures for their respective areas and have representation in the ACA governance structure, they do not have members in the same sense as in ACA divisions.

The ACA governance structure is unicameral. The ACA Governing Council includes the ACA president, past president, president-elect, treasurer, parliamentarian, executive director (from the headquarters permanent staff), and representatives from each of the divisions and regions. The ACA Governing Council meets at least biannually to conduct the association's business.

The benefits of ACA membership to professional counselors are too numerous to be listed here. However, some of the major benefits can be identified. First, in regard to professional publications, all ACA members receive the association's newsletter, *Counseling Today*, and the *Journal of Counseling and Development*. Members of ACA divisions and organizational affiliates also receive divisional newsletters. Most ACA divisions also publish journals that members receive. Next, ACA provides to members access to a wide variety of professional resources (e.g., films, videotapes, books, monographs, bibliographic search services, and other electronic media). Third, ACA provides a variety of insurance programs for its members, including professional liability, life, and health insurance. Fourth, ACA maintains an active political involvement system (including lobbyists) for interaction with the federal government. Relatedly, ACA has assisted with political involvement at state levels, particularly with regard to professional counselor licensure legislation. Fifth, ACA maintains a legal defense fund to which members can apply for funds if they become involved in work-related litigation.

Perhaps ACA's most visible benefit to its members is its annual national/international world conference (convention), held in the spring at a different site each year. The ACA world conference is a primary means for professional counselors to interact with one another, participate in professional development activities, and keep abreast of new professional activities, issues, and trends. A placement service for both students in counselor preparation programs and professional counselors also is provided at each ACA world conference. In addition, the ACA world conference typically attracts more than 100 exhibitors of professional materials and services.

ACA has 56 state and international branches, i.e., geographically restricted organizations whose purpose is to represent counselors in each geographic area. Each branch is a separate organization with its own membership requirements, dues, and structure, and each is defined geographically by state or regional boundaries (e.g., Ohio Counseling Association and the European Branch Counseling Association). However, membership is usually open to any professional who wishes to join. Typically, a primary organization (e.g., North Carolina Counseling Association or Florida Counseling Association) as well as state- or branch-level divisions parallel those in ACA, although most branches typically have fewer divisions than does ACA. The activities of the ACA branches typically reflect those of ACA. For example, most hold an annual convention, are involved in legislative activities (particularly those relating to counselor certification or licensure), publish newsletters, and provide a variety of professional resources. Some state branches also publish their own professional counseling journals. The primary difference between ACA and its branches is of course the scope of their respective efforts; the ACA branches focus their activities on matters particularly pertinent to the professionals in the specific geographic area represented.

ACA has corporate affiliates, each of which is a technically and legally separate organization with strong philosophical and theoretical ties to ACA. One is the Council for the Accreditation of Counseling and Related Educational Programs (CACREP). Another is the Counseling and Human Development Foundation (CHDF). This not-for-profit agency helps the counseling profession and ACA through the management of property and financial holdings and the provision of funds for activities with special significance to the counseling profession (e.g., research). ACA members and other professional counselors cannot join ACA corporate-affiliate organizations. The counseling professionals who manage them typically are selected by the organizations themselves. However, because most of the counseling professionals who operate the corporate affiliates are ACA members, these affiliates do have strong allegiance to ACA.

The American Association for State Counselor Boards (AASCB) is another organization closely aligned with ACA. Members of AASCB are representative counseling professionals from states having, or currently seeking, counselor licensure laws, or from other organizations (e.g., ACA or NBCC) with professional interest in counselor licensure. The primary purpose of AASCB is to provide a mechanism for communication and collaboration among states having licensure laws, and thus to promote and improve counselor licensure practices. AASCB also does not have an open membership for professional counselors, but rather is composed of persons selected by state and other organizations having interest in counselor licensure to represent those organizations.

Active membership in professional organizations is a primary way for professional counselors to exhibit professionalism. Professional organization membership allows members to acknowledge to themselves and others that they are concerned about people in the world vis-à-vis counseling services provided, and about their own competence and improvement as professional counselors. However, professional counselors can also demonstrate that they are concerned about professionalism in counseling through seeking pertinent professional credentials.

☐ Professional Credentials for Counselors

Professional credentialing is usually viewed as encompassing three major professional activities: (a) counselor (academic) preparation program accreditation, (b) certification, and (c) licensure (Loesch, 1988). In general, professional counselors seek these types of credentials in order to demonstrate that they have specific knowledge and skills for, and to be permitted to provide, certain types of counseling services. Thus, counselors who have certain professional credentials are presumed to be better able to provide certain types of counseling services in certain ways. The particular types or ways of counseling for which competence is presumed to be greater for credentialed than for noncredentialed counselors are reflected in the respective credentials.

Graduation from an Accredited Preparation Program

One credential a professional counselor can have is to be a graduate of an accredited preparation program. Because counselor preparation programs exist almost exclusively within institutions of higher education, almost all of them are accredited by some accrediting agency. The question then becomes, which accreditations are most pertinent to counseling? Many institutions of higher education are accredited by the regional Associations of Colleges and Schools (*x*ACS). For example, many institutions in the Southern United States are accredited by the SACS. Similarly, many colleges or schools of education are accredited by the National Council for Accreditation of Teacher Education (NCATE). However, these types of accreditations are very general in nature and have very little specific application to preparation for professional counseling. Thus, graduation from programs having only these types of accreditations is not a particularly strong credential for professional counselors. Comparatively, CACREP accreditation is specifically applicable to programs for the professional preparation of counselors. Therefore, graduation from a CACREP-accredited program is a much stronger professional credential for counselors. Moreover, this particular credential is increasingly providing advantages for attainment of other credentials (e.g., certifications or licensures) particularly appropriate for professional counselors. For example, graduates of CACREP-accredited counseling programs may participate in the NBCC's National Counselor Examination prior to completion of postgraduation experiential requirements and, if successful, become eligible for NBCC certification pending completion of other requirements. Similarly, some state counselor licensure procedures are expedited for graduates of CACREP-accredited programs.

Certification

Certification is the second type of credential important for professional counselors. Certification is a process whereby an agency, which may be either governmental or private, attests or affirms that an individual counselor has met the minimum qualifications established by the agency. The assumption underlying any certification process is that a certified counselor is able to do effectively the type(s) of counseling reflected in a particular certification (Loesch, 1988). Certification is usually referred to as a "title control" process because only the use of the title "certified" is restricted; who may engage in counseling activities or what types of counseling can be provided is not restricted. The primary advantage of any certification lies within the associated prestige, but such prestige has significant implications for professional counselors in several regards. For example, many employers give hiring preference to certified counselors. In addition, clients' initial perceptions of counselors are related to the potential for counseling effectiveness; the more favorable clients' initial impressions of counselors in terms of perceived competence, the more likely that counseling will be effective. Certification is one credential that usually increases clients' (initial) favorableness toward counselors (Wittmer & Loesch, 1986).

Professional certification activities for counselors have a relatively brief history; certification has been viewed as an important professional credential only since the mid 1970s. Although the exact reasons for this recent emphasis are unknown, one probable reason is that it is only recently that a need has arisen to be able to compare or equate counselors in a mobile society.

The most prominent certification processes are national, and in some cases international, in scope. That is, because the minimum qualifications for such certifications are set by national agencies, they are independent of local (e.g., state-level) counselor preparation program idiosyncracies. Therefore, all counselors certified by a particular agency are presumed to have the same minimum competence level regardless of the respective preparation programs from which they graduated. Accordingly, certification is one indication of minimal equivalence across counselors. This perspective is similar to the philosophy underlying CACREP's program accreditation thrust. The primary difference of course is that accreditation is focused on programs and certification is focused on individuals.

Although the counselor certification process implemented by the NBCC is not the oldest, it is rapidly becoming the widest known among those specific to counselors. Therefore, the NBCC's counselor certification processes will be exemplified here.

In the late 1970s, the Commission on Rehabilitation Counselor Certification (CRCC) and the National Academy of Certified Clinical Mental Health Counselors (NACCMHC) had been certifying rehabilitation counselors and mental health counselors, respectively. In addition, CACREP had accredited several counselor preparation programs, and several states had passed counselor licensure laws. These emphases on credentialing and the activities associated with them spawned within ACA (then AACD) interest in a counselor certification process. Thus, ACA mobilized its resources to evaluate existing counselor certification processes and to develop a plan for a broad-based counselor certification process. In 1981, ACA sponsored several meetings to develop specific plans. These actions eventually led to the first NBCC meeting in April of 1982, attended by representatives from ACA, other counselor certifying agencies, a state having a counselor licensure law, and a public representative. The group initiated plans for incorporation, established the initial criteria for certification, adopted an initial operating budget, developed a code of ethics, and established a schedule for subsequent activities. In addition, using information from a previous evaluative report that had identified deficiencies in existing assessment instruments for counselor certification processes, the group decided to initiate the development of a counselor certification examination specifically suited to NBCC's purposes (Loesch & Vacc, 1991).

Although both NBCC and CACREP are philosophically aligned with ACA, their respective governing bodies are constituted much differently. Whereas membership on the CACREP council is open to representatives from various ACA divisions as well as ACA itself, membership on the NBCC board of directors is not. Instead, the NBCC Board is composed of a chairperson, vice chairperson, treasurer/secretary, public representative, and five members elected by the board. The NBCC executive director is an ex officio member of the board. NBCC also employs three consultants, one each for technical assistance with examination development, research, and professional development activities, respectively. The NBCC headquarters is located in Greensboro, North Carolina.

Counselors certified by the NBCC are presumed to have fulfilled the minimum, basic knowledge and skill requirements applicable to all professional counselors. The National Certified Counselor (NCC) credential from NBCC is a general practice certification because it does not imply that NCCs can do any particular type of counseling, but rather that they have at least the minimum knowledge and skills necessary for any type of counseling. The competence inherent in the NCC credentialing process is based on the belief that, colloquially stated, all professional counselors must both know some things and be able to do some things (Loesch & Vacc, 1991).

The "know some things" component of the NBCC certification is evaluated in two ways, the first of which involves consideration of an applicant's prior academic preparation. The general, minimum academic requirement for any NBCC certification is a master's degree in counseling. However, specific academic course preparatory experiences also are required. In order to become a NCC, applicants must have successfully completed academic/curricular experiences encompassing a total of at least 48 semester or 72 quarter hours of graduate-level credit, each of the eight CACREP core curriculum areas, and at least two academic terms of supervised (counseling) field experience. These requirements are encompassed in any CACREP-accredited entry-level counselor preparation program.

The second part of the knowledge evaluation component involves participation in the NBCC's National Counselor Examination for Licensure and Certification (NCE). Different forms of the NCE are used for each administration because each form is developed from a large item pool. However, each form of the NCE has the same content format. That is, each form of the NCE covers the eight core curriculum areas of the CACREP standards and the NBCC work behaviors (as listed in Chapter 1). The current forms of the NCE each contain approximately 25 questions in each of the eight areas, with 20 per area being scored for certification purposes, resulting in a total possible score of 160. Note that not all of the NBCC work behaviors are covered in each form of the NCE. The remaining 40 questions on each form of the NCE are for item development purposes. Although subsection scores are reported, only the applicant's total score from the 160 items (i.e., the sum of the eight subsection scores) is used for performance evaluation purposes.

The NBCC uses a modified Anghoff procedure approximately every three years to establish a base form minimum criterion score for the NCE. In general, this method involves having a group of counseling professionals each make a probability judgment about the likelihood of a respondent answering each item correctly, summing the estimates across items, and averaging the summed judgments across judges (Loesch & Vacc, 1994). An applicant's total score is compared to the established minimum criterion score for each form of the NCE. For example, the minimum criterion score for the April, 1985 form of the NCE was 87; an applicant who scored 87 or higher on that form of the NCE passed the examination (Loesch & Vacc, 1991). The minimum criterion score for each form of the NCE subsequent to each base form is statistically equated to the minimum criterion score for the base form so that each minimum criterion score is statistically equivalent, or comparable, across forms of the NCE. Therefore, applicants do not have any particular advantage relative to surpassing the minimum criterion score in taking one form of the NCE as opposed to another (Loesch & Vacc, 1994). The NCE has been subjected to a wide variety of professional and empirical (e.g., Jaeger & Frye, 1988; Loesch & Vacc, 1991) analyses. In addition, respondents' comments about the NCE have been examined both subjectively and empirically (Vacc & Loesch, 1993). And finally, NCE results have been evaluated relative to current trends and movements in the counseling profession (Loesch & Vacc, 1988). Empirical evidence and subjective opinions overwhelmingly favor the reliability, validity, appropriateness, and defensibility of the NCE for use in the NBCC counselor certification process. Thus, NBCC's conjunctive use of academic preparation criteria and NCE performance are an effective means of evaluating counselors' professional knowledge.

The "be able to do some things" component of the NBCC certification process involves consideration of an applicant's previous supervised practice and professional experiences. All applicants must provide documentation of successful completion of a supervised practicum and internship. Applicants who have not completed a CACREP-accredited preparation program also must provide documentation of successful completion of (post master's degree) counseling experience that includes 3,000 client-contact hours and at least 100 hours of face-to-face supervision, all completed within a two-year period. This requirement is waived for graduates of CACREP-accredited programs because of the extensive requirements for supervised counseling experience in the CACREP accreditation standards. In addition, all applicants must provide letters of reference attesting to their minimum professional competence as counselors.

In the late 1980s NBCC implemented a special procedure intended to facilitate achievement of NCC status. Students enrolled in CACREP-accredited programs having a counseling emphasis are entitled to participate in the NCE during their last academic term of enrollment. Assuming they pass the NCE and graduate as scheduled with at least a master's degree, students exercising this option can become NCCs (almost) immediately upon graduation.

The initial NCC certification period is five years, with renewal contingent upon successful completion of professional development activities. In 1999, approximately 28,000 counselors held the NCC designation.

In 1985, the NBCC incorporated the certification process previously administered by the National Council for Credentialing of Career Counselors (NCCCC). The NCCCC was created by ACA's (then AACD's) National Career Development Association to implement a certification process specifically applicable to counselors specializing in career counseling (Sampson, 1986). The NBCC-NCCCC merger created a two-tier certification structure for the NBCC. Thus, the NBCC generic certification leading to the designation NCC is the basic tier and the NBCC specialized certification leading to the designation National Certified Career Counselor (NCCC) is a second tier. In 1999, only approximately 900 professional counselors had been designated as an NCCC. Therefore, this certification has been discontinued by NBCC. However, professional counselors holding the NCCC can maintain their certification and remain on a referral list for consumers.

In 1990 NBCC implemented two more specialty certifications, one leading to the designation National Certified School Counselor (NCSC) and another leading to the designation National Certified Gerontological Counselor (NCGC). However, the NCGC certification is no longer awarded by the NBCC, owing to an insufficient number of certificants. The NCGC status requires prior achievement of NCC status. However, it does not require participation in an examination in addition to the NCE. Rather, the eligibility criteria include specialized academic coursework, two years of professional experience, and a supervised internship in school counseling. In addition, completion of a self-assessment of competence and competence evaluations from a current supervisor and from a professional colleague with expertise in school counseling are required. For NCSCs, the colleague providing the competence evaluation must be an NCC or a state-certified school counselor.

Another NBCC certification appropriate for many professional counselors is that specifically for mental health counselors. This NBCC certification leads to the designation Certified Clinical Mental Health Counselor (CCMHC). The basic CCMHC criteria include:

1. graduation with a master's or higher degree from an accredited counselor preparation program that required appropriate coursework and a minimum of 60 semester or 90 quarter credit hours,
2. at least two years of post-master's, degree-relevant professional work experience which included a minimum of 3,000 client-contact hours,
3. a minimum of 100 clock hours of individual supervision by a professional counselor with CCMHC certification or equivalent credentials,
4. submission of an audio or video tape of a complete counseling session of at least 30 minutes duration, and
5. successful completion of the National Clinical Mental Health Counseling Examination (NCMHCE).

The newest certification currently available from the NBCC is that as Master Addictions Counselor. This certification has requirements similar to those for the CCMHC, but also includes requirements for specialized preparation and supervised experience in addictions counseling and successful completion of the Examination for Master Addictions Counselors (EMAC) (Page & Bailey, 1995). As for the other NBCC certifications, renewal is contingent upon succcesful completion of continuing professional development activities, such as participation in professional development workshops, additional courses, or home-study coursework.

A last certification currently available from the NBCC is the Approved Clinical Supervisor (ACS) credential. The certification is intended for experienced counselors who also have extensive training and experience in clinical supervision. Professionals who achieve this certification often are eligible to provide clinical supervision for potential certificants or licensees, and if so, are usually paid for such service. Achievement of this certification requires a minimum of five years experience in clinical supervision, professional preparation in clinical supervision (through formal coursework or professional development activities), an endorsement statement from a professional colleague familiar with the applicant's competence in supervision, and provision of self assessment and professional disclosure statements. The certification period is five years, with renewal contingent upon continuing professional development activities.

As the counseling profession evolves, so too will the certifications (and the associated requirements) provided by the NBCC. Current information of the various NBCC certifications can be found at its website (see Appendix A).

The Commission on Rehabilitation Counselor Certification (CRCC) provides another certification appropriate for many professional counselors. The CRCC awards the designation Certified Rehabilitation Counselor (CRC). The CRCC was created through the joint efforts of ACA's ARCA division and the National Rehabilitation Association. CRCC eligibility includes graduation with a master's or higher degree from a rehabilitation counselor education program accredited by the Council on Rehabilitation Education (CORE) that included a minimum 600-hour internship supervised by a CRC or from an essentially equivalent program; relevant, supervised professional work experience as a rehabilitation counselor for graduates of other than CORE-accredited programs; and successful completion of the CRCC examination. In 1999, there were more than 14,000 professionals holding CRC designation.

The American Association of Marriage and Family Therapists (AAMFT) provides a professional credential which is similar to, but not synonymous with, a certification for counselors. This credential is AAMFT Clinical Member status. The eligibility criteria include successful completion of specific academic experiences as specified by AAMFT, graduation from an AAMFT-accredited program, supervised work as a marriage and family therapist, and at least two years of post graduate degree professional work experience in marriage and family counseling.

Licensure

Being licensed is an important credential for professional counselors. As distinct from certification, licensure processes are stipulated in law, implemented at the state level, and geographically restricted in authority. Licensure is a legal process whereby a state agency regulates aspects of the practice of counseling within the state. State licensure laws are referred to as either "title" acts or "practice" acts. In the former, the states at least regulate who may identify themselves as "licensed counselors," and in many states even regulate who may identify themselves as "counselors."

Others may perform counseling-type activities, but they are prohibited by law from presenting themselves to the public as counselors. For example, healers, palmists, readers, advisors, and the like cannot use the word "counselor" in their advertisements in states having counselor licensure "title" acts. In the latter, the state regulates who may engage in activities legally defined as counseling as well as who may identify themselves as counselors.

There is one idiosyncracy to counselor licensure that merits digression. In general, counselor licensure laws are intended to control the practice of counseling within a state. However, school counselors in all states are given authority to practice counseling in schools through state school counselor certification procedures. Thus, with regard to school counseling only, state school counselor certification has essentially the same effects for school counselors as do licensure laws for other-than-school counselors.

Licensure laws pertinent to the counseling profession have both commonalities and wide variations within the United States. For example, all states have licensure laws for counseling activities under the aegis of the title "psychologist." Typically, psychologist licensure laws require a doctoral degree from a program accredited by the American Psychological Association, supervised professional work experience, an in-state residency period, letters of reference, and successful completion of an examination. Approximately half of the states also have license laws for marriage and family counselors or therapists, with requirements that are categorically similar to, but specifically different from those for psychologists (e.g., typically a master's degree is required instead of a doctoral degree).

In 1999, 45 states and the District of Columbia had enacted licensure laws for professional counselors. In the majority of those states, the title awarded is Licensed Professional Counselor (LPC); most others have a variation incorporating the phrase "professional counselor." Again, the eligibility criteria for counselor licensures are categorically similar, but specifically different, to those for psychologists.

A comparison of counselor certification and licensure processes reveals that there are many similarities, but a few distinct differences exist. Primary among the similarities is that both certification and licensure are voluntary in nature. Counseling can be done by many people who are neither certified nor licensed and so these credentials are not necessarily needed in order to do counseling. Rather, they are voluntarily sought by those who want to be truly professional counselors. Other similarities include requirements for payment of application, examination, annual renewal, and miscellaneous fees; specific types of prior academic preparation (usually a master's degree from a state, regionally, or nationally accredited institution); prior supervised counseling experience; prior work experience as a counselor; lack of negative personal characteristics (e.g., certain types of criminal convictions); and successful completion of an appropriate examination. In addition, certification and licensure are usually given for a specific time period, with renewal contingent upon successful completion of continuing professional development activities.

A primary difference between certification and licensure processes is the geographic region encompassed by the respective credential. Certifications are usually national in scope whereas licensure is granted for a specific state. Reciprocity agreements among states exist whereby one state agrees to honor all or most of the licensure criteria (e.g., performance on a licensure examination) of another state. However, complete reciprocity rarely exists between a certification and a state's licensure law even though many states use a certification examination, such as the NBCC's NCE, as (or in lieu of) a state licensure examination.

Graduation from an accredited program, certification, and licensure then are the primary credentials of professional counselors. Those professional counselors who hold such credentials do so to signify that they are interested in and actively striving toward providing the best possible counseling services. Moreover, they are in accord with the basic philosophical premise of all professional credentialing, which is to protect the public welfare through the provision of services only by competent practitioners (Shimberg, 1982).

☐ Developments in Counselor Credentialing

The counselor credentialing movement continues to improve in terms of both scope and substance. As professional counselors gain credibility for their work in more and more settings, they are becoming eligible for and included in a variety of specialized certifications such as those for pain management, behavioral medicine, and managed health care professionals. Thus, credentialing continues to grow in value for professional counselors.

Of the 45 states having passed counselor licensure legislation, 44 had operational licensure laws in 1999. Among the 44 having operational counselor licensure procedures, 38 either used exclusively or would accept the NBCC's NCE for fulfillment of the examination component. The widespread use of the NCE is basically attributable to the strong professional and psychometric properties of the NCE, and in part attributable to its 1990 endorsement by the AASCB as the examination of choice for counselor licensure.

☐ Counselors' Professional Development

Professional development is a general term used in the counseling profession to describe the activities in which professional counselors engage for the purpose of continuing to increase and improve their counseling knowledge and skills, primarily after they have become practitioners (i.e., after they have completed their counselor preparation programs). An abundance of professional development activities is available to professional counselors. Many counselors simply want to improve themselves and so participate upon their own initiatives. Also, as counselors progress through their careers, their functions and responsibilities evolve, and so they need new knowledge and skills to perform effectively. In addition, almost all counseling certification and licensure processes have continuing education (i.e., professional development) requirements for recertification or licensure renewal.

Given the extensiveness of professional development activities for counselors and the dearth of professional literature on professional development in counseling in general, it is surprising to discover what types of professional development activities are most appropriate and most effective. Indeed, although counselors' professional development makes sense conceptually, scant empirical support exists for the notion that it improves the ways counselors counsel. Why then are so many professional development activities being conducted?

The answer most likely lies in the changing nature of society. As society evolves, so too does its impact on people. People also evolve over the courses of their lives, and their needs that can be addressed by counseling services change, and perhaps increase, concomitantly. These ongoing changes necessitate that the counseling profession and its members be ever improving in order to maintain competence and be effective. Therefore, even though little evidence is available to support the impact or effectiveness of professional development activities in counseling, the need for them is only too obvious; professional counselors must constantly improve if they are to continue helping people effectively.

Perusal of the professional literature reveals that professional development activities for counselors have been suggested, developed, and implemented for literally every aspect of the counseling profession and for work with every type of person in society. Accordingly, to address all the types of activities here is not possible. However, a few of the major categories of activities can be addressed.

Counseling Skill Development or Refinement

Increasing personal knowledge and improvement of personal counseling skills is by far the most common type of professional development activity in which counselors engage. Because of knowledge and skill advances derived from theory development, research, and practical experience, existing counseling techniques are continually being improved and new techniques are being developed. Therefore, the professional counselor always has access to new, and presumably better, ways of doing things. Counselors extend their knowledge and improve their techniques primarily through participation in professional development activities such as continuing education or training workshops, in-service seminars, convention programs, and self-instruction modules, or through consultation activities. Among the alternatives, the most common type is professional convention programs. For example, typically, over 400 different programs are presented at the annual ACA world conference. Continuing education (i.e., professional development) activities, vis-à-vis convention programs, also are provided frequently at regional and state ACA conventions. Wilcoxon and Hawk (1990) surveyed ACA state branches in regard to provision of continuing education activities for their members and among other conclusions indicated that, "Perhaps the most notable finding in the study is the availability of CEU services at state levels" (p. 93).

Supervision Skill Development

Another major area of professional development for counselors is supervision skill development. Supervision may be defined generally as a specific type of consultation activity in which one professional counselor critiques another's work with clients toward the goal of maximizing the supervisee's skills and effectiveness. According to Dye and Borders (1990):

> Over the last 10 years counseling supervision has emerged as a separate specialty within the counseling profession. [C]ompetent supervisors are not only competent counselors but are also able to convey their counseling knowledge and skills (i.e., create learning environments) in ways that promote a supervisee's effectiveness and professional identity. (p. 27)

Because more and more counselors, as well as program administrators and managers, are becoming involved in supervision activities, an increase in professional development activities focusing on supervision has occurred. Impetus for this increase also has come from licensure laws and certification policies that require supervised experience for licensure or certification eligibility or renewal. More than ever the counseling profession is acknowledging that supervision, like counseling, requires a strong knowledge base and proven skills in order to be effective.

Use of Technology

Professional development in regard to use of technology also is currently being emphasized. So-called modern technology in general, and computer-based technologies in particular, have the potential to impact the counseling profession dramatically (Stevens & Lundberg, 1998). In discussing high technology in relation to the counseling profession, Harris-Bowlsbey (1984) presented three valid assumptions.

> First, high technology will never replace high touch in the human resource development field. Although robots may make automobiles better and faster . . . human beings will never be better counseled or guided by robots, computers, or interactive videodiscs. A second assumption is that high technology and high touch should be viewed not as opponents, but as potential partners. [. . .] Third, presumably the profession's thinking about the merger of high technology and high touch is new and tentative; therefore the counselors whom we educate and supervise will need preservice and in-service training. . . . (p. 7)

Harris-Bowlsbey's third assumption is true now more than ever and a multitude of professional development activities concerning the uses of computers in counseling are offered and are well-attended. Given the rapid advances in technology, this trend shows no sign of decreasing.

Burnout Prevention or Amelioration

A fourth major area of professional development for counselors is burnout prevention or amelioration. A classic question in the counseling profession is, who counsels the counselors? Counseling is an emotionally taxing activity that extracts an extremely heavy toll from counselors. Thus counselors, perhaps as much or more than people in any other profession, are susceptible to burnout, a state of emotional lethargy wherein motivation to perform is low and skills and talents are used inefficiently and ineffectively. Because of the increasing incidence of burnout among counselors, many professional development activities have been and are presented to help counselors avoid it. These activities are intended to enable counselors to monitor and moderate their professional (and sometimes personal) activities so that they are able to regenerate their professional energies continually and, in so doing, maintain and increase their level of effectiveness.

Participation in professional development activities is an important part of a counselor's professional orientation. These activities are the means by which professional counselors keep current, improve, and remain professionally motivated. As with participation in professional organizations and attainment of professional credentials, participation in professional development activities benefits both counselors and the clients to whom they provide services.

☐ Professional Contributions by Counselors

The fourth aspect of professional orientation, making contributions to the theoretical and knowledge bases of the counseling profession, is much smaller in scope than the first three because, unfortunately, only a small proportion of counselors are actively involved in it. That is, the primary means by which counselors may make contributions to the profession in general is through research and publication activities, and yet only a small proportion of counselors conduct research or write for publication in professional journals. Two primary reasons have been offered for this unfortunate circumstance: (a) counselors lack substantive research skills and therefore are not comfortable, capable, or confident in conducting or publishing research; and (b) counseling research results have not been readily applicable to counseling activities and therefore counselors see little value in it.

Goldman (1976, 1978) suggested that counselors are "turned off" to research because, among other reasons, during their training programs they were exposed to unreasonable expectations for research activities. He stated that the counseling profession has "sanctified precision, measurement, statistical methodology, and the controlled laboratory experiment" (Goldman, 1976, p. 545) and in so doing has set the standards for research and publication so high that most counselors or trainees feel incapable of achieving them, and therefore don't try. Empirical evidence to support this position is scant, but results of counselors' performance on the NCE seem to suggest that research is among counselors' lesser areas of competence. That is, scores on the Research and Evaluation subsection of the NCE consistently have been lower than those for other subsections (Loesch & Vacc, 1988). Thus, possibly, counselors in general do not have great degrees of proficiency in research. However, Goldman (1977) also has argued that extensive research skill proficiency is not really necessary for counselors to conduct meaningful research. Rather, he posited that counselors should strive to conduct research that is within their realm of competence.

Resolving the debate over counselors' needed levels of proficiency in research is unlikely. However, there is little reason to continue the debate. Even if counselors' research proficiency levels are low, forces within the counseling profession are present which will more than likely result in their elevation. Specifically, moderately high research proficiency levels are evident in all counselor preparation program standards (such as CACREP's) and in counselor certification (such as NBCC's) and licensure requirements. Therefore, most professional counselors now have to have at least minimal levels of research competence in order to achieve those credentials.

The lack of research results relevant to actual counseling practice has been decried by many authors. However, its relevance also has been acknowledged in the professional literature. For example, according to Engels and Muro (1986):

> Vacc and Loesch (1983) offered excellent general and specific suggestions and questions regarding the necessity for research as a means of self-regulation and self-evaluation, leading to a fruitful progressing and maturing in all aspects of the profession. We join in advocating inquiry as an integral, ongoing part of preparation programs and professional practice, with dedication to scientific and human inquiry and a healthy skepticism to generate a dialectic for ongoing improvements in effectiveness and data to document those improvements. (pp. 301–302)

Martin and Martin (1989) clearly summarized how research fits within the counseling profession:

> [W]hile appropriate research may not immediately change the field of counseling, the impact of research cannot be felt until clinicians accept applicable findings. Research results will never totally guide clinical practice; the number of variables is far greater than could ever be examined. However, research can be informative and help guide choices. Using research findings with sound clinical judgment helps counselors more ably assist their clients, which is the one common goal among researchers and clinicians alike. (pp. 491–492)

Thus, research and the subsequent publication of its results by professional counselors not only is consistent with the empirical counseling approach advocated in this book, but is also the primary means by which counselors improve the counseling profession.

☐ Summary

Becoming a professional counselor is not easy. Much has to be learned, many skills have to be developed, and an appropriate orientation has to be adopted. Further, learning and skill development must continue across the lifespan, and therefore being a professional counselor is not easy either. However, professional counselors enjoy many, many intrinsic and extrinsic rewards. These rewards are gained primarily through joining professional organizations, attaining professional credentials, engaging in professional development activities, and making contributions to the counseling profession. For the vast majority of professional counselors, the benefits gained far outweigh the efforts expended. More importantly, society and the people within it gain significantly from professional counselors participating in these activities. What greater good is there than that?

15

Professional Preparation of Counselors

The preceding discussions and those in Chapter 1 illustrate that neither singular nor simple answers exist to the questions "What is a professional counselor?" and "What does a professional counselor do?" There also is no singular or simple answer to the question "How should professional counselors be prepared?" Indeed, the question, "What should be done to produce a good counselor?" has been a source of continuous debate since the inception of the counseling profession. Given the current complexities of the counseling profession, a response to this question must necessarily be multifaceted. Further, underlying issues must be addressed before the responses can be understood.

☐ Issues in Counselor Preparation

It is obvious from historical perspective, research, observation, and just plain common sense that professional counselors are differentially effective in their counseling activities; some counselors simply are better than others. Yet while the effectiveness differential is readily acknowledged, causes of the differentiation remain issues of concern in the counseling profession. Some of the major issues involved can be best stated and addressed as questions.

1. Are professional counselors born or made?

The vast majority of professional counselors like to conceive of themselves as empathic, warm, caring, concerned, hopeful, and loving people whose primary goal in life is to help other people. The professional counseling literature also promotes these qualities as necessary for effective counseling (e.g., Corey, Corey, & Callanan, 1993; Neukrug, 1998; Nystul, 1999). Relatedly, counseling research generally shows that the greater the extent to which counselors convey these and related characteristics (such as those discussed in Chapter 1), the more effective they are in their professional counseling activities. Accordingly, considerable concern continues to be focused upon the personal characteristics of potential professional counselors. At issue is whether potential counselors must have certain types of personal characteristics before beginning counselor preparation or whether appropriate characteristics can (and must) be developed in potential counselors during their preparation programs.

From the 1950s into the 1980s, a substantial portion of the professional counseling literature and research focused upon the specification and determination of counselor characteristics associated with counseling effectiveness. This effort had potentially highly significant implications because if personal characteristics could be shown to be definitively associated with counseling effectiveness, then those characteristics could be used as selection criteria for persons entering counselor preparation programs. That is, applicants possessing the appropriate characteristics to a greater extent would be admitted to counselor preparation programs while those possessing the characteristics to a lesser extent would be denied admission, and therefore presumably denied access to the counseling profession.

The search for characteristics associated with counseling effectiveness has covered an amazingly diverse array of counselors' personal attributes and of aspects of counseling effectiveness, and has involved use of an equally diverse set of measurement and evaluation instruments and techniques and data analytic procedures. However, even though substantial effort has been invested, clear and definitive results have not been found. For example, Rowe, Murphy, and DeCsipkes (1975) conducted a comprehensive analysis of the 1960 to 1974 professional literature on the relationships between counselor and counselor trainee personality characteristics and counselor effectiveness, and concluded that further search for such relationships should be discontinued because the results of previous studies were "generally disappointing, often contradictory, and only tentative" (p. 241). Conversely, however, Wiggins and Weslander (1986) concluded that:

[Their own] study demonstrated some definite differences between groups of [school] counselors rated as effective or ineffective. Ineffective counselors are rated low by the supervisors, are dissatisfied with their jobs, have low self-esteem, have a low level of tolerance for ambiguity, and are not correlated significantly with the Holland environmental code for counselors. Effective counselors are rated high by the supervisors, are happy with their jobs, have high self-esteem, have a high level for tolerance for ambiguity, and have congruent Holland codes. (pp. 34–35)

It appears that the best statement that can be made is that some professionals believe that definitive associations have been established between personal characteristics and counselor effectiveness, while others believe such associations have not been determined. Thus, some counselor preparation programs use evaluation of applicants' personal characteristics for selection purposes, while many others do not. The search continues.

The alternative side of this issue holds that appropriate personal characteristics are developed within the context of counselor preparation programs. Again, however, conflicting evidence exists about whether desirable changes actually take place. For example, Zahner and McDavis (1980) concluded that "The results [of their study] . . . indicate that training for both the professional and paraprofessional groups [of counselors] has minimal influence on moral development of its current or past students" (p. 248). Conversely, Schwab and Harris (1981) concluded that "The results [of their study] suggest . . . that counselor trainees do change and grow toward being more self-actualizing from the time they enter to the time they graduate from their counselor training program" (p. 222). It is generally accepted that counselor preparation programs do change the personal characteristics of the people who participate in them. However, the exact nature and extent of these changes have not yet been fully determined.

The debate about whether good counselors are born or made has been deemphasized in counselor preparation practice today for two reasons. First, the relationship between counselor trainees' possession of measurable personal characteristics and the ability to convey desirable personal characteristics has not been shown to be direct. For example, because a concept such as empathy is extremely difficult to measure validly, researchers typically have focused upon related concepts, such as altruism, and inferred an associated ability to be empathic. However, a counselor trainee who scores high in altruism on a personality inventory is not necessarily inherently able to convey empathy in counseling processes. Thus the search for personal characteristics associated with counseling effectiveness is thwarted both theoretically and pragmatically and has not yielded results substantial enough to warrant continued emphasis.

Second, and more importantly, today most counselor preparation programs attend to both sides of the debate. That is, most attend to initial personal characteristics of applicants in their student selection procedures, although the nature and extent of the attention given varies greatly. Procedures employed range from the use of specific, multifaceted evaluations (e.g., personality inventories and personal interviews) to the use of global indicators of applicants' personal characteristics (e.g., reference letters and applicant goal statements). Most counselor preparation programs also incorporate activities intended to enhance participants' personal characteristics. Again, these procedures vary from very specific (e.g., sensitivity group activities to improve self-disclosure abilities) to general activities (e.g., lectures on professional commitment). Thus, a major professional issue has been deemphasized and avoided through accepted preparation practices.

2. What selection criteria are important?

Counselor preparation programs are similar to other professional preparation programs in that they are primarily graduate-level (i.e., post baccalaureate) curricula. However, a distinguishing feature of counselor preparation programs is the lack of a commonly associated undergraduate (i.e., baccalaureate) curriculum. For example, persons aspiring to be physicians typically must first complete a pre-med undergraduate curriculum and persons aspiring to be lawyers must complete a pre-law undergraduate curriculum. Similarly, persons aspiring to be counseling or clinical psychologists typically must first complete a psychology undergraduate curriculum. By comparison, no standard undergraduate curriculum typically must be completed before persons can enter counselor preparation programs. Institutions with undergraduate-level counselor preparation curricula exist, but they are extremely rare. Therefore, the undergraduate programs completed by applicants to counselor preparation programs are diverse. In fact, students in counselor preparation programs represent extremely varied previous academic preparations, including those in the areas of the social and hard sciences, liberal arts, fine arts, and business.

During the early years of the counseling profession, most professional counselors worked in educational institutions, primarily as secondary-school counselors. Persons seeking entry to counselor preparation programs usually held baccalaureate degrees in education and were working as teachers. In addition, many counseling professionals then viewed previous training and experience in teaching as necessary for becoming an effective school counselor and, relatedly, most state departments of education required prior teaching experience for certification as a school counselor.

As the counseling profession has evolved and become diversified, the relevance and importance of prior training and experience in teaching has been deemphasized for several reasons. First, the proportion of professional counselors who work in schools has decreased significantly and, therefore, the potential relevance of prior teaching experience has decreased proportionately. Second, a considerable number of states now certify persons to work as school counselors who have not had teaching experience but who complete school counselor preparation programs. Finally, research has not shown that school counselors with previous training and experience in teaching are more effective than school counselors without teaching experience; no empirical basis exists for suggesting that teaching experience is particularly beneficial to being an effective counselor. Even in light of these considerations, however, a substantial portion of professional counselors have completed baccalaureate curricula in education. One reason is that school counselors still constitute a significant portion of professional counselors in general and many of them have had prior training and experience in teaching. Another is that most counselor preparation programs are housed in schools or colleges of education within institutions of higher education and therefore undergraduate education majors typically have a greater probability than other undergraduate students of becoming familiar with counselor preparation programs.

When school counseling and the associated prerequisites were preeminent in the counseling profession, counselor educators could hold reasonable, relatively common assumptions about the previous academic and experiential backgrounds of students in counselor preparation programs. More importantly, they could build upon those assumptions in the construction of counselor preparation curricula. Today, however, to make generalized assumptions about students' prior training and experiences is not possible, and counselor preparation programs must be constructed to accommodate students with widely varying backgrounds.

Indicators of previous academic performance and current academic aptitude are perhaps the most widely used selection criteria for entry into counselor preparation programs. Undergraduate grade point average is the most commonly used indicators of applicants' academic performance. The most commonly used indicators of applicants' academic aptitude are scores on graduate-level academic aptitude tests, such as the Graduate Record Examination (GRE) (Hollis, 1998). Because counselor preparation programs are graduate-level curricula, students in them must have sufficient academic skills and aptitude to complete satisfactorily the academic requirements. However, research generally shows that these indicators are neither substantially related to nor particularly good predictors of counseling effectiveness. Therefore, academic performance and aptitude indicators continue to be used because they help to identify students who will complete counselor preparation academic requirements successfully, but not because they are good predictors of counseling effectiveness.

Counselor preparation programs generally require applicants to have letters of reference submitted with their applications for evaluating an individual's character, potential for academic success, potential for success as a counselor, or any combination of these factors. Hollis (1998) indicated that three letters of reference is the average requirement used by counselor preparation programs. Unfortunately, evaluations provided in reference letters usually add little if any discriminative power in the prediction of either academic success or counseling effectiveness. Thus, while the practice is common, the actual benefits of requiring applicant reference letters are few.

Some counselor preparation programs require applicants to submit a goal(s) statement that includes a brief explanation of what the applicant intends to do upon graduation from the program. Goal statements are used in evaluating the extent to which applicants have made decisions about their vocational aspirations. Generally, the more focused the applicant's goal statement, the more favorable is its evaluation because it is typically easier to define appropriate preparation activities for specific goals (i.e., specific work settings or counseling activities). Unfortunately, the nature of the counseling profession and counselor preparation programs often detracts from the usefulness of goal statements. Many students are unaware of the many different aspects of the counseling profession until after they have been admitted to counselor preparation programs (in part because of the lack of undergraduate programs). Thus, applicants' goal statements typically reflect a restricted knowledge base, which in turn restricts their usefulness. However, goals statements do provide a tangential benefit in the selection process; they allow program faculty to make at least a cursory evaluation of applicants' writing abilities. Such information is of some use for making judgments about applicants' abilities to complete graduate-level writing assignments effectively.

An increasing number of counselor preparation programs are using personal interviews as part of student selection processes. Typically, applicants are queried either individually or in groups by one or more program faculty about their prior educational and professional experiences, professional plans and aspirations, or other topics specific to particular preparation program situations. Personal interviews are useful for evaluation of applicants' verbal communication skills, language usage, general demeanor, and self-presentation.

Beyond these commonly used selection criteria (i.e., academic performance indicators, reference letters, goal statements, and interviews), there is only diversity. Indeed, additional selection criteria are almost as varied as are counselor preparation programs. Some of these selection criteria are related to requirements for counselor certification or licensure, others to specific theoretical orientations held by program faculty, and still others to specific intended job placements for program graduates. Thus, there are no universal academic or personal credentials that applicants to counselor preparation programs must possess. Even the few commonalities that are shared relate primarily to academic success rather than to potential counseling effectiveness. However, this situation should not be construed as bad, or even negative. Rather, it is an appropriate reflection of the diverse nature of the counseling profession. Various professional counselors fulfill many different roles and functions and, appropriately, people aspiring to be counselors should have equally varied credentials as they prepare to assume those roles.

3. How much academic preparation is necessary?

The delicate balance between efficiency and effectiveness is difficult to define, and even harder to achieve in many aspects of the counseling profession. For example, professional counselors always strive to provide the best possible services for their clients in the shortest possible time periods and with the least possible disruptions to or discomforts in clients' lives. In brief, professional counselors try to obtain for each client the best results as quickly and as easily as possible. An analogous situation exists for counselor preparation. The goal is to prepare effective professional counselors expeditiously. At issue is *how?*

One factor influencing the nature of counselor preparation program requirements is the nature of the students who enroll in them. Because students enter counselor preparation programs with widely varying backgrounds, such programs must build upon an uneven foundation; therefore, establishing a starting point for counselor preparation is difficult. If the starting point includes excessive preprogram requirements, many persons who otherwise might have entered counselor preparation programs will not do so because of the perceived extra work necessary just to start the programs. Conversely, persons who have had relatively extensive prior preparations may find the initial counselor preparation work to be mundane or redundant, and thus demotivating. Typically, counselor preparation programs respond to this situation by incorporating a few preprogram requirements. These are usually a few courses, such as those covering personality theories, abnormal psychology, learning theories, or basic statistics, that most applicants to the program have already completed. Students who have completed the preprogram requirements begin the basic counselor preparation program curriculum upon admission. Students who have not completed the preprogram requirements are usually required to take them soon after admission and before they begin the basic counselor preparation program curriculum. Thus, counselor preparation programs attempt to level the foundation by creating a happy medium among the diverse backgrounds of program applicants.

The length of time and amount of credit hours needed for counselor preparation also are confounded by external forces pertinent to professional practice. For example, state-level requirements for certification as a school counselor are typically less than counselor preparation program requirements because school-counselor certification requirements in most states are based on the assumption that school counselors will have had prior teaching experience. Requirements for school-counselor certification in those states are often merely listings of courses as opposed to a requirement for completion of a fully integrated counselor preparation program. Conversely, in many of the states that have counselor licensure laws, requirements for being licensed as a counselor are greater than most counselor preparation program requirements (e.g., in regard to supervised counseling experience). State legislatures have taken conservative approaches to protecting the public welfare in constructing their counselor licensure laws by including relatively extensive requirements.

In addition to state-level forces, national counselor certifying agencies have an influence on counselor preparation programs. These agencies typically have eligibility requirements approximating those of state licensure laws and therefore tend to exceed those of the majority of counselor preparation programs. To summarize, some external forces act to influence increases in the length of time and amount of coursework for counselor preparation while others, in effect, act to influence decreases or, at least, maintenance of the status quo.

A third aspect of this issue relates to the academic bases for specifying the time length and coursework for counselor preparation. Typically, guidelines for counselor preparation have specified that programs should be a specified minimum number of academic credit hours. Although this approach allows for relatively easy quantitative comparisons of minimum requirements across counselor preparation programs, it is fraught with pragmatic difficulties. For example, although quarter-hour credits can be converted to semester-hour credits (and vice versa) relatively easily, numeric conversions do not necessarily reflect content equivalence, even across courses having similar titles. Further, wide variations occur in minimum credit-hour requirements for similarly titled degrees across institutions within states and across states. For two counselor preparation programs to have essentially similar content (or course) requirements and to award similarly titled degrees, and yet have substantially different minimum credit-hour requirements is possible, and in fact quite common. This situation becomes even more confounded when variations in individual instructional styles and emphases are considered. That is, even when relatively specific guidelines have been presented for elements of counselor preparation programs, individual instructors have considerable freedom in interpretation and implementation of those guidelines and elements.

Partly in response to the difficulties in attempting to equate minimum credit hour requirements and partly for theoretical reasons, some counselor preparation guidelines specify enrollment in programs for a minimum period as well as for a minimum number of credit hours. The former requirement is based on the idea that the development of effective counseling skills entails more than the rote accumulation of knowledge. The belief is that effective counselors synthesize and apply knowledge learned in typical (i.e., didactic) courses, and that it then takes time and practice for counselor trainees to develop applied skills. Thus, the requirement of a minimum time period for enrollment is viewed as a way of ensuring that counselor trainees have had sufficient time to synthesize and integrate knowledge before they attempt to apply it in the actual practice of professional counseling.

Current guidelines for counselor preparation programs attempt to be simultaneously responsive to a wide variety of factors. Accordingly, they reflect a series of compromises between what is theoretically desirable and what is practical, and between what is desirable and what is possible. Fortunately, the guidelines generally have been effective in achieving the delicate balances among these considerations, primarily through increasing the length of counselor preparation programs in general and the supervised field-experience components of those programs in particular.

4. What should be the minimum degree?

Closely related to the question of what should be the minimum academic preparation necessary for counselors is which academic degree should reflect that minimum preparation? Because counselor preparation is almost exclusively provided at the post baccalaureate (i.e., graduate) level, there are basically two choices: master's or doctorate. If a broad, encompassing definition of who are counselors is accepted, then both degrees have been proffered as the required minimum. For example, clinical social workers and marriage and family therapists have long operated on the belief that the master's degree is the appropriate minimum for entry into the counseling profession while clinical and counseling psychologists have held that the doctorate is the necessary minimum.

A more focused definition of who counselors are has been presented in Chapter 1, and within that perspective the master's degree is clearly the accepted minimum (i.e., entry-level) degree. Acceptance of the master's degree as the minimum academic degree is apparently widespread because there are in fact far more master's-level than doctoral-level counselor preparation programs (see Hollis, 1998). Further, all states having counselor licensure laws and all national counselor certification agencies stipulate that the master's degree is the required minimum for licensure or national certification, respectively. Of course, state school counselor certification requirements have long stipulated that the master's degree is the necessary minimum for such certification. Thus, for professional counselors the master's degree is the accepted minimum academic degree required for entry into the counseling profession.

An interesting issue associated with acceptance of the master's degree as the minimum requirement is what should be the nature and purposes of the doctorate in counseling (i.e., in counselor education, as distinguished from the doctorate in clinical or counseling psychology)? At least one prominent counselor educator argued that the doctorate in counseling should be focused upon preparation of counselors having advanced clinical skills who would be best-suited for work in community agencies (Randolph, 1990). Others (e.g., Vacc, 1990; Wittmer & Loesch, 1990) argued that such a focus would be inconsistent with perspectives held in the counseling profession, and that emulation of other professionals would not be particularly fruitful for professional counselors. Lanning (1990) suggested that persons holding the doctorate in counseling should have an educator/practitioner orientation and fulfill four primary professional roles: (a) counselor educator/trainer, (b) counselor trainee supervisor, (c) researcher, and (d) counseling practitioner. More recently, West, Bubenzer, Brooks, and Hackney (1995) stated:

> CES doctoral graduates are employed in both direct service and academic positions. Because of the breadth of preparation (instruction, clinical practice, supervision, and scholarship), it would seem that CES doctoral graduates are equipped to consider a variety of societal needs, thus future employment opportunities for these graduates would appear strong. (p. 176)

It is unlikely that this issue will be resolved in the near future. However, regardless of debate about the issue, it is likely that the master's degree will remain the minimum academic degree for professional counselors.

5. What should be emphasized?

Two major issues are raised by this question. What content and skill areas and what method of instruction should be emphasized in counselor preparation programs? *Counselor Education and Supervision* is a professional journal devoted in part to the presentation of ideas, research, and practices in counselor preparation. Perusal of issues of this journal, for even a relatively small time span such as a year, reveals extremely large and diverse sets of knowledge and skills with which counselors are supposed to be familiar and adept. The idea can be gained from this journal, as well as from many others, that professional counselors are supposed to know about everything, be able to do anything, and be able to work effectively with many, many different types of people. Quite obviously this is not possible, and more importantly, it is probably not desirable. Counselors, like most other professionals today, tend to specialize, either in terms of clients to whom services are rendered or in terms of types of skills and activities used. Nonetheless, a common assumption in the counseling profession is that a basic body of knowledge and a set of basic skills should be possessed by all counselors regardless of professional specialization. Thus, it is a widely held belief in the counseling profession that a generic base of knowledge and skills must be learned and achieved by all professional counselors.

Considerable debate has existed over the nature of the generic knowledge and skill base for professional counseling. The recommendations for the various knowledge and skill areas to be included in this generic base are far too numerous to be elaborated here; suffice it to say that knowledge of almost all aspects of human functioning and almost all counseling skills have at one time or another been proffered as being essential for all professional counselors. As a result, over the last several decades, counselor trainers and professional counselors have been engaged in an effort to achieve a degree of consensus about the nature of generic preparation for professional counselors. Some of the results of this effort will be discussed later in this chapter.

A lack of consensus exists about relative emphases given to different methods of instruction in counselor preparation programs. Debated is the amount of instruction which should be didactic compared with how much should be experiential. Didactic instruction involves the presentation of knowledge by an instructor through lectures and material resources to typically large groups of counselor trainees; i.e., typical classroom instruction. Experiential instruction, however, means that counselor trainees learn by doing, typically under close supervision. Clearly, agreement that some of each of these types of instruction should be incorporated into counselor preparation programs exists, because some knowledge areas are covered most effectively through didactic instruction and some skills are taught most effectively through supervised experiential instruction. However, the most appropriate method is not readily apparent in many areas. For example, agreement exists that all counselor trainees need to have good understandings of professional ethics. Didactic instruction is usually a good way for counselor trainees to learn the content of various professional codes of ethics. However, the applications of professional ethics involve complex sets of intricate decisions and value judgments, and didactic instruction is probably less effective in this regard. Experiential instruction techniques, such as supervised role-playing, are usually better for teaching counselor trainees how to apply professional ethics. But the question remains, how much instructional time should be devoted to each type of instruction? For the most part, the answer to this question has been left to the discretion of counselor educators in their respective counselor preparation programs.

6. How should counselor preparation be evaluated?

The evaluation of counselor preparation program effectiveness has undoubtedly received the least attention of any of the major aspects of the counseling profession. While a considerable number of research investigations of the effectiveness of specific aspects of counselor training have been made, reports of total program effectiveness evaluations are almost nonexistent in the professional counseling literature. Ironically, this unfortunate state of affairs is in direct contradiction to increasing emphases on personal (i.e., individual) accountability for professional counselors. The professional counseling literature is replete with statements that professional counselors must be accountable for their professional and personal activities, but apparently counselor preparation programs are not holding themselves to similar standards.

In fairness, acknowledgment should be made that significant obstacles in conducting evaluations of counselor preparation programs exist, not the least of which is determining appropriate criteria for effectiveness. Further, counseling professionals typically receive little formal preparation in program evaluation strategies or techniques (Loesch, in press). Moreover, the counseling profession is not unique in these regards; few disciplines in the social sciences in general, or the helping professions in particular, have devoted much time and effort to preparation program evaluation activities. However, difficulties, lack of expertise, and common practice not withstanding, the fact remains that there is very little evidence to show that counselor preparation programs achieve what they are supposed to accomplish.

Professional counselors are frequently admonished to engage in individual accountability activities, and thereby have control over criteria for effectiveness, so as to avoid having criteria imposed upon them. This appears to be sage advice. However, the counseling profession apparently has not listened to its own advice, and with predictable results. External forces are having a significant influence on what constitutes effective counselor preparation. The most common forces in this regard are state and national counselor certification and licensure agencies. Professional counselor certification or licensure eligibility requirements literally define counselor preparation program effectiveness, at least for professional counselors seeking those credentials. Professional counselors have had significant input into certification and licensure requirements and therefore have had some say in what constitutes counselor preparation program effectiveness. However, other persons (e.g., legislators and lay persons) have had significant roles in establishing certification and licensure eligibility criteria. As a result, the counseling profession has relinquished at least part of the control over definition and determination of counselor preparation program effectiveness.

There is a hopeful side to this situation. Concern about the nature of counselor preparation has increased over the years, and in the early 1980s, substantial investments of thought, time, effort, and resources came to fruition in the establishment of commonly accepted standards of preparation for professional counselors. The establishment and application of counselor preparation program standards of course is not synonymous with counselor preparation program evaluation. However, the standards of preparation serve to reflect the counseling profession's definition of what constitutes effective minimum counselor preparation. Thus, the movement toward application of the standards of preparation is a significant and necessary step toward evaluation of those programs.

☐ Standards of Preparation

The counseling profession evolved from a few individuals' rather inauspicious concerns about the vocational developments of adolescents into a comprehensive and complex profession that attempts to address the multitude of mental health service needs of literally all people in society. Current philosophies, practices, and trends in the preparation of professional counselors have evolved along an analogous course. In the early, formative years of the counseling profession, relatively little disagreement about the professional preparation of counselors existed, primarily because little differentiation among counselors was present and the vast majority of professional counselors worked in schools and had been teachers. They had common backgrounds and common vocational goals, and preparation was simply facilitation of the transition from one role to another role in the school. However, as more and more distinct facets, roles, and functions emerged within the counseling profession, agreement about the nature of professional counselor preparation dissipated. In fact, considerable disagreement arose about the preferred nature of counselor preparation during the 1940s and 1950s. This situation prompted some members of the counseling profession to examine both what was happening and what should be happening in counselor preparation. Thus began the push for standardized professional preparation for counselors.

Historical Development

Similar to attempting to describe the evolution of the counseling profession in its entirety, to cover all the activities relevant to the evolution of current practices in counselor preparation is not possible. Therefore, the tactic of describing the evolution of one professional entity specifically concerned with counselor preparation will be used. That entity is the Council for the Accreditation of Counseling and Related Educational Programs (CACREP).

The CACREP lineage can be traced directly to the National Association of Guidance Supervisors (NAGS). One of the reasons for the founding of NAGS was to bring together individuals (i.e., supervisors of school guidance personnel) who had common concerns. Among those concerns was how to effectively supervise and administrate counselors whose roles and functions were changing and expanding and, concomitantly, whose preparations were becoming more diverse. This latter aspect prompted counselor trainers to become interested in and involved with the concern and, to a certain extent, led to the formation of the National Association of Counselor Supervisors and Counselor Trainers (NAGSCT) in 1952. Throughout the nine-year life span of NAGSCT, concern about and attention to counselor preparation were increasing. Relatedly, counselor trainers (educators) were becoming increasingly involved in the activities of the association, and eventually dominated its perspectives. This shift is partially reflected in the change of the name from NAGSCT to the Association for Counselor Education and Supervision (ACES), wherein counselor education/training and supervision are transposed.

The desirability of standardizing counselor preparation rose to prominence within ACES in the late 1950s and early 1960s, although the prominence was in fact fostered by a relatively small proportion of the ACES's membership. However, the ACES's membership was generally receptive to the idea of developing standards of preparation, and in 1963 that division endorsed an initial set of standards of preparation that would, theoretically, apply to all (graduate-level) programs preparing professional counselors. Perhaps more importantly, it also committed to continue to develop the initial (ACES's) standards of preparation. An interesting note, however, is that while ACES endorsed the standards of preparation and their further development, ACES did not endorse a requirement that counselor preparation programs adopt or abide by those standards.

As attention to standards of preparation continued to increase within ACES, other professional associations also became interested in the issues involved and initiated their own activities. For example, the American School Counselor Association (ASCA) adopted a set of specific guidelines for preparation of secondary school counselors in 1967, and another specific set for elementary school counselors the next year. Similarly, the American College Personnel Association (ACPA) in 1968 adopted specific preparation guidelines for student personnel (now student affairs practice) workers. Other associations did not formally adopt guidelines but instead increased their involvement through input and feedback to the members of ACES who were most involved in the development of the ACES's standards of preparation.

In response to the then relatively widespread interest in standards of preparation, the ACES's "Commission on Standards and Accreditation" was created in 1971. The significance of this event was two-fold. First, it was a reaffirmation of ACES's commitment to the development of standards of preparation. Second, and perhaps more important, it was the first formal acknowledgment of ACES's intent to establish procedures for accrediting counselor preparation programs. Thus, it signified ACES's commitment to implementing a plan wherein counselor preparation programs would be required to use and abide by the standards of preparation.

ACES's efforts relative to development of the standards resulted in the adoption of *Standards for Preparation of Counselors and Other Personnel Services Specialists* in 1973. This first set of standards delineated preparation guidelines for what is referred to as entry-level preparation, i.e., the minimum preparation necessary to assume a beginning position as a professional counselor. Subsequently, in 1977 ACES adopted the *Guidelines for Doctoral Preparation in Counselor Education* to be applied to doctoral-level counselor preparation programs. Both of these sets of standards were revised and, in 1979, adopted by ACES as the *Standards for Entry Preparation (Master's and Specialists) of Counselors and Other Personnel-Services Specialists* and the *Standards for Advanced Preparation (Doctoral) in Counselor Education*, respectively. Concurrent with the adoption of the 1979 revised standards, ACES began to accredit counselor preparation programs according to those standards. ACES worked closely with the California Association for Counselor Education and Supervision (CACES) because CACES had already accredited a few programs in California using their own standards, which were similar to the ACES's standards.

The initiatives shown by ACES in the development of standards of preparation and the implementation of preparation program accreditation activities were generally acclaimed in the counseling profession, but they also severely taxed the resources of ACES. Thus, in 1980 the ACA (then AACD) Board of Directors voted to adopt both sets of ACES's standards, to support further work on the standards, and to establish and support an entity to conduct broad-scale activities relative to counselor program accreditation. This latter commitment led directly to the formation of the Council for the Accreditation of Counseling and Related Educational Programs (CACREP).

CACREP held its first official meeting in September of 1981, at which time it officially adopted the ACES/ACA (then AACD) entry-level and advanced-level standards of preparation, recognized and accepted the accreditations awarded by ACES (and therefore by CACES), and established ideological and procedural guidelines for its own accreditation process.

CACREP is currently an organizational affiliate of ACA. This means that it is a legally distinct (i.e., technically separate from ACA), not-for-profit organization which focuses solely on activities necessary for the accreditation of counselor preparation programs. However, while CACREP is legally distinct from ACA and is not directly involved in ACA's functioning, it does have nontechnical linkages to ACA. For one thing, CACREP, like most other accrediting agencies, is not financially self--supporting and receives some financial support from ACA for its operations. For another, CACREP's membership is aligned with the ACA divisional structure; members of the Council are placed there by ACA and ACA divisions. For example, in 1999, the Council included representatives from ACES, AAC, AMHCA, ACCA, NCDA, AMCD, ARCA, ASGW, ASREVIC, IAMFC, IAAOC, and AHEAD. The Council also includes a representative from ACA (and therefore ACA is technically a member of the Council), two public representatives, and the CACREP Executive Director who serves as an ex officio member. Other ACA divisions are permitted to place representatives on the Council, but have not yet done so. This configuration allows CACREP to maintain close philosophical ties with ACA while functioning autonomously. For example, historically, CACREP incorporated several relatively minor changes in the standards of preparation being applied as well as guidelines for several aspects of preparation without obtaining approval from ACA. Thus, today, CACREP has its own standards of preparation and accreditation processes, although they are philosophically aligned with ACA purposes and goals.

CACREP accreditation is program specific; it accredits individual preparation programs instead of the academic units (i.e., departments) in which the programs are housed. Because of the diversity of individual preparation program titles used in different academic units in different colleges and universities, CACREP accredits programs only under the program titles it has adopted. The entry-level program titles currently used by CACREP are: (a) School Counseling (SC); (b) Student Affairs Practice in Higher Education (SA); (c) Marriage and Family Counseling/Therapy (MFCT); (d) Mental Health Counseling; and (e) Community Counseling (CC). Within some of these entry-level programs, more specific program emphases are possible, such as career counseling, gerontological counseling, or college counseling. The one advanced (i.e., doctoral) level program title used by CACREP is Counselor Education and Supervision (CE). As of the fall of 1999, programs accredited by CACREP were located in 137 different institutions of higher education spread across 43 states, the District of Columbia, British Columbia, and Puerto Rico. A current list of CACREP-accredited programs may be found at the CACREP website.

As CACREP's activities intensified and expanded as more programs sought accreditation, it has received more and more suggestions from various professional groups about what ought to be covered in the respective sets of standards. The burgeoning amount of both solicited and unsolicited input about its standards of preparation prompted CACREP to adopt, in 1984, a moratorium on implementation of new standards and a plan for periodic standards review or revision. CACREP thereafter instituted a five-year review cycle for possible revision of its standards of preparation. This plan stipulates that changes in the standards can be submitted for consideration by CACREP at any time, but changes can only be adopted for use at the end of (at least) a five-year period.

CACREP initiated its third standards review/revision process in 1997, with an intended implementation date in 2000. However, rapid changes in the nature of possible counselor preparation instructional delivery modalities, such as distance learning over the Internet, necessitated that the implementation date be reset at January 1, 2001. It is anticipated that the 2001 CACREP standards of preparation will retain essentially the same basic format as the 1994 CACREP standards (e.g., core curriculum plus specialty standards), but will incorporate additions to or changes in many of the specific standards. A draft version of the proposed 2001 CACREP standards may be found at the CACREP website.

The CACREP Orientation to Counselor Preparation

The CACREP standards of preparation and accreditation procedures are best understood within the context of what may be called the CACREP orientation to counselor preparation. It should be noted that this orientation is not unique to CACREP, rather, it evolved from within the ACA. In general, this orientation holds that persons who identify themselves as professional counselors should have successfully completed commonly agreed upon, or core, curricular experiences including learning in specified content/knowledge and skill areas and supervised counseling practice. In addition, all who identify themselves as professional counselors should have completed successfully specialized preparation in at least one specialization area (e.g., school, community, mental health, or marriage and family counseling/therapy). Thus, within this orientation, effective counselor preparation entails education and training in a specialized type of counseling for each aspiring counselor built upon core area preparation common to all counselors. Therefore, even though CACREP entry-level accreditations are given and titled by specialization area, it can be assumed that there is considerable commonality of preparation among graduates of any of the CACREP entry-level accreditation program areas.

The so-called CACREP orientation also holds that advanced-level (i.e., doctoral) preparation should be built upon entry-level preparation. Therefore, it is possible for a counselor preparation program to achieve CACREP advanced-level accreditation only if it encompasses all of the requirements of the CACREP entry-level accreditation standards for at least one specialization area. This tiered system helps to ensure that all professional counselors have evolved from and are operating upon common content/knowledge, skill, and experiential bases.

CACREP Standards Format

The 1994 CACREP entry-level standards of preparation are presented in the following six subsections:

Section I: The Institution.
Section II: Program Objectives and Curriculum.
Section III: Clinical Instruction.
Section IV: Faculty and Staff.
Section V: Organization and Administration.
Section VI: Evaluations in the Program.

The related CACREP advanced-level standards of preparation are contained in one section entitled Counselor Education and Supervision. Specialization standards are built upon the other (so-called generic) entry--level standards.

CACREP Standards for Entry-Level Preparation

Section I.   The first section of the 1994 CACREP entry-level standards identifies accreditation requirements for the institution and academic unit (e.g., department) in which the program for which accreditation is sought is housed. In general, this section specifies the needed identity of the program within the institution as well as the needed resources to conduct the program.

Some of the standards in this section relate to how the program is described in the institution's published materials (e.g., graduate school bulletin or catalog) and how the program is configured within the institution's organizational structure (e.g., within a department within a school or college). Others relate to needed financial support for the program operation and for the faculty specifically involved with the program. Standards in this section also specify necessary program resources (e.g., computer, library, and media facilities) for instructional and research activities associated with the program. Finally, a standard is included which stipulates that counseling services must be available to students in the program from other than program faculty. This latter standard is based on the belief that students in counselor preparation programs should have access to counseling services in ways that do not jeopardize their academic standings (as do other students in the institution).

Section II.   The second section of the standards incorporates several requirements directly related to the CACREP orientation discussed previously. For example, one standard requires that the entry-level program extend over 48 semester hours or 72 quarter hours of graduate-level credits for school counseling, community counseling, or student affairs practice in higher education programs and over 60 semester or 90 quarter hours for mental health counseling or marriage and family counseling/therapy programs. Another standard in this section stipulates that in cases where evaluations indicate that a student's participation and further continuation in the program are inappropriate, program faculty should assist the student to find a more appropriate academic or vocational placement.

Other standards in the second section relate the necessity for having clearly defined and stated program objectives and for effectively distributing those objectives to students and others associated with the program. Similarly, standards exist relating to the development and distribution of instructional materials (e.g., course syllabi and reference lists) to students. Also, some standards in this section are intended to facilitate students' professional involvements beyond classroom instruction. For example, standards are included relating to students' participation in research activities with faculty and in extracurricular professional development activities such as workshops, seminars, and colloquia.

The major portion of the second section delineates the eight so-called common core areas of academic preparation. These are the same areas identified and defined in Chapter 1: Human Growth and Development;

Social and Cultural Foundations; Helping Relationships; Group Work; Career and Lifestyle Development; Appraisal; Research and Program Evaluation; and Professional Orientation. As delineated previously, the possible specialty standards areas are presented separately from the entry-level standards even though they are considered as parts of the respective program objectives and curricula.

Section III. Because carefully supervised clinical practice has been, and is, at the heart of counselor preparation, the third section presents standards relating to supervised clinical (counseling) experiences and instruction for students. Some of the standards in this section relate to students' practicum and internship experiences. The practicum experience is viewed as the student's first experience with actual clients. Therefore, the standards call for students to have relatively limited but closely supervised counseling activities in practicum. A practicum must be a minimum of 100 hours, including at least 40 contact hours with clients in the setting. The internship is viewed as an advanced clinical experience for students and is permitted only after the student has had at least one practicum experience. The standards stipulate that the student participate in the internship in a setting similar to the one in which the student intends to work. The setting for the student's internship is important because during this experience the student is supposed to perform the functions and duties of a regular employee of the setting. An internship is a minimum of 600 hours, including a minimum of 240 contact hours with clients in the setting.

The other standards in section three relate to the nature of clinical supervision for students in practicum or internship. Indicated is that students in either practicum or internship must receive individual and group supervision on a regular, usually weekly, basis. Individual supervision is a meeting of at least one-hour duration between the student in practicum or internship and a program faculty member or another supervisor with equivalent professional credentials. Group supervision is a meeting of at least one-and-one-half-hours duration with several students in practicum or internship and a program faculty member or another supervisor with equivalent credentials. In addition, a student in practicum or internship is required to have an on-site (i.e., host) supervisor with whom the student meets according to a schedule they determine.

Other related standards in this section stipulate counseling laboratory facilities which should be available to the program for which accreditation is sought, necessary professional credentials for supervisors, and needed interactions among supervisors and program faculty.

Section IV. Needed credentials of faculty and assignments to and within the program for which accreditation is sought are described in the fourth section of the standards. For example, the standards indicate that an identified program leader or coordinator must be present, so that someone has ultimate responsibility for the program. In addition to the program leader, at least two other faculty must have instructional assignment to the program for which accreditation is sought. Also stipulated is that program faculty can only provide instruction in areas for which they have demonstrated expertise. Expertise, as used in this context, must be demonstrated through the program faculty members' recent involvements in professional activities such as research, publication, consultation, and/or participation in professional organization activities.

Section V.   The fifth section covers standards that address the operation of a program. Standards relating to required development and distribution of program informational materials and to program orientation activities for students are included. The need for clearly defined admissions policies and procedures also are addressed in this section. Of particular importance here are the standards relating to the specified minimum faculty-to-student ratio within the program and maximum faculty instructional loads. Standards also are included that relate to clear presentation and effective dissemination of students' requirements for matriculation through the program. Finally, standards requiring that students have a planned program of studies are included to ensure that students are following integrated curricula rather than just taking a collection of courses.

Section VI.   The last section of the entry-level standards focuses upon various types of evaluations conducted within the program. One subset of standards in this section relates to required evaluations of students by program faculty. In general, the program faculty is charged with the responsibility for determining whether students are progressing satisfactorily in the development of their knowledge bases, skills, and professional orientation. Other standards in this section relate to required evaluations of instructional and clinical supervision activities by students and the dissemination of the results of those evaluations to program faculty. Another subset of standards in this section calls for periodic evaluation of the program by graduates of the program and dissemination of those evaluation results to all persons associated with the program. This latter subset is the only formal requirement for evaluation of the effectiveness of the program in the CACREP standards.

The standards in these six sections are applied by CACREP to all entry-level programs for which accreditation is sought; thus they reflect the intent of generic or core preparation in entry-level programs. Concomitantly, the standards in the respective specialty standards subsections reflect professional area specializations.

CACREP Standards for Doctoral-Level Preparation

CACREP uses the term "advanced-level" preparation to mean counselor preparation beyond entry-level preparation. Therefore, the CACREP standards for doctoral-level preparation are used in addition to the standards for entry-level preparation. Again, a doctoral program in an academic unit can be accredited by CACREP even if no CACREP accredited entry-level program is included within the academic unit, however, the doctoral program must fulfill both the entry-level and advanced-level standards in order to be accredited. In general, the CACREP advanced-level standards extend the entry-level standards through greater emphases on supervised practice, research and statistics, and specific preparation in a professional specialization. The advanced-level standards also reflect the belief that preparation for professional leadership should be incorporated at this level. Therefore, specific standards are included that relate to activities presumed to facilitate development of professional leadership characteristics, abilities, and skills in doctoral students (West, Bubenzer, Brooks, & Hackney, 1995).

Accreditation Procedures

CACREP's accreditation process includes essentially five steps or stages. First, the faculty, with assistance from students in some cases, conducts a self-study of the program for which accreditation is sought. The purpose of the self-study is to determine the ways the program meets, or does not meet, the applicable CACREP standards and to document the degree of compliance with each of the standards. This step involves substantial investment of time, effort, and resources because: (1) each person associated with the program is supposed to be involved in the development of the self-study; (2) specific information is needed from each person associated with the program; and (3) collective, as opposed to individual, information or opinions about degree of compliance with each standard is required.

During the second step, the institution's application materials and self-study are evaluated by a three-person review committee, composed of CACREP representative (i.e., council or designated) members, to determine if the program is ready for a site team visitation. If the committee members reviewing the degree of compliance with the standards, as presented in the self-study, determine that the program (vis-à-vis the self-study) is not ready for a visitation by a site team, recommendations for needed changes or improvements, or both, are given and the self-study is returned to the institution. If the committee determines that the program is ready, the third step in the process (i.e., a visitation by a site team) is implemented.

CACREP site visitation team members are counseling professionals who have successfully completed training to act in accord with CACREP's accreditation procedures. The purpose of the site team visitation is to validate the institution's self-study, that is, to determine if that which is contained in the self-study is accurate. Upon conclusion of the site visit, the team members compose a report of their findings based on their review of the program's self-study and their visitation to the institution.

In the fourth step, the CACREP executive director returns the site visitation team's report to the institution. The program faculty, in turn, review the site visitation team's report and respond to it. This response is made only in regard to the accuracy of the site visitation team's report. This response is also delivered to the CACREP executive director.

In the last step, the CACREP council members review the institution's self-study, the site visitation team's report, and the institution's response to the site visitation team's report, and make a decision about the accreditation status to be awarded to the program.

One of three decisions may be rendered by CACREP about each program for which accreditation is sought: (a) Seven-year Accreditation, (b) Two-year Accreditation, or (c) Denial of Accreditation. Seven-year accreditation status is accorded to programs which essentially fulfill all applicable standards. Two-year accreditation status is accorded to programs which fulfill most applicable standards, but for which specific requirements remain to be fulfilled before seven-year accreditation status can be granted. If the program does not fulfill the stipulated requirements within the two-year period, denial of accreditation is assigned to the program. However, a program may be moved from two to seven-year accreditation status in less than two years if the requirements are fulfilled earlier.

Historically, CACREP has rendered the decision Denial of Accreditation to programs on very few occasions. This should not be construed to mean, however, that CACREP approves almost all programs for which accreditation is sought or is that it is lax in application of its standards of preparation. Rather, it is a reflection of CACREP's philosophy and its operating procedures. Philosophically, CACREP is dedicated to the enhancement of the counseling profession through assisting counselor preparation programs to improve their effectiveness through adherence to and application of the (CACREP) standards of preparation. This philosophy is operationalized primarily in step two. The initial review of the program's self-study provides the institution with an opportunity to delay the application for accreditation of the program until the program substantially meets CACREP's standards of preparation. Thus, only those programs for which a high probability exists for at least two-year accreditation status are processed through the subsequent steps in the CACREP accreditation process.

☐ Accreditation by Other Agencies

Several agencies, other than CACREP, also accredit specific counselor preparation programs. For example, the American Psychological Association (APA) accredits doctoral-level counseling psychology preparation programs, the National Council for Accreditation of Teacher Education (NCATE) accredits master's-level school counselor preparation programs, the Council on Rehabilitation Education (CORE) accredits master's-level rehabilitation counselor preparation programs, and the American Association for Marriage and Family Therapists (AAMFT) accredits master's-level marriage and family counselor preparation programs. Although there are unique aspects to the goals and processes of each of these agencies, they are all philosophically similar to CACREP in that they desire to improve the counseling profession through implementation of standardized counselor preparation practices.

☐ Summary

A strong movement exists within the counseling profession to improve counselor preparation through the application of standards of preparation within the context of program accreditation activities. For example, by the fall of 1999, approximately 137 of the more than 400 academic units in the United States, Canada, and United States' territories housing counselor preparation programs had CACREP approved programs. This proportion is substantial given that CACREP has had formal operations for only approximately a decade and a half. Applications to CACREP are increasing rapidly, indicating that the use of commonly supported and widely recognized standards of preparation is on the rise in the counseling profession. As much as any other current professional phenomenon, this movement stands to improve both professional counselors and the counseling services they provide.

16

Trends in Professional Counseling

Counseling is an emerging, evolving, and dynamic profession currently experiencing rapid growth and generally positive changes, particularly with regard to counselor preparation and professional credentialing. Other changes are more difficult to categorize because they are occurring in literally every aspect of the counseling profession. However, for discussion purposes, these changes may be subdivided into those taking place in professional counselors' work settings, and those concerning the clientele with whom professional counselors work. Relatedly, changes in where and with whom are often associated with how counselors work. Therefore, some changes in methods and techniques also are discussed.

☐ Trends in Settings
Where Professional Counselors Work

It has been noted that the counseling profession has its heritage in school counseling. Today, a substantial number of professional counselors still work in public and private schools and counselor employment in schools shows every indication of continuing to increase. This trend is evident not just because of an increasing number of students in schools, but rather because the perceived value and worth of having counselors in schools is becoming widely recognized. For example, a 1998 initiative from President Clinton called for having 100,000 more school counselors by the end of the first decade of the new millennium. The reasons for this increased recognition of the worth of school counseling are myriad. Unfortunately, one of the most prominent is the media attention to violence in schools during the 1990s. However, even unfortunate situations help to increase recognition of the benefits of having sufficient and effective school counseling services for all children.

This increased and improved recognition is due in large part to the fact that most school counselors fulfill their roles and responsibilities efficiently and effectively. This generalized effectiveness is due in part to the fact that there is considerable commonality in the nature of school counselors' roles and functions across school levels (Baker, 1996; Schmidt, 1998). For example, emphasis on developmental (i.e., preventive) approaches to helping children pervades the professional school counseling literature. However, there remains need for school counselors to be skilled in so-called remediative interventions as well. Baker (1996) stated the situation aptly:

> Current circumstances existing in the nation's schools and projections of socioeconomic conditions that will impact on the schools seem to demand systematic school counseling programs that are designed to respond to the developmental needs of children and adolescents in the elementary, middle, and secondary schools. Proactive programming designed to enhance student development transitions and reactive interventions that help students in danger of arrested development are both important and seem needed today and into the twenty-first century. (p. 2)

The commonalities of school counseling notwithstanding, some school counselor roles and functions are differentially emphasized across school levels (Coll & Freeman, 1997). Therefore, each of the three common school levels merits some individual discussion in regard to the work of school counselors.

Secondary Schools

Historically, counseling functions have been fulfilled in secondary schools since the second decade of the twentieth century. In the early years of school counseling, these functions were fulfilled by teachers, administrators, support personnel, or volunteers. Today, however, almost every secondary school has at least one full-time school counselor whose primary responsibility is to fulfill school counseling functions. Traditionally, counselors in secondary schools focused most of their efforts on college-bound students, spent some of their time collecting occupational information for use by students, and spent the remainder of their time in more mundane activities (e.g., class scheduling and attendance monitoring). The current trend, however, is for counselors in secondary schools to be highly involved in activities deemed appropriate by professional associations such as ASCA, even though there is variation in the attention given to particular activities (Schmidt, 1998). Clerical and administrative functions are decreasing in emphasis, and emphasis on activities that benefit students most is increasing.

Counseling in secondary schools now emphasizes greater attention to the needs of all students, not just those who are academically talented (Moles, 1991; Myrick, 1993). For example, counselors in secondary schools typically coordinate comprehensive career guidance programs suitable for students with widely varying circumstances, skills, abilities, and resources. Because such programs typically include use of computerized career development resources, most secondary school counselors also are using modern technology, especially computers, to be able to help more students. Relatedly, counselors in secondary schools are extending their effectiveness through greater use of group counseling, presentation of classroom guidance units, coordination of peer counseling programs, and involvement in teacher-as-advisor programs. Secondary school counselors also spend a considerable amount of time in consultation roles in helping teachers, administrators, and other school personnel to assist students with learning, personal, and other types of concerns. School counselors also are benefitting more now from improved collegial relationships with other school personnel, and therefore providing better services to students and others associated with schools (Benshoff & Paisley, 1996). Thus, counselors in secondary schools are now much more involved in professionally appropriate roles and functions, and considerably less involved in those activities that often fostered negative stereotypes of them.

Middle Schools

School counseling functions in middle (or junior high) schools are very similar to those at other, particularly secondary, school levels. However, implementation of school counseling services in middle schools is shaped by the nature of middle school students themselves. As early adolescents, sometimes referred to as transescents, middle school students present a wide array of personal and social characteristics and an even more diverse array of behaviors. Therefore, middle school counseling programs must be tailored specifically to this age group. Kottman (1990) indicates:

> The school counselor must design the guidance and counseling program to accommodate the attitudes and developmental needs of children in the early stages of adolescence. Active methods of counseling that require intense involvement on the part of both the counselor and students have been found to be most successful with children in junior high and middle school.

Methods that capitalize on the characteristic attitudes, behaviors, and development of junior high and middle school students are usually active and interactive. Many procedures are appropriate alternatives for traditional "talk" therapy, which may also be too passive or threatening for working with children at this level. (p. 138)

Kottman (1990) advocated use of therapeutic game play, stories and metaphors, and role-play and simulation as primary examples of counseling interventions particularly appropriate for middle school students. These types of activities are useful interventions for remediation of middle school students' concerns and problems. However, clearly the trend in middle school counseling is toward preventive and/or developmental counseling activities, especially for at-risk students (Keys, Bemak, & Lockhart, 1998; Myrick, 1993). Primary among activities of this nature are peer facilitator and teacher-as-advisor programs. Peer facilitator programs have been operational in schools for almost two decades, and involve students using so-called basic helping skills to assist their peers to cope with developmental and other concerns (Myrick, 1992). Teachers-as-advisors programs are newer, but also are rapidly being incorporated into schools, particularly middle schools. Describing the components of these programs, Galassi and Gulledge (1997) wrote:

They may be as disparate as "drop everything and read time," debates, discussions, peer mediation, celebrations of birthdays and holidays, and spirited sports competition. Packaged advisory curricula are available for sale to schools, or teachers may be left to their own devices to come up with activities. In some schools, students get both individual and group advising almost daily. Some advisory groups go on field trips or get together outside of school hours. (p. 55)

Middle school counseling programs sometimes necessitate unique approaches to students in a unique developmental stage (Murphy, 1997). Fortunately, many innovative and effective approaches to counseling services for middle school students are now commonly implemented.

Elementary Schools

The most significant advancements in school counseling over the last several decades have been in elementary school counseling. Substantial numbers of counselors first began working in elementary schools in the late 1960s and the early 1970s. Since then, the number of counselors in elementary schools has increased rapidly. This increase is attributable primarily to the realization that to do so is better for all concerned with schools—students, parents, or teachers, as well as persons whose involvement with schools is less obvious, such as professionals in community agencies. That is, the attempt to prevent students' problems before they arise is far more beneficial than to remediate problems after they have arisen. Thus, counselors in elementary schools spend most of their time and efforts focusing on preventive and developmental counseling activities (Baker, 1996; Coll & Freeman, 1997; Myrick, 1993). Myrick (1993) provided the basic assumption for the developmental counseling approach: "Developmental guidance and counseling assumes that human nature moves individuals sequentially and positively toward self-enhancement" (p. 25). He went on to clarify the primary objective of developmental guidance and counseling in schools:

> The developmental approach considers the nature of human development, including the general stages and tasks that most individuals experience as they mature from childhood to adulthood. It centers on positive self-concepts and acknowledges that one's self-concept is formed and reformed through experience and education. It further recognizes that feelings, ideas, and behaviors are closely linked together and that they are learned. Therefore, the most desired conditions for learning and re-learning are important considerations for development. The ultimate objective is to help students learn more effectively and efficiently. (p. 25)

Classroom guidance units, small group counseling, and parent and teacher consultation are primary methodologies used in developmental elementary school counseling. Newer technologies, such as multimedia computer software packages, also offer elementary school counselors a means to address students' developmental issues (Gerler, 1995). However, counselors in elementary schools also are involved in remediative counseling for students experiencing problems such as abuse, neglect, poor peer relationships, parental divorce, discrimination, or learning difficulties (Hardesty & Dillard, 1994). In essence, elementary school counselors provide a full range of counseling services, but focus upon developmental counseling activities.

Full Service Schools

Moving toward implementation of the concept of what are known as full service schools is currently very popular in American education. In general, this conceptualization holds that schools should be organized and operated so as to provide all the services that students could need, with specific attention to those services that affect learning. Within this framework, schools would either provide directly or be the primary referral source for any service that help children develop effectively. Services potentially offered through such schools might include those intended to enhance students' nutrition, physical health and well-being, socioeconomic condition, or mental health.

If the movement toward full service schools continues and becomes pervasive, then school counselors will play pivotal roles in the facilitation of services for the maintenance and enhancement of students' mental health. That is, school counselors should become the mental health services coordinators' in schools. This is truly an exciting possibility for the counseling profession because it holds the potential to meld the many facets of the profession into a unified service delivery unit. For example, there already exist schools wherein mental health counselors, and sometimes family counselors as well, provide their relatively specialized services to students or their families in the schools. In a relatively few schools, still other counseling services, such as rehabilitation counseling, also are provided in the schools. Typically, the provision of such services is coordinated by and through the school counselor. Whether full service schools continue to emerge remains to be determined. However, if they do, they will be of significant benefit to the counseling profession by allowing for greater professional collaboration in service delivery, increased recognition of counselors, and improved services to various clientele.

Colleges and Universities

Counselors have a long history of working in colleges and universities in counseling centers for students as well as in a variety of positions involving student affair activities such as admissions, residence life, student activities, and career placement. Traditionally, this conglomerate of activities has been represented in the counseling profession and in ACA by the American College Personnel Association (ACPA). However, the withdrawal of ACPA from ACA, and the accompanying exodus of professionals with primary interest in student affairs practice administration activities, has changed the situation. The emergence of the American College Counseling Association (ACCA) as an ACA division has clarified the counseling focus and allowed ACCA members to be more coherent in their professional views and interests. Concomitantly, ACA's International Association of Counseling Services (IACS), which accredits college and university counseling centers (among other activities), has intensified and extended its activities. Thus, there is a reemerging focus within ACA and the counseling profession on the provision of counseling services in colleges and universities.

Bishop (1990) noted that college and university counseling services are likely to focus in the future upon four broad categories of service areas: (a) crisis management, (b) career development, (c) special student populations, and (d) student retention. How services such as these are delivered, and the corresponding roles and responsibilities of professional counselors in colleges and universities, typically reflect the institution's size. Large colleges and universities tend to divide functions into highly specialized tasks and have counseling staff in each area, while smaller institutions have a few people responsible for many different functions.

Many professional counselors work primarily in counseling centers helping college students with vocational or social relationship/adjustment problems. However, computerized vocational development resources have done much to facilitate their career counseling work. Thus, more recently, they have been able to devote more of their attentions to students' personal concerns and problems. The growing recognition that college students are also people has greatly increased the types of problems to which counseling center counselors attend. For example, increasing numbers of college students experiencing problems such as parental divorce, anorexia, bulimia, marital difficulties, excessive stress, depression, anxiety, sexual harassment, interpersonal violence, or substance abuse are seeking the services of counseling center counselors (Bishop, 1995; Burns & Consolvo, 1992). Moreover, the increasing numbers of nontraditional students in colleges and universities (i.e., those who have returned to college after some lapse in their educational sequence) have necessitated that these counselors be able to help people with adult developmental and adjustment concerns. Thus, counselors in colleges and universities today are providing counseling services for the full range of problems evident in society, but their work is generally restricted to college students.

Community Agencies

Nowhere in the counseling profession has change been more dramatic than in the relatively recent increase in counselors working in community mental health agencies. This increase has greatly enhanced the identity of the counseling profession because it has brought about the recognition that professional counselors can provide valuable services to all people in society, not just students in educational institutions. The increase in counselors working in community agencies has allowed professional counselors to enjoy full membership status among the professions previously recognized as primary providers of mental health services.

Counselors working in community agencies are employed in many different types of agencies and involved with the provision of a wide variety of counseling services. They work in community agencies such as community mental health centers, abused or victimized person facilities, geriatric centers, substance (i.e., drug or alcohol) abuse programs (including both residential and out-patient facilities), crisis and hot-line centers, half-way houses, runaway shelters, vocational rehabilitation centers, nursing homes, residential facilities for the elderly, and shelters for the homeless. Within these types of settings counselors provide services such as personal adjustment, marriage and family, sex, career, grieving and loss, educational, wellness, and personal development counseling. They work with people of all ages, from very young children to very elderly people.

Traditionally, counselors working in community agencies have provided primarily remediative counseling services. That is, people have typically sought services from the agencies after problems have arisen. This is still a major emphasis in counseling in community agencies. More recently, however, counselors in community agencies also have become involved in preventive and developmental counseling. Further, counseling activities are now being provided in many community situations not previously having counselor involvements. For example, some counselors are now providing services in the context of Health Maintenance Organizations (HMOs). Forrest and Afferrian (1986) commented on the roles of counselors in HMOs:

> The educational model as well as the medical model provides an important vehicle for the delivery of primary prevention. Most MHCs [mental health counselors] are generally well prepared in this area. They are trained in group facilitation, and much primary and secondary prevention can be delivered in group settings. . . . The MHCs are aware that the patient's social support systems are a means of preventing physical illness, and MHCs commonly use processes for aiding in improving these systems. . . . (p. 69)

A related phenomenon is the increasing numbers of counselors working in the area of preventative medicine. Smith and Robinson (1995) stated:

> Mental health counseling brings a unique approach to the mental health care professions in that it offers a broader response to the definition of care than the traditional fields of psychiatry and clinical psychology. Historically, people who could benefit from mental health services were viewed as distinctly different from those who would be considered "healthy" (i.e., there is something "wrong" with them, or they are "ill" and therefore in need of treatment). If one considers mental health care to be a continuum based on needs of society with high-level wellness being on one end of the continuum and severe and persistent mental illness being on the other, virtually every person can improve their respective quality of life through the use of mental health services. Simply stated, mental health counseling believes that a person does not have to be sick to get better. (p. 74)

Thus, counselors working in community agencies are involved in literally all types of professional activities in the counseling profession.

A relatively small, but increasing, proportion of professional counselors are working in hospitals and other medical care facilities (e.g., renal care, cardiac, or trauma centers, or hospices). The counseling services provided by counselors in these settings are almost exclusively remediative or crisis-oriented in nature, primarily because clients enter the facilities to seek services for severe medical problems. Bereavement (i.e., grieving and loss) counseling is one of the major services provided by counselors in these settings, although they sometimes provide other types of services such as family, stress reduction, or sexuality counseling.

Private Practice

The establishment of counseling private practices is an obvious trend in the counseling profession today. Weikel and Palmo (1989) wrote:

> Probably the most exciting aspect of the expansion of mental health services has been the broadening of private practice to include all of the core providers [of counseling and/or therapeutic services], and not merely psychiatrists and psychologists. For MHCs [mental health counselors], this expansion has provided new opportunities for demonstrating their skills. . . . (p. 17)

Although the vast majority of counselors still are employed by agencies or educational institutions, the number of self-employed, and usually self-incorporated, professional counselors has increased significantly within the last few years. The increase is likely to continue, primarily due to the fact that a substantial number of professional counselors are able to be financially solvent, and in a few cases financially affluent, from the proceeds of their private practices. This financial solvency is in part linked to professional credentialing. That is, more and more professional credentials (e.g., licensures and certifications) of counselors are being recognized as indicators of professional competence. In turn, as the status of their credentials increases, so do the costs of their services and the willingness of people and agencies to pay those costs. For example, most insurance company policies now cover the services of professional counselors who are licensed or certified. Payments by other than counseling service recipients (e.g., insurance companies) are known as third-party payments. Similarly, a growing number of companies and corporations are providing third-party reimbursements to credentialed counselors in private practice for services rendered to company employees because it is often less expensive for the companies to pay private practitioners than to provide in-house counseling services.

The counseling services provided by various counselors in private practice run the gamut of the various services found in the counseling profession. Private practitioner counseling services can be found for any imaginable human mental health need. However, the vast majority of counselors in private practice have focused their activities on counseling children, marriage and/or family counseling, substance-abuse and addictions counseling, or personal adjustment counseling. In addition, most counselors in private practice are heavily involved in consultation activities, particularly those relating to facilitation of human and interpersonal relations development and the provision of training workshops. Thus, most counselors in private practice are involved in multiple, but few, major professional activities in order to generate income.

An Interjection About Managed Care

Clearly managed care is the major concern for counselors working in either community agencies or private practice. In brief, managed care means that third-party payers, usually insurance companies, determine how much money will be paid for how much service (usually a specified number of counseling sessions) for which type of client problem (usually reflected in a particular psychodiagnosis). Managed care is a significant concern for the counseling profession in several regards. First, it involves an outside entity specifying how much counseling is necessary to "fix" a client's problem and therefore takes control of the counseling process from the counselor and the client. Second, it is apparently based on the assumption that all clients experience the same problem in the same way, which of course is contrary to all major theories of personality and human development. Third, it forces counselors to focus upon (immediate) problem resolution as opposed to more broad-based healthy emotional functioning. Fourth, it greatly restricts client options about counseling because of the necessity to focus upon very specific problem symptoms, as opposed to underlying problem dynamics. Fifth, it restricts the counseling approaches that counselors may draw upon for resolution of client problems. And finally, it certainly limits the amount of money counselors may make for services rendered.

Managed care is the bane of the entire health care industry, including counseling. How the impact of managed care will play out in the counseling profession in particular remains to be seen. However, there is no doubt that it is already having significant impact on the provision of counseling services and concomitantly on how counselors lead their professional lives. It is certainly likely that counseling professionals will continue to do battle with managed care; but how it will all fall out nobody knows.

Business and Industry

A trend that continues to increase, albeit slowly, is employment of counselors in business and industry. Employment of counselors in business and industry is based primarily on the adage that a happy employee is a good employee. That is, an employee who is free from major personal problems is likely to be productive, punctual, have a low rate of absenteeism, and show allegiance to the employer. Counseling services in business and industry therefore are intended primarily to keep employees happy, that is, functioning effectively in their work, personal, and familial lives.

Counselors in business and industry settings are usually employed within the context of human resource development (HRD) or employee assistance programs (EAPs). Gerstein and Bayer (1988) indicated that:

> Clearly, counselors have the potential to play an important role in the EAP arena. . . . [C]ounselors are needed to assist with program evaluation, quality service assurance, program administration, theory development, research, and marketing. (p. 296)

Both of these types of programs typically involve provision of services such as interpersonal and employee relations training, career and lifestyle development (including leisure counseling), stress and time management training, consultation about a variety of mental health concerns, and not surprisingly, personal and familial counseling services. Counselors also have become involved in relocation facilitation in response to employee and familial stresses resulting from geographic relocations. Thus, as in other settings, counselors in business and industry settings become involved in many different types of counseling service provision.

Religious Congregations

An interesting mixture of professions is evident in the growing number of clerics (e.g., ministers, priests, sisters, or rabbis) who have completed counselor-preparation programs. Members of religious congregations often turn to their respective clerics for spiritual guidance and counseling about problems in their lives. Many clerics have realized that some of these people need assistance that is not readily amenable by religious or spiritual guidance alone; thus, they have need to provide counseling services in accord with the interpretations used throughout this book. The types of counseling services provided by clerics are many, but three seem to be most prevalent. One is bereavement (i.e., grieving and loss) counseling. In the difficult times following loss situations (e.g., deaths of loved ones), members of congregations typically seek solace from clerics. Facilitation of the bereavement process is therefore a common counseling activity for clerics. A second is marriage and family counseling. Again, in times of marital or family discord or crises, clerics are among the first to whom members of congregations turn for assistance. A third primary counseling activity for clerics is referral. That is, when people have problems, they often approach their respective clerics first, probably because they are aware that their clerics will maintain confidentiality about the problems. In these situations, clerics are instrumental in deciding whether the problems can be resolved through religious and spiritual guidance, counseling provided by the clerics themselves, or counseling services from (other) professional counselors. If the latter option is selected, these clerics also have to decide to whom to refer the people and how to facilitate the referral process. Given the large numbers of people with whom clerics typically work, these latter activities are quite common.

Conversely, it also is common for counselors to refer clients to pastoral counselors to work on spiritual issues, and it is recommended that these clergy be chosen based on their demonstrated ability to maintain confidentiality, to have the client's best interests in mind, and to understand the principles of counseling (Faiver, O'Brien, & McNally, 1998). Counseling, in some relatively restricted forms, thus is common in many religious congregations.

Legal Systems

A small, but growing, segment of professional counselors is working in the criminal justice and other parts of legal systems. For example, counselors working in correctional institutions primarily provide personal adjustment and career and lifestyle counseling for incarcerated persons, particularly those for whom release is imminent. Counselors working in other offender rehabilitation programs, such as those for sex-offenders or spouse (or other family member) abusers, focus primarily on remediation of the dynamics and situations underlying the offenses, as well as other types of counseling for problems related to the offenses. More recently, some professional counselors have become involved in providing counseling services within another part of the legal system: divorce litigation. These counselors are employed by the legal system (i.e., employed by a court as opposed to being employed by either of the litigants) to provide divorce mediation services prior to trial. The goal of counseling in this situation is to enable the litigants to achieve a mutually accepted marriage dissolution agreement instead of having it decreed by a judge. In essence, divorce mediation counseling is a very specialized form of marriage and family counseling.

These then are the major trends in the settings where professional counselors work. Collectively, they reflect the general trend in the counseling profession of counselors working in almost all types of settings. Indeed, identifying settings where counselors do not work is difficult.

☐ Trends in Clientele with Whom Counselors Work

Just as the number of settings in which counselors work has expanded greatly since the beginning of the counseling profession, so too has the number of different types of people with whom counselors work. This general trend is of course partially a function of the increase in the number of settings in which counselors work. However, it is also a function of professional counselors actively having involved themselves in a greater variety of counseling services so that they could effectively serve more and different types of people. Thus, professional counselors have been and continue to be proactive in their efforts to serve increasing numbers of people. The people served can be categorized in several different ways, one of which is by stage in the life span.

Preschool Children

One of the newest client groups for professional counselors is preschool children. The counseling profession's emphasis on developmental counseling in elementary schools has prompted some counselors to extend the emphasis to children before they enter school. There are potentially significant advantages to working with children before they enter formal educational systems. Hohenshil and Brown (1991) wrote:

> Prekindergarten children are at an age when interventions have the best probability of success. . . . From a developmental perspective, the earlier the interventions are begun, the better the success rate whether children are at risk or not. This is the fundamental rationale upon which prekindergarten programs rest. (p. 3)

Accordingly, some counselors are now providing services such as learning skills training, interpersonal relationships facilitation (e.g., with siblings and other family members), and social skills enhancement to very young children. Relatedly, because some young children have problems which need remediation, some professional counselors use techniques such as play counseling, bibliotherapy, and art therapy to help these children. Counselors working with young children also often work with the children's parents to help the parents develop better parenting, behavior management, and child motivational skills. In general, counselors' efforts with very young children often are intended to help the children get a good start in life, and sometimes to help them overcome the problems (e.g., abuse and/or neglect) they have already encountered.

Elementary School Age Children

The vast majority of elementary school age children receive needed or desirable counseling services from counselors working in schools. However, counselors working in community agencies and private practice increasingly also are providing services to elementary school age children. Several reasons exist for this trend. One is that school counselors simply have too many children with whom to work and too many other school-related responsibilities to provide effective services for all who need them. As a result, some parents are seeking other sources of assistance for their children.

A second reason is that some parents (inappropriately) fear that a stigma will be attached to their child(ren) if they are counseled in the school setting, and so seek less public counseling services for them. A third is that because school counselors must be able to provide many different types of counseling services, it is difficult for them to specialize in particular types of counseling; counselors in community agencies or private practice typically specialize and therefore (in some cases) are able to provide better services.

A final, although rarer, reason is that court-ordered counseling for children is increasing as more and more judges now understand the nature and benefits of counseling services for children. An example of this is the increasing number of children who are being required by courts to receive counseling for problems resulting from parental divorce. Typically, judges order such counseling services to be provided by counselors in community agencies or by counselors in private practice who have contractual arrangements with the judicial system.

Middle School Age Children

Thornburg (1986) listed eight developmental tasks, across three developmental areas, with which counselors could help transescents:

Physical development
Becoming aware of increased physical changes
Intellectual Development
Organizing knowledge and concepts into problem-solving strategies
Making the transition from concrete to abstract symbols
Social Development
Learning new social and sex roles
Identifying with stereotypical role models

Developing friendships
Gaining a sense of independence
Developing a sense of responsibility (pp. 170–171)

In borrowing counseling techniques from those appropriate for elementary school age children and for adolescents, as well as developing techniques specifically appropriate for transescents, counselors have made great strides in provision of effective counseling services for middle school age children. In addition, the increase in family counseling by counselors outside of school settings has been very successful in helping both transescents and their families cope with pertinent developmental and transitional issues. In so doing, they have done much to facilitate transescents' successful passage through an often difficult developmental period.

Secondary School Age Students

For reasons similar to those for elementary and middle school age children, increasing numbers of secondary school age children (i.e., adolescents) are being counseled not only by school counselors but also by professional counselors in community agencies or private practice. Adolescence is a difficult period in any person's life because of normal problems such as emerging sexuality, changing peer relationships, academic pressures and strains, identity development, career exploration, disengagement from family and parents, and value conflicts. However, today's adolescents also are increasingly confronted with problems related to drug and alcohol abuse, delinquency, depression, violence, parental divorce, step-family acclamation, physical or sexual abuse, and a host of societal problems such as unemployment and racial or sexual discrimination.

Many parents are unable to help their children through the difficulties of adolescence and so seek professional counseling services for their children. In addition, many youth themselves also are seeking counseling assistance with problems. In extreme cases, youth with severe problems receive counseling services from crisis centers or residential treatment (e.g., substance abuse) facilities. However, more typically, they receive counseling services from counselors in community agencies or private practice who specialize in working with youth.

Persons in Mid-Life

Among the newer groups for whom counseling services are being more frequently provided are persons in mid-life. This time period is difficult, if not impossible, to define in terms of an age range because of changes in human longevity as well as conflicting interpretations about to which life it applies; is it the middle of actual life, marital or family life, or career life? More appropriately, the term mid-life applies to a person's situation in life in general. That is, the term mid-life is usually applied to people who have established relatively stable lifestyles, careers, familial situations, and behavior patterns, and who are not yet preparing for retirement. Some people in this situation are so stable that stability becomes a problem for them. Colloquially, these people are asking themselves the question, "Is this all there is?" The problems manifested by people in mid-life who are experiencing generalized disenchantment are many and include such things as identity confusion, depression, marital or familial strife, career dissatisfaction, or substance abuse. Women at mid-life, in particular, are undergoing a multitude of changes, such as menopause, role transitions, and the empty nest syndrome (Lippert, 1997). Accordingly, these people seek counseling for a variety of purposes, and generally want to find new directions for themselves and their lives.

Older Adults

The graying of America is a colloquial phrase used to reflect the rapidly increasing average age of people in society, an increase that is attributable to increasing human longevity. The large number of older people in society has in turn brought (overdue) greater attention to their life situations, needs, and problems. Approximately two decades ago, Riker (1981) wrote:

> [T]he need for help is great among older citizens in this country. Even a cursory look at statistical information regarding alcoholism and suicide among older persons highlights some of the extremes of mental health problems. Less extreme, but certainly suggestive of a general mental health problem of older persons, are the results of a 1980 nationwide study of 514 randomly selected Americans, 60 years of age and older. This study places those interviewed in three descriptive categories, as enjoyers (27%), survivors (53%), and casualties (20%). . . . The designation for each category seems to be self-explanatory, with casualties referring to those experiencing major difficulties in areas such as health, finances, or living conditions. For whatever reasons, the majority of this older population sample are survivors, while an additional 20% are facing major problems. The range of the problems is considerable, the intensity varies, but the extensiveness among older persons seems inescapable. (pp. xvii–xviii)

The study Riker cited may be dated now, but the conditions among older persons he focused upon are not. Even though older persons in the United

States constitute a significant and increasing proportion of the United States population, the problems they experience (e.g., health, financial, or familial concerns) have not been addressed or alleviated substantially. In addition, they continue to fall victim to mistaken stereotypes about them, such as that most older persons live in residential care facilities and require extensive nursing services, are a significant drain on the economy, or would rather live under the care of others as opposed to being functionally independent. Thus, older persons are a proportionately significant clientele for counselors and it is likely that their counseling needs will increase and expand.

One response to this situation has been an increase in counseling services specifically suited to older persons, services often referred to as gerontological counseling (Myers, 1995). Older persons experience the myriad problems experienced by younger persons, but their life situations often add at least one major confounding factor: the perception of not having enough time left in their lives to resolve the problems. Moreover, the counseling needs of individual older persons tend to be generalized within their respective lives; if they have needs for counseling, they tend to have the needs in many aspects of their lives as opposed to in specific parts of their lives (Myers & Loesch, 1981). Thus, counseling services for older persons need to be comprehensive in scope, and professional counselors who work with older persons must be able to provide a variety of types of counseling services.

Intellectually Gifted and Talented People

In addition to life span divisions, the clientele for professional counselors also can be categorized by other human characteristics. Some of these are groups of people who would not ordinarily be expected to be in need of counseling services. For example, Myers and Pace (1986) summarized the professional literature and found the following problems to be evident among various intellectually gifted and talented people: depression, underachievement, perfectionism and overachievement, suicide, delinquency, peer relationship problems, career development problems related to potential for multiple careers, problems in making long-range plans, difficulties in dealing with deferred gratification, early career closure, and value conflicts with peer groups, family, and society. McMann and Oliver (1988) indicated that the presence of a gifted child in a family may cause significant intrafamilial difficulties. More recently, Peterson and Colangelo (1996) wrote:

> [W]hen highly intelligent adolescents are turned off by school or are struggling to stay involved during adolescent or family upheaval, their under-

achievement may represent great pain and frustration, not to mention loss of potential adult productivity (p. 399).

While there is much knowledge about gifted people's needs, counseling strategies specifically effective for them have not been adequately developed or investigated. Gifted and talented persons are a group for whom individual, group, or family counseling services are often appropriate, but also a group to whom professional counselors have only recently turned their attentions.

Culturally Differentiated Populations

Recognition of the unique characteristics of persons from various cultural groups (sometimes referred to as racial or ethnic minorities) has prompted the counseling profession to be responsive to their needs through the provision of multicultural counseling services specifically suited for them. Culturally differentiated persons, of course, experience any of the problems for which counseling services are appropriate. However, they also may experience problems associated with their unique characteristics and life situations. Moreover, counseling service delivery modes appropriate for persons in society's majority may not always be appropriate for culturally differentiated persons. Das (1995) wrote:

> To effectively work with clients belonging to a particular racial or ethnic minority, the counselor has to acquire a specific knowledge about the particular group. The counselor also needs a general understanding of the socio-political systems operative in the United States with respect to the minorities and the institutional barriers that prevent minorities from using mental health services. [T]he multicultural counselor also needs to understand those aspects of social organization and cultural norms and values that generate stress in the lives of people and that lead to psychological distress and dysfunction. (p. 47)

Similarly, Patterson (1996) noted:

> All clients . . . belong to multiple groups, all of which influence the client's perceptions, beliefs, feelings, thoughts, and behavior. The counselor must be aware of these influences and of their unique blending or fusion in the client if counseling is to be successful. (p. 230)

Thus, professional counselors who provide counseling services to them must be thoroughly knowledgeable of both the characteristics of various cultural groups and counseling approaches and techniques effective for working with them.

Attention to multicultural issues in counseling is probably the major focus of the counseling profession as the new millennium begins—and well it should be given the rapid changes in the composition of American society (Axelson, 1999; Ivey, Ivey, & Simek-Morgan, 1996). The current emphasis on the need for counseling to be mutliculturally sensitive and effective has resulted in many new professional resources to assist counselors to be more sensitive to multicultural situations, issues, and concerns (e.g., Lee, 1997; Lee & Walz, 1998; Pedersen & Locke, 1996), have more and better multicultural counseling skills in general (e.g., Sandhu & Aspy, 1997; Arrendondo, Toporek, Brown, Jones, Locke, Sanchez, & Stadler, 1996), and have multicultural counseling skills suitable for use in relatively specific circumstances or purposes (e.g., Kammen & Gold, 1998; Lee, 1996; Wehrley, 1996).

Genders

Provision of gender specific counseling services is another major trend in the counseling profession. The need for such specialized counseling services first became evident with recognition of the changing roles and status for women in society. As women entered the labor force in increasing numbers and as they pursued redefined (i.e., nontraditional) roles in familial and interpersonal situations, they encountered problems which often made the transitions difficult. Westervelt (1978) stated:

> Counselors know that [women's] changed or changing perceptions of self and society generate new sources of conflict and ambivalence and of guilt and shame, as well as new sources of motivation and new patterns of aspiration. (p. 2)

Thus, counseling services and techniques specifically for women evolved from their unique needs and situations, particularly the need to help women achieve their potentials and adjust effectively to new behavior patterns (Aspy & Sandhu, 1999). Counseling services and techniques specifically for men evolved for similar reasons (i.e., changing roles and life situations), but at a slower rate. Scher (1981) stated that:

> Most men are hidden from themselves and from others. Pressures from intimates and society, however, as well as self-engendered possibilities, are creating a slow push toward greater openness to new potentials. The conflicts and problems that this push creates will and have brought men to counseling. (p. 202)

In summarizing the state of affairs, Scher and Good (1990) wrote:

> [I]t is necessary to examine what we know about the intersection of conceptions of gender and counseling. We believe that conceptions of gender have a powerful effect on the counseling process. This is caused by the gender roles of the participants, the gender role history of the client, and

the expectations of our culture as to how members of each sex are to be-have, think, and view the world. (p. 389)

In general then, gender specific counseling helps males or females to con-tend with their respective problems and difficulties associated with their sex-role developments.

Persons Differentiated by Sexual Orientation

Recognition of the rights of persons differentiated by sexual orientation is increasing in society, and concomitantly in the counseling profession. However, there is much to be learned and known before counselors can effectively counsel such persons. Dworkin and Guiterrez (1989) presented the challenge with which the counseling profession is confronted:

> In order to counsel gay, lesbian, and bisexual clients, counselors must be-come familiar with the culture of their clients and the "folkways" that are pertinent to these people's lives, from the client's perspective, so that "these continuous methods of handling problems" that they learn in the counsel-ing session are relevant. Just as counselors would not use the same method to treat Anglos as to treat Blacks, a counselor cannot always use the same methods that work in a heterosexual context to counsel clients living in and existing within a gay, lesbian, or bisexual context. (p. 6)

Yet while the counseling profession has demonstrated increased sensitiv-ity to the issues involved in counseling individuals differentiated by sexual orientation, few specific techniques have been developed and little re-search has been done on what is effective in counseling them. Thus, the counseling profession is just beginning to develop specialized counseling approaches for persons differentiated by sexual orientation.

Abused Persons

Another subset of clientele groups receiving increased attention and greater services from professional counselors includes persons having particular types of problems. One of the most striking subgroups in this category is abused persons. Abuse is usually used to refer to physical abuse (i.e., batter-ing), but it also may include verbal abuse or neglect (i.e., necessary atten-tion not provided). Abused persons include those from the very young to the elderly, all ethnicities, and both genders. The incidence of abuse is staggering; "every five years, the number of deaths of persons killed by friends and acquaintances equals that of the entire Viet Nam War" (Wetzel & Ross, 1983). Although abuse occurs among all types of people, women are by far the most frequently abused persons. Abuse against women most frequently occurs in two forms: physical abuse (e.g., by a spouse) and sexual assault (i.e., rape).

Any type of abuse results in at least a psychological trauma, and often an associated physical trauma, for the victim. Thus, counseling for abused persons is primarily remediative in nature. Counseling abused persons also typically necessitates that professional counselors work collaboratively with other professionals such as physicians, law enforcement officers, and attorneys. Counseling abused persons is among the most difficult types of counseling, yet it is also one in which more and more professional counselors are becoming involved.

Addictions Counseling

Substance, typically alcohol or drug, abuse is another major problem for which increasing numbers of people are seeking counseling. Page and Bailey (1995) wrote that:

> It is important to note that addictions not only include chemical addictions but also eating disorders, sexual addictions, gambling addictions, and countless others; therefore, the number of people in the United States who have addictions problems may actually be greater than 250 million people. (p. 167)

Humans at literally any age after conception may encounter substance abuse problems. Indeed, substance abuse problems are so pervasive that almost everyone in society will be touched, either directly or by close association, by the problems. Professional counselors are increasing and intensifying their counseling services for substance abusers. Both remediative and preventive counseling services and strategies are being used in the effort to combat substance abuse problems.

Traditionally, substance abuse counseling was most prevalent in community (mental health) agencies, schools, and residential treatment facilities. However, substance abuse counseling is increasingly being provided by counselors in private practice or as a part of employee assistance programs (EAPs) in business and industry. A wide variety of counseling approaches and strategies have been used to attempt to alleviate substance abuse problems. Unfortunately, no clear patterns of effectiveness have appeared. Thus, although professional counselors are making concerted efforts with regard to the provision of substance abuse counseling, proven tactics have not yet been established and counselors must continue to explore and use a wide variety of counseling methodologies to help people with substance abuse problems.

Wellness/Holistic-Health Proponents

One group of people for whom counseling services are being provided more frequently are those interested in holistic health. Gross (1980) stated that:

> Holistic health is an approach to well-being of people that includes the prevention of illness, alternative ways of treating illness, and the means by which good health and the full enjoyment of life can be achieved. The term *holistic* . . . means whole in the sense that a living entity is more than the sum of its parts. It also connotes an interdependent system in which a change in one part of the system makes for changes in all other parts of the system. The application of holism to health is an attempt to overcome the mind/body dualism that has long characterized Western science and medicine. (p. 96)

Myers (1991) provided the context for counselors to assist in such an approach to well-being:

> Wellness refers to the maximizing of human potential through positive life-style choices. This holistic paradigm offers a philosophical base for counseling and development that provides guidelines for intervention and at the same time emphasizes the uniqueness of our approach as counseling and human development professionals to mental health concerns. (p. 183)

A number of different terms have been used to refer to counseling aimed at facilitating holistic health, including wellness counseling, health counseling, and holistic counseling. Regardless of the term used however, the goal is to help people achieve better mental and physical health through greater reliance on their own innate physiological and psychological maintenance systems. To achieve this end, professional counselors typically use some remediative activities (e.g., help people to stop smoking) and some preventive activities (e.g., stress management training). Such counseling is provided by counselors in a variety of settings, and is especially common in employee assistance programs. Unfortunately, the potential for holistic/wellness counseling has not yet been achieved fully, primarily because the focus in wellness programs has been on physical well-being. Myers (1991) indicated:

> The mental health component of existing wellness programs is probably understated. The strong link between physical and mental health leads to emotional benefits as a by-product of wellness programs. Ultimately, the potential exists for mental health to be a direct target of wellness interventions. The foundation exists; it needs only to be further developed and implemented. (p. 189)

Individuals with Sexual Problems

People with problems related to human sexuality are another major clientele for professional counselors. Unfortunately, however, the number of professional counselors who are able to provide effective sexuality counseling is limited. Schepp (1986) commented that only a few counselor preparation programs offer a specialization in sexuality counseling and that "to enter the field, one must usually obtain general professional preparation first and then take additional sexuality courses and [sexuality counseling] supervision" (p. 183).

In general, clients with problems related to sexuality may be divided into two subgroups: heterosexuals and persons differentiated by sexual orientation. In regard to the first group, the major problems for which counseling is sought usually relate to sexual functioning, such as problems of inability to achieve orgasm, premature ejaculation, or painful intercourse. In regard to the second group, the major problems for which counseling is sought sometimes relate to sexual functioning, but more often relate to problems such as sexual identity confusion, guilt, or generalized anxiety from generally unexpressed sexual preferences. Accordingly, professional counselors providing human sexuality counseling must be competent to counsel with regard to both the physical and psychological aspects of human sexuality.

Individuals with Marital or Familial Problems

Finally, the fastest growing clientele for professional counselors are persons experiencing marital and familial difficulties. Relatedly, Hollis and Wantz (1993), based on their longitudinal study of counselor preparation programs, indicated that specialization in marriage and family counseling is one of the most prominent trends among professional counselors and the most popular academic program major among students in counselor preparation programs. Thus the current high level of interest in marriage and family counseling is likely to continue for quite some time.

Movement by professional counselors into the realm of marriage and family counseling is by no means complete, and has not been and will not be without difficulty. Historically, persons involved in marriage and family counseling aligned themselves with AAMFT. More recently, a significant number of ACA members have provided marriage and family counseling services, a situation which led to formation of IAMFC. This situation, in turn, has led to considerable debate about which organization most effectively represents marriage and family counselors. The debate has both philosophical and pragmatic components. With regard to the former,

AAMFT has put forth the proposition that marriage and family therapy [counseling] is a profession onto itself whereas IAMFC (and therefore ACA) has viewed marriage and family counseling as a specialty built upon generic counseling expertise (cf. Brooks & Gerstein, 1990a, 1990b; Everett, 1990a, 1990b). Regardless of the outcomes from the debates about which organization best represents marriage and family counselors or should be allowed to accredit their professional preparation programs, there is at least one significant commonality among marriage and family counselors: adoption of a systems theory approach to counseling. Everett (1990a) wrote that:

> The application of systems theory in understanding family behaviors and dynamics represents both the foundation and integrating force in marital and family therapy [counseling].
>
> Family systems theory identifies the interactional milieu of the family as central to emotional development, behavioral patterns, and values and loyalties for individual members. The appearance of symptomatology is an expression of systemic dysfunction. Such dysfunctions, or imbalances, may appear in an early generation and be passed across numerous generations, displayed variously as symptoms in individuals, marriages, or parent-child relationships. (p. 499)

Using this generalized framework, professional counselors conduct counseling with entire families to attempt to resolve problems of one or more family members. The problems addressed are myriad, including marital disharmony, single-parenting, drug abuse, children's delinquency, alcoholism, step-family adjustments, sexuality, and physical and sexual abuse. Although many counselors in many different settings provide marriage and family counseling, it is primarily provided by those in community agencies and in private practice.

☐ Conclusion

The counseling profession is an interesting and exciting one of which to be a part. The counseling profession has made great strides in its quest to become a recognized and appreciated profession. The trials and tribulations that have been overcome in this quest stand as testimony to the competence and high levels of professionalism of professional counselors. Those yet to be faced stand as challenges, not to be feared but rather to be embraced because of the potential positive benefits. The vast majority of professional counselors are truly fine people who care deeply about what they do and about how well they do it. Counseling is both a true and noble profession. Our society is far better off because of the excellence in the counseling profession.

REFERENCES

Adler, A. (1958). *What life should mean to you*. New York: Capricorn Books.

Adler, A. (1964). *Problems of neurosis*. New York: Harper & Row.

Adler, A. (1926/1972). *The neurotic constitution*. Freeport, NY: Books for Libraries Press.

Amborose, D. M., & Lennox, L. (1988). Strategic market positions for mental health services. *Journal of Mental Health Administration, 15*(1), 5–9.

American Counseling Association. (1999). *ACA Code of Ethics* and *Standards of Practice*. Available: http://www.counseling.org/resources/codofethics.htm

Anderson, B. S. (1996). *The counselor and the law* (4th ed.). Alexandria, VA: American Counseling Association.

Anderson, D. (1992). A case for standards of counseling practice. *Journal of Counseling and Development, 71*, 22–26.

Andersen, M. J., & Ellis, R. (1995). On the reservation. In N. A. Vacc, S. B. DeVaney, & J. Wittmer (Eds.), *Experiencing and counseling multicultural and diverse populations* (3rd ed.) (pp. 179–198). Bristol, PA: Accelerated Development.

Arrendondo, D. R., Toporek, R., Brown, S. P., Jones, J., Locke, D., Sanchez, J., & Stadler, H. (1996). Operationalization of the multicultural counseling competencies. *Journal of Mulitcultural Counseling and Development, 24*, 42–78.

Aponte, J. F., Rivers, R. Y., & Wohl, J. (1995). *Psychological interventions and cultural diversity*. Boston: Allyn and Bacon.

Arthur, G. L., & Swanson, C. D. (1993). *Confidentiality and privileged communication*. The ACA legal series (vol. 6). Alexandria, VA: American Counseling Association.

Aspy, C. B. & Sandhu, D. S. (1999). *Empowering women for equity: A counseling approach*. Alexandria, VA: American Counseling Association.

Association for Gay, Lesbian, and Bisexual Issues in Counseling. (1999). *Association for Gay, Lesbian and Bisexual Issues in Counseling Home Page*. Available: http://www.aglbic.org/

Association for Specialists in Group Work. (1998). *Group work best practice guidelines*. Alexandria, VA: Author.

Atkinson, D. R., Morten, G., & Sue, D. W. (1989). *Counseling American minorities: A cross cultural perspective* (3rd ed.). Dubuque, IL: W. C. Brown.

Axelson, J. A. (1998). *Counseling and development in a multicultural society* (3rd ed.). Pacific Grove, CA: Brooks/Cole.

Bacon, C. L. (1990). *Celebrating diversity: A learning tool for working with people of different cultures*. Washington, DC: American Association of Retired Persons.

Baker, S. B. (1996). *School counseling for the twenty-first century* (2nd edition). Englewood Clifs, NJ: Prentice Hall.

Bandura, A. (1977). Self-efficacy—Toward a unifying theory of behavior change. *Psychological Review, 84*, 191–215.

Bandura, A. (1982). The psychology of chance encounters and life paths. *The American Psychologist, 37*(7), 747–755.

Bardon, J. I., & Bennett, V. C. (1974). *School Psychology* Englewood Cliffs, NJ: Prentice-Hall.

Barlow, D. H., Hayes, S. C., & Nelson, R. O. (1984). *The scientist practitioner.* New York: Pergamon.

Bartlett, W. E., Lee, J. E., & Doyle, R. E. (1985). Historical development of the Association for Religious and Values Issues in Counseling. *Journal of Counseling and Development, 63*(7), 448–451.

Baruth, L. G., & Manning, M. L. (1991). *Multicultural counseling and psychotherapy,* New York: Macmillan.

Benshoff, J. M., & Paisley, P. O. (1996). The structured peer consultation model for school counselors. *Journal of Counseling and Development, 74,* 314–318.

Bergan, J. R., & Kratochwill, T. R. (1990). *Behavioral consultation and therapy.* New York: Plenum Press.

Bergland, B. W. (1974). Career planning: The use of the sequential evaluated experience. In E. L. Herr (Ed.), *Vocational guidance and human development* (pp. 350–380). Boston: Houghton Mifflin.

Bernard, J. M. (1987). Ethical and legal considerations for supervisors. In L. D. Borders & G. R. Leddick, *Handbook for counseling supervision* (pp. 52–57). Alexandria, VA: Association for Counselor Education and Supervision.

Bishop, J. B. (1990). The university counseling center: An agenda for the 1990's. *Journal of Counseling and Development, 68*(4), 408–413.

Bishop, J. B. (1995). Emerging administrative strategies for college and university counseling centers. *Journal of Counseling and Development, 74,* 33–38.

Blake, R. R., & Mouton, S. S. (1983). *Consultation.* Reading, MA: Addison Wesley.

Borders, L. D., & Leddick, G. R. (1987). *Handbook in counseling supervision.* Alexandria, VA: Association for Counselor Education and Supervision.

Bordin, E. S. (1990). Psychodynamic model of career choice and satisfaction. In D. Brown, L. Brooks, & Associates (Eds.), *Career choice and development* (pp. 102–144). San Francisco, CA: Jossey-Bass.

Bordin, E. S., Nachmann, B., & Segal, S. J. (1963). An articulated framework for vocational development, *Journal of Counseling Psychology, 10,* 107–116.

Brooks, D. K., & Gerstein, L. H. (1990a). Counselor credentials and interprofessional collaboration. *Journal of Counseling and Development, 68*(5), 477–484.

Brooks, D. K., & Gerstein, L. H. (1990b). Interprofessional collaboration: Or shooting yourself in the foot only feels good when you stop. *Journal of Counseling and Development, 68*(5), 509–510.

Brown, D., & Srebalus, D. J. (1988). *An introduction to the counseling profession.* Englewood Cliffs, NJ: Prentice-Hall.

Bullis, R. K. (1993). Law and Management of a Counseling Agency or Practice. ACA Legal Series (vol. 3). Alexandria, VA: American Counseling Association.

Bumpass, L. L. (1990). What's happening to the family? Interactions between demographic and institutional change. *Demography, 27,* 483–498.

Bumpass, L. L., & Sweet, J. A. (1989). Children's experience in single parent families: Implications of cohabitation and marital transitions. *Family Planning Perspectives, 21,* 256–260.

Bureau of the Census. (1992). *Census of population and housing summary* (Tape File 1C) (CD-ROM). Washington, DC: Government Printing Office.

Burn, D. (1992). Ethical issues in cross-cultural counseling and training. *Journal of Counseling and Development, 70*(5), 578–583.

Burns, C. F., & Consolvo, C. A. (1992). The development of a campus based substance abuse prevention program. *Journal of Counseling and Development, 70*(5), 639–641.

Butler, R. N., & Lewis, M. I. (1982). *Aging and mental health (3rd ed.).* St. Louis, MO: Mosby.

Cabral, A. C., & Salamone, P. R. (1990). Chance and careers: Normative versus contextual development. *Career Development Quarterly, 39*(1), 5–17.

Caplan, G. (1970). *The theory and practice of mental health consultation.* New York: Basic Books.

Capuzzi, D., & Gross, D. R. (2000). Introduction to the counseling profession (3rd ed.). Boston: Allyn & Bacon.

Carroll, M. R., & Levo, L. (1985). The Association for Specialists in Group Work. *Journal of Counseling and Development, 63*(7), 452–454.

Castro Martin, T., & Bumpass, L. L. (1989). Recent trends in marital disruption. *Demography, 26,*37–51.

Chartrand, J. M. (1991). The evolution of trait-and-factor career counseling: Person × environment fit approach. *Journal of Counseling and Development, 69*(6), 518–524.

Chickering, A. (1987). *Education and identity.* San Francisco, CA: Jossey-Bass.

Cohen, E. D. (1990). Confidentiality, counseling, and clients who have AIDS: Ethical foundations of a model rule. *Journal of Counseling and Development, 68*(3), 282–286.

Coleman, E., & Schaefer, S. (1988). Boundaries of sex and intimacy between client and counselor. In W. C. Huey & T. P. Remley, Jr. (Eds.), *Ethical and legal issues in school counseling,* (pp. 286–298). Alexandria, VA: American School Counselor Association.

Coll, K. M., & Freeman, B. (1997). Role conflict among elementary school counsleors: A national comparison with middle and secondary school counselors. *Elementary School Guidance and Counseling, 31,* 251–261.

Corey, G. (1995). *Theory and practice of group counseling* (4th ed.). Monterey, CA: Brooks/Cole.

Corey, G. (1996). *Theory and practice of counseling and psychotherapy* (5th ed.). Pacific Grove, CA: Brooks/Cole.

Corey, G., Corey, M. S., & Calanan, P. (1988). *Issues and ethics in the helping professions* (3rd ed.). Pacific Grove, CA: Brooks/Cole..

Corey, G., Corey, M. S., & Calanan, P. (1993). *Issues and ethics in the helping professions.* (4th ed.). Pacific Grove, CA: Brooks/Cole.

Corey, M. S., & Corey, G. (1987). *Groups: Process and practice.* Monterey, CA. Brooks/Cole.

Cormier, W. H., & Cormier, L. S. (1991). *Interviewing strategies for helpers.* Belmont, CA: Brooks/Cole.

Costa, L., & Altekruse, M. (1994). Duty to warn guidelines for mental health counselors. *Journal of Counseling & Development, 72,* 346–350.

Coven T. M. (1992, Winter). Freedom of choice, supervision and signing off by mental health professionals. *FMHCA Newsletter,* pp. 1, 3–5.

Cox, W. E. (1985). Military Educators and Counselors Association. *Journal of Counseling and Development, 63*(7), 461–463.

Crawford, R. L. (1994). Avoiding counselor malpractice. ACA Legal Series (Vol. 12). Arlington, VA: American Counseling Association.

Crites, J. O. (1973). Career Maturity Inventory. Monterey, CA: California Test Bureau/McGraw-Hill.

Cronbach, L. J. (1990). *Essentials of psychological testing* (5th ed.). New York: Harper & Row.

Das, A. K. (1995). Rethinking multicultural counseling: Implications for counselor education. *Journal of Counseling and Development, 764,* 45–52.

Davenport, L. D. (1992). Ethical and legal problems with client centered supervision. *Counselor Education and Supervision, 31*(4), 227–231.

Davis, T. & Ritchie, M. (1993). Confidentiality and the school counselor: A challenge for the 1990's. *The School Counselor, 41* (1), 23–30

Dawis, R. V. (1996). The theory of work adjustment and person-environment-correspondence counseling. In D. Brown, L. Brooks, and Associates (Eds.), *Career Choice and Development* (3rd ed.) (pp.75–115). San Francisco: Jossey-Bass.

Dean, L. A., & Meadows, M. E. (1995). College counseling: Union and intersection. *Journal of Counseling and Development, 74,* 139–142.

DiMichael S. G., & Thomas, K. R. (1985). ARCA's journey in professionalism: A commemorative review on the 25th anniversary. *Journal of Counseling and Development, 63*(7), 428–435.

Drummond, R. J., & Ryan, C. W. (1995). *Career Counseling: A Developmental Approach.* Columbus, OH: Merrill.

Dworkin, S. H., & Guiterrez, F. (1989). Introduction to special issue. Counselors be aware: Clients come in every size, shape, color, and sexual orientation. *Journal of Counseling and Development, 68*(l), 6–8.

Dye, H. A., & Borders, L. D. (1990). Counseling supervisors: Standards for preparation and practice. *Journal of Counseling and Development, 69*(l). 27–29.

Edwards, P. B., & Bloland, P. A. (1990). Integrating leisure guidance into a career counseling center. *Journal of Career Development, 16,* 185–194.

Eddy, W., & Lubin, B. (1971). Laboratory training and encounter groups. *Personnel and Guidance Journal, 49*(8), 625–635.

Egan, G. (1997). *The skilled helper: A problem-management approach to helping.*(6th ed.) Pacific Grove, CA: Brooks/Cole.

Ellis, A., & Dryden, W. (1997). *The practice of rational-emotive behavior therapy* (2nd ed.). New York: Springer.

Engels, D., Wilborn, B. L., & Schneider, L. J. (1990). Ethics curricula for counselor preparation programs. In B. Herlihy and L. B. Golden (Eds.) *Ethical standards casebook* (4th ed.) (pp. 111–126). Alexandria, VA: American Association for Counseling and Development.

Engels, D. W., & Muro, J. J. (1986). Silver to gold: The alchemy, potential, and maturing of ACES and CES. *Counselor Education and Supervision, 25*(4), 289–305.

Emener, W. G., and Cottone, R. R. (1989). Professionalization, deprofessionalization, and reprofessionalization of rehabilitation counseling according to criteria of professions. *Journal of Counseling and Development, 67*(10), 576–581.

Erikson, E. H. (1963). *Childhood and society* (2nd ed.). New York: Norton.

Erikson, E. H. (1968). *Identity and crisis.* New York: Norton and Company.

Erickson, S. H. (1990). Counseling the irresponsible AIDS client: Guidelines for decision making. *Journal of Counseling and Development, 68*(4), 454–455.

Erikson, S. H. (1993). Ethics and confidentiality in AIDS counseling: A professional dilemma. *Journal of Mental Health Counseling, 15,* 118–131.

Everett, C. A. (1990a). The field of marital and family therapy. *Journal of Counseling and Development, 68*(5), 498–502.

Everett, C. A. (1990b). Where have all the "gypsies" gone? *Journal of Counseling and Development, 68*(5), 507–508.

Faiver, C. M., O'Brien, E. M., McNaly, C. J. (1998). "The friendly clergy": Characteristics and referral. *Counseling and Values, 42,* 217–221.

Fischer, L., & Sorenson, G. P. (1995). *School law for counselors, psychologists, and social workers.* (3rd ed.) New York: Longman.

Fong-Beyette, M. L. (1988). Do counseling and marketing mix? *Counselor Education and Supervision, 27*(4), 315–319.

Forrest, D. V., & Affemian, M. (1986). The future of mental health counselors in health maintenance organizations. *American Mental Health Counselors Association Journal, 8*(2), 65–72.

Fosler, R. S., Alonso, W., Myer, J. A., & Kern, R. (1990). *Demographic change and the American future.* Pittsburgh, PA: University of Pittsburgh Press.

Freud, S. (1911). Formulation regarding the two principles of mental functioning. *Standard edition,* vol. 12. (pp. 218–228).

Fuchs, D., Fuchs, L. S., Dulan, J., Roberts, H., & Fernstrom, P. (1991). Where is the research on consultation effectiveness? (Report No. EC301226). Nashville, TN: Vanderbilt University (ERIC Document Reproduction Service. No. ED. 345465)

Fujimara, L. E., Weis, D. M., & Cochran, J. R. (1985). Suicide: Dynamics and implications for counseling. *Journal of Counseling and Development, 63*(10), 612–615.

Fuqua, D. R., & Newman, J. L. (1989). Research issues in the study of professional ethics. *Counselor Education and Supervision, 29*(2), 84–93.

Galassi, J. P., & Gulledge, S. A. (1997). The middle school counselor and teacher-advisor programs. *Professional School Counseling, 1,* 55–60.

Gay, L. R. (1996). *Educational research: Competencies for analysis and application* (5th ed.). Upper Saddle River, NJ: Prentice Hall.

Gazda, G. M. (1978). *Group counseling: A developmental approach.* Boston: Allyn & Bacon.

Gazda, G. M. (1989). *Group counseling: A developmental approach* (4th ed.). Boston: Allyn & Bacon.

George, R. I., & Dustin, D. (1988). *Group counseling: Theory and practice.* New York: Prentice Hall.

Gerler, E. R., Jr., (1995). Advancing elementary and middle school counseling through computer technology. *Elementary School Guidance and Counseling, 30,* 8–15.

Gerstein, L. H., & Bayer, G. A. (1988). Employee assistance programs: A systemic investigation of their use. *Journal of Counseling and Development, 66*(6), 294–297.

Gilbert, S. P. (1992). Ethical issues in treatment of severe psychopathology in university and college counseling centers. *Journal of Counseling and Development, 70*(6), 695–699.

Gilchrist, L. A., & Stringer, M. (1992). Marketing counseling: Guidelines for training and practice. *Counselor Education and Supervision, 31*(3), 154–162.

Ginzberg, E. (1972). Restatement of theory of occupational choice. *Vocational Guidance Quarterly, 20*(3), 169–176.

Ginzberg, E., Ginsburg, S. W., Axelrod, S., & Herma, J. (1951). *Occupational choice: An approach to general theory.* New York: Columbia university Press.

Gladding, S. T. (1988). *Counseling: A comprehensive profession.* Columbus, OH: Merrill.

Gladding, S. T. (1991). *Group counseling: A counseling specialty.* New York: Macmillan.

Gladding, S. T. (2000). *Counseling: A comprehensive profession* (4th ed.). Columbus, OH: Merrill.

Goldenberg, I., & Goldenberg, H. (1996). *Family therapy: An Overview* (4th ed.). Pacific Grove, CA: Brooks/Cole.

Goldman, L. (1976). A revolution in counseling research. *Journal of Counseling Psychology, 23,* 543–552.

Goldman, L. (1977). Toward more meaningful research. *Personnel and Guidance Journal, 55,* 363–368.

Goldman, L. (Ed.). (1978). *Research methods for counselors.* New York: Wiley.

Gonzalez, E. (1989). Hispanics bring "corazon" and "sensibilidad." *Momentum, 20,* 10–13.

Gray, L., & Harding, A. K. (1988). Confidentiality limits with clients who have the AIDS virus. *Journal of Counseling and Development, 66*(5), 219–223.

Gredler, M. E. (1996). *Program evaluation.* Englewood Cliffs, NJ: Prentice-Hall.

Green, J. W. (1995). *Cultural awareness in the human services* (2nd ed.). Boston: Allyn and Bacon.

Gross, D. R., & Robinson, S. E. (1987). Ethics, violence, and counseling: Hear no evil, see no evil, speak no evil? *Journal of Counseling and Development, 65*(7), 340–344.

Gross, S. J. (1980). The holistic health movement. *Personnel and Guidance Journal, 59*(2), 96–102.

Grunwald, B. B., & McAbee, H. V. (1998). *Guiding the family: Practical techniques* (2nd ed.). Muncie, IN: Accelerated Development.

Hadley, R. G., & Mitchel, L. K. (1995). *Counseling research and program Evaluation.* Pacific Grove, CA: Brooks/Cole.

Hansen, J. C., Rossberg, R. H., & Cramer, S. H. (1994). *Counseling: Theory and process* (5th ed.). Boston: Allyn and Bacon.

Hanson T., Warner, R., & Smith, E. (1980). *Group counseling: Theory and process.* Chicago: Rand McNally.

Hardesty, P. H., & Dillard, J. M. (1994). The role of elementary school counselors with their middle school counterparts. *Elementary School Guidance and Counseling, 29,* 83–91.

Harris, T. A. (1967). *I'm OK-You're OK.* New York: Avon.

Harris-Bowlsbey, J. (1984). High touch and high technology: The marriage that must succeed. *Counselor Education and Supervision, 24*(1), 6–16.

Harris-Bowlsbey, J., Dikel, M. R., and Simpson, J. P., Jr. (1998). The Internet: A tool for career planning. Alexandria, VA: National Career Development Association.

Havinghurst, R. S. (1972). *Developmental tasks and education* (3rd ed.). New York: McKay.

Heppner, P. P., Kivlighan, D. M., & Wampold, B. E. (1998). *Research design in counseling* (2nd ed.). Pacific Grove, CA: Brooks/Cole.

Herlihy, B., & Sheeley, V. L. (1988). Counselor liability and the duty to warn: Selected cases, statutory trends, and implications for practice. In W. C. Huey & T. P. Reniley, Jr. (Eds.), *Ethical & legal issues in school counseling* (pp. 137–142). Alexandria, VA: American School Counselor Association.

Hernandez, H. (1989). *Multicultural education: A teacher's guide to content and practice.* Columbus, OH: Merrill.

Herr, E. L. (1985). AACD: An association committed to unity through diversity. *Journal of Counseling and Development, 63*(7), 395–404.

Herr, E. L. (1986). Life-style and career development. In M. D. Lewis, R. L. Hayes, & J. A. Lewis (Eds.), *An introduction to the counseling profession* (pp. 167–214). Itasca, IL: F. E. Peacock.

Herr, E. L. (1989). *Counseling in a dynamic society: Opportunities and challenges.* Alexandria, VA: American Association of Counseling and Development.

Herr, E. L., & Cramer, S. H. (1995). *Career guidance and counseling through the lifespan* (5th ed.). Boston: Little, Brown.

Hittleman, D. R., & Simon, A. J. (1997). *Interpreting educational research: An introduction for consurmers of research* (2nd ed.). Columbus, OH: Merrill.

Hock, E. I., Ross, A. O., & Winder, C. L (Eds.). (1966). Professional preparation of clinical psychologists. *Proceedings of the Conference on the Professional Preparation of Clinical Psychologists* meeting at the Center for Continuing Education, Chicago, Illinois August 17–September 1, 1965. Washington, DC: American Psychological Association.

Hohenshil, T. H., & Brown, M. B. (1991). School counselors and prekindergarten children. *Elementary School Guidance & Counseling, 26*(1), 3.

Holcomb-McCoy, C. C., & Myers, J. E. (1999). Multicultural competence and counselor training: A national survey. *Journal of Counseling and Development, 77,* 294–302.

Holland, J. L. (1966). *The psychology of vocational choice.* Waltham, MA: Blaisdell.

Holland, J. L. (1985). *Making vocational choices: A theory of vocational personalities and work environments* (2nd ed.). Needham Heights, MA: Allyn & Bacon.

Holland, J. L. (1997). *Making vocational choices: A theory of careers.* (3rd ed.). Englewood Cliffs, NJ: Prentice-Hall.

Hollis, J. W. (1998). Is CACREP accreditation making a difference in mental health counselor preparation? *Journal of Mental Health Counseling, 20,* 89–92.

Hollis, J. W., & Wantz, R. A (1993). *Counselor preparation 1993–95: Programs, personnel, and trends* (8 ed.). Muncie, IN: Accelerated Development.

Hopkins, B. R., & Anderson, B. S. (1996). *The counselor and the law* (4th Ed.). Alexandria, VA: American Counseling Association.

Hopson, B. (1982). Counseling and helping. In R. Holdsworth (Ed.), *Psychology for career counseling* (pp. 61–79). London: Macmillan Press.

Hotelling, K. (1988). Ethical, legal, and administrative options to address sexual relationships between counselor and client. *Journal of Counseling and Development, 67*(4), 233–237.

Houser, R. (1998). *Counseling and educational rsearch.* Thousand Oaks, CA: Sage.

Hoyt, K. B. (1972). *Career education: What it is and how to do it.* Salt Lake City, UT: Olympus.

Hoyt, K. B. (1974). *An introduction to career education.* U.S. Office of Education Policy Paper. Washington, DC: Author.

Hummel, D. L., Talbutt, L. C., & Alexander, M. D. (1985). *Law and ethics in counseling.* New York: Van Nostrand Reinhold.

Isaacs, M. L. (1997). The duty to warn and protect: Tarasoff and the elementary school counselor. *Elementary School Guidance and Counseling, 31*(4), 326–342.

Ivey, A. (1971). *Microcounseling: Innovations in interviewing training.* Springfield, IL: Charles C. Thomas.

Ivey, A. (1994). *Intentional interviewing and counseling: Facilitating client development in a multicultural society* (3rd ed.). Belmont, CA: Brooks/Cole

Ivey, A. E., Ivey, M. B., & Simek-Morgan, L. (1996). *Counseling and psychotherpy: A multicultural perspective* (4th ed.). Boston: Allyn and Bacon.

Jacobs, E., Harvill, R., & Masson, R. (1988). *Group counseling: Strategies and skills.* Springfield, IL: Charles C. Thomas.

Jaeger, R. M., & Frye, A. W. (1988). An assessment of the job relevance of the National Board for Certified Counselors Examination. *Journal of Counseling and Development, 67*(1), 22–26.

Johnson, C. S. (1985). The American College Personnel Association. *Journal of Counseling and Development, 63*(7),405–410.

Johnson, D. W., & Johnson, F. P. (1987). *Joining together* (3rd ed.). Englewood Cliffs, NJ: Prentice-Hall.

Jones, L. K. (1994). Frank Parsons' contribution to career counseling. *Journal of Career Development, 20,* 287–294.

Kagel, J. D., & Kopels, S. (1994). Confidentiality after Tarasoff. *Health & Social Work, 19*(3), 217–222.

Kain, C. D. (1988). To breach or not to breach: Is that the question? A response to Gray and Harding. *Journal of Counseling and Development, 66*(5), 224–225.

Kalichman, S. C. (1993). *Mandated reporting of suspected child abuse: Ethics, law, and policy.* Washington, DC: American Psychological Association.

Kamman , C., & Gold, J. (1998). *Call to connection: Bringing sacred tribal values into modern life.* Alexandria, VA: American Counseling Associaiton.

Kemp, C. A. (1970). *Foundations of group counseling.* New York: McGraw Hill.

Kerlinger, F. N. (1986). *Foundations of behavioral research* (3rd ed.). New York: Holt, Rinehart and Winston.

Keys, S. G., Bemak, F., & Lockhart, E. J. (1998). Transforming school counseling to serve the mental health needs of at-risk youth. *Journal of Counseling and Development, 776,* 381–388.

King, P. M. (1978). William Perry's theory of intellectual and ethical development. In 1 Kriefelkamp, C. Widick, & C. A. Parker (Ed.), *Applying new developmental findings* (pp. 35–54). San Francisco, CA. Jossey-Bass.

Kitchener, K. S. (1986). Teaching applied ethics in counselor education: An integration of psychological processes and philosophical analysis. *Journal of Counseling and Development, 64*(5), 306–310.

Kitchener, K. S. (1988). Dual role relationships: What makes them so problematic? *Journal of Counseling and Development, 67*(4), 217–221.

Kitchener, K. S., & Harding, S. S. (1990). Dual role relationships. In B. Herlihy & L. B.

Golden (Eds.), *Ethical standards casebook* (4th ed., pp. 146–154). Alexandria, VA: American Association for Counseling and Development.

Kohlberg, L. (1966). A cognitive-developmental analysis of children's sex-role concepts and attitudes. In E. E. Maccoby (Ed.), *The development of sex differences* (pp. 82–172). Stanford, CA: Stanford University Press.

Kottler, J. A., & Brown, R. W. (1999). *Introduction to therapeutic counseling* (4th ed.). Pacific Grove, CA: Brooks/Cole.

Kottman, Y. (1990). Counseling middle school students: Techniques that work. *Elementary School Guidance and Counseling, 25*(2), 138–145.

Kurpius, D., Gibson, G. Lewis, J., & Corbet, M. (1991). Ethical issues in supervising counseling practitioners. *Counselor Education and Supervision 31*(1), 48–57.

Lago, C., & Thompson, J. (1996). *Race, culture, and counseling.* Philadelphia: Open University Press.

Lanning, W. (1990). An educator/practioner model for counselor education doctoral programs. *Counselor Education and Supervision, 30*(2), 163–169.

Lee, C. C. (1996). *Saving the native son: Empowerment strategies for young Black males.* Alexandria, VA: American Counseling Association.

Lee, C. C. (Ed.). (1997). *Multicultural issues in counseling: New approaches to diveristy* (2nd Ed.). Alexandria, VA: American Counseling Association.

Lee, C. C., & Walz, G. R. (1998). *Social action: A mandate for counselors.* Alexandria, VA: American Counseling Association.

Lipper, L. (1997). Women at midlife: Implications for theories of women's adult development. *Journal of Counseling and Development, 76,* 16–22.

Loesch, L. C. (in press). Counseling program evaluation: Inside and outside the box. In J. E. Myers, E. Herr, & D. C. Locke (Eds.), *The handbook of counseling.* Thousand Oaks, CA: Sage.

Loesch, L. C. (1988). Preparation for helping professionals working with diverse populations. In N. A. Vacc, J. Wittmer, & S. Devancy (Eds.), *Experiencing and counseling multicultural and diverse populations* (2nd ed.). Muncie, IN: Accelerated Development.

Loesch, L. C., & Vacc, N. A. (1988). Results and possible implications of the National Board for Certified Counselors Examination. *Journal of Counseling and Development, 67*(1), 17–21.

Loesch, L. C., & Vacc, N. A. (1991). *Technical manual for the National Counselor Examination.* Alexandria, VA: National Board for Certified Counselors.

Loesch, L. C., & Vacc, N. A. (1994). Setting minimum criterion scores for the National Counselor Examination. *Journal of Counseling and Development, 73*(2), 211–214.

Lofquist, L. H., & Dawis, R. V. (1991). *Essentials of person-environment-correspondence counseling.* Minneapolis, MN: University of Minnesota Press.

Mabe, A. R., & Rollin, S. A. (1986). The role of a code of ethical standards in counseling. *Journal of Counseling and Development, 64*(5), 294–297.

Martin, D., & Martin, M. (1989). Bridging the gap between research and practice. *Journal of Counseling and Development, 67*(81), 491–492.

Maslow, A. H. (1954). *Motivation and personality.* New York: Harper & Row.

Maslow, A. H. (1968). Toward a psychology of being (2nd ed.). New York: Van Nostrand Reinhold.

McClure, B. A., & Russo, T. R. (1996). The politics of counseling: Looking back and forward. *Counseling and Values, 40,* 162–174.

McDaniels, C., & Gysbers, N. C. (1992). *Counseling for career development: Theories, resources, and practice,* San Francisco. CA. Jossey-Bass.

McFadden, J., & Lispcomb, W. D. (1985). History of the Association for Non-White Concerns in Personnel and Guidance. *Journal of Counseling and Development, 63*(7), 444–447.

McMann, N., & Oliver, R. (1988). Problems in families with gifted children: Implications for counselors. *Journal of Counseling and Development, 66*(6), 275–278.

Mehrens, W. A., & Lehmann, I. J. (1991). *Measurement and evaluation in education and psychology* (4th ed.). New York: Holt and Winston.

Meyer, D., Helwig, A. Gjernes, O., & Chickering, J. (1985). The National Employment Counselors Association. *Journal of Counseling and Development, 63*(7),440–443.

Miars, R. D., Burden, C. A., & Pedersen, M. M. (1997). The helping relationship. In D. Capuzzi & D. Gross (Eds.), *Introduction to the counseling profession* (2nd ed.) (pp. 64–84). Boston: Allyn and Bacon.

Miller-Tiedeman, A., & Tiedeman, D. V. (1990). Career decision making: An individualistic perspective. In D. Brown, L. Brooks, and Associates (Eds.), *Career choice and development* (pp. 308–337). San Francisco, CA: Jossey-Bass.

Minkoff, H. B., & Terres, C. K. (1985). ASCA perspectives: Past, present, and future. *Journal of Counseling and Development, 63*(7), 424–427.

Moles, O. C. (1991). Guidance programs in American high schools: A descriptive portrait. *The School Counselor, 38*(3), 163–177.

Moreno, J. L. & Kipper, D. A. (1968). Group psychodrama and community-centered counseling. In M. Gazda (Ed.), *Basic approaches to group psychotherapy and group counseling* (pp. 27–79). Springfield, IL: Charles C. Thomas.

Murphy, J. J. (1997). *Solution-focused counseling in middle and high schools*. Alexandria, VA: American Counseling Association.

Myers, J. E. (1991). Wellness as the paradigm for counseling and development: The possible future. *Counselor Education and Supervision, 30*(3), 183–193.

Myers, J. E. (1995). From "Forgotten and Ignored" to standards and certification: Gerontological counseling comes of age. *Journal of Counseling and Development, 74*, 143–153.

Myers, J. E. & Loesch, L. C. (1981). The counseling needs of older persons. *The Humanist Educator, 20*(1), 21–35.

Myers, R. S., & Pace, T. S. (1986). Counseling gifted and talented students: Historical perspectives and contemporary issues. *Journal of Counseling and Development, 64*(9), 548–551.

Myrick, R. D. (1977). *Consultation as a counselor intervention.* Ann Arbor, MI: ERIC Counseling and Personnel Services Information Center.

Myrick, R. D. (1992). *Helping skills for middle school students.* Minneapolis, MN: Educational Media.

Myrick, R. D. (1993). *Developmental counseling and guidance: A practical approach* (3rd ed.). Minneapolis, MN: Educational Media.

National Association of Hispanic Publications. (1995). *Hispanics/Latinos: Diverse people in a multicultural society.* Washington, DC: Author.

National Board for Certified Counselors. (1993). *A work behavior analysis of professional counselors.* Greensboro, NC: NBCC, and Muncie, IN: Accelerated Development.

NCDA Professional Standards Committee. (1992). Career counseling competencies. *The Career Development Quarterly, 40*(4), 378–386.

Nelson, P. L. (1992, July). Lawsuits, legal matters and liability claims hit the profession. *AACD Guidepost*, p. 17.

Neukrug, E. (1998). The world of the counselor: An introduction to the counseling profession (2nd Ed.). Pacific Grove, CA: Brooks/Cole.

Nugent, F. A. (1994). *An introduction to the profession of counseling* (2nd ed.). New York: Merrill.

Nystul, M. S. (1999). *Introduction to counseling: An art and science perspective.* Boston: Allyn and Bacon.

O'Bryant, B. J. (1992, Summer). Something's wrong. *The American Counselor*, p. 36.

Ohlsen, M. M. (1970). *Group counseling.* New York: McGraw-Hill.

Page, R. C. (1985). The unique role of the Public Offender Counselor Association. *,Journal of Counseling and Development, 63*(7), 455–456.

Page, R. C., & Bailey, J. B. (1995). Addictions counseling certification: An emerging counseling specialty. *Journal of Counseling and Development, 74,* 167–173.

Paisley, P. O., & Borders, L. D. (1995). School counseling: An evolving specialty. *Journal of Counseling and Development, 74,* 150–153.

Paniagua, F. A. (1998). *Assessing and treating culturally divers clients.* Thousand Oaks, CA: Sage Publications.

Parker, W. M., & Myers, J. E. (1991). From ANWC to AMCD: Goals, services, and impact. *Journal of Multicultural Counseling & Development, 19,* 52–64.

Parsons, R. D. (1996). *The skilled consultant.* Boston: Allyn and Bacon.

Pate, R. H., Jr. (1992, Summer). Student suicide: Are you liable? *The American Counselor,* pp. 14–19.

Patterson, C. H. (1996). Multicultural counseling: From diversity to universality. *Journal of Counseling and Development, 74,* 227–231.

Pavlov, I. P. (1927). *Conditional reflexes.* London: Oxford Press.

Peatling, J., and Tiedeman, D. (1977). *Career development: Designing self.* Muncie, IN: Accelerated Development.

Pedersen, P. (1988). *A handbook for developing multicultural awareness.* Alexandria, VA: American Association for Counseling and Development.

Pedersen, P. B. (1999). *Multiculturalism as a fourth force.* Philadelphia: Brunner/Mazel.

Pedersen, P. B., & Locke, D. C. (1996). *Cultural and diversity issues in counseling.* Alexandria, VA: American Counseling Association.

Perloff, R., Craft, J. A., & Perloff, E. (1984). Testing and industrial application. In G. Goldstein & M. Hersen (Eds.), *Handbook of psychological assessment* (pp. 421–440). New York: Pergamon.

Perry, W. C. (1970). *Forms of intellectual and ethical development in the college years.* New York: Holt, Rinehart and Winston.

Peterson, G. W., Sampson, J. P., Jr., & Reardon, R. C. (1991). *Career development and services: A cognitive approach.* Pacific Grove, CA: Brooks/Cole.

Peterson, J. S., & Colangelo, N. (1996). Gifted achievers and underachievers: A comparison of patterns found in school records. *Journal of Counseling and Development, 74,* 399–407.

Peterson, J. V., & Nisenholz, B. (1999). *Orientation to counseling* (4th ed.). Boston: Allyn and Bacon.

Piaget, J. (1964). *Judgement and reasoning in the child.* Patterson, NJ: Littlefield.

Pitz, G. F., & Harren, V. A. (1980). An analysis of career decision-making from the point of view of information processing and decision theory. *Journal of Vocational Behavior, 16,* 320–346.

Pope, K. S. (1988). How clients are harmed by sexual contact with mental health professionals: The syndrome and its prevalence. *Journal of Counseling and Development, 67*(4), 222–226.

Priest, R. (1991). Racism and prejudice as a negative impact on African American clients in therapy. *Journal of Counseling and Development, 70,* 213–215.

Rafuls, S. E. (1997). Qualitative research methods. In L. C. Loesch & N. A. Vacc (Eds.), *Research in counseling & therapy* (pp. 65–67). Greensboro, NC: ERIC Clearinghouse on Counseling & Student Services.

Randolph, D. L. (1990). Changing the nonpsychology doctorate in counselor education: A proposal. *Counselor Education and Supervision, 30*(2), 135–147.

Remley, T. P., Jr. (1988). More exploration needed of ethical and legal topics. *Journal of Mental Health Counseling, 10*(3), 167–170.

Remley, T. P., Jr. (1992a, Spring). You and the law. *The American Counselor,* pp. 33–34.

Remley, T. P., Jr. (1992b, Summer). You and the law. *The American Counselor*, pp. 31–33.

Remley Jr., T. P., Herlihy, B., & Herlihy, S. B. (1997). The U.S. Supreme Court Decision in Jaffe v. Redmond: Implications for counselors. *Journal of Counseling and Development, 75*(3), 213–218.

Riker, H. C. (1981). Preface. In J. E. Myers (Ed.), *Counseling older persons (vol. III): Trainer's manual for basic helping skills* (pp. xvii–xx). Washington, DC: American Personnel and Guidance Association.

Rinas, J., & Clyne-Jackson, S. (1988). *Professional conduct and legal concerns in mental health practice*. Norwalk, CT: Appleton & Lange.

Ritchie, M. H. (1989). Enhancing the public image of school counseling: A marketing approach. *The School Counselor, 37*(1), 54–61.

Robinson, S. (1991). Ethical and legal issues related to counseling: Or it's not as easy as it looks. In D. Capuzzi & D. R. Gross (Eds.), *Introduction to counseling perspectives for the 1990s* (pp. 447–468). Boston: Allyn and Bacon.

Robinson, S. E., & Gross, D. R. (1989). Applied ethics and the mental health counselor. *Journal of Mental Health Counseling, 11*(3), 289–299.

Roe, A. (1956). The psychology of occupations. New York: Wiley.

Rogers, C. (1951). *Client-centered therapy*. Boston: Houghton Mifflin.

Rogers, C. (1970). *Carl Rogers on Encounter Groups*. New York: Harper & Row.

Rogers, C. (1971). Facilitating encounter groups. *American Journal of Nursing, 71*(2), 275–279.

Rosenhan, D. L., Teitelbaum, T. W, Teitelbaum, K. W., & Davidson, M. (1993). Warning third parties: The ripple effects of Tarasoff. *Pacific Law Journal, 24,* 1165–1232.

Rowe, W., Murphy, H. B., & De Csipkes, R. A. (1975). The relationship of counselor characteristics and counseling effectiveness. *Review of Educational Research, 45,* 231–246.

Saltmarsh, R. E., Jenkins, S. J., & Fisher, G. L. (1986). The TRAC model: A practical map for group process and management. *Journal for Specialists in Group Work, 11,* 30–36.

Sampson, J. P. (1999). Integrating Internet-based distance guidance with services provided in career centers. *The Career Development Quarterly, 47,* 243–254.

Sampson, J. P., Jr. (1986). *Preliminary technical manual for the NBCC career certification examination*. Washington, DC: NBCC.

Sampson, J. P., Jr. (1990). Ethical use of computer applications in counseling: Past, present, and future. In B. Herlihy & I. B. Golden (Eds.), *Ethical standards casebook* (4th ed.) (pp. 170–176). Alexandria, VA: American Association for Counseling and Development.

Sampson, J. P., Jr., Kolodinsky, R. W., & Greeno, B. P. (1997). Counseling on the information highway: Future possibilities and potential problems. *Journal of Counseling and Development, 75,* 203–212.

Sandberg, D. N., Crabbs, S. K., & Crabbs, M. A. (1988). Legal issues in child abuse: Questions and answers for counselors. In W. C. Huey & T. P. Remley, Jr., (Eds.), *Ethical and legal issues in school counseling* (pp. 173–181). Alexandria, VA, American School Counselors Association.

Sandhu, D. S., & Aspy, C. B. (1997). *Counseling for prejudice prevention and reduction*. Alexandria, VA: American Counseling Association.

Schein, E. (1969). *Process consultation: Revisited*. Reading, MA: Addison-Wesley.

Schepp, K. F. (1986). *Sexuality counseling: A training program*. Muncie, IN: Accelerated Development.

Scher, M. (1981). Men in hiding: A challenge for the counselor. *Personnel and Guidance Journal, 60*(4), 199–202.

Scher, M., & Good, G. E. (1990). Gender and counseling in the twenty-first century. What does the future hold? *Journal of Counseling and Development, 68*(4), 388–391.

Schilson, E. A. (1991). Strategic therapy. In A. M. Horne & J. L. Passmore (Eds.), *Family counsleing and therapy* (2nd ed., pp. 141–178). Itasca, IL: F. E. Peacock.

Schlossberger, E., & Hecker, L. (1996). HIV and family therapists' duty to warn: A legal and ethical analysis. *Journal of Marital and Family Therapy, 22*(1), 27–40.

Schmidt, J. J. (1998). *Counseling in schools: Essential services and comprehensive programs* (3rd ed.). Boston: Allyn & Bacon.

Schwab, R., & Harris, T. L. (1981). Personal growth of counselor trainees. *Counselor Education and Supervision, 20*(3), 219–224.

Seligman, L. (1994). *Developmental career counseling and assessment* (2nd ed.). Pacific Grove, CA: Brooks/Cole.

Shaffer, J. B., & Galinsky, M. D. (1989). *Models of group therapy.* New York: Prentice-Hall.

Sharf, R. S. (1996). *Applying career development theory to counseling.* Pacific Grove, CA: Brooks/Cole.

Sheeley, V. L. (1992). Beyond 40: Past presidents' perceptions. *Journal of Humanistic Education and Development, 31,* 2–11.

Sheeley, V. L., & Herlihy, B. (1989). Counseling suicidal teens: A duty to warn and protect. *The School Counselor, 37*(2), 89–95.

Shimberg, B. (1982*). Occupational licensing: A public perspective.* Princeton, NJ: Educational Testing.

Siassi, I. (1984). Psychiatric interview and mental status examination. In G. Goldstein & M. Hersen (Eds.), *Handbook of psychological assessment* (pp. 421–440). New York: Pergamon.

Skinner, B. F. (1938). *The behavior of organisms: An experimental analysis.* New York: Appleton-Century-Crofts.

Slimak, R. E., & Berkowitz, S. R. (1983). The university and college counseling center and malpractice suits. *Personnel and Guidance Journal, 61*(5), 291–294.

Smith, H. B., & Robinson, G. P. (1995). Mental health counseling: Past, present, future. *Journal of Counseling and Development, 74,* 158–162.

Smith, M., & Glass, G. (1977). Meta-analysis of psychotherapy outcome studies. *American Psychologist, 32,* 752–760.

Smith, R. L., Carlson, J., Stevens-Smith, P., & Dennison, M. (1995). Marriage and family counseling. *Journal of Counseling and Development, 74,* 154–157.

Solomon, C. (1982). Special issue on political action: Introduction. *Personnel and Guidance Journal, 60*(10), 580.

Sonstegard, M. A. (1998). A rationale for group counseling. *Journal of Individual Psychology, 54*(2), 164–175.

Sporakowski, M. J. (1995). Assessment and diagnosis in marriage and family counseling. *Journal of Counseling and Development, 74,* 60–64.

Spitzer, R. L., Endicott, J., & Robins, E. (1978). Research diagnostic criteria: Rationale and reliability. *Archives of General Psychiatry, 23,* 41–55.

Stadler, H. A. (1990). Counselor impairment. In B. Herlihy & L. B. Golden (Eds.), *Ethical standards casebook* (4th ed.) (pp. 177–187). Alexandria, VA: American Association for Counseling and Development.

Stadler, H. A., Willing, K. L., Eberhage, M. G., & Ward, W. H. (1988). Impairment: Implications for the counseling profession. *Journal of Counseling and Development, 66*(6), 258–260.

Stanard, R., & Hazler, R. (1995). Legal and ethical implications of HIC and duty to warn for counselors: Does *Tarasoff* apply? *Journal of Counseling and Development, 73,* 397–400.

Stevens, D. T. & Lundberg, D. J. (1998). The emergence of the Internet: Enhancing career counseling education and services. *Journal of Career Development, 24,* 195–208.

Strein W., & Hershenson, D. B. (1991). Confidentiality in nondyadic counseling situations. *Journal of Counseling and Development, 69*(4), 312–316.

Sue, D. W. (1998). *Multicultural counseling competencies.* Thousand Oaks, CA: Sage.

Sue, D., Ino, S., & Sue, D. M. (1983). Nonassertiveness of Asian-Americans: An inaccurate assumption? *Journal of Counseling Psychology, 30,* 581–588.

Sue, D. W., Ivey, A. E., & Pedersen, P. B. (1996). *A theory of multicultural counseling and therapy.* Pacific Grove, CA: Brooks/Cole.

Sue, D. W., & Sue. D. (1985). Asian-Americans and Pacific islanders. In P. Pederson (Ed.), *Handbook of cross-cultural counseling and therapy,* 141–146. Westport, CT: Greenwood Press.

Sue, D. W., & Sue, D. (1995). Asian-Americans. In N. A. Vacc, J. Wittmer, & S. DeVaney (Eds.), *Experiencing and counseling multicultural and diverse populations* (2nd ed., pp. 63–90). Muncie, IN: Accelerated Development.

Sundel, M., & Sundel, S. S. (1999). *Behavior change in the human services* (4th ed.). New York: Wiley.

Super, D. E. (1957). *The psychology of careers.* New York: Harper & Row.

Super, D. E. (1969). Vocational development theory: Persons, positions, and processes. *The Counseling Psychologist, 1,* 2–9.

Super, D. E. (1976). *Career education and the meaning of work* (Monographs of Career Education). Washington, DC: Office of Career Education, U.S. Office of Education.

Super, D. E. (1990). A life-span, life-space approach to career development. In D. Brown, L. Brooks, and Associates (Eds.), *Career choice and development* (pp. 197–261). San Francisco, CA: Jossey-Bass.

Super, D. E., Thompson, A. S., Lindeman, R. E., Jordaan, J. P., & Myers, R. A. (1979). *Career development inventory.* Palo Alto, CA: Consulting Psychologists Press.

Swenson, L. C. (1996). *Psychology and the law for the helping professions.* (2nd ed.) Pacific Grove, CA: Brooks/Cole.

Talbutt, L. C. (1988). Libel and slander: A potential problem for the 1980s. In W. C. Huey, & T. P. Remley, Jr. (Eds,), *Ethical & legal issues in school counseling* (pp. 131–136). Alexandria, VA: American School Counselor Association.

Talbutt, L. C., & Hummel, D. L. (1982). Legal and ethical issues impacting on counselors. *Counseling and Human Development, 14*(6), 1–12.

Tarasoff v. Regents of the University of California, 529 P.2d. 553 (S.C. Cal 1974).

Tennyson, W. W., & Strom, S. M. (1986). Beyond professional standards: Developing responsibleness. *Journal of Counseling and Development, 64*(5), 298–302.

Thompson, B. (1992). Two and one-half decades of leadership in measurement and evaluation. *Journal of Counseling and Development, 71,* 434–438.

Thornburg, H. D. (1986). The counselor's impact on middle-grade students. *The School Counselor, 33*(3), 170–177.

Thorndike, E. I. (1932). *The fundamentals of learning.* New York: Teachers.

Tidwell, B. J. (1997). *The black report: 1997 edition.* Lanham, MD: University Press of America.

Tiedeman, D. V. & O'Hara, R. P. (1963). *Career development: Choice and adjustment.* New York: College Entrance Examination Board.

Trotzer, J. P. (1989). *The counselor and the group: Integrating theory, training, and practice.* (2nd ed.). Muncie, IN: Accelerated Development.

Trussell, J. (1988). Teenage pregnancy in the United States. *Family Planning Perspectives, 20,* 262–272.

Tyler, L. E. (1969). *The work of the counselor* (3rd ed.). Englewood Cliffs, NJ: Prentice-Hall.

Uba, L. (1994). *Asian Americans: Personality patterns, identity, and mental health.* New York: Guilford Press.

Udansky, M. L. "Diverse fits naotion better than normal," *USA Today,* May 2, 1992, Section A, pgs. 1 and 7.

Vacc, N. A. (1999). Appraisal. In L. C. Loesch (Ed.), *The Official Study Course for the National Counselor Examination for Licensure and Certification (NCE):* Workbook, 189–211. Philadelphia, PA: Taylor and Francis.

Vacc, N. A. (1990). Changes and continuity for counselor education. *Counselor Education and Supervision, 30*(2), 148–155.

Vacc, N. A. (1992). An assessment of the perceived relevance of the CACREP standards. *Journal of Counseling and Development, 70,* 685–687.

Vacc, N. A., & Loesch. L. C. (1993). A content analysis of opinions of the National Counselor Examination. *Journal of Counseling Development, 71,* 418–421.

Vacc, N. A., Wittmer, J. & DeVaney, S. (Eds.) (1995). *Experiencing and counseling multicultural and diverse populations* (3rd ed.). Muncie, IN: Accelerated Development.

Van Hoose, W. H. (1986). Ethical principles in counseling. *Journal of Counseling and Development, 65*(3),168–169.

Vander Kolk, C. J. (1985). *Introduction to group counseling and psychotherapy.* University of Michigan, Ann Arbor: Books on Demand.

VanZandt, C. E. (1990). Professionalism: A matter of personal initiatives. *Journal of Counseling and Development, 66*(3), 243–245.

Vasquez, M. J. T. (1988). Counselor-client sexual contact: Implications for ethics training. *Journal of Counseling Development, 67*(4), 238–241.

Vasquez, M. J. T., & Kitchener, K. S. (1988). Introduction to special feature. *Journal of Counseling and Development, 67*(4), 214–216.

Walter, M. I., & Handelsman, M. M. (1996). Informed consent for mental health counseling: Effects of information specificity on clients' ratings of counselors. *Journal of Mental Health Counseling, 18,* 253–262.

Watson, J. B. (1930). *Behaviorism* (2nd edition). Chicago: University of Chicago Press.

Wattenberg, B. J. (1991). *The first universal nation: Leading indicators and ideas about the surge of America in the 1990s.* New York: The Free Press.

Wehrly, B. (1996). *Counseling interracial individuals and families.* Alexandria, VA: American Counseling Association.

Weikel, W. J. (1985). The American Mental Health Counselors Association. *Journal of Counseling and Development, 63*(7), 457–460.

Weikel, W. J., & Hughes, P. R. (1993). *The counselor as expert witness.* ACA Legal Series (vol. 5). Alexandria, VA: American Counseling Association.

Weikel, W. J., & Palmo, A. J. (1989). The evolution and practice of mental health counseling. *Journal of Mental Health Counseling, 11*(1), 7–25.

Welfel, E. R. (1998). *Ethics in counseling and psychotherapy: Standards, research, and emerging issues.* Pacific Grove, CA: Brooks/Cole.

West, J. D., Bubenzer, D. L., Brooks, Jr., D. K., & Hackney, H. (1995). The doctoral degree in counselor education and supervision. *Journal of Counseling and Development, 74,* 174–176.

Westervelt, E. M. (1978). A tide in the affairs of women: The psychological impact of feminism on educated women. In L. W. Harmon, J. M. Birk, L. E. Fitzgerald, & M. F. Tarmey (Eds.), *Counseling women* (pp. 1–33). Monterey, CA: Brooks/Cole.

Wetzel, L., & Ross, M. A. (1983). Psychological and sociological ramifications of battering: Observations leading to a counseling methodology for victims of domestic violence. *Personnel and Guidance Journal, 61*(7), 423–427.

Whiston, S. C., & Emerson, S. (1989). Ethical implications for supervisors in counseling of trainees. *Counselor Education and Supervision, 28*(4), 318–325.

Wiggins, J. D., & Weslander, D. L. (1986). Effectiveness related to personality and demographic characteristics of secondary school counselors. *Counselor Education and Supervision, 26*(1), 26–35.

Wilcoxon, S. A., & Hawk, R. (1990). Continuing education services: A survey of state associations of AACD. *Journal of Counseling and Development, 69* (1), 93–94.

Wilkinson, W. K., & McNeil, K. (1996). *Research for the helping professions.* Pacific Grove, CA: Brooks/Cole.

Wittman, P. P. (1988). Marketing counseling: What counseling can learn from other health care professions. *Counselor Education and Supervision, 27*(4), 308–314.

Wittmer, J. (2000). *Managing your school counseling program: K-12 development strategies.* Terre Haute, IN: Educational Media Group.

Wittmer, J., & Loesch, L. C. (1990). Roses, ducks, and doctoral degrees in counselor education. *Counselor Education and Supervision, 30*(2), 156–162.

Wittmer, P. J., & Loesch, L. C. (1986). Professional orientation. In M. D. Lewis, R. L. Hayes, & J. A. Lewis (Eds.), *An introduction to the counseling profession* (pp. 301–330). Itasca, IL: Peacock.

Wittmer, P. J., & Myrick, R. D. (1974). *Facilitative teaching: Theory and practice.* Pacific Palisades, CA: Goodyear.

Yalom, I. D. (1995). *Theory and practice of group psychotherapy,* (4th ed.). New York: Basic Books.

Yell, M. L. (1996). Reporting child abuse and neglect: Legal requirements. *Preventing School Failure, 40,* 161–163.

Zahner, C. J. & McDavis, R. J. (1980). Moral development of professional and paraprofessional counselors and trainees. *Counselor Education and Supervision, 19*(4), 243–251.

Zunker, V. G. (1997). *Career counseling: Applied concepts of life planning* (5th ed.). Pacific Grove, CA: Brooks/Cole.

ABOUT THE AUTHORS

Nicholas A. Vacc, Ed.D., is the Joe Rosenthal Excellence Professor in the Department of Counseling and Educational Development at The University of North Carolina at Greensboro, and a past recipient of the Hitchcock Distinguished Professional Service Award. He is a National Certified Counselor (NCC), an examination consultant for the National Board of Certified Counselors (NBCC), a fellow in the American Orthopsychiatric Association, and past president of the Association for Assessment in Counseling (AAC). He is also former editor of *Measurement and Evaluation in Guidance* (currently known as *Measurement and Evaluation in Counseling and Development*), past chair of the American Counseling Association (ACA), Council of Journal Editors, and past president of the North Carolina Association of Measurement and Evaluation in Counseling and Development. He is currently co-chairperson of the Joint Committee on Testing Practices, a group that develops and recommends policy and practice pertaining to professional testing.

Larry C. Loesch, Ph.D., is a Professor in the Department of Counselor Education at the University of Florida. He has published over 100 journal articles, book chapters, and books, and has given over 75 professional presentations. He is a former editor of *Measurement and Evaluation in Guidance*, and has served on the editorial board of *Counselor Education and Supervision*. He is past president of several professional organizations, including Chi Sigma Iota, the Association for Measurement and Evaluation in Guidance, and the Southern Association for Counselor Education and Supervision. He has received the ACA's Research Award as well as its Hitchcock Distinguished Professional Service Award. He is a member of the Chi Sigma Iota's Academy of Leaders and received that organization's 1998 Sweeney Professional Leadership Award.

INDEX